BYPASS COURT
A DISPUTE RESOLUTION HANDBOOK

FOURTH EDITION

GENEVIEVE A. CHORNENKI
CHRISTINE E. HART

LexisNexis®

Bypass Court: A Dispute Resolution Handbook, Fourth Edition
© LexisNexis Canada Inc. 2011
March 2011

Members of the LexisNexis Group worldwide

Canada	LexisNexis Canada Inc, 123 Commerce Valley Dr. E. Suite 700, MARKHAM, Ontario
Australia	Butterworths, a Division of Reed International Books Australia Pty Ltd, CHATSWOOD, New South Wales
Austria	ARD Betriebsdienst and Verlag Orac, VIENNA
Czech Republic	Orac, sro, PRAGUE
France	Éditions du Juris-Classeur SA, PARIS
Hong Kong	Butterworths Asia (Hong Kong), HONG KONG
Hungary	Hvg Orac, BUDAPEST
India	Butterworths India, NEW DELHI
Ireland	Butterworths (Ireland) Ltd, DUBLIN
Italy	Giuffré, MILAN
Malaysia	Malayan Law Journal Sdn Bhd, KUALA LUMPUR
New Zealand	Butterworths of New Zealand, WELLINGTON
Poland	Wydawnictwa Prawnicze PWN, WARSAW
Singapore	Butterworths Asia, SINGAPORE
South Africa	Butterworth Publishers (Pty) Ltd, DURBAN
Switzerland	Stämpfli Verlag AG, BERNE
United Kingdom	Butterworths Tolley, a Division of Reed Elsevier (UK), LONDON, WC2A
USA	LexisNexis, DAYTON, Ohio

Library and Archives Canada Cataloguing in Publication

Chornenki, Genevieve A.
        Bypass court: a dispute resolution handbook / Genevieve A. Chornenki, Christine E. Hart. — 4th ed.

Includes bibliographical references and index.
ISBN 978-0-433-46299-6

    1. Dispute resoulution (Law) — Canada. I. Hart, Christine E. II. Title.

KE8615.C458 2005   345.71'09   C2005-900602-1
KF9084.C458 2005

Printed and bound in Canada.

For William Henry Jackson,
beloved and friend.

And for Katie Elizabeth Xue,
whose sparkle and sunny spirit has enriched my life more than
words can tell.

ABOUT THE AUTHORS

Genevieve A. Chornenki is an independent DR practitioner who provides non-partisan services such as mediation, arbitration, independent complaint-handling and contract ombuds services. She was inaugural chair of the ADR section of the Ontario Bar Association and received its first Award of Excellence in ADR in 1999. In 2000, she also received an Excellence in Teaching Award from the University of Toronto. Genevieve holds an LL.M. in ADR together with the dual practice designations of Chartered Mediator and Chartered Arbitrator (ADR Institute of Canada). She served as a Director of the Sport Dispute Resolution Centre of Canada and continues as a member of the Local Mediation Committee of the Ontario Mandatory Mediation Program, Toronto Region. She is a founding member of the Estate Mediation Group, which helps people and their professional advisors resolve contested estate and challenging estate planning situations through mediation, conflict coaching and family conferences.

Christine E. Hart, President of Accord/hart & associates inc., is one of Canada's leaders in conflict management. She has practised for 30 years in the field of dispute resolution — as a lawyer, mediator, facilitator, arbitrator and dispute systems designer. After successfully creating and implementing the first court-connected mediation program in Canada, in Ontario's Superior Court, Christine went on to found Canada's first comprehensive conflict management practice as a partner and President of KPMG Conflict Management Solutions Inc. In 1998, she founded Accord/hart & associates inc. (AHA!), where her work has focused on preventing and resolving business and governance disputes. Christine is an accredited Corporate Director (2005), and since 1979 has been a director/governor of a variety of organizations including the Greater Toronto Airports Authority (GTAA), Goodwill Toronto, Sheridan College, Ontario Bar Association, Canadian Psychiatric Research Foundation, the Canadian Stage Company and Kingsway College School. She is a former Member of Provincial Parliament (1987) and Minister of Culture and Communications for Ontario (1989), and is a past Chair of the Ontario Bar Association Alternative Dispute Resolution (ADR) Section.

PREFACE

This is a book about dispute resolution — ways that disputes can be settled, solved or finally determined. It explains and organizes these ways with lots of examples and commentary from the authors' experiences. It helps readers to choose a suitable way and gives them practical advice and information about using some specific dispute resolution processes.

WHAT IS MEANT BY THE TERM "DISPUTE RESOLUTION"?

In our first edition we were somewhat dogmatic about our labels. We chose the term "dispute resolution" over "*alternative* dispute resolution" because the word "alternative", which usually distinguishes court and non-court methods, suggested that some ways of settling or solving disputes stand in opposition to others. We wanted to get away from "either/or" thinking.

We still want to avoid polarizing people but we have become more relaxed about our labels. In this, our fourth edition, we use DR and ADR interchangeably because we consider them to be omnibus terms that encompass many options for resolving disputes, including litigation and administrative hearings.

In other words, our definition is inclusive. DR or ADR contain both court and non-court possibilities.

This book concerns a collection of methods that can be used for all or part of any dispute. We identify these methods as *consensual*, *informative*, *adjudicative*, *democratic*, *mechanical* or *coercive*. Each kind of method has its attributes, its benefits, its drawbacks. We explore these in more detail.

For us, ADR has always been about understanding and working with all available choices. It has not been about promoting one procedural choice to the exclusion of another. We continue to discourage questions about whether a particular choice is morally right or wrong, or whether its attributes are generally superior or inferior. Such questions tend to provoke defensive reactions and to unnecessarily align people with opposing idealistic camps.

We prefer a series of more pragmatic, recurring questions. Why, if at all, is any particular dispute amenable to resolution? What DR process, if any, is appropriate for all or part of any dispute? And how can any particular process be carried into operation, and with what result?

WHAT MAKES THIS BOOK SPECIAL?

The fourth edition of *Bypass Court* continues in the form of a *handbook*, not a treatise or an academic textbook. It is expressed in colloquial (sometimes informal) language, and it draws upon our experience in the field. It is intended to be fully used — to be read, written on, underlined, highlighted and referred to.

This handbook provides basic principles, examples, forms, checklists and sample documents. It integrates theory and practice. It aims to deliver useful information so that readers can formulate realistic expectations about various DR choices.

While the book covers a collection of DR processes including the court-like procedure of arbitration, it emphasizes methods which do not involve decisions by outside authorities. When the idea for this handbook was conceived and when we wrote the first edition, we were aware of no Canadian book that focused on these other DR possibilities — and certainly none that took the form of a handbook. That said, in this fourth edition we decided that it was time to address arbitration because it is a legitimate form of dispute resolution that is being used with increasing frequency where consensual methods like mediation do not lead to resolution.

FOR WHOM IS THIS BOOK INTENDED?

This handbook is intended for anyone who may be involved in an existing or potential dispute. The involvement may be direct and personal — two cottage owners disagreeing about a boundary line, for instance, or the beneficiaries of an estate in controversy over the interpretation of a will. The involvement may be less direct, organizational, perhaps — the director of human resources, for example, who must negotiate the terms of a severance on behalf of his or her company, or the principals of two businesses who must work out a disagreement about price, quantity or quality. The involvement may be theoretical or academic, such as students of dispute resolution or existing practitioners: mediators, arbitrators, dispute resolution educators. And finally, the involvement may be as a professional or other advisor to people or organizations in conflict. We define such advisors broadly. Although occasional portions of the text address the modes of thinking and behaviour relevant to lawyers, there is a wide assortment of advisors — accountants, architects, business agents, counsellors, engineers, ministers, ombuds, trustees in bankruptcy, valuators and so forth — who will find this book valuable.

This handbook can respond to the needs of each of these individuals. A beginning student or initiate can focus on Chapter 1, which describes a DR universe. A lawyer might pinpoint Chapter 7, for a quick, elementary review of relevant legal principles. A business executive concerned with the earliest, most cost-effective resolution of disputes can concentrate on Chapter 2, about negotiation. And an individual going to arbitration can learn what to expect in the new Chapter 8, which concerns the arbitration process.

WHAT ARE THE DIFFERENT USES OF THIS HANDBOOK?

Since this book was first published, we have heard from readers who play different roles in DR: actual DR participants such as claims adjusters or professional negotiators, lawyers and others who advise people in conflict, DR students, DR teachers and trainers, fellow DR practitioners and people with just a general interest or curiosity about the field.

This handbook continues to have many applications. It can be used by people considering or about to participate in a DR process such as negotiation or an initial mediation. It will assist their preparation and planning by suggesting what to think about, anticipate and do, both before and during the process.

This handbook can be used by professional advisors — those who regularly come in contact with people and organizations in controversy. For example, lawyers have used it to understand what someone means by the term "interest-based negotiation". This book lets advisors guide their clients and customers in choosing a suitable DR process and forms a basis for decisions about what role the advisor should play.

Persons on the same side of a controversy can share the book as they determine what, if anything, can be done about their common concerns. What's the difference between mediation and arbitration, and which one should they choose? Such persons may be association members who find themselves unable to support their representatives, ratepayers who want to be sure that a development meets their needs, purchasers of goods and services who worry about the quality of what they buy, and so on.

This handbook can also be a gift to those on the other side of a controversy as an invitation to consider a route to resolution. One warring partner to another. A franchisor to franchisee. Opposing experts. Contending advocates.

This handbook can be a reference guide in dispute resolution courses and seminars. It can serve as a foundation text for those who teach basic DR principles. It can be the starting point for enquiry, discussion, debate.

This handbook can stand as an introduction by dispute resolution practitioners to the people and organizations they serve or wish to serve. It will inform DR consumers about the services DR practitioners can deliver and introduce them to the complexities of DR.

WHAT MOTIVATED US TO WRITE THIS BOOK?

In 1996 we were motivated to produce a handbook as a way of focusing the thinking around dispute resolution and helping to increase its legitimacy in Canada. It was not so long ago that processes like mediation were considered "flaky and soft" or, alternatively, "dangerous". One episode of *Street Legal*, the defunct Canadian television serial about lawyers, showed mediation as an unpredictable process where people were bullied out of their rights.

How things have changed! Canadian courts have taken a shine to mediation, and judges themselves want to play the role of mediator. Canada's DR universe is still expanding, and every human activity or undertaking — from organized religion to the Olympics — seems to have incorporated ADR.

Our initial goal was to clarify and synthesize DR concepts. Much of our initial work in the first edition involved clarifying our own attitudes and thinking about DR, a necessary prerequisite to putting ideas down on paper. We constantly struggled with two somewhat opposing tasks: how to extract general principles from our experience and observations for the benefit of the reader and avoid groundlessly generalizing about DR and foreclosing its many possibilities.

Often we would grapple with the organization of a chapter, only to detect an exception just beyond the structure that we had worked so hard to erect. We would see overlap, convergence and similarities where precision, clarity and difference were intended.

In this edition we are more sanguine. We eroded or discarded some of our earlier generalizations and invented others. We incorporated some of the philosophical and practical changes brought on by close to a decade of mandatory mediation, and added new information about partnering and Canadian initiatives. We have drawn on our experience and tried to illustrate our ideas with more frequent and concrete examples. We hope we have succeeded in making this book more useful for our readers.

Although ADR is now our paid work, we both have backgrounds and training in law with ample experience in the litigation system. Our interest in dispute resolution began independently of each other in the 1980s, prompted by our observations about the civil justice system from which we made our living. We were attracted to the possibilities outside that system and wanted to find a way to incorporate them into our working lives, being of the do-what-you-love-and-the-money-will-follow school of thought. DR and a mutual friend brought us together.

Seeing the application of consensual dispute resolution to civil disputes, Genevieve struck out on her own at a time when *mediation*, *medication* and *meditation* were routinely confused. She was also instrumental in the creation of the ADR section of the Canadian Bar Association. For a few years Genevieve carried on an ADR business with partners, but in 1990 she resumed her status as a solo practitioner. You can read more about her personal experiences in Chapter 13, "Epilogue: Why Dispute Resolution Still Matters to Us".

In 1990, following her stint in provincial Parliament and as a Cabinet Minister, Christine built on her recognized skills for bringing people together around issues, trained as a mediator and began practising in the field of Dispute Resolution — principally with grievance mediations, as that was available in the field at the time. She was recruited in 1994 by the Chief Justice of the Superior Court and by the Attorney General for Ontario to lead the joint federal-provincial ADR Centre Pilot Project — the first of its kind in Canada. In that role, Christine introduced mediation to the Toronto business and legal communities for the first time in a non-labour context, fine-tuned and evaluated the prototype and worked with all the stakeholders to develop a consensus on an appropriate model to be used in connection with the courts. Mediation is now a fundamental part of civil litigation in Ontario's Superior Court, which has been described by the Court Rules Committee as the most significant change in the civil court process in the last 100 years. Until its advent, the superior courts in Canada had never actively assisted litigants to bring about early resolutions of their disputes. In 1996, Christine was recruited by a large consulting firm to spearhead and develop its national practice in conflict management, but decided to strike out on her own. Since 1998, her firm, Accord/hart & associates inc. (AHA!) has been providing comprehensive DR services across Canada, including advising boards on conflictual issues.

Christine pursued her interest in DR within an existing law firm at first, but was ultimately appointed director of the first court-connected DR project in Canada in 1994. When that assignment was successfully fulfilled (and court-connected DR was embraced on a permanent basis), she surrendered her law career in favour of full-time DR.

Being fortunate to have participated in some early Canadian DR activities and to have seen DR in a wide variety of contexts — labour, business, regulated professions, environment — we initially recognized a knowledge gap between users and their professional advisors. We decided to collaborate on this handbook to provide practical advice about how to select, prepare for and operate in a dispute resolution process not based on the adversarial model of point and counterpoint. Producing a practical, portable, economical and accessible source of information has been our primary goal throughout.

A decade later, we are pleased to report on DR's continuing growth in Canada. In Chapter 12 we talk about the number of Canadian programs and illustrate a few of them. Government and industry initiatives abound, including some impressive evaluation statistics. The knowledge gap has been considerably reduced and DR's mystique is dissipating in favour of pragmatic, yet thoughtful, use. Businesses and individuals are initiating DR procedures for their disputes and putting DR clauses into their contracts. Universities and community colleges are offering certificates and degrees in DR. At the grade school level, children are learning communications skills and practising win-win solutions with each other and at home. Dispute resolution has become a life competency. Some employers even consider it a job requirement.

To be sure, the field is still developing, but it has come a long way in a short time. DR thinking has more depth, and superficial debates have generally abated. The volume of Canadian books and essays on DR has increased impressively. We welcome past and current developments and enthusiastically anticipate those of the future.

BYPASS COURT: WHAT DOES THE TITLE CONNOTE?

In naming our book *Bypass Court*, we anticipated at least two reactions to the first edition. We predicted that there would be those who would want to do what the title suggests: eliminate or minimize the impact of our court system on their own particular problems. The transaction costs as well as the emotional, time and timing problems associated with going to court are well known and often intolerable for many people, companies and institutions.

We predicted that there would be others who would want to protect, shelter or foster the court system, possibly because they earn their living working and advocating in the system and they enjoy the status that it endows, or possibly because they believe that it delivers protections and clarification not available through private systems of social ordering, such as negotiation.

Given our legal training and backgrounds, we are familiar with how the court system works, with who plays and who pays. We have experienced and observed both its weaknesses and its strengths for all those it affects: litigants, the public, judges, lawyers, paralegals and court administrators and staff. We are familiar with the system's constancy and its caprice, its vigour and its torpor, its respect for some and its contempt for others, its rigidity and its fluidity, its ravages and its rewards.

Like each of the processes discussed in this book, the litigation system is a human one, and, put into perspective, it represents but one possibility in a collection of choices. How prominent a space it occupies in that collection is for each reader to decide.

The question about the role of the court lost some of its charge in the years since our first edition because people were able to get actual experience in ADR and move beyond mere hopes and fears. Their participation in mediation or arbitration, for instance, gave them knowledge and information that enabled them to act, not react, in the face of a dispute. ADR turned into a meaningful choice instead of an abstract idea to improve the world.

CONCLUSION

This handbook is intended more as a starting place — opening the reader's mind to the full range of DR possibilities, and helping them to decide whether and how a particular DR process can work for them. The next step is to begin thinking about how such disputes can be avoided or better managed in the future.

As our economy becomes enmeshed with others to the south, and eventually around the world, interactions between people and institutions will, depending on how you see it, create more conflict or more opportunities. It should come as no surprise that we take the optimistic view. We might even go out on a limb and say that the future presents brilliant and favourable prospects for dispute resolution, especially for Canadians.

Genevieve A. Chornenki
Christine E. Hart
Toronto, Ontario
January 2011

ACKNOWLEDGMENTS

We wish to acknowledge and thank the following for peer review, helpful suggestions and gentle edits. Any shortcomings remain our responsibility.

Dave McNabb, Deputy Ombuds, Royal Bank of Canada
Judith Michael of Judith Michael & Associates
Kimberly Morris, Barrister & Solicitor
Sam Posner of Posner Legal, Toronto
John Rooke, Associate Chief Justice of the Court of Queen's Bench of
    Alberta
Rick Russell of Agree Dispute Resolution Inc.

Genevieve A. Chornenki
Christine E. Hart

TABLE OF CONTENTS

1

THE DISPUTING WORLD: WHAT CHOICES EXIST?

Disputes exist in a complex world of infinite variety where people, groups and corporations think and behave in unique ways. Their values may clash, their objectives may be at odds, or they may have vastly different access to resources. Their feelings and attitudes may also diverge dramatically.

Disputes vary in importance and scope. Noise through a party wall may unbalance one person but seem trivial to another whose passion is chemical runoff from a golf course. A partnership spat about vacation times is devastating at first but pales in relation to a complaint from a major customer. And if there is only $1 million of public money when $5 million is needed, the consequences of how each dollar is spent is more dramatic than a scenario of unlimited cash flow.

Disputes exist over time: what simmers today boils over tomorrow; what exploded yesterday may dissipate today. Feelings evolve as time passes, sometimes subsiding, sometimes erupting.

Disputes evoke varying behaviours. One person may go away alone to reflect, ashamed at what has happened. Another person may tell the world and try to enlist the support of everyone in sight. A third person may quietly send a broadcast e-mail, attacking the other person, and enjoy the process of getting even.

If a snapshot could be taken of the universe of disputes at any given time, the picture would be multicoloured and complex. It would show multiple contexts: home, school, workplace, boardroom, council chamber, legislature and nation. It would depict innumerable sources of conflict: values, interests, beliefs, information, resources, actions, interpretations, consequences, feelings and so on. The photo would capture the relative importance people attach to things: their preferences, attitudes, behaviours and other responses.

Among the disputes in the snapshot would be those amenable to resolution *at this moment*. These would represent a subgroup, a portion of all disputes in existence. Chances are that the resolvable disputes are those in which the parties involved view the costs and negative consequences of the conflict as too high and seek to minimize or eliminate them. For these, the timing is right, the attitudes ripe.

This book is about dispute resolution for those situations. It is about ways that willing parties can resolve disputes when they are ready and prepared to attempt settlement. They may not come together with the same degree of commitment to a resolution. They may come with differing ideas of an acceptable outcome and how it might be reached. They may want to use different methods along the way. But they come together at least with a desire to see if and how far they can go towards a settlement.

THE SIX GENERAL DR CATEGORIES

When people and companies want to resolve disputes, there are many possibilities for *how* to do so. To understand the range of choices available, consider the following simple image:

Figure 1-1

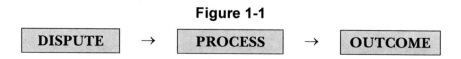

A dispute can be about all kinds of things, but if it is to be resolved, something must happen to it. It must undergo some sort of process so that the situation changes and there is a new result. The result can be an agreement, a decision, new information, a changed situation or a random event depending on the process used.

Dispute resolution processes may be divided into six general categories.[1] A process may be one of the following:

1. Consensual — If a process is *consensual*, it seeks an outcome with which everyone can agree. For example, condominium members may sit down and together try to figure out what to do about noise complaints. In consensual Dispute Resolution (DR), disputants try for agreement on their own or with the help of an outsider like a mediator. The results are subject to agreement of the people involved, who have the right to accept or reject a proposed resolution. In a consensual process, there is an outcome only when everyone buys into a proposal.

2. Adjudicative — If a process is *adjudicative*, its outcome is based on a decision from an outside authority who decides (adjudicates) the issues between the parties. For example, an arbitrator's decision can

---

[1]   Some authors use "interests", "rights" and "power" to sort dispute resolution options. If a process responds to people's needs, it is an interest-based process. If it adjudicates rights, it is a rights-based process. If it uses strength, authority or even arms, it is a power-based process. See C.A. Cosantino & C. Sickles Merchant, *Designing Conflict Management Systems: A Guide to Creating Productive and Healthy Organizations* (San Francisco: Jossey-Bass Publishers, 1996) at 45. We find that interests, rights and power are at play in all dispute resolution processes, so we sort them by means of how people participate and what outcomes they produce.

fix the price of live chickens between the chicken producers and their processors for a particular period of time. That means that the parties have no opportunity to approve or veto the price once it is set. They only get to argue their views beforehand. In an adjudicative process, disputants take part, not by talking things out amongst themselves but by making presentations aimed at convincing the adjudicator to decide in their favour. The adjudicator then decides for them; the parties do not. Adjudicative processes which come about by agreement between individuals or companies are *private*. For instance, shareholders' agreements often provide for arbitration of shareholder disputes. Adjudicative processes that are funded with public resources and created or sanctioned by the state, such as the civil courts, are *public*. A civil trial is the best example of that.

3.   Informative — If a process is *informative*, its purpose is to obtain or put together information for the use of the disputants. A valuation of a commercial building is an informative process in that it tells people how much the building is worth. Then they can decide what to do with it on a more educated basis. An informative process can produce factual information or opinions and recommendations, such as how to remedy faulty construction or what to do about a troublesome employee. The information may be obtained for only one disputant or for all jointly. Informative processes are supplementary because they do not bring a dispute to a close. Instead, they supplement or inform the steps that can lead to a resolution. For example, the value of the commercial building may be presented at an arbitration to support one side's view of how much it is worth. The other side could present a competing valuation. *Non-dispositive* is another term for informative processes, as they do not dispose of or finish up a dispute or issue directly.

4.   Coercive — If a process is *coercive*, it seeks to influence an unwilling disputant to do something that otherwise will not be done voluntarily. For example, a strike is a coercive process. It is used to influence management to make concessions that it will not willingly make. Other examples of coercive processes are civil disobedience, hostage-taking, embargoes or boycotts. Coercive processes are highly variable according to context and may be of an individual or a collective nature. They are all, however, unilateral (not collaborative) attempts by one side to get what it wants by making the situation unpleasant or intolerable for the other side.

5.   Democratic — If a process is *democratic*, it is essentially numerical and involves determining what most people in a group want to do. Voting for or against a resolution at a meeting is a democratic process. Group members may indicate their preference by a show of hands, written ballot or other recorded method and calculations are done to see if enough people favour a particular course of conduct. The

outcome or result is the one supported by the greatest number of people who have expressed their opinion in the predetermined method.

6.   Mechanical — If a process is *mechanical*, it relies on a simple mechanism or system to achieve an outcome that is usually *one* part of a binary choice or *one* possibility of many. If two speakers toss a coin to see which one goes first, they have used a mechanical method to resolve the order of speakers. Other examples of the mechanical process include drawing straws, picking names out of a hat, lottery or a random computer selection. Mechanical systems generally connote an element of chance or randomness — they are impersonal.

ADR MENU

The six general dispute resolution categories described above together form a menu of options for the resolution or prevention of disputes. For an illustration of this menu, see Figure 1-2, below, which supports the notion that ADR stands for Appropriate Dispute Resolution, an array of choices available to meet the needs of the parties and their situation. One size does not fit all.

Figure 1-2 also reminds us to take care with the term ADR and to clarify what people mean when they use it. In this chapter, we are using ADR as an omnibus term, an acronym that encompasses many options, including litigation. Some people see ADR as meaning everything but litigation or an administrative hearing. To them, it means an alternative to established dispute resolution norms. Still others use the term ADR to mean consensus-based processes like mediation and negotiation. For example, the Immigration Appeal Division of the Immigration and Refugee Board has an "ADR" program which is essentially an hour-long mediation session conducted by a division member for the early settlement of cases. That is a totally different meaning for ADR than the one we are using here. It is not wrong, just different. Therefore, it is a good idea to clarify what people mean when they talk about "ADR".

Figure 1-3 expands the ADR menu by showing specific process options within each general category. Here is where methods like mediation and arbitration are listed. But note that there are more choices than just these two old workhorses. In the consensual category, for instance, six separate processes are identified. There are generic processes like negotiation and mediation as well as more specialized choices like partnering (used in construction) and restorative justice conferencing (used to deal with young offenders).

Figure 1-3 hints at how rich and varied the ADR menu really is, but it is by no means exhaustive. It does not, for example, include any of the participative processes used in the change management field,[2] which is arguably a close cousin to ADR. Nor does it hive off a separate category for "preventative" ADR like "preventative mediation", which is intended to avoid grievances, or "conflict coaching", which teaches negotiation and mediation skills.

New ADR processes and adaptations are continually evolving as people tailor them to their needs and as practitioners expand their markets. Some adaptations do not result in a discrete ADR process. Instead, they infuse existing professions or practices with new attitudes and approaches. Collaborative Family Law, a movement which first appeared in British Columbia, would be an example of that. It is a non-adversarial and multi-disciplinary approach to divorce where clients, lawyers and other professional advisors work through issues collaboratively and on the understanding that legal proceedings will not be commenced while the search for solutions proceeds.[3]

Thus, there are many more ADR permutations and combinations than can be listed in Figure 1-3. ADR adaptations by industrial, regulatory, religious, ethnic or cultural groups are coming into being all the time. Whether they are cousins, siblings or old ADR friends with a makeover, we welcome them all.

SPECIFIC ADR PROCESSES

What follows is a brief description of some of the processes set out in Figure 1-3.

Keep in mind as you read the following summaries that they provide a thumbnail sketch only. They do not show the dynamics involved in any process and cannot capture the lush variety that exists in practice out in the field. Variations result from the different needs and contexts as well as the different personalities, philosophies, experience and training of those involved. None of our summaries are intended to limit or prescribe the adaptations that now exist or will develop for any process.

Figure 1-3 places litigation in perspective by showing that it is one component of a dispute resolution world, not the default choice or necessarily even the first choice. To be sure, going to court has its place. We are supporters of a strong and accessible public system. Our judicial system is an indispensable foundation and a safeguard for Canadian society. It is not to

---

[2] For example, see L. Ackerman Anderson & D. Ackerman, *The Change Leader's Roadmap: How to Navigate Your Organization's Transformation* (San Francisco: Jossey-Bass/Pfeiffer, 2001) and, by the same authors, *Beyond Change Management: Advanced Strategies for Today's Transformational Leaders* (San Francisco: Jossey-Bass/Pfeiffer, 2001).

[3] See Ontario Bar Association, Alternative Dispute Resolution Section, Newsletter, "Collaborative Family Law: A Fresh Approach to Resolution", 11:4 (April 2003).

be underestimated or disrespected. The courts interpret public rules and documents for the benefit of all. They set precedents and give rulings that enable citizens to guide their behaviours. They expose systemic injustices and hold individuals, companies and public officials to account. In addition, the civil litigation system makes people sit up and take notice; it brings unwilling negotiators to the table. Still, litigation is not for everyone. Some people cannot afford it. Some people cannot stomach it. And some simply cannot get their real needs met that way. That is why it is helpful to have other choices that replace or work hand in hand with litigation.

Figure 1-2: DR Process Categories

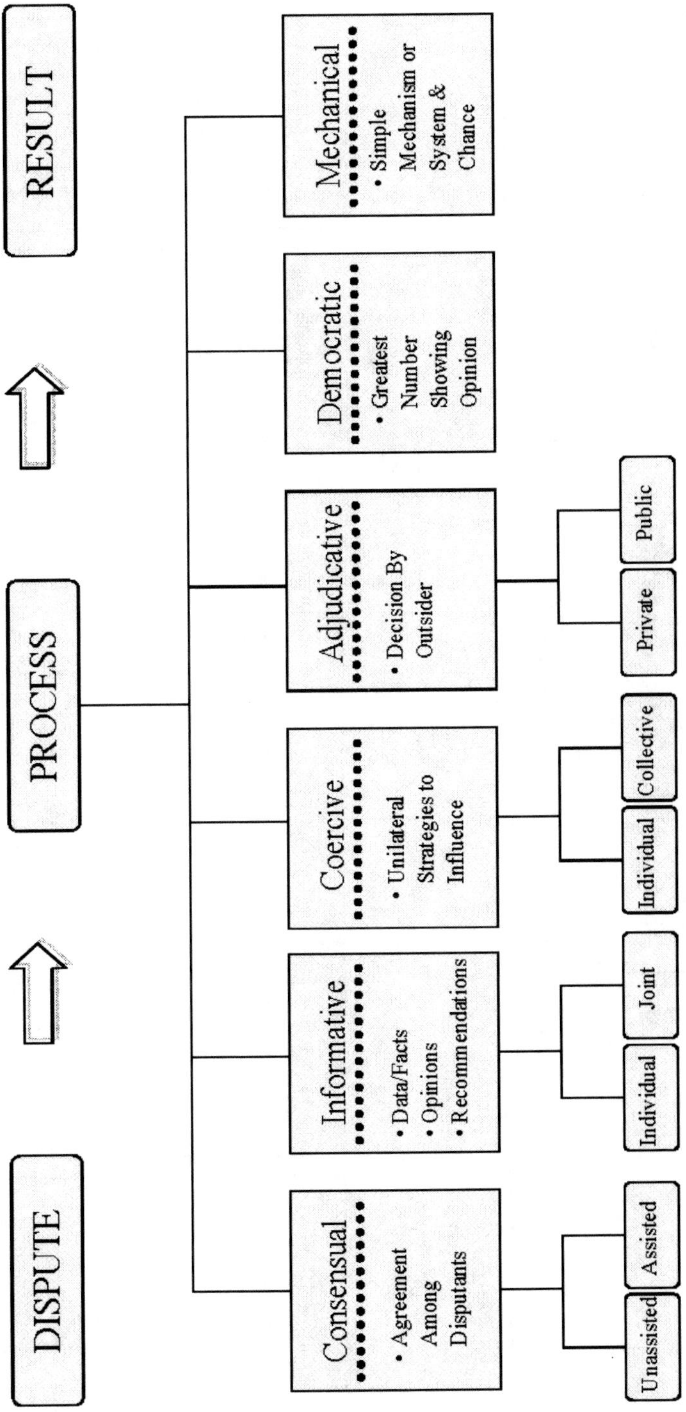

Figure 1-3: Specific DR Processes Within Categories

DISPUTE			PROCESS			RESULT
Consensual	Informative	Coercive	Adjudicative	Democratic	Mechanical
• Negotiation	• Fact Finding	• Stone Walling	• Arbitration	• Voting	• Coin Toss
• Mediation	• Neutral Evaluation	• Strike	• Binding Fact Finding	• Election	• Lottery
• Mini-Trial	• Advisory Board	• Civil Disobedience	• Binding Valuation	• Referendum	• Names in a Hat
• Facilitation	• Valuation	• Boycott	• Administrative Tribunal		• Random Computer Selection
• Partnering	• Expert Opinion	• Embargo	• Litigation		
• Restorative Justice Conferencing	• Technical Inspection	• Armed Action			

In the rapidly evolving field of civil/commercial DR, there is no standardized meaning attached to the labels for these general processes. Thus, it is necessary to look at the meaning ascribed to these processes in this handbook. These are set out below. Recognize, however, that within any process, there are variations based on the personalities, attitudes, beliefs, training and experience of the parties and of the outsider involved. These definitions cannot capture the rich variety that exists in the implementation of any particular process.

- *Negotiation* occurs when two or more parties in dispute communicate and engage in behaviour to see whether they can come up with something that is superior to what they have now or to what each of them could accomplish unilaterally. Negotiation takes place when two potential business partners get together and talk about their respective roles and responsibilities in a new venture. They may work out an acceptable business arrangement or they may decide that they are not suited to work together. They still negotiate, however. Parties can negotiate in person or through representatives. The negotiation process is dealt with in more detail in Chapter 2.

- *Mediation* occurs when two or more parties in dispute permit an outsider to assist them with their negotiations. The outsider does not tell them how their dispute must be settled and has no authority to impose a solution, but instead analyzes the dispute and directly or indirectly gives the parties the benefits of this analysis. For example, if labour and management have been unable to resolve their differences, resulting in a strike, a mediator may be appointed to help the two sides reach agreement. To do so, the mediator will use various approaches and techniques, but at the end of the day the union (labour) and management must consent to any deal. In some models of mediation, the mediator may provide an opinion about what might happen if the matter goes forward to trial or to an administrative hearing. The mediation process is dealt with in more detail in Chapter 3.

- An *Advisory Board* or *Dispute Review Board* is a body or group of outsiders (who may or may not be representatives of the parties) asked by the parties in dispute to consider the various aspects of the dispute and to make recommendations about how it can be settled or managed. For example, a financial institution may offer customers an advisory board for disputes over the operation or granting of credit. The customer's nominee, the financial institution's nominee and a neutral chair can then work together to generate a recommendation for the financial institution and the customer to use in going forward with the banking relationship.

- *Neutral evaluation* occurs or *expert opinion* is sought when two or more parties in dispute ask an outside expert to give them an opinion about some aspect of their dispute. The outsider's opinion may or may not influence the negotiations. If, for instance, an owner and a contractor disagree about why ground water is seeping into a foundation, they may ask a qualified person to provide them with an explanation. Depending on the opinion, one or the other of them might alter their negotiating position and agree upon remedial action and/or the allocation of costs. Neutral evaluation is dealt with in more detail in Chapter 4.

- *Valuation* occurs when two or more parties in dispute ask an outsider with relevant knowledge and training to assign a value to or to quantify some aspect of their dispute, such as the appropriate price for shares or the value of a diamond brooch. As the name suggests, valuation concerns value, quantum or price. For example, the executor of an estate which contains a factory can employ a valuator to assist in fixing an appropriate price range for that particular asset.

- A *mini-trial* or *private mini-trial* is a settlement technique, not a trial, that occurs when two or more parties (usually corporations or large institutions like government) convene executive decision-makers, who listen to abridged presentations. An outsider leads the process. After the presentations, the decision-makers consider whether to negotiate. For example, the chief executive officers of competing computer software companies could attend and listen to abbreviated versions of both sides of a copyright infringement dispute. Afterwards, they can discuss ways to settle that dispute. The outsider may help the executives with the negotiation. Mini-trials are discussed in more detail in Chapter 6.

- A *Judicial mini-trial* is broadly defined as a settlement technique which has been introduced to expedite the resolution of a dispute within the civil litigation system.[4] In some provinces it may be ordered by a judge,[5] but that is not the case in Alberta.

- A *Judicial Dispute Resolution* or *JDR* in Alberta, has been defined very much like a judicial mini-trial, as being "any process that involves a justice, or a judicial officer, in resolving a dispute, after litigation has commenced in an action before the Court (thereby invoking the jurisdiction of the Court to do a JDR with the parties' consent), that is different from a *pure adjudication*".[6]

- *Facilitation* occurs when an outsider called a facilitator works with a group to help it improve its process (how it goes about doing its tasks).

---

[4] See address by former Chief Justice of the Court of Queen's Bench for Alberta, W.K. Moore, *Address to the Arbitration Group* (6 February 1995) at 3. Alberta Law Reform Institute, *Civil Litigation: The Judicial Mini-trial*, Dispute Resolution — Special Series, Discussion Paper No. 1 (August 1993) at 4, online: <http://www.law.ualberta.ca/alri/docs/dp001.pdf>.

[5] For example, in British Columbia, the Northwest Territories, and Newfoundland and Labrador.

[6] We are greatly indebted to Associate Chief Justice John D. Rooke, Court of Queen's Bench of Alberta, for sharing his paper, "Improving Excellence: Evaluation of the Judicial Dispute Resolution Program in the Court of Queen's Bench of Alberta" (1 June 2009) at 83, online: Canadian Forum on Civil Justice <http://cfcj-fcjc.org/clearinghouse/hosted/22338-improving_excellence.pdf>.

The facilitator does not tell the group what tasks it is supposed to do but leads the group through its process and guides it along using certain skills and techniques. A facilitator may be called in to help an executive group create a strategic plan. A facilitator may also be asked to work in conflict situations, such as when group members are having difficulty getting along.[7]

- *Partnering* does not focus on the resolution of a particular dispute like mediation. Instead, it focuses at the front end on the working relationships in a complex and/or long-term joint project. Partnering occurs when the people involved get together in a collaborative, facilitated session and intentionally work out the details of their relationship, including how disputes and issues will be handled in the future. The Greater Toronto Airport Authority's new Terminal One at Pearson Airport benefited from a partnering process. Partnering may be viewed as a specialized adaptation of facilitation.

- *Restorative justice conferencing* is a way to deal with young offenders within the community. It occurs by means of a meeting attended by the offender and his or her family and supporters, the victim and his or her family and supporters and anyone from the community who has been materially affected by the crime. Through dialogue and discussion, participants focus not only on the event itself, but also on who has been impacted and how.

- *Fact-finding* occurs when one or more parties in dispute ask an outsider to listen to them and/or conduct an investigation in order to make factual conclusions or to draw inferences from existing facts. For instance, in response to a complaint of racial or gender discrimination within a certain faculty, a university may engage a fact-finder to conduct an investigation and prepare a report about whether the alleged behaviour occurred and what to do about it. The fact-finder may or may not make recommendations in addition to determining facts. Fact-finding may be binding or non-binding, meaning that the disputants may determine in advance whether they will abide by the fact-finder's report or whether they will remain free to reject or challenge it.

- *Arbitration* occurs when two or more parties in dispute ask an outsider to listen to their facts and arguments and to decide for them how the dispute must be resolved. The decision is often (but need not be) binding and can be enforced through the courts by means of the arbitration legislation that exists throughout Canada. For instance, automobile manufacturers and importers in Canada have set up a system where consumer warranty and defect claims can be resolved by

---

[7]   See R.M. Schwarz, *The Skilled Facilitator: Practical Wisdom for Developing Effective Groups* (San Francisco: Jossey-Bass Publishers, 1994).

an arbitrator who listens to both sides and makes a ruling on the validity of the claim and the remedy, if any, available to the consumer. Arbitration can be of a binding or non-binding nature.

- *Pre-trial conferences*, also called *settlement conferences*, occur as part of the litigation process when lawyers for the parties in the lawsuit (and sometimes the parties) attend before a judge of the court to talk about whether and how the lawsuit can be settled.

- *Litigation* occurs when disputants use the courts (our public justice system) to prosecute or defend their rights and responsibilities in accordance with the law and following the relevant procedural rules of court. If a dispute proceeds all the way through litigation, it will typically culminate in a trial or other form of hearing and decision-making by a public official (judge).

The categories and processes shown in Figure 1-3 tend to be somewhat permeable, and different categories may share characteristics. They may not stand out in stark relief, and one process sometimes merges into another. The informative process of fact-finding, in which an outsider makes an investigation and reports, has elements of an adjudicative process like arbitration. The fact-finder determines facts from evidence, directly and by inference. So does an arbitrator. The difference is that an informative fact-finder does not bind the parties while an arbitrator typically does.

A boycott or strike can have democratic aspects if they are the product of collective decision-making. At the same time, they can be coercive processes, designed to influence a party to do something that it will not voluntarily do.

The adjudicative processes of binding arbitration and litigation also have coercive aspects about them. Both are backed by the machinery of the state in that an arbitrator's orders can be enforced through court orders and judgments. Those in turn can be enforced by methods of execution (garnisheeing wages, seizing and selling property) or by contempt of court for which the ultimate penalty is imprisonment.

We also point out that except for the original "self-help" process of negotiation, each of the methods described above makes use of an outsider or neutral who guides participants through a process and plays a role in resolution whether as decision-maker, process leader or expert. Typically, this outsider has no other relationship with the parties and has no stake in the controversy, but as we discuss in Chapter 3, this does not have to be the case. The "outsider" may actually be a specialized "insider" who has an identified ADR role on behalf of an organization. The person who leads the ADR process may or may not have training in a particular DR process and may or may not have knowledge of the subject matter of the dispute.

This brings us to the issue of subject-matter expertise. It is an open question in the DR field as to whether the outsider needs to know the subject matter of the dispute. There are pros and cons both ways.

An outsider with subject-matter knowledge may understand context and terminology. This gives that person credibility and engenders respect. It also saves time, as there is no need to pause and explain. The knowledgeable person understands what really goes on in the field and is aware of the causes and consequences of disputes. He or she may also be adept at devising solutions to problems and bringing forward helpful practices and suggestions.

The downside is that an expert may define a dispute too narrowly and may not see other dimensions beyond her or his own expertise. For example, a social worker may see only the relationship aspects of a dispute and may overlook some of the more practical or financial components. A lawyer may tend to frame topics only in terms of legal theory. Another danger is that the outsider may become an advocate for one point of view and insist on one particular outcome. The professional ego may get engaged and begin to interfere. For instance, in a construction case, an engineer can become wedded to a single method of remediation when other methods are available. Instead of exploring those carefully with the parties so that they can make informed decisions, the expert may give short shrift to other options or summarily dismiss them. This can reinforce or create an impasse. It can also cause people to question the expert's objectivity.

An outsider without subject-matter knowledge may not readily understand context, terminology or how things work. This can give the impression of confusion or uncertainty and result in a loss of confidence in the outsider. Extra time and other resources may also be needed for explanations, at least the first time. More subtle consequences or implications resulting from the facts may be lost on the outsider. The practicality of outcomes may not be questioned and oversights or erroneous assumptions may not be caught. The non-expert outsider may have little to contribute by way of suggestions to address the substantive complaint, since he or she would be unaware of how others have handled similar problems.

The upside is that a non-expert outsider may bring a fresh and open mind and an ability to see beyond conventional boundaries. He or she may thus identify new or different opportunities for resolution, not obvious to those close to the dispute. This kind of outsider may be the only one prepared to say, "Hey, the Emperor has no clothes!", thus freeing the parties from convention and unstated strictures. In Chapter 3 we give an example of how a non-expert mediator helped in a difficult manufacturing dispute by pointing out to the parties that their complex and technical presentations did nothing to identify the real areas of dispute. They could not distinguish the forest from the trees.

DR PROCESS SELECTION

Sometimes people will be clear on what dispute resolution process to use. It is an intuitive matter, a case of what feels or seems "right". At other times, no single, obvious process choice arises. Several processes may seem like good candidates.

Choosing among several possibilities involves identifying and ordering people's concerns and seeing which DR method best addresses them. This is not a mechanical or computational process where numbers are plugged into a formula to produce an answer. It is somewhat more subtle than that. Two plus two might not equal four in every situation.

Process selection usually involves sorting through a variety of considerations. Sometimes a dominant concern or a restriction rises to the top and points to one particular process. For example, if a person definitely wants to resolve a dispute but is not prepared to compromise or take responsibility for the solution, an adjudicative choice like arbitration or litigation is appropriate. Adjudicative methods give a final outcome without asking participants to compromise or agree. That suits some people just fine.

Keep in mind that it is not necessary to choose just one process. It is possible to mix and match. DR processes can be either stacked like the fillings in a sandwich or laid out in a string.

People can work through one process and come out the other side into another process. The Staffing Policy of the Canadian Food Inspection Agency, for instance, starts with simple discussion as a means of resolving staffing concerns, such as complaints about how job competitions were run. Mediation is a next step if the parties think that it would help. If consensual methods do not work, an adjudicative method is used. The matter gets referred to an outside adjudicator in a decision-making process called "Independent Third Party Review".[8] In other words, staffing complaints are resolved by means of an ADR ladder.

Another option is to combine processes horizontally by using one process to support or supplement another. For example, the Canadian Motor Vehicle Arbitration Plan is primarily an arbitration program where independent arbitrators decide warranty or defect issues between consumers and manufacturers. However, an arbitrator can refer an issue to an independent technical inspector[9] who inspects the consumer's vehicle and replies with a written report. The result of the inspection, an informative process, is fed back into the adjudicative process. The arbitrator can use the inspector's findings and

---

[8] For more about this program, see Chapter 10, "Canadian Initiatives and Onward".

[9] For more about this informational process, see Chapter 10, "Canadian Initiatives and Onward".

opinions in deciding the case. The inspection is a subsidiary process or subroutine in the arbitration.

Tables 1 through 5, below, gather together specific considerations for each type of process, but before we focus on those, here are some general questions for choosing a DR process:

- What are the costs and consequences of the dispute (both positive and negative)? What is their relative impact on the parties? If the costs are low, this will probably tell you something about their commitment and willingness to resolve things.

- How important is it to find a resolution to the dispute and for what reasons? Are the costs and consequences tolerable or do people really want to get rid of them? A person who is satisfied with the status quo or benefits from it is not a good candidate for consensual processes which presume a willingness to alter the status quo.

- What level of trust do the parties repose in each other and how relevant is that to the dispute? If trust is low, there may be more reliance on a powerful outsider or more need to have a pronouncement from someone in authority. Alternatively, a consensual process will have to move slowly in an attempt to establish trust.

- Do the parties expect to be active participants in the DR process? If so, of what will their participation consist — putting forward facts and arguments to convince another person or actively negotiating? Consensual processes have an appealing conversational informality whereas adjudicative processes tend to have an adversarial format. That takes a bit of getting used to.

- If an outsider were to be involved, what would that person be expected to do? Manage the discussion? "Control" someone? Provide information? Influence people? Coerce them? If the parties are looking for "head banging", then a purely facilitative mediator would not meet their expectations. If they want authoritative, factual advice, they will need an expert, not a generalist.

- Who is accountable for the outcome and to whom? Are the parties or their representatives ready, willing and able to take responsibility for an outcome or do they prefer to delegate that to appropriate outsiders? As we have said before, consensual processes make people responsible for participation as well as the outcome. Someone else has responsibility for the outcome in adjudicative processes. Mechanical processes are completely impersonal and do not hold anyone to account for the choice.

- Does the organization or "culture" support the kind of participation and outcomes that they profess to prefer — through lines of authority, money, other resources, ethics, behavioural and other norms? If not, what limits does this place on process choice? It is no use sending someone to negotiate if no one else in the organization will support a deal. It is a bad idea to hold consultations or votes if no one will pay any attention to the results.

- Will the process or its outcome involve or affect parties other than those directly named? If so, how will this occur or be achieved? Is this desirable, undesirable or neutral? If there are vulnerable, statutory or other public interests involved, a public process may be required or a private process may need to be modified to provide openness and accountability.

- How will the outcome be used? How can it be implemented or enforced? It is often easier to enforce a court order or arbitration award against an unwilling party than a settlement agreement. On the other hand, authoritative measures are not likely to elicit cooperation in many modern workplaces.

- Are the parties able and willing to give "recognition"[10] to each other, to paddle around in each other's canoe? If they are shuttered in their own rooms with no ability to look out, they may not be able to participate in the give and take of consensual processes like mediation, facilitation or restorative justice conferencing.

- Are the parties equipped with all of the facts, expertise and judgment necessary or desirable for an outcome? If not, how can this be obtained and at whose expense? An informative process like fact-finding or a reliable agreement to equalize the distribution of information might be in order.

- What standards or norms (if any) are appropriate for this dispute? Who will select them? How are they to be applied or enforced? If the parties cannot agree on the rules or facts that govern their dispute, someone else may need to settle the rules or facts by means of an informative or adjudicative process.

The foregoing questions elicit information much richer and infinitely more useful than a simple review of the benefits of DR: speed, efficiency,

---

[10]   "Recognition" is a term borrowed and adapted from R.A. Baruch Bush & J.P. Folger, *The Promise of Mediation: Responding to Conflict Through Empowerment and Recognition* (San Francisco: Jossey-Bass Publishers, 1994). It is used in this handbook to describe the capacity of a party to recognize aspects of a dispute *beyond itself*. This includes an ability and willingness to consider, entertain, examine and listen to other points of view, whether of the facts, the law, the inferences to be drawn from the facts, the motivations of another party, the meaning that can or might be attached to words used, the technical explanations for the problem, and so on. Recognition is a critical phenomenon for *consensual* DR processes, because a party that is never able to acknowledge these other possibilities is an unlikely candidate for a process which bases its outcome on agreement. That party is unlikely to be able to perform a related task which involves the ability and willingness to consider possible ways to resolve the controversy that take into account the multiple aspects of the problem, including the needs, wants or concerns of another party. In our experience, it does not matter whether this recognition is given out of enlightened self-interest or whether it is a genuine extension of the self based on strength and compassion. The presence of some form of recognition, even if it is weak, seems to predict suitability for *consensual* DR processes whereas its absence does not.

economy, privacy. Chances are that the very act of reviewing such questions will lead a party in dispute to a clearer, more profound understanding of its needs. Principles and priorities will automatically emerge, and the appropriateness of the general categories — consensual, informative, coercive or adjudicative — will come into focus. The exercise is a blend of logic and intuition. It involves judgment, skill and accurate knowledge of what each kind of process entails.

Once you have answered these general questions, you can shift your focus to Tables 1 through 5, which collect together specific considerations which tend to favour a specific DR choice.

Table 1
Choosing a Consensual DR Process

Here are some considerations that point to a consensual process like negotiation or mediation.

[ ]   Do you want to convey the impression of responsiveness and caring, such as to vulnerable persons?

[ ]   Do you want more participation in the process than just the presentation of evidence and arguments?

[ ]   Is it necessary or desirable for non-parties or the broader public to take part?

[ ]   Are there cultural differences which cannot be adequately respected or accounted for in an adjudicative model?

[ ]   Is there a need for a composite, non-legal or creative remedy not available through adjudication (*i.e.*, are legal remedies too limiting)?

[ ]   Are you looking for finality on your own terms?

[ ]   Do you want increased certainty through a customized outcome that you help to make?

[ ]   Do you want to avoid the caprice or uncertainty of a decision-maker like a judge or arbitrator?

[ ]   Are you unable or unwilling to face the risk of loss if you put the matter to a judge or arbitrator?

[ ]   Are you unable or unwilling to accept coercive power?

[ ]   Do the monetary or non-monetary costs of an adjudicative model (*i.e.*, legal fees, expenses, executive time and strained relationships) exceed anticipated benefits?

[ ]   Will the real issues become distorted or limited if they have to be framed as a question of right or accusation? Is there a risk that an either-or framing would leave the *real* issues unaddressed?

[ ]   Are you willing and able to convert your positions to interests and to listen to the interests of the other side?

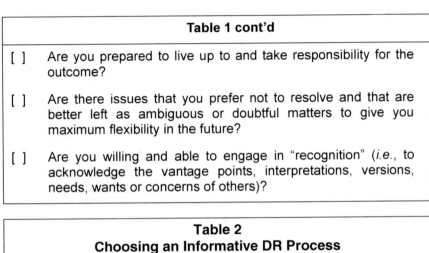

Table 1 cont'd

[ ]   Are you prepared to live up to and take responsibility for the outcome?

[ ]   Are there issues that you prefer not to resolve and that are better left as ambiguous or doubtful matters to give you maximum flexibility in the future?

[ ]   Are you willing and able to engage in "recognition" (*i.e.*, to acknowledge the vantage points, interpretations, versions, needs, wants or concerns of others)?

Table 2
Choosing an Informative DR Process

Here are some considerations that point to an informative process like fact-finding.

[ ]   Are the people involved missing relevant, necessary information or data to support a voluntary, informed choice?

[ ]   Are you missing relevant, necessary information to convince a decision-maker or to promote the "best" decision by an outsider?

[ ]   Are the people involved unable or unwilling to convert positions to interests? Is there a direct, irreconcilable clash of interests that cannot be worked around?

[ ]   Do you expect additional information will be of a persuasive value? Do you think the result of more information would be to influence the ultimate outcome in your favour?

[ ]   Are the people stuck because there are different versions of fact or inferences drawn from fact (including expert opinion) which are central to the dispute and need to be resolved as a first step?

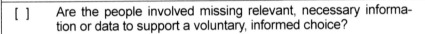

Table 3
Choosing a Coercive DR Process

Here are some considerations that point to a coercive process that can be carried out unilaterally without the other side's agreement.

[ ]   Are you unable or unwilling to convert interests into positions because there are:

   • irreconcilable value differences that cannot be bridged, compromised or superseded with some more important value?

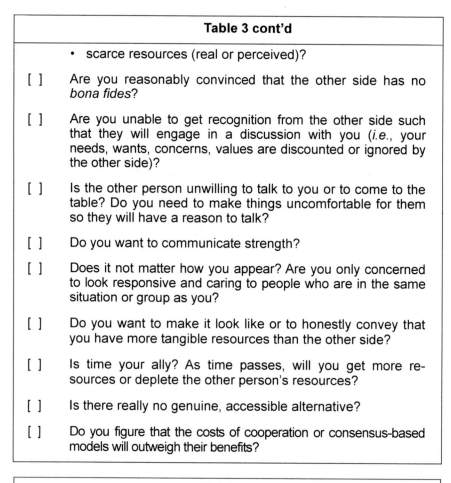

Table 3 cont'd

- scarce resources (real or perceived)?

[ ]   Are you reasonably convinced that the other side has no *bona fides*?

[ ]   Are you unable to get recognition from the other side such that they will engage in a discussion with you (*i.e.*, your needs, wants, concerns, values are discounted or ignored by the other side)?

[ ]   Is the other person unwilling to talk to you or to come to the table? Do you need to make things uncomfortable for them so they will have a reason to talk?

[ ]   Do you want to communicate strength?

[ ]   Does it not matter how you appear? Are you only concerned to look responsive and caring to people who are in the same situation or group as you?

[ ]   Do you want to make it look like or to honestly convey that you have more tangible resources than the other side?

[ ]   Is time your ally? As time passes, will you get more resources or deplete the other person's resources?

[ ]   Is there really no genuine, accessible alternative?

[ ]   Do you figure that the costs of cooperation or consensus-based models will outweigh their benefits?

Table 4
Choosing an Adjudicative DR Process (Public or Private)

Here are some considerations that point to an adjudicative process like arbitration.

[ ]   Are you concerned about the abuse of power by a public body or official?

[ ]   Are you facing a claim that is genuinely frivolous or opportunistic and that should be tested for its *bona fides*?

[ ]   Is a legal precedent unavailable and genuinely needed to govern future similar cases? Do you have the resources to fund the quest for such a precedent?

[ ]   Is it important to label or categorize something in a formal or authoritative way? For example, is it income or capital? Does it meet eligibility criteria or not?

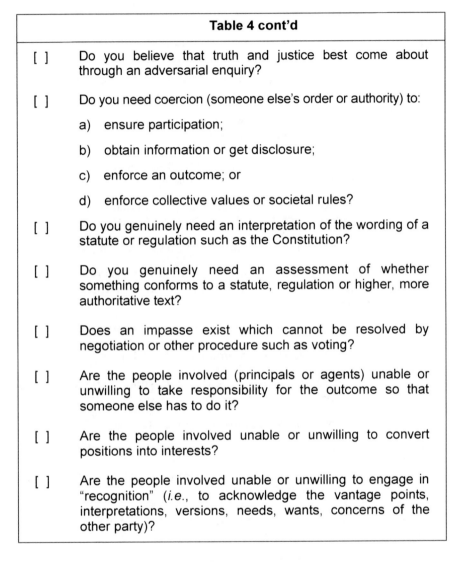

Table 4 cont'd

[ ] Do you believe that truth and justice best come about through an adversarial enquiry?

[ ] Do you need coercion (someone else's order or authority) to:

a) ensure participation;

b) obtain information or get disclosure;

c) enforce an outcome; or

d) enforce collective values or societal rules?

[ ] Do you genuinely need an interpretation of the wording of a statute or regulation such as the Constitution?

[ ] Do you genuinely need an assessment of whether something conforms to a statute, regulation or higher, more authoritative text?

[ ] Does an impasse exist which cannot be resolved by negotiation or other procedure such as voting?

[ ] Are the people involved (principals or agents) unable or unwilling to take responsibility for the outcome so that someone else has to do it?

[ ] Are the people involved unable or unwilling to convert positions into interests?

[ ] Are the people involved unable or unwilling to engage in "recognition" (*i.e.*, to acknowledge the vantage points, interpretations, versions, needs, wants, concerns of the other party)?

Table 5
Choosing Someone to Help with a
Consensual DR Process

Here are some considerations that point to whether an outsider like a mediator or facilitator will add value to a consensual process.

[ ]   Do the people need help converting positions to interests — their own or the other party's?

[ ]   Do the people need help with conflict analysis (*i.e.*, what is fuelling and maintaining the conflict)?

[ ]   Do people feel comfortable talking to each other or would it be more comfortable to use an intermediary?

[ ]   Do the people need help to figure out why they are stuck?

[ ]   Would people benefit from a neutral framing of the issues, information or goals instead of their individual partisan versions?

[ ]   Do you want an objective, safe place or repository to:

• share sensitive information;

• determine whether and how to share sensitive information with the other party;

• construct a palatable way of expressing an idea;

• canvass possibilities for settlement; or

• explore risks and rewards of settlement and non-settlement?

[ ]   Could someone else help to design, assemble and test possible solutions?

[ ]   Would a measure of detachment and objectivity help? Would the people benefit from the overview of an objective person with no stake in the issues or outcome?

[ ]   Would a fresh perspective on the problem make a difference?

[ ]   Would an "event" with an outsider focus everyone's attention and help direct their energies towards settlement?

[ ]   Are you having trouble on your own getting recognition from the other party?

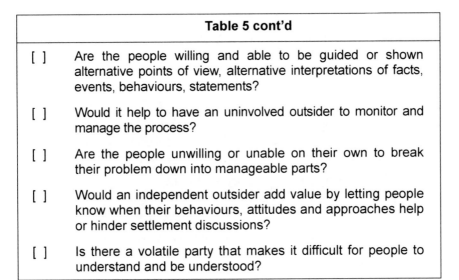

Table 5 cont'd
[ ] Are the people willing and able to be guided or shown alternative points of view, alternative interpretations of facts, events, behaviours, statements?
[ ] Would it help to have an uninvolved outsider to monitor and manage the process?
[ ] Are the people unwilling or unable on their own to break their problem down into manageable parts?
[ ] Would an independent outsider add value by letting people know when their behaviours, attitudes and approaches help or hinder settlement discussions?
[ ] Is there a volatile party that makes it difficult for people to understand and be understood?

PROCESS SELECTION — AN EXAMPLE

Let us now consider how these considerations might apply to a specific situation which is not uncommon, a shareholder dispute.

Two business owners disagree about how to allocate $1 million of profits from their manufacturing business. To date, they have always divided the profits equally in the most tax-effective way. They have also always made equivalent but different contributions to the business. One has been responsible for production. The other has been responsible for sales. However, in the last fiscal year, one of them (with the other's consent) reduced his time commitment by 25 per cent. He wanted to "slow down". There was no appreciable effect on revenues or profitability so he feels entitled to an equal share of all profits subject only to a modest reduction in salary. The fully active partner disagrees. She argues that an unequal time commitment means unequal remuneration in all respects — unequal salary, dividends and bonuses. She says that the ownership structure should also change as a result of his semi-retirement.

What process or combination of processes should these partners employ?

Looking in and without more information, any one of a number of processes could work. They could use arbitration, expert advice, mediation or direct negotiation. The most suitable process is going to depend on the partners themselves and on the details of their situation.

A *democratic* method like voting would not work where the partners have the same number of votes, since deadlock would be the obvious result.

Face-to-face negotiation seems to be the cheapest and most direct method, provided emotions are not running so high that they will interfere with or destroy communications. If that is an issue, the partners can get their lawyers to negotiate on their behalf or they can call in the services of a mediator.

Assuming that they have all necessary information and/or can agree to a voluntary exchange of relevant information and that they both want to actively work things out, then *consensual* DR like negotiation or mediation remains suitable. These presuppose some measure of goodwill and flexibility.

If, however, it is more important for the partners to get a resolution on the numbers than to work things out together and possibly address other issues, they could use a *mechanical* process or an *adjudicative* one.

A *mechanical* process like drawing names from a cup (your allocation or my allocation) is an efficient, albeit crude, way to break the impasse. The partners simply write their solutions out, put them into a hat and agree to abide by the one that gets picked. If they want, they can ask an outsider to draw out the winning solution for them. This is a blunt and somewhat random method, but its speed, economy and impersonal nature may commend it.

Arbitration is another option, either the conventional adversarial format or final offer acceptance (a more sophisticated version of names in a hat). An arbitrator can listen to each of them and then decide on the allocation of profits, using any one of a number of standards, including the arbitrator's own sense of fairness or simply by picking the final offer of one over the other. An arbitrator decides things for the partners and relieves them of any obligation to compromise or be flexible. The arbitration award may break the impasse and move things forward. Then again, it might not. It all depends on how pivotal the monetary question is for the partners. If the money question is a proxy for other issues like business philosophy, fairness or control, then both a mechanical method and an adjudication on money will leave these deeper issues untouched. One would, of course, wonder how these partners will continue together if they cannot reach a negotiated outcome, but such situations have been known to occur. Indeed, they may need to come to terms with whether to end their relationship or devise a new one with modified duties and remuneration.

Suppose that the partners prefer to reach their own solution and that they are also willing to address the issues other than the monetary one. They may still meet a stumbling block if they require external touchstones or data to legitimize their choices or help them work things out. What do others in this situation do? Is there any practice in their industry? Are there tax implications to consider? The owners may agree that a *consensual* process like negotiation is desirable, but want their decision to be an informed one. Thus, an *informative* process using an expert opinion can be used. An accountant or small business advisor can give the partnership advice or make recommendations to both owners based on what is "usual" in the industry and provide structural suggestions as to how the problem can be solved. Such assistance might influence the negotiations and help the partners achieve their own informed outcome.

Suppose now that one partner is less committed to reaching a solution than the other and fails to show up for meetings set specifically to discuss the matter. The more committed partner might then employ some *coercive* measures to encourage the other's participation, such as involving influential people whose opinions matter, commencing litigation or refusing to co-sign cheques. These measures may eventually influence the uncommitted partner to participate in another DR process or some combination of them. In short, they might get the partner to the table.

BYPASS COURT: GO TO SOLUTION

One simple, commonplace scenario, such as the partners in disagreement above, lends itself to a number of DR possibilities depending on the parties and their situations. The variations and permutations identified and imaginable from that scenario demonstrate the peril of a glib decision about which DR process to use without a more detailed enquiry.

The scenario also shows that:

1.   Disputes exist in and over time so that one DR process may be appropriate later or earlier in the dispute. Negotiation might flow from a coercive method designed to get someone to the table.

2.   Disputes can have many dimensions. Different components might call for different processes. A jointly retained expert (or individual experts) can tell the partners what they need to know about the tax and corporate aspects.

3.   One DR process can be related to another. A coercive or adjudicative process can be worked in tandem with a consensual or informative one. An informative process can be fed back into a consensual process or an adjudicative one. A mediator could help these partners have a constructive dialogue. A valuator or tax expert could provide data to use in that dialogue so that informed, realistic decisions are made.

Figure 1-4, below, brings this all together. Using the analogy of a board game, Figure 1-4 illustrates the various paths to a solution for all or part of a dispute. Taking the partnership dispute as an example, or one from your own experience, note how it is possible to move into and out of a process as circumstances require. How many times around the board must you travel before arriving at a solution?

Figure 1-4: Paths to Solution

2

NEGOTIATION

NEGOTIATOR PERCEPTIONS

When students of negotiation are asked what the purpose of negotiation is, most say that it is "to reach agreement". When they are asked what their goals for the negotiation course are, most speak of wanting to learn "skills and techniques" to improve their negotiation abilities. They do not want to be caught "giving away the store", or "giving too much" in the course of a negotiation.

These responses reveal some interesting attitudes about negotiation. They suggest that negotiation connotes compulsion (to reach a deal) and involves pressure to perform to some unstated yet governing standard. The responses also suggest that, properly instructed, negotiators will be equipped to perform just the right move at just the right time, contributing to a result that gets them what they want.

We take a different view of negotiation, adopting a problem-solving, not a performance-based approach. We examine negotiation as a goal-oriented, yet exploratory, exercise. Experience has shown us that negotiation is enhanced more by thought, preparation and conflict analysis than by in-the-moment techniques. And we hold that a negotiator's orientation and mindset informs the techniques, behaviour, strategy and tactics that he or she employs.

Further, we identify negotiation as a process at the crossroads of DR choices, the access point to a variety of other processes that can be undertaken to inform and supplement the negotiation itself, or to resolve impasses not amenable to negotiation. Not every dispute is appropriate for negotiation, and negotiators need to recognize when and to what extent that might be so.

CHAPTER GOALS

The goal of this chapter is to give the negotiator some useful analytical tools and insights. It does this largely through a negotiation worksheet, to be used by negotiators in a wide range of contexts. The worksheet is completed first by Andrea Lang, a hypothetical negotiator in a dispute between Lang Systems Ltd. and the Solo Professionals Association of Western Canada. Her negotiation choices and conflict analysis are recorded as she works her way to a resolution of the dispute. At the end of the chapter is a blank negotiation worksheet for your direct use.

The negotiation worksheet has a particular orientation that appears repeatedly throughout this handbook. It is an *interest-based* orientation, which emphasizes the *interests* of the parties over their *positions*.

POSITIONS AND INTERESTS

Positions are the "demands", "solutions" or "conclusions" that parties bring to the table. They do not present much scope for crafting a resolution that will satisfy both parties, as they offer only a simple "yes or no" choice — your way or my way. For that reason, they are not usually the end of the story in a negotiation.

The following examples illustrate that the full measure of the conflict between two disagreeing parties cannot be understood by hearing their competing *positions*:

- An employee who has been fired and is later broached with the idea of being reinstated in his job: "They couldn't pay me enough to take the treatment they dished out again."

- A supplier who is trying to collect: "I refuse to deliver any more shipments unless my bill is paid."

- An investor whose sell order to his long-time broker was missed: "Conrad has to apologize before I will even consider how much he owes me."

Interests are the "motivations", "needs" or "concerns" that lie behind the positions of the parties. An interest is the "why" behind the "what". Your *position* is what you have decided upon. Your *interest* is what caused you to decide.

The following examples illustrate how a focus on interests can open up the discussion to consider a broader range of options:

- "They couldn't pay me enough ..." is an expression of concern that the employer did not value the employee's services before, and that "they are now just thinking with their pocketbooks." It suggests a need by the employee for recognition of his or her worth to the employer.

- "I refuse to deliver any more shipments ..." is an expression of concern that "I'm a small operator and I'm putting my own business at risk to finance my customer's prosperity."

- "Conrad has to apologize ..." is a conclusion resulting from "I am concerned that even after so many years of doing business together, Conrad does not appreciate the consequences of his conduct and its effect on me."

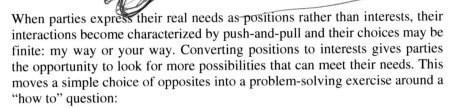

When parties express their real needs as positions rather than interests, their interactions become characterized by push-and-pull and their choices may be finite: my way or your way. Converting positions to interests gives parties the opportunity to look for more possibilities that can meet their needs. This moves a simple choice of opposites into a problem-solving exercise around a "how to" question:

- *Reinstate/Pay me* becomes: How can the employee achieve his need to be valued and his reputational and long-term financial needs in a small industry while the employer gains seasoned expertise at a time when it is experiencing cash-flow problems? An equity share, more say in the direction of the business, more time to write a book on a particular area of expertise all suggest themselves as possibilities.

- *Refuse/Can't pay* becomes: How can the supplier's cash flow concerns be met while at the same time providing an adequate supply of materials to the customer to ensure the revenue to pay their debts? Payment over time with a security element, exchange of services, or alternative financing might be examined here.

- *Apologize/I won't apologize* becomes: How can Conrad become aware of the general and specific consequences of his conduct? Direct discussions with those affected come to mind.

You may be able to think of other creative possibilities not mentioned here for each of the above situations. The point of the examples is not to demonstrate that agreement will inevitably follow or that the possibilities will always be acceptable to the people involved; the examples are simplified, without much context and with little detail about the people themselves.

WORKING WITH INTERESTS

There are three kinds of interests. When interests relate to the subject matter of the dispute, they are substantive. When they relate to the feelings or inner state of the participants, they are psychological. When they relate to "how" things are done, they are procedural. Look behind the positions in most disputes, no matter what kind, and you will find all three kinds of interests operating.

Consider the following exchange between an elderly, infirm parent and an adult son or daughter.

Parent: *I'll not move from this house! You have no right to make me move.*

Child: *You can't live by yourself anymore. You've got to move. And, I'll get a court order if I need to!*

The face-off positions here are, on the one hand, "Move from this house" and, on the other hand, "I'll not move from this house." The positions are diametrically opposed and cannot readily be reconciled. Beneath these positions could be many different interests. The substantive interests relate to appropriate care for the elderly parent: What is the right living facility? What treatment decisions should be made? Who would be the best caregiver and in what context? The psychological interests relate to the non-tangible, emotional and feeling concerns: feelings of frustration at reduced physical capabilities; guilt or sadness about the condition of a loved one; deep fear about the loss of privacy and independence. The procedural interests relate to how the controversy is handled: what level of participation the parent will have in deciding what living facility is appropriate; whether all relevant family members are able to take part in the discussion; and how family and friends will learn about the parent's change of residence.

These interests need to be identified and sorted out in order to transform this tug-of-war into a problem-solving exercise. This also entails the formulation of a problem-solving question which takes into account the interests of each side. This is sometimes called a *joint question* or a *"how to" question*. In this situation, such a question could be, "How can the elderly parent be physically safe and receive the necessary level of care, while at the same time maximizing his or her personal privacy, dignity and independence?"

In interest-based negotiation, the exercise is the same regardless of the context. Interests are elicited or deduced and then combined into a joint problem-solving question.

Parties in dispute can have interests in common, interests that are mutually exclusive and interests that are diametrically opposed to each other. Interest-based negotiation tries to meet as many of those interests as possible. The goal is to give each side as much as is possible, hence the notion of "win-win".

Consider the case of two neighbours, Bob and Jane, engaged in a lawsuit. A drainage ditch ran across the back of Jane's yard, where it abutted Bob's yard. Jane had filled in the ditch. Bob sued Jane for trespass when she refused to excavate the ditch. Their positions were diametrically opposed: "Dig out that ditch!" and "I will not dig out that ditch!"

When one begins to ask questions, interests are revealed. Why does Bob object to filling in the ditch? It seems that rainwater is no longer draining by means of the ditch and Bob's yard is flooded. Why did Jane fill in the ditch to begin with? Fill was added in order to increase the usable area of Jane's backyard.

While the positions are diametrically opposed, the interests are not. They can both be met. The question is, "How can Jane increase the usable area of the backyard while at the same time giving Bob's yard drainage?" There are several possibilities to be considered. These include using more porous fill so that drainage can occur, inserting a culvert into the area before adding fill or establishing some kind of permeable platform across the ditch. These possibilities or options need to be tested and funded, of course, but they raise the prospect that both neighbours' substantive interests can be met.

The substantive interests in the foregoing example are not common interests. The common interests are things like a joint desire to resolve the problem amicably or a common desire to end the monetary and emotional costs of the conflict, or even a common desire to avoid the risk inherent in litigation. The point is that if you think about this particular problem, it is those common interests which can motivate the parties to look for an answer to their substantive concerns.

Of course, the neighbours may still have interests which are diametrically opposed. Assuming that they can find a suitable option to extend the usable area of Jane's yard at the same time providing drainage, that option must be funded. Who will pay? This issue may again be one of tension and the parties will need to determine whether the impasse can be broken in an interest-based way or whether some other mechanism is necessary. The cost allocation may be resolved through simple compromise, by reference to some external standard, through the decision of an outsider like an arbitrator or through a random means like a coin toss. These are just some possibilities.

Consider the familiar "orange story", an example frequently used to illustrate the utility of interests. In that story, two siblings squabble over the last orange in the fridge. The wise parent, resisting the instinct to simply slice the orange in half, asks each child why they want the orange. Miraculously, one child claims the orange for the peel (to make marmalade or cake) and the other claims the pulp (to eat outright). Thus, it is possible to satisfy 100 per cent of each child's interest.

But what would happen if both children claimed the peel or both children claimed the pulp in light of the fact that there is only one orange? Here we run into a "distributive" problem which concerns the allocation of a limited resource. That is the same kind of problem facing Jane and Bob when it comes to determining who should pay for the remedial work.

There are several possibilities with respect to the orange, but because it is currently a limited resource, these do not involve completely satisfying either child's substantive interest. The possibilities include dividing the orange in half (simple compromise); giving one child the orange and the other child something else of value (exchange); establishing some rules to guide the distribution, i.e., the last orange goes to the hungriest child (principles); awarding the orange to the child who invents the best short story (contest); giving this orange to one child and promising the next orange to the other (timelines); and so forth.

Not all parts of every controversy can be satisfied by integrating the interests of the parties. As illustrated above, distributive aspects of a dispute still may involve some aspect of compromise or trade-off. This is commonly seen in personal injury disputes, where an important question is the quantum of damages payable in respect of the injury. Our message is that in every controversy, the inquiry should at least be made to see whether and to what extent interests can be met. This entails a curiosity about the interests of the other side and a willingness to investigate how those interests might be satisfied.

An interest-based approach does not require a negotiator to become credulous or to abandon judgment or intuition. An interest-based approach does not mandate blanket disclosure and indiscriminate trust. It *does* involve an ability to look beneath the surface — both for yourself and for the other parties. It *does* challenge parties to recognize that others have needs that may differ from their own. And it *does* challenge parties to try to simultaneously meet the needs of themselves and others — at least on some level.

APPROACHING INTERESTS WITH CAUTION

A word of caution about an interest-based approach to negotiation is appropriate here. In recent years, this orientation has become popular in business, management and dispute resolution publications. It *is* an attractive approach, one that engenders optimism, confidence and creativity. However, this popularization has led to certain myths that need to be debunked:

1.   *An interest-based analysis is a complete conflict analysis.* In fact, an interest-based analysis is just one possible frame of reference. Another is that negotiation is about "trading": What can I give you that will be a fair exchange? You want money. I want a release. Let's bargain about that.

     Alternatively, negotiation may be about the division and distribution of limited resources: What you get, I don't. What I get, you don't. There is a fixed sum of money available for the design and development of the marketing software. I am entitled to more of that sum for my contribution than you are for yours.

     Interest-based proponents often argue that each of the above examples could be converted to an interest-based situation — and to some extent this is true — but an interest-based analysis cannot alter the fact that some situations have significant distributive aspects. Joint venturers in the mining industry, for instance, can do their best to increase revenue from the venture — but at the end of the day, there will be a finite pool of money to divide. If the joint venturers explore their real needs, wants and concerns in the context of their business enterprise, this may help them to devise a system or set of principles to allocate the profits, but it will not eliminate the need for distributing those profits, which are finite.

2. *An interest-based approach will always lead to settlement; ergo, all disputes or issues are negotiable.* We have already observed in Chapter 1 that only a subgroup of all existing disputes are amenable to resolution at any given time. Within that group, a further subgroup will be appropriate for negotiation, and what this means is that there must be a sufficient overlap of (common) interests between the parties relative to conflicting ones. When the common interest is too small in comparison to the competing interests, negotiation may not work.

For example, a patient complains to a disciplinary body about the behaviour of a nurse, causing an investigation and a pending disciplinary hearing. The patient may find the events leading up to the complaint disturbing. He may also want the controversy over and done with because it takes up too much of his time. The nurse, for his part, may find the fact of the complaint threatening and disturbing too, and may want it to be over because of the uncertainty that he faces in a disciplinary hearing. The overlapping area of interests exists in the common desire of the patient and the nurse for an end to the dispute. That area, however, may be inadequate to support a negotiation. If the patient's primary interest is revenge or infliction of harm and the nurse's primary interest is vindication or affirmation of his professional standing by his peers, those interests may pull in opposite directions. Further, if each person places priority on such concerns, they may prevail over the common concerns for an end to the dispute. In these circumstances, it may be that only a decision-making process can achieve what each of them seeks, and both may be prepared to accept the risks involved in that process, namely, that they get all or nothing.

3. *Interest-based negotiation is morally superior to other orientations and other processes.* This view often prevails because interest-based negotiation is often called "principled" negotiation. It is promoted in a normative fashion as the right or proper thing to do. The implications of the term "principled" are obvious.

While there may be aspects of morality within any DR process (matters of honesty and integrity, for instance), an analytical orientation need not have any moral component. A person is not good because he or she engages in interest-based negotiation and bad because he or she declines to do so. Criticism is not warranted because parties pick litigation over mediation or coercive measures over adjudicative ones. As many of the examples in this handbook will illustrate, interest-based negotiation may at times be either inappropriate for or inaccessible to the parties.

THE BENEFIT OF INTERESTS

So why frame a discussion of negotiation around an interest-based orientation if it has limitations and imperfections?

We do so because our experience shows it to be a useful tool for analyzing conflict. Interests give us information about what the dispute is *really* about. They take us to a deeper level where a rich inventory of equipment may be found to assist in designing both resolutions and processes. Interests help us to understand some impasses and to sort negotiable problems from non-negotiable ones.

In our experience, when you work to understand and meet other people's interests, then they:

- tend to feel heard and are more apt to be in a position to listen to you;

- are more likely to be satisfied with or "buy into" the outcome;

- find it easier to cooperate in a problem-solving exercise;

- consider letting go of hard-fought positions when they see the prospect of having their needs met; and

- become open to options that were previously rejected, some of which may satisfy your own important needs.

NEGOTIATION AS EXPLORATION

Negotiators who view negotiation as a quest for inevitable agreement place themselves under enormous and unnecessary pressure. While agreement may sometimes be highly desirable and the alternative consequences unpalatable, presuming that agreement will flow from every negotiation places the cart before the horse. If the word "exploration" replaces "agreement" and the word "curiosity" replaces "compulsion", quite a different picture emerges.

Negotiation is a process whereby two or more participants with an actual or perceived clash of interests interact (with spoken and written words, with direct and indirect behaviour) in an *attempt* to reach a joint decision on matters of common concern. Whether or not the participants succeed in making that joint decision, they are still engaging in negotiation.

We adopt the view that negotiation inevitably involves *some* element of interdependence. Whether it is the union and company trying to work out the wording of the collective agreement, the divorcing spouses determining the distribution of matrimonial property, the product user seeking damages from a manufacturer, or the injured shopper seeking damages from the store, each participant is reliant upon or connected to the other, if only during the currency of their dealings. Their interdependence may spring from an ongoing relationship or from a one-time transaction. The participants may resent the interdependence or revel in it, or be aware of or oblivious to it, but it is present nevertheless. Negotiation comprises their efforts to define, redefine or extinguish that interdependence.

In this chapter, we define *negotiation* as a process by which parties interact to see *whether* and *to what extent* they can create a result that is *more desirable* to them than the one that already exists. If it is superior, then they may adopt the result, thus achieving agreement. If it is not, they may reject it, thus maintaining the status quo or moving on to another DR process.

THE ROLE OF THINKING IN NEGOTIATION

As is said of alpine skiing, 90 per cent of negotiation takes place in the mind. It is the negotiator's ability to analyze the dispute, to identify its component parts, to spot the sources and causes of impasse, and to devise activities that respond to the analysis, that is most helpful to the negotiator. In negotiation, although a party may be required to respond in the moment, no amount of technique can substitute for sound conflict analysis. This is infinitely more important than such details as who makes the first offer, where the negotiation takes place or the shape of the table. These details flow from the analysis; they do not govern it.

In performing a conflict analysis, the negotiator will observe multiple opportunities to access other DR options. These can be used to inform the negotiation, to attempt to change the dynamics at the table, to achieve leverage or to break impasse. Negotiation as a hub or central DR access point is examined later on in this chapter.

Now, let us examine a hypothetical dispute, using an interest-based approach and the negotiation worksheet. The worksheet is divided into two basic parts: preparation and analysis.

Case Study One

In this dispute, Lang Systems Ltd. and the Solo Professional Association of Western Canada (SPAWC) disagree about their contractual obligations. The negotiation will be approached from the perspective of Lang Systems Ltd., a small incorporated business.

Lang Systems Ltd. is in the business of selling and servicing computerized billing and accounting systems to a range of small- and medium-sized businesses. It is owned and operated by Andrea Lang and generates gross annual revenues of about $500,000. Approximately one third of Lang's gross revenues include the design and delivery of customized training courses targeted at specific market segments such as professional people who practise independently. These courses deal generally with office systems (of all sorts) and with the software and hardware combinations available to satisfy accounting and billing needs. The courses generate revenue *and* provide access to potential purchasers of systems. Andrea Lang is a chartered accountant by training but has not actively practised accounting for five years since she established Lang Systems Ltd.

SPAWC is an incorporated not-for-profit association with a membership of about 325. It is affiliated with a national organization known as CSPA, the Canadian Solo Professional Association. SPAWC has been in existence for over 20 years but its membership has remained small, declining slightly over the last three years. Internal problems and infighting have continually plagued SPAWC over the years, such that much of its energies are diverted from membership service and development. This prevents it from exploiting the potential membership of 1,000 to 1,500 members.

Lang used to be on the board of directors of SPAWC but did not run for office once her term expired, figuring that better use could be made of her time in her own fledgling business.

SPAWC is badly in need of revenue. It used to be the exclusive service provider to a large insurer of prepaid multi-disciplinary services, but that contract was not renewed this year.

Three months ago, Lang agreed to design and deliver a 30-hour course in cooperation with SPAWC entitled "Office Systems for the Sole Practitioner". The opportunity to do this came up rather unexpectedly and the deal was put together in the space of a week. Lang submitted a proposal to SPAWC which its board accepted without modification.

The terms of the deal are that Lang "is responsible for all aspects of design, development, delivery and administration, including course materials, location, registration and phone line". The proposal further stated that: "The only responsibilities that SPAWC has will be the promotion of the course through advertising and mailings (*i.e.*, through the SPAWC newsletter and through its quarterly journal, *The Professional Alone*), plus the delivery of a certificate of completion to members under seal of SPAWC within 20 days of completing any course." The certificate is important, as it represents an educational credit leading to a special designation within SPAWC.

Lang was to run the course twice in six months. Course fees were to be payable to Lang Systems Ltd. The price was $750 for non-members and $699 for members of SPAWC. For each registrant, SPAWC was to get 25 per cent of the gross. The minimum registration was 30 participants for each course. At 28 registrants, Lang Systems Ltd. would break even on any particular course and recover one quarter of its course development costs.

Now, seven days before the start of the first course, there are only 25 registrants. Lang attributes this to the fact that SPAWC has done virtually no advertising and promotion except one mailing to members and wait-listed registrants last month. In Lang's view, a mailing to members is of minimum use, since many members would not need the educational credit, and it is *potential* members that should be sought. Of those currently registered for the first course, only three per cent are existing SPAWC members.

The following is an example of how Andrea Lang can use the negotiation worksheet in conducting her negotiation with SPAWC. The worksheet is completed by Andrea as she thinks about and takes action on the problem. Follow along and see how you, too, could use this worksheet in your own negotiation.

NEGOTIATION WORKSHEET: Part I — Preparation

YOUR NAME:　　　　　　　　**Andrea Lang**
　　　　　　　　　　　　　　　Lang Systems Ltd.

CONCERNING:　　　　　　　　**Solo Professionals**
　　　　　　　　　　　　　　　Association of
　　　　　　　　　　　　　　　Western Canada
　　　　　　　　　　　　　　　(SPAWC) Courses

I-1: WHAT GIVES RISE TO THE DISPUTE?

Looking at the dispute from your own perspective, describe it here. Consider its practical impact on you and what causes it to demand your attention at this time.

DESCRIBE THE PROBLEM

- SPAWC is not promoting our joint course as it is supposed to do under the contract. The contract is very specific and says that SPAWC is responsible for "publication of the course through mailings and advertising." I am responsible for all other aspects.

WHAT ARE THE CONSEQUENCES OF THIS PROBLEM?

- Registrations for the first course are at or below the minimum registration number.
- I am in danger of losing my investment in the design of the course.
- The course will not be profitable. It will be operated at or near break-even and if so, is not a viable business activity. Lang Systems Ltd. exists to make a profit.

A dispute often manifests itself in the form of a problem for one or both parties when negative consequences flow from the problem and demand a person's attention. A useful starting point in negotiation preparation is to describe the problem and the consequences briefly from the negotiator's vantage point.

I-2: SHOULD I NEGOTIATE? — A PRELIMINARY ASSESSMENT

What are the reasons that you and the other side would invest the time and effort negotiating? Are the costs and consequences of negotiating better or worse than not doing so at this time? Complete this analysis for both yourself and the other side.

ABOUT YOU	ABOUT THEM
WHAT ARE THE CONSEQUENCES OF NOT REACHING AGREEMENT? HOW LIKELY ARE THESE TO OCCUR?	WHAT ARE THE CONSEQUENCES OF NOT REACHING AGREEMENT? HOW LIKELY ARE THESE TO OCCUR?
PROBABILITY: HIGH/MEDIUM/LOW	PROBABILITY: HIGH/MEDIUM/LOW
1. I don't recoup my investment — High 2. I lose money — Medium 3. Lang loses business credibility — Medium 4. SPAWC sues me — Low	1. Loses potential opportunity to increase membership — High 2. Loses credibility with 3 per cent of members who registered — Medium 3. Loses needed revenue from the courses — High 4. Lang sues them — Medium
ARE THERE OTHER POSSIBILITIES FOR SOLVING THE PROBLEM THAT DO NOT REQUIRE INTERACTING WITH THE OTHER SIDE? IF SO, HOW DESIRABLE ARE THEY?	ARE THERE OTHER POSSIBILITIES FOR SOLVING THE PROBLEM THAT DO NOT REQUIRE INTERACTING WITH THE OTHER SIDE? IF SO, HOW DESIRABLE ARE THEY?

DESIRABILITY: HIGH/MEDIUM/LOW	DESIRABILITY: HIGH/MEDIUM/LOW
1. Abandon course altogether and go on to more profitable activity — Medium 2. Find alternative partner — Low 3. Take on promotion myself and withhold SPAWC's share to cover my extra expenses — Low	1. Withdraw sponsorship of course — Medium 2. Find alternative partner — Low
BASED ON THE ABOVE, WHAT IS MY LEVEL OF COMMITMENT TO ACHIEVING A RESOLUTION?	BASED ON THE ABOVE, WHAT IS MY LEVEL OF COMMITMENT TO ACHIEVING A RESOLUTION?
HIGH/MEDIUM/LOW — Medium	HIGH/MEDIUM/LOW — Medium

Resolving the problem jointly is going to take time and effort for both Lang and SPAWC. The negotiator needs to make a preliminary assessment of whether this investment is worth it and what incentives the other side has to negotiate. In so doing, the negotiator looks at other possibilities, away from the bargaining table, which in some instances may be more attractive and may lead to an abandonment of the negotiation.

I-3: WHO IS INVOLVED IN THIS NEGOTIATION?

With whom are you negotiating? What characteristics do the participants bring? Who else is relevant? Again, complete this part for both yourself and the other side.

ABOUT YOU	ABOUT THEM
NEGOTIATOR'S NAME: Andrea Lang	NEGOTIATOR'S NAME: Helen Antonova, Chair, SPAWC Education Committee

CIRCLE ONE: Individual / Partnership / Corporation / Institution / Board / Agency / Govern- ment Department / Other	CIRCLE ONE: Individual / Partnership / Corporation / Institution / Board / Agency / Government Department / Other
REPRESENTING: Lang Systems Ltd.	REPRESENTING: SPAWC
PAST DEALINGS:	PAST DEALINGS: • Antonova is a good per- son but I question whether the board can pull things together.
CHARACTERISTICS (KNOWN & SUPPOSED):	CHARACTERISTICS (KNOWN & SUPPOSED): • SPAWC is a very dysfunc- tional organization. It has no clear mandate. Its board of directors is generally frac- tious and it can't seem to get anything done.
IS THERE A READINESS AND WILLINGNESS TO BARGAIN? • Yes	IS THERE A READINESS AND WILLINGNESS TO BARGAIN? • Not sure
IS THERE AN ABILITY TO BARGAIN? • Yes	IS THERE AN ABILITY TO BARGAIN? • Limited

WHAT ARE OUR RELATIVE RESOURCES?

Lang has expertise in the design and delivery of courses. SPAWC has limited experience. My course is ready to go. I am a small business with limited cash. SPAWC has no cash to speak of. Lang Systems Ltd. is a profit-making enterprise and I am its sole owner and operator. Every hour I spend in negotiating this problem is an hour not devoted elsewhere in the business. SPAWC is a board of volunteers. They would have less at stake than I do because it's not their own money, but would also find negotiating time to be non-profitable. Each board member is also a professional in sole practice, carrying all aspects of the business himself or herself.

In moving forward with the negotiation analysis, it is useful to consider the characteristics of the parties involved. This includes those at the negotiating table, those whom they represent and those who might be influenced or affected by what transpires. This analysis will typically contain a mixture of subjective and objective information and may reveal assumptions, prejudices or conclusions relating to parties, which may need to be re-examined for their soundness.

Who else is likely to influence any decisions taken in the negotiation? To whom must any outcome be justified and on what basis?

YOU	OTHER PARTICIPANT
IDENTITY OF INFLUENTIAL PARTIES: • Current and potential course registrants.	IDENTITY OF INFLUENTIAL PARTIES: • Current and potential course registrants. • Current Board members.
BASIS FOR INFLUENCE: • They were promised things in the course flyer that should be lived up to.	BASIS FOR INFLUENCE: • They were promised things in the course flyer that should be lived up to.

	• Decision-making authority of the negotiator is not clear or consistent.
	• They want to retain credibility with Board and members.
JUSTIFICATIONS NECESSARY:	JUSTIFICATIONS NECESSARY:
• I need only justify the deal to myself.	• SPAWC needs to be able to justify a deal to its board and members.

I-4: WHAT IS THE ENVIRONMENT IN WHICH THE NEGOTIATION TAKES PLACE?

What else is likely to influence any decisions taken in the negotiation? Is there anything about the circumstances, situation or environment in which you are negotiating that is relevant? This could include family, ethnic, political, economic, geographic, timing, organizational or any number of other factors, including the presence or absence of lawyers in the negotiation.

YOU

CONTEXT OF NEGOTIATION:

• The marketplace for systems training is becoming quite competitive, as there are no barriers to entry.

SIGNIFICANCE OR IMPACT:

• Lang must distinguish its courses — a certificate from SPAWC does this.
• Lang Systems Ltd. now has at least four competitors whereas two years ago it had none and was the first in the marketplace.

Negotiations seldom, if ever, occur in isolation. Rather, they take place in a context — a milieu or environment that constrains, influences or aggravates the dispute. The context can be of many sorts — family, ethnic, organizational, religious, historic, economic, political — and more than one context may be operational at any one time. The context may infuse the dispute with its own values, beliefs, language, modes of communication, behaviour and other norms. For example, in a commercial context, behavioural norms often prevent the express acknowledgment of the role of feelings in human activities. "It's just money", people often say. "There's very little emotion here, unlike a family problem." Yet, feelings may be very powerfully present and influential, despite the taboo against acknowledging their legitimacy. Thus, the negotiator needs to think about the context(s) in which the negotiation occurs and how it will influence the negotiation.

I-5: PROCEDURE — HOW WILL I NEGOTIATE?

What is the preferred method of approach to meet your needs? How can the negotiation best be carried out?

YOU	OTHER PARTICIPANT
I have already sent a letter to Helena Antonova, Chair of SPAWC's Education Committee, setting out my concerns and explaining that I will not pay SPAWC 25 per cent of the gross per head in these circumstances. She wrote back saying that their promotional obligation is *limited to* using their communication organs, namely the Newsletter and Journal, and does not extend to outside advertising. She said it was my job to bring this up earlier if it was a problem, not wait until the last minute. Although I prefer to deal by memorandum or letter because that gives me a chance to think things through, this is inefficient and the start date for the course is approaching. Therefore, I must speak directly with her. Telephone will do.	Helena Antonova is busy. She does not really have time for letters, and generally prefers to deal by telephone — especially in this case since our offices are at opposite ends of town.

Negotiation need not occur purely in the course of a face-to-face meeting. It can happen with a range of words and actions carried out in several ways — letters, diagrams, charts, pictures, telephone calls, meetings, email — and in various combinations and permutations. The negotiator needs to give some thought to the combination that will be most effective in the circumstances. This will include consideration of a variety of factors such as timing, duration, identity and numbers of people involved, personal communication preferences (some people write better than they speak, others speak better than they write) and availability.

I-6: INTERESTS — A PRELIMINARY VIEW

What is really at stake in this negotiation? Try to go beneath the pet solutions that each party is lobbying for in order to understand the root causes. Expose as many interests as you can.

INTERESTS

WHAT HAVE I DEMANDED OR INSISTED UPON?

- I told SPAWC that unless it immediately promotes our joint course and gives me a promotional plan, I'm refusing to pay 25 per cent of the gross.

WHAT NEEDS OF MINE LIE BENEATH MY DEMAND?

- To punish SPAWC — make it get its act together.
- Need for a business solution — to make course profitable or cut my losses.
- Stability — I cannot have "moving parts" in an ongoing business venture.
- Recoup my course development costs of $40,000.
- Minimize *my* cash outlay in promotion.
- Increase registrations.
- Keep profitability at $20,000 per course.
- Maintain credibility in the marketplace — delivering a first rate course.
- Get courses known.
- Distinguish course in marketplace from other similar courses.
- Preserve the right to a certificate from SPAWC.

DO ANY OF THESE NEEDS CONFLICT WITH EACH OTHER?

- Possibly punishing SPAWC conflicts with a business solution. I cannot imagine SPAWC would voluntarily agree to punishment.

IF I COULD HAVE ONLY ONE OF THE CONFLICTING NEEDS, WHICH ONE WOULD IT BE?

- Business solution — I'm a *for*-profit enterprise, not a regulatory or policing body.

WHAT HAS THE OTHER SIDE DEMANDED OR INSISTED UPON?

- SPAWC insists that its promotional responsibilities are limited to using its own internal communications vehicles and still wants 25 per cent per head.

WHAT NEEDS MIGHT LIE UNDERNEATH THE OTHER SIDE'S DEMAND?

- Reduce its cash outlay.
- Maximize its revenue.
- Serve members — member services.
- Attract new members.

Earlier in this chapter, emphasis was placed on the distinction between positions and interests. Negotiators were urged to convert positions to interests to minimize the chances of impasse and increase the prospect of a meaningful result that responds to needs. Before engaging in further words and actions with the other side, the negotiator needs to stop and consider what *needs* each side has that might be bundled up inside its opening shot. Typically, negotiators do this most easily for themselves, although at this stage not all of a negotiator's own interests may be clear. Such clarity will come. Negotiators also tend to look at interests less easily and less readily for the other side as if stating the other's interest will make it come true. Keep in mind that the exercise is at this point a private one done for the negotiator's own information only, and that uncovering or speculating about interests is not the same thing as disclosing them. Disclosure questions will be dealt with next.

Looking for the real needs behind the positions may not be easy because needs can be vague, undeveloped, unconscious or conflicting just as they may be clear, developed, conscious and complementary. When a negotiator's needs conflict, it may be necessary to pick one over the other. Interests can also occur at many levels and one need may lie beneath another. Try to go as far beneath the surface as you can in identifying these needs.

I-7: THE LAW AND THE LITIGATION SYSTEM

In considering whether to call upon the law and the legal system in the negotiation, the negotiator may need to consult a lawyer for advice. Such advice should enable the negotiator to complete the following questions as part of preparation for the negotiation.

COURT PREPARATION

IF THIS WENT TO COURT, WHAT QUESTION WOULD THE COURT BE ANSWERING?

- The court would determine the proper interpretation of the contract between Lang Systems Ltd. and SPAWC, specifically what the words "the promotion of the course through advertising and mailings (*i.e.*, through the SPAWC Newsletter and through its quarterly journal, *The Professional Alone*)" mean.

WOULD THIS RESOLVE THE DISPUTE?

- Possibly. It would certainly clarify our respective responsibilities.

WHAT ARE THE CHANCES THAT THE QUESTION WILL BE ANSWERED IN MY FAVOUR?

- Hard to say. Arguments go both ways. 40 to 60 per cent chance.

WHAT WOULD MY INVOLVEMENT BE?

- Give lawyer all relevant paperwork.
- Review draft documents prepared by lawyer.
- Instruct lawyer in person and by phone.
- Attend examination for discovery.
- Prepare for trial.
- Be a witness at trial.

HOW MUCH WOULD THIS COST?

- $10,000 to $40,000.
- Lower end of range if other side agrees to simply submit wording of contract to a judge for interpretation.

HOW AND TO WHAT EXTENT WOULD ANY OF THIS MEET MY NEEDS?

- A decision would certainly clarify responsibilities and possibly vindicate my interpretation but:

1. It would do nothing to *create* resources for promotion and I remain concerned that SPAWC doesn't have what it will take to promote the course in any event.
2. It does not assure the *best* use of promotional dollars even if SPAWC has the money. It's important to me to know *where* the course is being promoted.
3. It would divert time and money away from my existing business and I am its sole owner and operator.
4. It would publicize the dispute between SPAWC and Lang Systems Ltd. with the result that confidence in the course might be undermined.

Canada is to some extent a rights-based society; its people think about their entitlements and obligations at law. They are able to establish and defend those rights through our court system, which is publicly funded and backed by the sanction of the state. Therefore, it is legitimate, indeed natural, for negotiators to consider whether and to what extent the law and the legal system are useful in the resolution of a dispute. Sometimes "the legal system" means litigation. At other times it means the relevant agency, board or commission that is created to deal with specialized matters, such as a securities commission, a labour relations board or a professional regulatory body. These too are publicly funded and backed by the sanction of the state.

In most instances this entails seeking the advice of a lawyer who is licensed and qualified to tell the negotiator about the relevant law, the appropriate procedures and the costs and consequences of both. Consideration must then be given to how this information meets the negotiator's needs.

I-8: ANTICIPATED WORK PRODUCT

Without regard to the specifics of the situation, what outcome or work product, if any, is anticipated from the negotiation?

YOU	OTHER PARTICIPANT
WORK PRODUCT EXPECTED: • An agreement in principle that the board can approve; I want a directors' resolution confirming any deal reached.	WORK PRODUCT EXPECTED: • A firm proposal to take to the board?

When engaging in a negotiation, the negotiator should give thought to the kind of work product expected to result and what is realistic in the circumstances. In some cases, a handshake will suffice and an oral under-standing is all that is required. At the other extreme, a detailed formal document drawn and vetted by lawyers may be in order. In between is an agreement in principle with varying amounts of detail. The anticipated work product will also be influenced by the nature of the dispute and the disputants, the degree of authority possessed by the negotiator, the costs and consequences of the format, and other variables.

I-9: TRUST AND DISCLOSURE

Before embarking on direct discussions with the opposite side, a negotiator should reflect on related issues of trust and disclosure. How important is trust and to what extent should it prevail? What information should be disclosed and to what extent? In either case, are there concerns that can be addressed without taking the negotiator to extremes?

ISSUES

DO YOU TRUST THE OTHER PARTY? WHY OR WHY NOT?

- SPAWC is moderately trustworthy. Its continuing need for cash and its changing board of directors tend to make it a slow and inconsistent organization. It cannot be counted on to act promptly. In the past, I've had to wait up to 12 months for an accounting with respect to joint training.

ARE YOU GOING TO BE PERCEIVED AS TRUSTWORTHY?

- Yes. I have always done what I have said I was going to do and I have an excellent reputation in the field. Some SPAWC members could even attest to the fact that I have accommodated their changing office needs at a reduced cost or even at a loss to the business in order to generate good will.

WHAT IS IMPORTANT ABOUT TRUST?

- If SPAWC agrees to pay for all or part of the necessary promotion, I need to be assured that the money will be available without further argument.
- Also, my trust relates to my willingness to engage in the negotiation — I need to feel that SPAWC has a *bona fide* intention to reach a settlement.

WHAT ARE THE RISKS IF YOUR TRUST IS UNWARRANTED?

- I will have "wasted" the time spent negotiating. That time has opportunity costs.

WHAT ARE THE REWARDS IF YOUR TRUST IS WARRANTED?

- Lang Systems Ltd. and SPAWC stand a good chance of working something out and I can stop spending this unproductive time.

BALANCING THE RISKS AND REWARDS, IS THERE ANY WAY TO MEET YOUR CONCERNS ABOUT TRUST?

- With respect to the money, I can proceed without trust. Since I collect the course fees, Lang Systems Ltd. is in a position to deduct SPAWC's share of promotion from its entitlement.

- I am prepared to invest time working out a solution but up to a maximum of 10 hours. After 10 hours I will reassess the situation and may withdraw from the negotiation.

HAVING THOUGHT ABOUT YOUR INTERESTS (NEEDS, WANTS, CONCERNS) AND THE OPPORTUNITIES THAT YOU HAVE AWAY FROM THE TABLE, LIST ANY CONCERNS YOU HAVE ABOUT DISCLOSURE, TOGETHER WITH THE BASIS FOR THE CONCERNS.

- I do not want SPAWC to know that I would seriously entertain the idea of cutting my losses and abandoning the course altogether even before the first one runs. My concern is that if they learn this, they may not think I am genuine in my search for a resolution and may decline to talk to me.
- I do not want to reveal my costing and budget for the courses because it is confidential business information. I am concerned that this would put SPAWC in a position to compete with me directly in the training business and that other members who are my direct competitors may get access to the information.

WHAT ARE THE RISKS ASSOCIATED WITH DISCLOSURE?

- Educating competitors (see above).

WHAT ARE THE REWARDS OF DISCLOSURE?

- If SPAWC understands my business needs at least in a general way, it will legitimize my position. SPAWC members are all business people too.

> ### BALANCING THE RISKS AND REWARDS, IS THERE ANY WAY TO MEET YOUR CONCERNS ABOUT DISCLOSURE?
>
> * I don't need to mention my alternatives until I see what a possible solution looks like. As to my costing and budget, I can talk in general terms about my business needs.

The related issues of trust and disclosure bedevil many a negotiator and many a negotiation.

Trust is the element of confidence, faith or reliance that one negotiator places — or declines to place — in another to mean what he or she says, to do what he or she promises, and to act without malice or malevolence towards him or her. Trust is a two-sided coin. The negotiator may trust but not be trustworthy — or be trustworthy but not trustful.

Disclosure is about telling — releasing information or informing the other side. "Whether", "when" and "how much" are recurring questions about disclosure in negotiation.

Trust and disclosure each exist along continua and often stand in direct relation to each other: the amount of disclosure varies with the degree of trust reposed in the other side. High levels of mutual trust can facilitate negotiation by promoting exchange of relevant information and problem-solving, whereas high levels of mutual distrust can make it virtually impossible to deal. Additional difficulties arise when there are disproportionate levels of trust — for the exchange of information and the use to which it is put can be quite uneven, especially where unwarranted reliance is placed in another who comes to the table without *bona fides*.

The problem with trust is that the negotiator can only tell in hindsight whether it has been appropriately placed. That will give the negotiator information for future dealings but scarcely assist in the moment. The matter is further complicated by the fact that trust is a complex phenomenon originating in a blend of rational thought, visceral reaction, personal experience, objective information, direct observation, inference and more.

The negotiation worksheet focuses the negotiator on the pragmatic aspects of trust and disclosure. What are the costs and consequences of disclosure? The costs and consequences of secrecy? Do the benefits outweigh the risks? There are no easy answers here and each negotiator needs to formulate an answer in each particular case.

Elsewhere, this chapter has emphasized that interest-based negotiation does not require indiscriminate trust and blanket disclosure. That would be tantamount to the negotiator abandoning judgment. Instead, the negotiator should *think about* trust and disclosure, identifying concerns and try to find ways to meet them. Is there a way to proceed independently of trust? This is sometimes a possibility.

Identifying or hypothesizing about interests is not tantamount to communicating them. The negotiator should separate these two aspects of negotiation preparation. First, the negotiator should convert from positions to interests. *Then* the negotiator should consider the extent to which it is comfortable to talk about them.

NEXT STEPS

Having concluded her preparation, Andrea Lang was able to arrange a telephone call with Helena Antonova. She had no specific ideas about how the conversation should end, but planned to explain to Antonova why she could no longer consider paying the organization 25 per cent of the gross revenue from the course. She wanted Antonova to understand why SPAWC's behaviour was a problem to Lang Systems Ltd., and to make it clear that the situation was a business problem and not a personal one, from her perspective. Lang was aware that all too often in the past, the board of directors simply attacked a member personally if it disagreed with what he or she was saying. At the same time, Lang wanted to get as much information as she could to determine whether and to what extent the association was prepared to do anything. Of prime concern to Lang was preserving the certificate of completion that would come from SPAWC, enabling registrants in this course to earn credit towards a certificate program administered by SPAWC. It is this certificate that distinguishes Lang Systems Ltd. courses from other similar courses in the marketplace at this time.

The telephone conversation between Lang and Antonova was cordial but businesslike. They discussed various aspects of the problem, including their differing interpretations of SPAWC's obligations with respect to promotion. Although Lang disagreed with SPAWC's interpretation and could not persuade Antonova to her point of view, she began to see how SPAWC had arrived at its interpretation and started to realize that the clause could be interpreted in SPAWC's way just as easily as it could be interpreted her way.

Antonova mentioned that SPAWC was operating in the red this year, especially due to the fact that it had lost an important revenue-producing contract in the last six months. The income from that contract had constituted over 75 per cent of its revenues and the association was struggling to make it up. Lang accepted this information because: (a) the percentages were consistent with those when she was on the board of directors; and (b) Antonova knew that she could easily verify the information from the interim financial statements to which each member was entitled. The practical implications of this were that SPAWC would not have the resources to promote and advertise the course the way it ought to be done even if a court were to clarify its written obligations.

Lang also learned the following during the conversation:

• Antonova was willing to try to work things out because she liked her, but she was a volunteer and there was a limit on how much time she could spend on the negotiations. She would work with her so long as their process was efficient and clear.

• Lang's initial letter and Antonova's response had already come before the board for consideration. Antonova was authorized by the board to discuss the matter with Lang and to return to the board with an agreement in principle for their approval.

• The board of directors would be meeting in three days and could ratify any agreement at that time.

• There was a new division taking place within SPAWC. The board of directors was hungry for cash — any cash from almost any source — and tended to take a short-term view of things. The education committee, however, which Antonova chaired, was interested in quality. It was in the process of bringing back to the board for final approval a series of educational criteria which all course deliverers would have to meet to offer courses in conjunction with SPAWC and to grant certificates from SPAWC for credit towards its certificate program. The result of this change would be to open the marketplace to Lang Systems Ltd.'s competitors so that its courses would no longer be distinctive in the marketplace. Antonova assured Lang that her course would have no difficulty meeting the criteria but stated that Lang Systems Ltd. would have to go through the approval process nonetheless. Antonova anticipated that the new course guidelines would be up and running within the next three to four months.

• Antonova could see Lang's point of view and interpretation of the disputed clause. She wished that she had raised the matter earlier so that they could have put their minds to it before Lang made its investment in the course.

Using the information gained thus far in the telephone call, Lang can conduct a further analysis. In particular, she may return to this preliminary list of interests to verify her own needs and those of SPAWC. Lang may be obliged to do this during the course of the conversation or she may arrange for a short period of time to give the matter additional thought in light of the new information.

NEGOTIATION WORKSHEET: Part II — Analysis

YOUR NAME: Andrea Lang
                              Lang Systems Ltd.

CONCERNING: Solo Professionals of
                              Western Canada
                              (SPAWC) Courses

II-1: INTERESTS REVISITED — MUTUAL NEEDS

Revisit the preliminary list of interests and consider how it can be modified in light of what you have heard. Think about the information you have obtained and how it is meaningful and useful to you in the negotiation.

INTERESTS

WHAT IS THE MOST IMPORTANT INFORMATION THAT YOU LEARNED IN YOUR COMMUNICATIONS WITH THE OTHER SIDE?

- Lang Systems Ltd. is about to lose the unique feature of its course — SPAWC's certificate.
- Antonova is authorized to cut a deal subject to board ratification available in three days.
- SPAWC needs money.

WHAT ARE THE IMPLICATIONS OF THIS INFORMATION?

- Lang Systems Ltd. will lose a marketing advantage.
- SPAWC cannot afford to sue me or be sued.
- SPAWC cannot afford to buy the kind of advertising that is required to maximize acceptability.
- A deal should give SPAWC income.
- Time is of the essence — I can close this one off soon if I move quickly.

GIVEN WHAT I HAVE LEARNED, WHAT ARE MY MOST IMPORTANT NEEDS?

- Maintain the distinctiveness of Lang's course for as long as possible.
- Preserve certificate for this course.

- Finalize the negotiation — end the opportunity costs of negotiation.
- Get the best possible contribution towards promotion for the courses.
- Recoup my course development costs.
- Run a profitable course.
- Get stability for this course.

WHAT ARE THE MOST IMPORTANT NEEDS OF THE OTHER PARTY?

- Cash!
- Cash!
- Cash!
- Increased memberships.
- Consistency of quality in courses — consistency of approach towards all course providers.
- Membership development.

DO ANY OF THESE NEEDS DIRECTLY CONFLICT? IF SO, HOW IS THIS SIGNIFICANT?

- Yes. SPAWC's need for cash conflicts with my need to get the highest possible contribution from SPAWC for promotion. Even if I held back 100 per cent of SPAWC's entitlement, it would not cover all promotional costs and SPAWC has no other resources to draw upon. If this goes ahead, it is inevitable that Lang Systems Ltd. will be paying the bulk of the promotional costs. If I could run the course at least five times in all, I can recover my development costs in totality.

By thinking about interests during preparation, the negotiator is able to form a preliminary view about what is important and what might drive a deal. This view should not be held too firmly so that new information arising during the course of the negotiation may be taken into account. The negotiator's preliminary view of the interests of the opposite party may constitute a hypothesis, and direct discussion may be necessary to confirm, nullify or modify the hypothesis. Different and unexpected information may be learned, giving rise to possibilities not considered before. Even the negotiator's own interests may shift — some may recede in importance, others may stand out in stark relief, and others may appear at odds. The negotiator must be alert and open to new information, especially that which has a bearing on the needs of the parties at the table.

At the same time, the negotiator needs to determine whether and to what extent the other person's needs are complementary or conflicting and what importance the other person attaches to the various needs. Often — although not always — a situation which looks like a direct clash of interests turns out to be one in which the needs of the parties can happily coexist.

II-2: STATING THE PROBLEM-SOLVING EXERCISE

Now, restate what the negotiation is about, this time using a "how to" question and incorporating as many of your needs and those of the other participant as you can. Make this a joint question, such as: How can I protect the unique aspects of my invention while at the same time giving you sufficient information to make a buying decision?

JOINT "HOW TO" QUESTION

How can I recoup my development costs for the course, get the largest possible contribution toward promotion and preserve its distinctiveness (for as long as possible) while satisfying SPAWC's need for cash and its expressed intention to treat all future course providers the same?

Once an adequate degree of clarity is achieved around the question of needs, the challenge is to think of how to meet those needs — as many needs as possible. This is the true problem-solving aspect of negotiation. A useful way to do this is to restate the problem as a "how to" question as discussed at the beginning of this chapter. Such a question incorporates the needs of *both* the negotiator *and* the other party and thus encompasses a certain amount of tension. Parties often focus on their own concerns to the exclusion of those of the other party out of fear that legitimizing another person's concerns will prevent theirs from being met. This is an understandable emotional reaction, but unless the needs are truly in opposition, such as disputants claiming all of a fixed and limited resource, it is not one that needs to be true.

II-3: PROBLEM SOLVING — POSSIBLE AND PREFERRED SOLUTIONS

Thinking about the joint "how to" question and working alone or together with the other person, list as many possibilities as come to mind for responding to the question. Construct a composite sketch if you can, incorporating as many ideas from both sides of the table as you can. Try to add new or novel ones. Then step back and examine what has been created.

YOU

RESTATE THE "HOW TO" QUESTION:

- How can I recoup my development costs for the course, get the largest possible contribution toward promotion and preserve its distinctiveness (for as long as possible) while satisfying SPAWC's need for cash and its expressed intention to treat all future course providers the same?

POSSIBLE WAYS TO SOLVE THE PROBLEM:

- Run the course as many times as possible before the new system comes in.
- Lang Systems Ltd. does promotion itself — finds spots, writes ad text, *etc.*
- Lang Systems Ltd. and SPAWC share advertising costs in some reasonable proportion to be determined.
- Some of SPAWC's entitlement goes to promotion.
- SPAWC does those aspects of promotion and advertising that it can do at a low or no cost, such as piggy-backing ads with existing mailings, including notices in its newsletters.
- SPAWC promotes association membership to registrants of Lang Systems Ltd. course via personal letter from the president, talk from membership chairman, distribution of brochures.
- Raise course fees.
- Deliver inferior product (*i.e.*, cut back on course materials).
- Reduce course length.
- SPAWC delivers certificates.
- Pay SPAWC only if minimum number of registrants is reached.
- Pay SPAWC on a sliding scale.
- SPAWC provides instructors at no cost to Lang Systems Ltd.

DO ANY COMBINATIONS MAKE SENSE? OF THE ABOVE WAYS, WHICH ONES DO THE BEST JOB OF SATISFYING AS MANY OF OUR CONCERNS AS POSSIBLE?

The greater the amount of cash available to SPAWC, the greater the chances of a proposal being accepted by the board at its meeting in three days. The more times I can run the course, the more value can be derived from every advertising dollar (since multiple courses can be advertised in one ad) and the greater the ability to amortize course development costs. Changing the course structure or content would involve redesign of existing literature, and SPAWC-appointed instructors would be learning Lang's course methods at no cost and to the potential detriment of Lang Systems Ltd.

A combination of the following satisfies each side's primary needs:

- Lang Systems Ltd. to run course as many times as possible (but not less than six times) before the end of the next 18 months.
- SPAWC to receive no money if minimum registration number not reached (course may be cancelled at Lang's discretion).
- Otherwise, SPAWC to receive 25 per cent per head.
- 35 per cent of SPAWC's entitlement from any course to be held back by Lang as reimbursement for promotional or advertising costs.
- SPAWC to provide certificate of completion for each course which will also serve as credit towards its certificate program.
- SPAWC's president to provide customized letter of welcome to each course registrant, outlining benefits of membership.
- SPAWC to arrange with Lang Systems Ltd. other opportunities for contact with participants during the currency of any course.

Early on, the negotiator begins to imagine possibilities for the ultimate resolution of the dispute. Because negotiation is a dynamic process involving at least one other person or party, this early picture will be influenced by information obtained during the negotiation. The totality of this information, especially the final list of needs and priorities, forms the backdrop for the ultimate exploration of a solution.

In private, jointly or some combination of both, the negotiator needs to construct a picture of what is possible and realistic in the circumstances. Returning to the joint "how to" question, consideration should be given to the manner in which it might be answered. Sometimes, the answer may be obvious and one-dimensional. Other times it may be obscure and multi-faceted. Whatever the case, some degree of effort and thought is in order.

By generating a list of possibilities for the resolution of the dispute, the negotiator will be able to construct a composite picture. This can then be examined to determine whether and to what extent it meets the negotiator's needs. The options can be narrowed. A preferred solution may emerge.

II-4: MAKING A COMMITMENT — OR NOT

In this chapter, we have defined negotiation as an exploratory, problem-solving process, that is, an interaction through which parties determine whether and to what extent they can make a more desirable outcome than one that exists. Thus, before committing to an outcome available through negotiations, the negotiator needs to compare that result to opportunities. By doing this in an informed, careful manner, negotiators exercise choice.

YOU

IS THERE ANY SIGNIFICANT WAY IN WHICH THE PREFERRED SOLUTION DOES NOT MEET YOUR PRIORITIES AND NEEDS?

- I would have preferred to make SPAWC solely responsible for promotion in order to minimize Lang Systems Ltd.'s outlay — but this is not realistic. First, SPAWC does not have the money and, second, it does not have the same commitment to profitability.

LIST THE VARIOUS OPPORTUNITIES THAT YOU HAVE "AWAY FROM THE TABLE" (ELSEWHERE) TO MEET YOUR CONCERNS, ALONG WITH THE RESOURCES, DEGREE OF RISK AND THE POSSIBLE REWARDS THAT EACH WILL ENTAIL.

Lang Systems Ltd. can:

1. Abandon the courses altogether — bail out — and cut its losses. This involves no risk and no further resources, but will result in a loss as the course development costs will not be recovered and Lang Systems Ltd. will lose visibility in the marketplace.
2. Continue on as is, do its own promotion but withhold any money from SPAWC. Involves further capital and entails risk that SPAWC will withhold its certificate from course registrants, thus giving rise to participant dissatisfaction or lawsuits.
3. Team up with another association or fund another partner. This is future market development that should be done anyway but could not possibly be explored or implemented within three days. Further, it should be done in addition to and not in substitution for the deal with SPAWC.

DO YOU PREFER ONE OF THESE OTHER OPPORTUNITIES?

- No. I think the rewards of going forward with the preferred solution from this negotiation will outweigh the risks. Lang

Systems Ltd. will continue to occupy a pre-eminent position in the training market at least for another 18 months with SPAWC's certificate.

WHY WOULD THE OTHER SIDE BUY INTO THE PRE-FERRED SOLUTION?

- It maximizes its cash return without the need for any upfront investment or any significant cash outlay. It provides SPAWC with a readily available course and with access to potential members, during the time that its new course system is coming into play. In short, there is little, if any, downside for SPAWC.

The formulation of possible solutions and the emergence of a preferred solution is inextricably linked with the evaluation of that solution and an assessment of its probabilities for acceptance. In fact, the two stages may merge into one comprehensive whole.

Here, the negotiator takes the final steps to determine whether, and to what extent, commitment is appropriate. In doing this, the negotiator can return once again to the list of priorities and needs as well as to a consideration of opportunities away from the table. It is only if the possibilities created in the negotiation are superior to the opportunities away from the table that the negotiator is likely to make the necessary commitment.

But the analysis is not complete. The negotiator then needs to ask: Is this a realistic outcome? Why would the other side agree to that? The other side is likely going through a comparable analysis and only if the preferred solution meets its priorities and needs and is better than its opportunities away from the table is it likely to agree.

II-5: RECORDING THE COMMITMENT

WRITTEN AGREEMENTS

TO WHAT EXTENT IS WRITING NECESSARY?

- Helena Antonova needs something to take to the board, and Lang Systems Ltd. wants a directors' resolution ratifying the deal. An agreement in principle or points of agreement will suffice.

> **HOW CAN THE DEAL BE RECORDED IN A WAY THAT IS ACCEPTABLE TO BOTH SIDES?**
>
> - Helena Antonova and I recorded the commitment in a memo.
> - This will be taken to the board in three days for its ratification.

The value of recording the commitment in writing is that it obliges the negotiators to focus on what they have created and to think things through in a more concrete or practical form. If the step is carefully done, it increases the likelihood that areas of ambiguity or impracticality will be identified early and can be remedied or discussed.

Writing up a deal also documents it so that the negotiators can return to it in the future should recollections dim about the nature and extent of the commitments. The parties are creating evidence of their intentions. A short pencil, it is said, is better than a long memory.

Recording the commitment can be simple or elaborate, depending on the nature of the dispute, the characteristics and needs of the disputants and the milieu in which their negotiation takes place. In the negotiation of repetitive "like" claims, the commitment can be reduced to a form with a series of check-off boxes or blanks to complete. In other instances, points of agreement or points of principle may suffice. In still other situations, formal legal documentation may be in order. No one standard is right for all cases.

The SPAWC board of directors unanimously adopted the agreement in principle that Lang and Antonova had negotiated, with one exception. The period in which Lang was to run the course with the benefit of SPAWC's Course was reduced from 18 to 14 months, because by then the association's new course system would be fully operational. This change was not significant to Lang Systems Ltd., as it could easily repeat its course a sufficient number of times within 14 months to recoup its development costs. It accepted the change, without objection.

REVIEWING OUTCOME

Negotiation, as has previously been stated, is a human process subject to countless variations and variables. It holds promise but not guarantees; possibilities but not necessarily perfection. In reviewing the outcome achieved by Lang Systems Ltd. on the negotiation worksheet, you might easily think about other appropriate possibilities, other attitudes that could infuse the negotiation, other approaches that Andrea Lang could have taken. Why didn't she just refuse to pay the SPAWC anything when it defaulted and keep all the money for herself? Why did she acknowledge the legitimacy of its educational plans that would put her competitors on an equal footing in the marketplace?

Isn't she at fault for not taking more care with her business arrangements to begin with? Should she have agreed to restore the 25 per cent of gross to SPAWC at the end? Couldn't she have negotiated a "better" deal in the circumstances? Indeed, another negotiator might have emerged with a different result — or none at all.

For Lang Systems Ltd., it was the intersection of many things that contributed to the progress of the negotiation and the ultimate result. Important among them were the personal characteristics of its sole owner and operator, Andrea Lang — her tolerance for risk, her sense of and approach to time, her attitude towards ambiguity, her personal morality and standards of fairness, the emphasis that she placed on certain of her needs, and so on. The condition of the marketplace and the characteristics and needs of SPAWC also played significant roles. Change any one of the variables, such as the emphasis that Lang placed on certain needs or even one aspect of her personal value system, and a different result would ensue. Whether it is a better, worse or just different result is ultimately for the negotiators to say. Andrea Lang achieved what was realistically possible for herself and her business within her frame of reference and set of priorities. To suggest that she could have got everything she wanted to the exclusion of the other side is to invest negotiation with potential that it stands very little chance of achieving.

NEGOTIATION AS A HUB

In the transportation industry, carriers are often obliged to pass through a hub — a central collection point from which things are then distributed, and which may also serve as an administrative or maintenance heart. This is a useful image or analogy for negotiation which can be the hub or access point for other DR processes in the journey to resolution.

The negotiation worksheet example of Lang Systems Ltd. and SPAWC was a straightforward one. Trust was not an insurmountable issue. Information was equally available to each. Feelings were present but not overbearing. Impasse, while always possible, did not surface to stymie the negotiators.

Other negotiations can be more troublesome and can be less suitable for a one-time negotiation such as that which took place between Andrea Lang and Helena Antonova. These may suffer from delay, disinterest, bad faith or other conditions that may set the negotiator to wondering whether there can be a negotiation at all.

In such challenging circumstances, it is useful to examine the nature and source of the impasse and to consider whether and to what extent some other DR process may provide a complete resolution or supplement and inform the negotiation itself, so as to move it into a more productive mode.

To illustrate the possibilities that exist for applying other DR processes to all or part of any dispute, a further example is in order.

Case Study Two

The Halifax Central Non-Profit Housing Corporation hired Neiman Sloan as its general contractor for the construction of a 120-unit housing complex called McGuiness Centre in the downtown core. The affairs of the corporation are run by a volunteer board of nine members who vote on all matters of significance and are responsible for the conduct of its affairs.

Sloan was awarded the contract for the construction of McGuiness Centre over the serious reservations of two members of the board. They had heard negative things about Sloan's reputation and believed that the corporation was taking an unwarranted risk in awarding a construction contract funded with public money to a contractor with questionable integrity. Those members preferred Zanthan Construction over Sloan, even though Zanthan's bid was significantly more expensive.

Although the McGuiness Centre was substantially completed and ready for occupancy six months ago, there are problems. Neither the general contractor nor his mechanical subcontractor has been able to balance the air conditioning system. This is serious. Residents, many of whom are disabled, are either freezing in their units or boiling or both in rapid succession. A subcommittee of the board has been trying to work things out with Sloan for the last four months, but many visits to the site by Sloan's crew have produced no result. The constituency of the board of directors has changed in that 25 per cent of its membership turns over in any one year. However, members Abella and Rappaport, who opposed Sloan, still serve as directors.

The board has generally lost confidence in Sloan's ability to remedy the mechanical problem but believes itself bound to find a practical remedy to the problem as soon as possible. After all, its job was to contract with competent contractors for a functioning building in accordance with the plans and specifications.

On top of that, one member of the board recently received information in confidence from two former members of Sloan's staff which explains the real problem. They claim that Sloan made unauthorized changes to the mechanical system, such as reducing the overall size of ducts and crawl spaces, substituting less efficient ventilation fans and reducing the amount of insulation by 15 per cent. Their position is that Sloan hid these reductions from the owners, but used the savings to pay himself for cost overruns elsewhere on the project. This information was disclosed to the full board of directors during its recent monthly meeting.

What is the board of directors to do? The first question to consider is whether and to what extent the board can negotiate a resolution to the practical problem and the alleged deception directly with Neiman Sloan. This will involve an analysis of whether and for what purposes Sloan would come to the table, and whether the board can have sufficient confidence in his *bona fides* to make the negotiation productive. Remember, not every problem is a negotiable one at any one point in time.

Chances are that the absence of trust would be so significant as to constitute an initial barrier to negotiation. This barrier may eventually be overcome but not at the outset. Not only would the board doubt that Sloan would do what he promises to do in any negotiation, they would place little reliance on any information he might convey.

In such a situation, two possibilities present themselves. Would Sloan consent to an independent fact-finding and investigation with respect to his administrative practices on this contract, with a report being made back to him *and* the board? And, if so, will the investigation be conducted on a with prejudice or a without prejudice basis; what use would be made of the investigation results; and could the investigator be called to give evidence for or against Sloan at a later date? A fact-finding of this nature is an *informative* process. The results could be used as a basis for negotiations between the parties, or to provide relevant information to a decision-maker, such as an arbitrator or judge, in the future. It is, however, a voluntary process. If the informant's accusations are unsound, Sloan may agree to this to demonstrate his *bona fides*.

Alternatively, if Sloan would not voluntarily agree to a fact-finding exercise, the board of directors could obtain information through the compulsion of the litigation system. In accessing the litigation system, the board of directors can frame the case as one of negligence, breach of contract and, probably, civil fraud. Litigation is an *adjudicative* process, but one with significant *coercive* aspects as discussed in Chapter 1. During the course of the litigation, Sloan would be obliged to produce all documents relevant to the legal issues and to testify under oath in the discovery process. Not only would the litigation process provide compulsion for the collection of information, but it may also expose Sloan to significant risk, causing him to cooperate in the resolution of the practical problem as well.

The practical heating problem lends itself to another *informative* process by way of neutral evaluation or expert evaluation. The parties could jointly agree on an outsider with relevant expertise to examine the problem and render an opinion about its causes and possible solutions, together with an appropriate cost estimate. A mechanical engineer may be the appropriate outsider. Alternatively, each side could retain its own expert, as is commonly done in litigation, and could see whether and to what extent the experts' diagnoses and prescriptions coincide.

Suppose that the parties each do hire independent experts who are in agreement as to both the causes of the problem and its remedy, but who disagree significantly as to the costs. The board of directors and Sloan may simply agree to average the costs or they may refer the disagreement to a different outsider, who listens to competing facts and arguments for either side and then decides — arbitrates — what the appropriate repair costs ought to be. Such an *adjudicative* process may provide an efficient end to the factual impasse and thus may resolve a portion of the dispute.

But there are other non-monetary aspects to the dispute. The board of directors feels deceived, and those members who served at the time that Neiman Sloan was awarded the contract experience embarrassment in that they will be seen to have surrendered their judgment and failed to adequately perform the terms of their public trust. For them, no amount of investigation, fact-finding or decision-making will remedy things. There is something more that they require. Here, a mediator may assist. By converting from positions to interests, and by working all parts of the controversy to a whole, the mediator may succeed in constructing a creative and composite solution with the parties that incorporates both monetary and non-monetary aspects. The mediator can identify and work with the legitimate and pervasive human component of the dispute. This may result in an acknowledgement from Sloan that he understands the reaction of the board and their conclusion that he betrayed the trust that they necessarily reposed in him. Attention to the non-monetary aspects of the dispute at the same time as the monetary aspects may facilitate a resolution that is acceptable to all of the interests at the table.

Finally, if the parties are prepared to try a consensual process such as mediation but want to be assured that their participation gives rise to a final resolution, the parties may engage in a *hybrid process* of mediation-arbitration. This can engage an outsider as a mediator in much the same way as described above, but if a mutually agreeable settlement is not reached, then the outsider can listen to the parties and determine for them how the issues are to be resolved. In authorizing the outsider to decide the matter in the final event, the parties can stipulate that the arbitrator decides the dispute in accordance with law, or alternatively in accordance with "equity and good conscience" without regard for specific legal principles or technicalities.

Thus, a single dispute with multiple aspects can benefit in whole or in part by a variety of DR processes, some of which supplement and inform negotiation, others of which replace or supplement negotiation. This is the ultimate beauty of DR: the ability to adopt and adapt to a variety of DR choices for the benefit of those involved.

NOTES

3

MEDIATION

INTRODUCTION

Mediation is a process in which people involved in a dispute (the parties) meet and work with an outsider (the mediator). The mediator leads the negotiation process and helps the parties work their differences out to mutual satisfaction.

Since our first edition of *Bypass Court* in 1996, there has been an exponential increase in the situations where mediation is used. Almost every imaginable kind of dispute has been successfully mediated to conclusion, for example: lenders enforcing security against debtors; family members challenging the legitimacy of a relative's will; separate hospitals ordered to merge into one; young offenders brought face-to-face with their victims; corporations or individuals alleging libel and slander; or investors suing over bad advice.

In addition to *ad hoc* or one-off use, there has been a proliferation of mediation programs. There are initiatives to mediate disputes in amateur sport, residential school claims, the location of natural gas pipelines, the protection of vulnerable children and neighbourhood fence fights.

In all of these situations, the mediator uses skills and knowledge to understand the essence of the dispute and help the parties figure out what they need to do or stop doing in order to bring about a resolution. The mediator cannot make them do anything they do not want to do and does not issue binding decisions like an arbitrator. For example, the mediator cannot force an insurance company to compensate a homeowner for water damage under the homeowner's policy. Instead, the mediator tries to influence the parties to take steps to resolve things themselves and manages a forum for the constructive discussion of the problem. The mediator might help the insurance company see that the denial of coverage is based on a clause in the policy that is open to other, equally valid interpretations. The mediator might help the homeowner to see that the denial of coverage was not an arbitrary and mean-spirited decision after all, but one based on genuinely different interpretations of the wording in the policy.

Mediators conduct the mediation process based on their individual backgrounds, training, experience and general philosophy, as well as the nature of the parties and the dispute.

In Canada, the term "mediator" usually refers to an independent person who has no stake in the dispute or its outcome and is at arm's length to the disputing parties. There are, however, other legitimate kinds of mediators, such as human resource advisors employed by public or private organizations who work to resolve issues between internal stakeholders, or dispute resolution officers at quasi-judicial tribunals who help to bring about settlements that take the public interest into account and respect relevant legislation.

In all cases, however, the essence of the mediator's job is to work with the appropriate individuals and organizations to bring about a mutually acceptable resolution to the issues. The goal of the mediation is a voluntary, negotiated settlement to which everyone can commit. That is why mediation is often called "assisted negotiation". The mediator — whether completely independent or not — assists the parties to negotiate more effectively than they could on their own and maximizes their ability to find a solution that works for them. The mediator is supposed to add value to the negotiation and bring an extra something that begins to untie the knots of conflict. In this chapter we show what that means on a very practical level.

There are many trained mediators in Canada, most of whom have been taught to use the principles of interest-based or principled negotiation in their work (see Chapters 1 and 2). This means that these mediators look for the explicit and implicit interests (*e.g.*, needs, wants, fears, aspirations) of each side and are alert to whether and how those interests can be addressed. If the concern is privacy, can some kind of confidentiality be assured? If the concern is cash flow, can the payment be made over time? If the concern is being understood, will a detailed acknowledgment make a difference? If the concern is fear of loss, can some safety measures be adopted? As will be shown, interest-based principles hang on an underlying three-stage mediation process.

MEDIATION'S BASIC FEATURES

Certain terms are used to describe the basic features of mediation and mediators and while these do not give a concrete picture of mediation in action, it is useful to canvass them here. They are the philosophical underpinnings of mediation. The legal aspects of some of these terms are examined in more detail in Chapter 7.

Confidential — This refers to the secrecy or privacy that is supposed to be an essential component of the mediation process. Typically, in mediation there is a promise given by the mediator to the parties and by the parties to each other that the discussion and outcome of mediation will not be shared with others who are not involved in the process. This promise is made explicit in a written mediation agreement like the ones shown at the end of this chapter. The promise may also be implicit because most people take it for granted that settlement talks are off the record. On a general policy basis, confidentiality is understood to be necessary to encourage people to speak honestly and freely as they work towards settlement without fear that they will be penalized for compromising or making admissions. It is the notion that your words will not come back to haunt you.

In the second edition of this book, we wrote that "Mediation in Canada is virtually always confidential and 'off the record' in the commercial context", but the Ontario Court of Appeal cast doubt on the absolute quality of that statement when it refused to sanction a breach of confidentiality in a court-connected mediation with the remedy of contempt. See Chapter 7.

Consensual — This refers to the fact that mediation is a process of agreement and all mediation participants must agree to a settlement before there is a substantive outcome resulting from the mediation process. If the homeowner wants $35,000 and the insurance company is prepared to pay only $5,000, the mediator has no power to impose a number by way of resolution no matter how close the parties may be to a deal. It is only if the parties commit to a settlement themselves that they are then bound by the outcome. This differs significantly from arbitration, where once the parties agree to that process, they are legally obliged to accept the arbitrator's award, subject only to rights of appeal or judicial review. If the home-owner's position is $35,000 and the insurance company's position is $5,000, an arbitrator could award one amount, the other amount or any number in between that is supported by the evidence. At mediation, that could not occur by mediator's fiat.

In mediation, the parties submit to a process of negotiation but not to a guaranteed outcome. They use the mediator's negotiation assistance as described in this chapter, but they do not submit to the mediator's imposed solution. Another way of expressing the consensual aspect of mediation is to call it a *non-binding* dispute resolution process. In such a process, no one binds anyone to a deal.

Voluntary/Mandatory — These words relate to how the parties come to be at mediation in the first place. If they come of their own accord, even though subject to the stresses and pressures of the dispute or the fear of litigation, then they take part in a voluntary mediation. An estate trustee and a possible dependant may agree to mediate a dependant's relief claim before any legal proceedings are commenced. They will select a mediator, agree on a date and convene with the mediator to talk things out in a voluntary mediation. No outside body is exerting force to get them to the table. The practicalities of the case and their willingness to try to settle bring them to the table.

On the other hand, once a claim is formally launched in court, the es-tate trustee and claimant may be required to attend at mediation whether they want to or not by order or rule of the court. Then mediation is called mandatory; their attendance is mandated. Requiring parties to attend might impact their general attitude towards mediation and reduce their willingness to cooperate with the mediator, but it does not really change the mediation process; the mediator still uses the three-stage process illustrated in this chapter and tries to help the parties to negotiate their own resolution.

Neutral — This much debated word is an adjective that describes the mediator.[1] Basically, it refers to an independent-minded mediator who has no stake in the controversy and has no personal or business connection with any of the parties.[2] By being neutral, the mediator brings an emotional detachment to the dispute and approaches the issues with more objectivity than the parties themselves. This is the quality that frees up the mediator to be able to diagnose the dispute, influence the negotiators to be flexible and realistic, and make suggestions that the parties could not make on their own.

We are not talking about a fictional human being, however. We are referring to people who can separate themselves from the disputants and their issues, and who can treat everyone with even-handedness. Of course, mediators do bring their own values and thoughts to each file. If those thoughts and values are so strong that the mediator is advocating for them to the exclusion of all else or is siding with one party and renouncing another, then the mediator has slipped out of the neutral role. Resistance, complaints or a general loss of confidence in the mediator may follow.

Some mediators can identify people or topics that they know will push their buttons and impair their detachment. These mediators will decline or terminate assignments involving such hot issues. For example, a colleague has an aversion to parenting plans that will separate siblings. She recognizes that she cannot be neutral in the face of such proposals and is upfront with parents that she will not participate in the development of plans that will separate brothers and sisters. Her approach to such mediation assignments flows from an awareness of her internal state and how it will impact her role as a mediator.

THE THREE STAGES OF MEDIATION

A mediation is an event. It is an in-person get-together for the purpose of talking and coming up with a settlement. A date and time will have been

---

[1]   See C. Morris, "The Trusted Mediator" in J. MacFarlane, ed., *Rethinking Disputes: The Mediation Alternative* (Toronto: Emond Montgomery, 1997) at 301.

[2]   Some mediators are employees of one of the parties. A labour relations specialist at the Ontario Labour Relations Board, for example, helps management and labour resolve issues that would otherwise be adjudicated at the Board and brings the Board's practices, policies, procedures and concerns into the negotiation. It is as if the employed mediator has a dual mandate, being at once mediator and negotiator. That said, the employed mediator is at arm's length to the other two parties and deals with them in an open-minded and even-handed way.

reserved and a special place set aside or rented for the occasion with a main room and one or more break-out rooms. A written confirmation will have gone out from the mediator to the parties, often with a draft agreement to mediate attached. Meetings will have been held by each side to prepare for the day. Written statements will have been put together setting out the parties' demands, facts and arguments. Back-up documents will have been exchanged. Experts or support persons may have been arranged.

If all of this is done in anticipation of the event, what happens when everyone arrives? How does an in-person mediation occur? In keeping with our practical handbook approach, we will divide the mediation process into three basic stages and discuss them in a way that marries theory and practice.[3] The three stages are:

1. exchange of information and understanding the conflict;

2. feedback to and from the parties; and

3. actual bargaining.

For a more academic approach, see the many fine textbooks for mediators that divide the mediation session into more stages and describe more detailed models.[4]

Stage 1: Exchange of Information and Understanding the Conflict

At the very beginning, the mediator convenes the parties in the same room and says some opening words to put people at ease, to confirm the purpose and nature of the session, to outline the various roles and responsibilities around the table and to let people know what to expect by way of general procedure. Some mediators have a set script that they deliver in every case, running through everything from a definition of mediation to a detailed list of behavioural rules (one person at a time and so forth). More experienced mediators tend to tailor what they say to the circumstances and the parties in each case. They would not instruct sophisticated business executives or senior government officials to take turns talking or remind repeat labour relations players that a mediator is not a judge. However, an experienced mediator might have a word or two to say about civility and the practical purpose of the mediation session if the face-off positions of the parties are extreme and acrimonious. The mediator's interventions here, as elsewhere in the process, need to be appropriate to the context and the participants.

---

[3] We gratefully acknowledge our colleague, Dominique F. Bourcheix, Mediator and Arbitrator of Montreal, Quebec for her assistance in compiling this section. It was she who first condensed mediation into these practical steps and synthesized the activities at each stage.

[4] See, for instance, L. Boulle & K.J. Kelly, *Mediation: Principles, Process, Practice* (Toronto: Butterworths, 1998).

Once the preliminaries are adequately dealt with, the mediation usually evolves into a face-to-face exchange of information where each side talks about the situation from its own point of view. All mediation participants — parties, lawyers, experts and mediators — hear about all aspects of the dispute.

At this stage, people do not actively negotiate with each other or make final decisions about how to resolve the matter. Instead, they give and get information.

Sometimes this stage begins with each side making unstructured oral presentations and demonstrating facts by means of statistics, photographs, videotapes, maps or plans. There is a fair amount of advocacy. For example, the 18-year-old driver will describe how the motor vehicle accident has impacted his life, sports and studies and why a significant monetary award is in order. The automobile insurer will explain how the injuries, though real, are relatively minor in nature and justify only a nominal payment and, perhaps, question why the 18-year-old switched lanes without signalling or checking his blind spot?

Sometimes, as in a complex multi-party construction case, the information exchange begins not with oral advocacy from the parties but with the mediator synthesizing what he or she has learned from reading their written briefs and expert reports. This short-circuits the adversarial exchanges and leads the parties into a more focused and specific discussion.

The point is that there are a number of ways to initiate the discussion in the first stage of a mediation and there is no need to follow a prescription or cookbook approach.

Initially, each side tends to speak on its own behalf and from its own perspective. As a result, the first stage of mediation can have an adversarial or tit-for-tat quality. Instead of listening to understand, or presenting to educate and elucidate, people often advocate to convince or ridicule, and listen for admissions or anticipated lies. For example, the purchaser of the defendant's building rhetorically asks, "How could you not have known about the mould?" The vendor defensively responds, "Well, if it was that obvious, how did your own inspector miss it?" In this sort of exchange, there is only so much that a mediator can or should suppress. To some extent, these exchanges are normal and to be expected. That does not mean they are to be encouraged or promoted throughout the mediation. At the end of the day, mediation calls for a hard-headed — not hot-headed — approach. The parties will ultimately need to alter their behaviours if they want to get the most out of the mediation; it is well known that people's ability to think logically and rationally is impaired when they are emotionally upset.

An important goal of Stage 1 is to generalize the information distribution so that everyone has the same factual basis for their analysis. Often at the start of mediation, information is fragmented and looked at through a partisan lens. Through a joint information exchange the parties can begin to appreciate new or different things, such as facts, proofs, interpretations, arguments or attitudes. It is important to be open to new and different information because it may provide openings for settlement.

In one mediation, a businessman was convinced that his public relations specialists had ruined his company's product expansion in North America. He felt that it was their fault that he had lost the chance to be first out of the starting block. Now his company was doomed to be a small, insignificant player and he would never be rich. To him, the public relations company had let him down deliberately or through gross incompetence. The discussion in joint session, however, showed that the businessman had been operating under his own private assumptions, none of which had ever been made explicit, let alone set out in the written agreement for services. It became abundantly clear to everyone that there was either a huge miscommunication where the businessman had failed to make his assumptions clear or else there were two different but equally valid interpretations of the public relations company's mandate. Since none of this had ever been identified in any prior discussions, there had been no previous opportunity for clarification or action. The mediation became a forum to look at the problem in a new way to see whether and how the situation could be addressed. Against the background of the joint discussion, the public relations company was prepared to offer a significant amount of money to be rid of a problematic client. The businessman knew a good thing when he saw it. He told himself that the money was compensation for a lost business opportunity and, pocketing the money, he continued on as the owner of a modest, local business.

In Stage 1 clues often come out that explain the key to the whole conflict. The parties and the mediator need to be alert to this. These clues may explain how to solve the problem or, conversely, suggest why the problem cannot be resolved through mediation after all.

One mediation involved a complex series of sequential business transactions. These were to culminate in the payment of $75,000 in return for which one party was to become the owner of a valuable piece of property. One of the many issues between the parties was the transfer of title. The prospective owner insisted that the $75,000 had been paid, not directly, but through a series of elaborate and convoluted contras or credits, such that the real property now belonged to him. In Stage 1 of the mediation, this confusing aspect of the dispute began to come into focus, although, at first, neither side could admit to what was going on. The argument about contras and credits was the prospective owner's solution to a psychological impediment.

Two years earlier, the parties had met privately and negotiated a deal between themselves. However, before the deal was signed, an extra $75,000 was tacked on at the insistence of one party's lawyer who did not think the deal was sweet enough for his client. The prospective owner signed the revised deal and appeared to agree to the additional payment, but, in reality, there was no psychological or moral commitment to do so. In fact, there was tremendous resentment against the other side for failing to abide by the private deal and there was strong resistance to paying more than the original price no matter what the written agreement said.

As Stage 1 progressed, it became increasingly obvious that the prospective owner was so bitter about the $75,000 that he would not pay it voluntarily unless the other party was prepared to make some serious adjustments to the overall transaction or until a court ordered it to be paid after trial and appeal. However, the other side insisted on the letter of the written agreement and was not prepared to accept or respond to the prospective owner's interests. Since each side was equally inflexible and affluent, and neither feared the risks and costs of litigation, the parties eventually concluded that a negotiated settlement was not possible at mediation.

Stage 1 can yield overt conflict and can seem pointless, since the positions may be both well known and irreconcilable. Nevertheless, this stage needs to be carried out as far as possible because both sides should have the broadest possible range of information in order to analyze the situation and decide what to do. It helps if the people can remember that even if they disagree with the version or vision of the other side, they should learn as much as they can about it. One of our colleagues puts it well in reminding parties that "listening is not agreeing". Her point is that whatever goals a person brings to mediation, it is helpful to know what the other side wants, since there is almost always some element of a trade needed to accomplish those goals. Simply put, results in mediation are achieved cooperatively, not unilaterally.

Stage 1 is a time to ask and answer questions, particularly if this can be done courteously and helpfully. Skilled lawyers and savvy parties know how to go about this in a way that moves the mediation along. Mediators also need to be able to do this. They try to be objectively curious, attentive and to concentrate on the messages the people are sending (what they say, do not say and cannot bring themselves to say). Once the parties have had an opportunity to ask their own questions, the mediator asks questions to move the mediation along. This requires courage, restraint and judgment on the part of the mediator: courage because the mediator may be the only one in the room prepared to admit that something is confusing; restraint because the mediators must take care not to prematurely limit the debate; and judgment because the mediator has to determine what to ask publicly and what to save for private questioning.

In one mediation, after a two-hour exchange of information among several experts representing the parties, the mediator asked if they were satisfied that they had properly summarized their positions. Everyone declared satisfaction and said that there was nothing more to add. The mediator then explained that to an outsider, the presentations were both general and non-responsive and that even with the best will in the world, it was impossible to understand what was defective among the 22 components of the machinery in the factory, let alone appreciate what corrective action had been taken, at what cost and to what effect. It was therefore useless to begin a discussion about which party was responsible for what had happened to the machine. There were too many questions outstanding. When the parties followed the mediator's suggestion that they go back over things, item by item and in detail, they were able to reduce the scope of the problem by identifying areas of agreement and disagreement and walking through their more manageable list of disagreements one at a time.

Stage 2: Feedback to and from the Parties

Each in-person mediation usually comes to a point where the parties have gone as far as they can in a joint information-sharing meeting. They have given and received to the extent possible in that open forum. They then come to the second stage of mediation, where they consider what they have heard and discuss it with the mediator in private, away from the pressure and presence of the other side. These private meetings are called caucuses and they are discussed in more detail later in this chapter.

In a Stage 2 caucus, the parties give feedback and get feedback from their lawyers and experts as well as from the mediator. They need an opportunity to evaluate and integrate what they learned in joint session and to determine how it might make a difference. But they are not yet ready to actively bargain or make any final decisions about how to resolve the matter.

There are many different types of exchanges that go on in the privacy of a caucus and it would be impossible to describe all of the permutations and combinations here, but some examples follow.

Sometimes the parties need the opportunity to react privately and to share those reactions with the mediator. The person who sat quietly through innuendo about his or her integrity or the person who resisted reacting to being called a "welfare bum" will be clear and explicit that he or she completely disagrees with and resents the remarks. He or she will express hurt, resentment, anger or frustration — any one of a number of justifiable reactions. He or she might even lodge his or her own private attack on the other person to show what he or she could have said or what he or she wishes he or she had said, but could not think of at the time. These reactions may require no more of an intervention on the mediator's part than respectful listening.

A party might also like to share and get feedback on its own perceptions of the other side. For example, "She seems deadly serious about her
claim" or "He's fallen in love with his own theory" or "Gee, physically, he
seemed rather more frail than I anticipated." People make all kinds of
observations in a plenary session and incorporate these observations into
their decisions about what to do next. They want to check out their impressions and see whether others have made the same interpretations that they
did.

Stage 2 is an appropriate time for interested parties to ask for and receive meaningful feedback from the mediator on many things. The mediator
may have impressions to share as well, or questions about what was said in
the plenary session. The mediator may also have a view of the merits of the
case or overall position if it is politic to share these views. It is our experience, at least in civil mediation, that the parties are grateful to receive the
honest feedback from an independent third party which has been privy to an
overview of the conflict, provided that this is done diplomatically and
objectively. It is as if the mediator's impressions are a proxy for the ultimate
views of a trial judge or tribunal; people use them as a yardstick to measure
their own view of the situation. People are under no obligation to accept a
mediator's feedback; however, most welcome and value it if the mediator is
not dogmatic or insulting but genuinely interested in being of help. The
mediator's views help people formulate their own risk calculations and
consider whether to revise their naturally partisan views of the conflict.

One mediation concerned an oral contract between two men, one of
whom had died. The claimant asserted that he had performed services which
the deceased had both needed and wanted and that in exchange the deceased
had promised the claimant a monthly support allowance. The claimant and his
counsel expressly petitioned the mediator in caucus, "What do you think of
our chances in court? What do you think of the optics of our case? Please tell
us directly, as we will value what you say." Because the explicit request was
consistent with the mediator's philosophy and practice, the mediator gave a
personal impression of the case based on the written materials and the oral
exchanges in the plenary session. The claimant and his lawyer used that to
decide how hard to bargain in Stage 3.

In another mediation, the plaintiff started privately itemizing for the
mediator how he and his wife could earn extra money to fund their lawsuit:
he could work overtime and take on additional assignments; she could work
through her holidays; they could start to cut back on certain things at home;
and so forth. They would need about $60,000 — quite a bit of after-tax
money to get to trial. The plaintiff felt that he had been cheated and needed
to stand up for himself as a matter of personal integrity. His lawyer thought
that the case could be won, so the $75,000 investment (what he had paid and
what he needed to earn) seemed tempting. The plaintiff had a sense of
dissonance over the matter and asked the mediator point-blank, "What

would you do if you were me?" The mediator replied, "I can't answer that. I can't pretend that I am you. People make decisions for different reasons and your reasons may not be mine. Speaking only for myself, I would look at things in terms of my life energy: how much life would I have to give in exchange for the $60,000 and is there something else I would rather be doing? In other words, is this the highest and best use of my life?" The plaintiff looked relieved and said that the idea of life energy made sense to him; he often used that yardstick to determine what to do, especially after a recent illness. The plaintiff thanked the mediator for the frank answer. Then in discussion with his lawyer, he decided how to approach the defendant about a compromise solution without appearing to capitulate.

If the parties are open during Stage 2, they will be able to see things that did not occur to them before and they may be surprised at what they learn. Two commercial parties met with a mediator before taking their dispute to their regulatory tribunal. They were debating the interpretation of a statutory provision that the tribunal had never interpreted before. The parties were locked in a tug-of-war over their opposing interpretations, each convinced that theirs would prevail. However, the mediator pointed out a third possible interpretation which would leave both sides worse off than the status quo. This prospect had not occurred to the parties, but once it was raised they both saw it as viable. Now, they had an impetus to work out a solution on their own.

Stage 2 is a stage of analysis, consolidation and synthesis. The parties take into consideration their preparation and what they learn in the plenary session. They add to that feedback from their own professional advisors and feedback from the mediator, who is able to approach the problem in an objective and detached way without any partisan obligations. They analyze everything and try to figure out their short-term and long-term course of action. If the parties can be open-minded, they will see things that were not apparent to them before — risks and opportunities, questions and explanations, pathways and impediments. With the mediator's help they will begin to get a sense of what is possible and what they can do (or stop doing) to make it become a reality.

Stage 3: Actual Bargaining

After impressions and information are privately shared in Stage 2, people move into Stage 3, where they begin to actively bargain or negotiate. While there is nothing stopping the parties from meeting face-to-face, fairly often negotiation takes place through the mediator, who goes back and forth between the parties, trying to assemble the foundations of a settlement. Just how this happens will largely depend on the kind of file.

In a partnership dispute, the mediator may begin, not with offers and counter-offers, but with a general settlement outline. Before getting specific, the mediator will need to confirm that all partners want to move in the same direction. As a start they may agree, for example, that instead of fighting over the dissolution of the firm, the disgruntled partner will leave the firm and sell her interests to the remaining partners within 90 days (assuming for the moment that a mutually satisfactory price can be reached), that the departing partner may take all of her files and work-in-process, that they will jointly work out the words and means to inform the clients and professional colleagues, and that everything will be subject to appropriate tax and accounting advice. Of course, this is not a final settlement agreement, but the beginning of a mutually acceptable resolution that is refined through various iterations as the mediation progresses.

In a distributive file such as a personal injury mediation, the parties will actually exchange quantified offers through the mediator. The plaintiff will begin by asking for $100,000 consisting of $75,000 for general damages, $15,000 for past income loss and $10,000 for loss of competitive advantage. The insurance company will counter with an offer of $20,000 which consists of $25,000 for generals, $15,000 for past income loss and nothing for loss of competitive advantage minus 50 per cent for contributory negligence. In round 2, the plaintiff will reduce its claim and the defendant will increase its offer. In round 3, there will be less movement but the numbers will gradually approach each other. After some skirmishing through the mediator, there will finally be a monetary settlement. The insurance company will pay the plaintiff the agreed-upon amount in exchange for a full and final release.

Of course, not every proposal or offer will or should pass through the mediator. Concessions, offers and proposals can be delivered face-to-face. In one mediation, a woman and man were being sued in connection with a real estate transaction. The man was added as a defendant because he had signed the transfer of title and the plaintiff assumed that this meant he had an unregistered, beneficial interest in the land. In a plenary session the man explained that he had signed the transaction without protest or question because a lawyer told him to do so, but that he was not a spouse at the time of the transaction and had no interest in the land whatsoever. Upon hearing the man's explanation and being satisfied about his *bona fides*, the plaintiff (with his lawyer's concurrence) agreed to discontinue the action against him and limit the claim to the woman.

Throughout Stage 3, the mediator is much more than a passive conduit, mechanically transmitting offers or ideas from one party to the other. The mediator is very actively helping each side to:

1.   understand what is important to them and what priorities they assign to their goals;

2.   figure out how to put words to their ideas and communicate them effectively;

3.   understand what the other side is looking for and what they are not looking for;

4.   determine whether and how they can address the needs of the other side;

5.   get a sense of what is possible and what is realistic, predict what is likely to be accepted and what is not and why;

6.   evaluate and respond to offers and proposals from the other side; and

7.   keep their emotional charge under control so that they are responding, not reacting, to what is happening in the mediation.

The mediator has much to contribute but does not act unilaterally.

In one mediation, a small employer sued his former senior manager for breach of fiduciary duty. The manager had gone to work for a competitor and the employer sought an injunction against both of them. The defendants' team spent a lot of time trying to draft a set of voluntary restrictions that would be palatable for the employer only to have their hard work summarily rejected.

The mediator brought the parties back together to clarify the plaintiff's real concerns and to educate the defendants as to why their carefully crafted proposal would not work. "It's way too complicated", said the employer. "It would take too much monitoring and too many resources. All I really care about are the customers up for renewal in the next six months." This was new. The employer had never said this before, primarily because up until now he had been reacting to the situation with anger instead of thinking through his needs. Still, no one heard what he had said. The defendants continued to try to sell their proposal.

But the mediator heard something significant. "Wait a minute", the mediator said. "I think you are all missing something really important. The employer just said that all he really cares about are the customers coming up for renewal in six months. If that's the case, then all this is beside the point. Did I get that right?" The employer confirmed that this was so and within minutes the parties agreed to a written restriction with a clear, defined duration and scope. Once the employer became clear on his needs, the defendants could see that it was an eminently reasonable concern and one that the law would likely protect in any event.

Bit by bit in Stage 3, through trial and error, the parties and the mediator assemble the basis for a settlement. Where issues are distributive, they negotiate a number through offers and counter-offers or come up with some principles or formulae to arrive at an amount. Where issues are distributive, they generate and evaluate options to see whether and how their interests can be met. When everyone can say yes to everything on the table, a settlement is achieved and then it can be written up in the form of minutes of settlement or points of agreement.

The best mediation practice is to immediately document any agreement that is reached before parties and their advisors leave the session. It may be inconvenient, but experience tells us that it will save both time and the momentum towards resolution. Working out acceptable language on the spot is far easier with all present and in the atmosphere of goodwill engendered by the positive outcome, than it would be if it was piled on top of existing paperwork back at the office. Writing it down and having everyone sign brings a satisfactory sense of closure to the dispute, even if what is being signed is an agreement in principle. That may be why mediated settlements are noted for their durability.

Mediation is a very accommodating process and consequently a useful addition to your DR toolbox. It is not a cure-all and not for every case. Nor is it a quick fix; it takes work. But for a wide variety of conflicts, mediation can bring about the changes in perspective necessary to resolve them. It can be done quickly — even before litigation is launched. It is low cost, often taking less than a day; it is low risk, being "off the record"; and it challenges all of your creative negotiating skills. Best of all, it gives you a very good shot at finality — enabling you to close the file and focus your attention on new business issues, or on the cases that really do need litigating.

EXCEPTIONS TO THE THREE STAGES OF MEDIATION

Every generalization has exceptions, and this is true of a three-stage mediation model as well. Some mediations do not follow this model at all because it is not suited to the people involved or their circumstances. The mediator has to adapt the process to respond to each situation on its own terms. These adaptations can include reordering the stages of mediation, extending the timelines or making use of technology.

In one workplace mediation, three co-workers were not getting along and they agreed to participate in mediation but were very reluctant to meet face-to-face. They all wanted to be able to do their jobs in an environment of harmony and respect, but mistrust, resentment and fear formed a powerful barrier. On top of that, they had all used incomplete and inaccurate information to perpetuate very negative images of each other.

Eventually, an in-person plenary session took place, but this meeting, which typically forms Stage 1, was the very last thing that happened in the mediation.

Instead of a joint meeting, this mediation began with many one-on-one communications between individual co-workers and the mediator using in-person meetings as well as telephone, voicemail, email and facsimile. Many of these exchanges concerned individual fears and reservations that prevented the workers from moving forward. Each co-worker had the same concerns, but they did not know that.

A variety of interventions were necessary before a plenary session was possible. The mediator had to educate and re-educate each worker about the mediation process; ensure each worker's willingness and ability to participate in mediation; obtain permission to share private information not previously available; arrange for and distribute information from new sources; discuss the matter with third party advisors; encourage the workers to clarify and then write out their own concerns, questions and proposals; assist each worker to review and respond to the other workers' lists; integrate all workers' lists into a tentative written agreement for discussion only; distribute the tentative agreement and provide sufficient time for private deliberation; and assist the parties to prepare for the plenary session. Only after these many interventions and more could the mediator convene an in-person meeting, where the three co-workers spoke directly with each other.

When the in-person plenary session took place, it did not resemble Stage 1 described above. There was no general oral sharing of information; this had been done electronically beforehand. These workers needed the comfort of a draft agreement before they could meet face-to-face. They used that draft as an agenda for their meeting until they felt comfortable enough to talk freely with one another. The mediator's earlier interventions created the necessary zone of comfort for them to finally meet in person and when they finally got together, the situation was not as emotionally charged as they imagined it would be.

The co-workers began with their draft agreement as a focal point and guide. They began a constructive conversation with the mediator's help, gradually taking more responsibility for the content and their behaviours. Ultimately, they agreed on the steps each of them would take to begin to restore workplace stability. They understood that the mediation session was a new start, not a final step. The mediation process ultimately let them admit that they each contributed to the problem and that in the future they had to prevent small personal differences from escalating into major workplace conflict. They concluded the plenary session with a signed agreement containing a dispute resolution process for the future as well as a set of mutually acceptable rules for their workplace. They agreed to give these a try as a basis for a renewed working relationship.

For the most part, mediation in Canada is an oral, in-person process where issues are explored and conflicts settled by means of explicit, personal discussion. However, as the above example suggests, this does not have to be the case for every situation and the mediation model can (and should) be adapted as needed.

Telephone, teleconferencing and web-based technologies are other adaptations. These allow for people to take part in mediation while living and working at great distances from each other. They bring mediation right into the office, workplace or home, making it accessible and convenient. These technologies make geographic location irrelevant and eliminate the costs of moving people and documents around.

There is an important evolving form of dispute resolution called "online dispute resolution" ("ODR"),[5] that takes advantage of the fact that the World Wide Web is now part of mass culture. ODR is dispute resolution that is implemented largely using web-based information management and communication and, in some cases, database applications. Essentially, it takes original in-person processes and converts them from off-line to online models. People are required to access sites and download or submit information from the Internet after which they engage in various processes such as direct negotiation, mediation and arbitration, all in electronic form.

An example of an online mediation program is offered by Property Mediation Zone,[6] where one party to a dispute arising from the ownership, management or rental of property can file a case on the website, and through direct and/or mediated communications online with the other party in a secure environment, can develop a mutually agreeable solution. This is just one of many examples of online mediation that have been developed around the world.

At this stage in the evolution of mediation, only real purists insist that eyeball-to-eyeball mediation is the only way to go. Experienced mediators will do what it takes to convenience the parties and get the job done, understanding that there are limitations to every model and modality of mediation.

Online mediation lacks the immediacy of face-to-face mediation and limits the available information to what is on the screen. There is a whole human dynamic that cannot yet be reproduced online. The same limitation applies to telephone mediation. People often regret that they cannot see a person's face and read his or her body language over the phone. Indeed, telephone mediation can be challenging because it relies so heavily on hearing, a secondary sense for most people. Information is taken in only through the ears, whereas 80 per cent of sensual information usually comes to us through the eyes. So, if telephone mediation is used for any extended period of time (particularly telephone conferencing), its high energy demands may lead to fatigue. It is easier for a mediator to deal with one

---

[5]   See, for example, online: <http://odr.info>.
[6]   See online: Property Mediation Zone <http://www.propertymediationzone.co.uk>.

person at a time in telephone mediation or to confine the discussion to procedural matters.

Even the oral, in-person form of mediation has limits, and every perceptive mediator has noticed them. In-person mediation compels people to talk things out when talking may not be their preferred form of communication or problem-solving. Some people simply prefer writing instead of talking. That is how they order their world and synthesize their experiences. There are also people who do not respond well to pressure and cannot make decisions on the spot, something that an oral, fixed time mediation requires. There are parties — and lawyers — who are like that. They simply lack the skills to assimilate new information quickly and the pressure of in-person mediation only makes things worse. For these participants, extended breaks, adjourned sessions, one-at-a-time telephone conversations or email communications provide the extra reflective time that they need. Again, it is a question of adapting the mediation process to the people, not the people to the process.

PLENARY SESSIONS AND CAUCUSES

The examples in this chapter show that mediation is like a play composed of different scenes. The scenes can be placed in any order and the content of each scene will vary.

Some scenes involve all of the characters in the play. These are the plenary sessions or joint meetings. Other scenes involve a subset of the characters, such as the mediator and one party only. These are the caucuses, individual meetings or "time outs".

As discussed in the section on Stage 1, an in-person plenary session lets all participants get the same information from the same source at the same time. It gives them a chance to say what is important to them in their own way and to directly influence the other side. It also gives the parties a chance to observe the other person and his or her professional advisor first-hand and to form a variety of impressions about the people and the problem.

In contrast, a caucus gives the parties a chance to talk to the mediator without the pressure of the other side. They can get the mediator's objective view about the case, try out options for settlement or simply blow off steam. A caucus also lets the parties talk privately to their own advisors.

It should also be added that sometimes a mediator will caucus with just lawyers or professional advisors without the clients. For example, the mediator may meet both lawyers. This gives the lawyers a chance to discuss the law with greater flourish and try to influence each other directly or to see what they can both do to move the mediation along. They might candidly discuss what they would be prepared to recommend to their clients as a final settlement.

The mediator might also meet with one lawyer at a time, on request or at the mediator's initiative. Sometimes a lawyer has an unrealistic or recalcitrant client and the lawyer wants to enlist the mediator's help to bring some reality to the discussion. On other occasions, the mediator has an idea that might move the mediation along but wants advice on whether and how to present it to the client.

Typically, but not always, a mediation begins with a plenary session and moves to caucuses when the plenary discussion starts to produce diminishing returns. The mediator then holds several caucuses and goes back and forth between the parties, shuttling like a crab. He or she will try to clarify interests, see what the parties intend to do, establish the principles or parameters of settlement or help formulate and relay offers.

When settlement is reached, the parties reconvene in a plenary session to put the finishing touches on their settlement. If there is no settlement, the last plenary may be used to summarize the progress that has been made and to agree on the next step or on an agenda for future resolution.

The number of plenary sessions and caucuses will vary with the mediation. In the general three-stage model, Stage 1 takes place in plenary and Stage 2 in caucus. Stage 3 occurs through a combination of caucus and plenary. However, it is worth repeating that the three-stage model is a generalization and many permutations and combinations exist. Sometimes, the entire mediation occurs in plenary session and the parties have no need to split up. In other cases, the parties begin in plenary, break into caucus and do not meet again at all, even if a settlement is reached. This will happen, for instance, if the parties have a great deal of antipathy towards each other and form a combustible mix when put together in an enclosed space. There are still other mediations where the parties never meet face-to-face for reasons as diverse as geography and discomfort.

Plenary sessions and caucuses can be combined in whatever way suits the participants, and any combination can be valid. Here is a visual representation of some ways that we have seen plenary sessions and caucuses combined:

1. This Mediation begins and ends with a plenary session. One caucus in between.

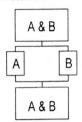

2. This Mediation begins and ends with caucuses. One plenary session in between.

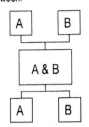

3. This Mediation consists of a series of caucuses culminating in a final plenary session.

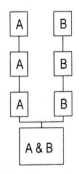

4. In this Mediation, the parties never meet in a plenary session; the mediator goes back and forth in a series of caucuses.

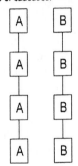

These mediations show that symmetry is not necessarily always present in a mediation format:

5.

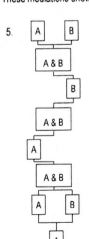

In #5, each side requested a caucus at different times.

In #6, Party B required more attention. B could be an employee and A an institutional employer, for example.

6.

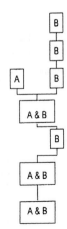

CAUCUS RULES

Before conducting a caucus, the mediator typically discusses what use will be made of information received privately in the absence of the other party. Usually, the mediator will adopt one of two common caucus confidentiality models:

1.   The mediator may take *nothing* out of the individual caucus without the party's express permission.

OR

2.   The mediator may take *anything* out that has not been specifically identified as confidential by the party in the caucus session.

If the mediator neglects to clarify his or her practice concerning caucuses, the participants should speak up and seek clarification. This aspect of mediation is not ordinarily negotiated by the parties; it is the mediator's practice preference which forms the default.

Some mediators add that even if a party wants a disclosure made in caucus to be kept confidential, the mediator may challenge the request and discuss the basis for and consequences of the request. A common example here is surveillance. An insurer or an employer may have photographs or videotapes which it is convinced demonstrate that the other side is lying or malingering. It will tell the mediator about the surveillance for the express purpose of impressing on the mediator how sure its case is and how dishonourable the other party is. It will further expect the mediator to agree that the other side should reduce its monetary demand or give in because of the surveillance. And yet, it does not want the mediator to tell the other side about it. It wants to "save it for trial". In this case, a discussion about priorities is in order. Which does the insurer or employer want more — to preserve a position at trial or influence the other side's perception of its chances of success right now in the negotiation? The two are mutually exclusive. If the mediator cannot share the information, what was the purpose of the disclosure? Ultimately, it is the opposite party that needs to be influenced to modify its demand, not the mediator.

If, at the end of a caucus, it is clear that a party objects to the sharing of specific information, the mediator must respect the confidence. However, there are ethical and/or legal exceptions to this and a mediator should mention these limitations. One exception relates to the threat of harm to human life and safety, even to property. If a disgruntled employee threatens to sabotage an important piece of production equipment and has both the means and the apparent intent to do so, should that confidence be respected? This disclosure is not a withholding of a "bottom line", which tends to be a moving target anyway. Nor does it concern the employee's legitimate self-help remedies if settlement cannot be reached. It is about a threat of criminal activity, something outside the parameters of *bona fide* negotiation. In such a situation, the mediator has the option of disclosure or termination of the mediation or both.

ONE MEDIATOR OR TWO?

A typical in-person mediation involves a single mediator, but two mediators (co-mediators) can be used. A panel or team of mediators can also be used as is the case with some community mediation initiatives where one mediator is the lead and others are in supporting roles.

Multiple mediators can be used in an attempt to reflect the diversity of the constituents (male/female, for example), for training purposes (experienced mediator/trainee), or when the parties simply cannot agree on a single person. Multiple mediators can combine several skill sets or substantive backgrounds. A social worker or therapist may co-mediate with a family law lawyer for matters of matrimonial property and children, or an accountant may co-mediate with an engineer on a complex construction matter with a delay claim. We know of one model where two staff members of a tribunal were co-mediating, one to manage the process and one to provide expert advice on what had happened in other similar cases or how the parties could legitimately meet their interests in the context of the governing legislation. As so often happens, it is a question of what the case calls for and what works.

Of course, in a fee-paid mediation, multiple mediators can add to the expense as well as the time, since the parties are paying for two mediators, not one, and must take an extra professional calendar into account when finding a convenient date. Where the co-mediators are not compatible or experienced in working together, this arrangement can also create dissonance (one mediator proposes one intervention, one mediator proposes another) and can prolong the time required for the mediation. These reasons probably explain why co-mediation is a possible but not common mediation model.

WHAT DO MEDIATORS ACTUALLY DO?

The mediator's role is often described in abstract terms. We say, for instance, that a mediator "facilitates communication" or "assists in the negotiation". These descriptions are accurate but they are like aerial views 35,000 feet up. They do not give sufficient practical details to help a person navigate on the ground. To get a real sense of what mediators actually do, it is necessary to look at their strategies and tactics — what they do in the field.

The mediator's strategy is his or her mission or goal statement, the big-picture philosophy that sets the parameters of the process. A mediator's strategy influences his or her tactics, those individual activities that contribute to the overall goal. A mediator needs a well-defined strategy as a touchstone to sustain him or her in the frequent turbulence of mediation. Thus, the strategy is generally less fluid than the tactics.

There is a limited range of mediator strategies, with caricatures at each extreme. At one end are mediators who drive deals. These pure pragmatists unambiguously define settlement as the goal. At the other end are mediators who foster personal, moral growth without regard for tangible outcomes.

The majority of mediators fall mid-range. They view mediation as a means to make informed decisions about whether and how to settle. Success is a range of outcomes from a complete deal with reconciled relationships through to a wisely chosen trial.

A few years ago, some Canadian mediators were informally asked to elaborate on their tactics and strategies.[7] To begin with, they explained their strategies or "big picture" approach to mediation. Here is what they said:

> The "mission" or "goal" or "objective" (used interchangeably) of mediation is to assist in creating an environment in which all parties are able to make a (subjectively) good decision, all things considered.

> Until proven wrong, I assume that the parties are there because they want a deal and my job is to help them find that deal. It is as if they are in a room and they want out. My job is to help them find the exits.

> As a mediator, my job is not to create a deal. My job is to uncover one if it exists.

> I frame the mediation process as a decision-making process, not a settlement process. The goal of a mediation, to me, is to give the parties better information so they can decide whether to settle or proceed. My role, in concert with that of counsel (if there are counsel), is to get the best information out so that the clients can make an informed choice.

> Getting a deal is a big picture strategy but it is not my overriding strategy. Mine is to have each party make an informed decision about settlement. That means I help them hear each other, help them understand their own and the other's interests, and see all possible ideas for settlement. Then, I don't care if they settle.

> My job is to help the parties to determine whether and how they might settle. It's not simply about getting a deal, although that is often important. The parties have to see if they can create something better than they currently have. If so, they will settle. But, if the status quo remains appealing, they will stick with that, and rightly so.

Note that these strategies are infused with values. Rational, individual decision-making is revered and swaddled in a strong urge "to help". Like the general terms of mediation, these strategies operate at the philosophical level. In the service of the mediators, there are countless tactics with both

---

[7]   This segment originally appeared in *The Advocates' Quarterly* in the fall of 2001 under the title "Mediator Strategies and Tactics".

pragmatic and psychological aspects. These tactics are how mediators bring about their strategy or put their philosophy into action directly and indirectly, verbally (through questions and statements) and non-verbally (through demeanour and actions).

Here are some of the favourite tactics identified by mediators. They are grouped into categories, together with commentary and anecdotes. Like the Deadly Sins, these categories number seven.

Tactic #1 — Having Tea

A trial may not be a tea party, but to some extent mediation can be described that way. Mediators have to survey the scene, get to know who is at the party and minimize anxiety. While not everyone will have a good time, mediators have to encourage them to stay until the cake arrives. The tactic most frequently mentioned by mediators was "making people comfortable" and "establishing rapport". In fact, one mediator mentioned it as his "primary" tactic, from which all else flows.

Mediators establish rapport in many ways ranging from social niceties, for example, mentioning the local sports team generally — "How about them Jays, eh?" — through to making educated guesses about the players. Much depends on the available time, problem, people or context and the mediator's personality.

One outstanding mediator (whom we would choose as our mediator) routinely sees parties independently at first, if only briefly. She hears their stories and permits them to connect with her, a stranger in a one-on-one setting, without the pressure of the other party's presence. The goodwill she builds is money in the bank for later.

Other mediators start to get a feel for who is involved and what is important to them by reading briefs and background documents. From these they deduce the parties' interests. (See Tactic #3.)

The notion of rapport may seem soft and fluffy, but nothing could be further from the truth. The mediator needs a kind of authority. If he or she is dismissed every time he or she opens his or her mouth, he or she will not be effective. His or her opinions have to count for something, be received as credible. One mediator explains, "I try to connect with the parties, find ways to get them to identify with me and care what I think. This increases my ability to influence them or at least to earn a hearing from them. If it is apparent to disputants that you are sincere and motivated to help, you can overcome any number of missteps procedurally or technically and still be effective."

Tactic #2 — Lending an Ear

North American mediation is an extroverted, oral affair. People are expected to come together and talk explicitly about the situation, to exchange information and make rapid decisions. This model challenges everyone — mediator, counsel, parties — to listen openly and without judgment.

Frequently, the mediator is the only one in the room who listens with indiscriminate respect. Listening is a powerful mediator tactic as it connotes a genuine, ongoing effort to fully understand the verbal and non-verbal messages exchanged. This is more complex than regurgitating what someone says after the preface, "What I hear you saying is …". Listening invokes the whole mediator, body and soul.

Like other tactics, listening has both pragmatic and psychological aspects. On a pragmatic level, it helps to establish whether the parties are talking about the same thing. Surprisingly, they often are not. Sometimes they use words, like "fairness", "damage" or "justice", with different meanings. Frequently they think they know what the other side is saying but are clinging only to presumptions. And, occasionally, parties think they are disagreeing when they are not.

Listening also unlocks doors. During an intractable personal injury mediation, the plaintiff talked about a young man who had rescued him during the accident. Defence counsel labelled the story irrelevant. Plaintiff's counsel rolled his eyes, and the fellow's own son tried to silence him. But the mediator was rapt by the descriptions of the radiant Good Samaritan who had intervened. Suddenly, the mediator knew. "Why, you believe that you were visited by an angel?" "Yes! Yes!" came the reply, "I was." What the mediator thought about angels was irrelevant. His non-judgmental listening counted more.

Tactic #3 — Sniffing Things Out

Like tracking dogs, mediators love to sniff things out. We call it "uncovering hidden interests", those tangible and intangible motivators which lie beneath demands. Is a claim for $1 million about economic loss, self-esteem, publicity, prophylaxis or retribution? The mediator is curious because these different interests suggest an array of solutions, some without price tags.

Mediators classify interests as: substantive if they relate to the subject matter; psychological if they relate to feelings; and procedural if they relate to how things are done. Interest-based mediators elicit interests to convert a tug-of-war into a problem-solving exercise. Mediation then moves from a contest of competing demands into a joint question — how do we meet both sets of needs?

One mediation concerned an apparent fight over a patent. When the mediator exposed the interests, however, ownership of the patent fell away. One party simply wanted to be recognized as a creative inventor. The other's goal was commercial exploitation. Instead of debating entitlement to the patent, the parties cut a business deal.

Tactic #4 — Sharing a Canoe

One mediator summarized nicely, "To succeed in mediation, you really have to get into the other guy's canoe and paddle around a bit. It's no use berating him or wishing that the world were different. The trick is seeing things through the other person's eyes." This means that the mediator, the parties and counsel have to acknowledge the other side's point of view and engage in some measure of empathy. In mediator-speak we call this "recognition". As the label suggests, this is about getting one side to recognize that there is at least one other possible way of looking at things. This can be enormously difficult,[8] yet it is of intense practical importance because there is a direct relationship between "recognition" and settlement.

Encouraging one party to paddle in another's canoe does not mean forcing him or her to satisfy the other person's needs. It means inviting him or her to consider those needs and why it might be useful to take account of them. In one mediation, a financial institution had a perfectly logical explanation for closing a customer's account and wanted to repeat this explanation several times. But the customer's focus was the impact of the closure, which no amount of explanation would address. The financial institution came to understand that its investment in explanations would net fewer settlement points than attention to the consequences of its actions.

Tactic #5 — Giving Needles

Sometimes people are ready to settle. But often, one (or both) party is frozen in impenetrable blocks constructed of what "really" happened, how much the party suffered, the demonic nature of the other side or the "right" solution. Then, the mediator's job — in the face of conscious or unconscious resistance — is to effect a thaw. This is a little like administering an unwelcome inoculation. It is ultimately beneficial, but the needle can hurt, especially if the person is resistant and tense.

Mediators give this tactic many names. One mediator calls it "debunking" or deflating unrealistic expectations, like correcting arrogant predictions of absolute victory or complete annihilation of an opponent. Another

---

[8]   This difficulty often flows from the fact that "recognition" is the opposite of what adversarial proceedings call for. For the purposes of trial or arbitration, counsel concedes uncontested or inconsequential points and understands the other person's point of view to be able to rebut it, not satisfy it.

mediator calls it "asking painful questions" that draw people to uncomfortable areas of weakness or risk. Another talks of "untethering people from the past — regardless of what their conflict is about". That mediator speaks "as much as possible in future-directed language, the future tense. I am not as interested in hearing where they are 'coming from' as 'where they want to go'".

Although this tactic yields pragmatic results, it frequently has a large psychological component. In one mediation, the plaintiff had to jump through fire to get to a deal. There was no fire, of course, just the perception of one. Settlement would mean letting go of his victim mentality and the stereotypes he nurtured about the defendant. These invaded his being. His palpable fear (which he could not actually articulate) was of the internal vacuum that would replace this dispute once it settled. His counsel had grown impatient. The defendant labelled him a calculating, if immature, gold-digger. It took a long time — weeks — to help that plaintiff let go. It took the same amount of effort to persuade the defendants to extend time. When the plaintiff finally jumped, he found that the chasm was small and he landed upright. After the mediation the plaintiff proclaimed that settling with the defendant was the best thing he ever did.

Another mediator had a similar situation in a professional negligence file which called for this tactic. The defendant, an experienced and well-respected professional, invested significant time and effort justifying her past judgment. If that continued, there would be no movement towards resolution. Finally, after another rendition of justification, the mediator said straight out: "Madam, I understand all that, as we have discussed it many times before, but I am trying to take you someplace else." "I know", the professional said sadly, "and I have been resisting going there."

Tactic #6 — Carrots and Sticks

One familiar tactic concerns risk assessment. The mediator reviews what a party stands to lose without settlement. In more extreme cases, the mediator exaggerates, "You are bound to lose your house if you carry on!" Threats comprise one (crude) version of this tactic where the mediator searches for the right concrete motivator. This involves a comparison of the proposed settlement to available alternatives like trial. The mediator asks, "What will happen if this file does not settle?" Or, "Can we talk about your past and future costs if litigation proceeds?" Since this tactic clips counsel's turf, it is sometimes provocative.

Social science research shows that people are generally risk averse. They prefer to protect what little they have than wager larger gains. When mediators canvass the costs of outstanding conflict (out-of-pocket, unrecoverable costs, lost opportunities, personal stress) they instinctively apply this research. In one mediation, a lone counsel pleaded with the co-defendants, "It's not right to settle! We could do far better at trial." He had a moral point, but no one wanted to fund it.

Of course, not all parties are risk averse. Some enjoy a good fight. Some are well-heeled and careless of cost. Some can scrutinize risk and thoughtfully assume it. Mediators adapt this tactic to these parties. One mediator explains, "I usually size up the case to see what is larger, the carrot (opportunity) or the stick (risk of a poor alternative "WATNA" (worst alternatives to a negotiated agreement) coming to pass). They say that a smart lawyer will argue the law when she has the law and the facts when she has the facts. I analogize this to my private mediator's practice: If there is a great opportunity they could lose, I focus on the opportunity. If there is a BATNA (best alternatives to a negotiated agreement) risk to avoid, I 'walk them down the BATNA road,' taking time to smell the disturbing aromas and painting a colourful picture."

Tactic #7 — Passing the Ball Back

"About every five years I have a mediation that is going nowhere and I simply put on my coat and start to leave. Once I even went to the lobby and sat for a while in my overcoat. Soon, they came looking for me."

Every (truthful) mediator has had files that did not settle. The mediator has to pack his or her bags and leave. That is not usually theatrics. It is the ultimate deferral to individual choice. If mediators frame mediation as individual decision-making, they have to accept decisions not to settle.

Mediators remind themselves that if they are the hardest working ones in the room, they are hogging the ball and assuming too much responsibility. They have to pass the ball back.

One mediator remembered spending all night between sessions trying to unpick a tangled dispute, without success. The next morning in exasperation she asked, "What is there about the present situation that makes it so desirable?" "I beg your pardon?", the parties answered. "Well, you are stuck and I am wondering what is so compelling about your current situation that makes you want to stay there?" "Well — nothing!", they exclaimed. That exchange provoked the necessary flexibility. The file settled, but only after the mediator really let go.

Knowing some common mediator strategies and tactics together with the underlying assumptions can help people participate more effectively in the process. By the same token, people should understand that there are some things a mediator will not do.

One thing a mediator will *not* do in a traditional interest-based mediation is jointly deliver to the parties in plenary session an opinion as to who has the better case, essentially picking a winner. The traditional interest-based mediation model is used in the Ontario, British Columbia and Saskatchewan court-connected mediation programs and by a great many private mediators. In that model of mediation, the mediator will resist the temptation or a party's request to give a general public opinion on the merits of the claim, or on the range of damages likely to be awarded at trial. Many mediators will do this privately, but that is a different thing. See the section "Mediation as a Process of Influence", below.

The difficulty with a joint, public evaluation is that it can be counter-productive to the negotiation because it drives the parties further apart rather than bringing them closer together. This is especially true if the evaluative opinion is significantly out of line with the parties' expectations of what it will be. A frequent reaction is that the "winning" party wants to forget the mediation and press on to trial, and the "losing" party wants to end the mediation so it can retreat and lick its wounds. The mediator must then employ all of his or her skill to get the parties talking again, to re-establish the idea that there are risks on both sides, and to help them find a creative way to save face and come to an honourable resolution.

A few mediators, including some former judges, will openly evaluate a case in a process which they also call "mediation". They typically have a depth of experience in the subject matters of the disputes they are mediating or a certain measure of institutional or reputational authority, so that their opinions will carry weight with the parties. There is a continuing debate among mediators as to whether such an evaluative process can be called "mediation" when it is really a hybrid form of "neutral evaluation". This debate is not likely to be resolved soon, and it is enough for our purposes that the two forms exist.

While the debate in the mediation community is not over with respect to certain kinds of conduct by mediators, many would agree that parties in mediation can expect the following:

1.   A mediator will not act as any party's lawyer by giving partisan legal advice as opposed to providing general information about the legal process or typical elements of a certain kind of case.

2.   A mediator will not coerce a settlement by intimidation, threats, misrepresentation or other forms of unsavoury behaviour.

3.   A mediator will not make a decision for or impose his or her judgment on any party.

4.   A mediator will not pick favourites such that he or she becomes the advocate or agent of one party to the exclusion of the other or hold active biases for or against anyone, *i.e.*, big bad bank versus beaten down little customer. This does not mean that a mediator treats all parties exactly the same. The mediator has to reach out to each party as he or she

finds them; however, the mediator must treat them even-handedly and not openly prefer one party or one cause over another.

5.   A mediator will at all times maintain the confidentiality of the parties with respect to the dispute.

Again, we stress that there is no single "correct" role for a mediator. The same mediator will take different approaches to different fact situations and different parties. One secret of the success of mediation in helping parties to resolve their differences is that it is such an endlessly flexible process. The aim of this section is not to describe what the ideal mediator does in every mediation. Rather, it is to give you some idea of what to expect from your mediator, and to help you ask the right questions in making your choice.

MEDIATION AS A PROCESS OF INFLUENCE

We have met DR practitioners who insist that a mediator must take care not to influence the negotiations between the parties during the course of the mediation. According to them, a mediator is detached from the content of the dispute and simply provides an even-handed process that lets the parties have a constructive discussion about their differences. "The mediator owns the process and the parties own the content", these practitioners like to say, and they would never dream of giving their own impressions of what is going on or offering any sort of opinion even if one participant was under a mistaken impression about a key part of the dispute.

The reason given for this hands-off approach is that a mediator must achieve true detachment in order not to compromise "neutrality". It is as if the mediator is a waiter at a cocktail party, indifferent to whether the glasses on the tray contain whiskey or champagne, and simply responsible for distributing the drinks equally among the guests.

We have no difficulty with the notion that the parties in mediation must ultimately decide whether and how to settle their dispute. After all, it *is* their dispute and the mediator's mandate is not to make a decision for them. Still, our experience tells us that mediation is a process of influence and that affecting the negotiators is an integral part of the mediator's role. So we disagree with the prohibition on a mediator giving impressions, opinions and concrete feedback concerning the dispute. This is completely contrary to our experience as mediators. The mediator's feedback is often just what the parties are looking for.

Recently, an employee of a financial institution took part in his first mediation. "I'm a complete rookie in this process", he said, "my aim is to make it work for me in order to settle this dispute." When the plenary session ended and the caucus began with his side, the first words out of his mouth were, "Opinions, opinions, opinions. I want to have your opinion about this situation." This participant, who had not been schooled in the philosophical niceties of mediation, intuitively felt that the views of an outsider would help with his decisions. He welcomed and wanted those opinions.

It is our observation that in order to help the parties approach or achieve agreement, the mediator has to become involved, get engaged and roll up his or her sleeves. That is quite the opposite of being a detached process-minder. It means that the waiter actually has to know rye from scotch and distinguish good champagne from cheap wine. He has to operate with discretion, charm and attention. He has to encourage people to try new drinks, provide prompt refills and take orders for unanticipated brands. He must respect the abstainer and restrain the indulger without threats or altercations. The good waiter may be invisible in his success, but all the while he is influencing the outcome of the event. Like waiters, mediators influence outcomes by paying attention and participating fully in their roles.

And why shouldn't that be so? The mediator is supposed to add value to the equation. Without a mediator, the parties are engaged in a different process — direct negotiation — and they don't have to spend a cent to do that. They pay for the services of a mediator who has to be more than an indifferent traffic cop.

To be sure, the mediator has to do this skilfully and to employ honesty as well as tact. He or she does not make up facts or conjure up risks that do not exist, but gives honest, genuine feedback.

To understand the inevitability of mediator influence, it helps to remember that mediation is a system made up of components and subsystems. These components include people with all of their individual backgrounds, cultures, personal preferences and peccadilloes plus the content and context of their dispute. These components interact and affect each other all the time.

As a system, mediation resembles a hanging mobile. Touch one part, even with the gentlest pressure, and all of the parts move. The mobile reconfigures itself. The mediation system is very dynamic (occasionally volatile) and the components of the systems are always influencing and impacting upon one another. What this means is that at its heart mediation is a process of influence. Each participant is trying to influence every other participant throughout the process.

When we think of mediation as a dynamic system, it does not seem possible that a mediator could get into the middle of a conflict without having some impact, intended or not. The purpose of getting involved to begin with is to make some kind of a difference and if the parties were satisfied with the status quo, there would be no conflict and no call for mediation. A mediator's job is to make the negotiation more effective.

When thinking about a mediator's role, it is important to distinguish influence from coercion. Influence is unavoidable; coercion is out of place. Coercion is a situation in which the parties feel that they have no choice but to do what the mediator says because the mediator bullies them, lies to them or intimidates them. That is not appropriate. What is appropriate, indeed inevitable, is that a mediator will always have an impact on the negotiations and will influence what goes on. That is the purpose of the mediator being involved, and, as we explained in the stages of mediation, honest and open feedback is an integral part of the process.

The impulse and ability to influence is not limited to mediators. When a dismissed employee comes to a mediation, she comes for several reasons. To have her say, perhaps. To be heard, to vindicate herself. But, she also comes to influence her former employer to pay her the largest sum of money possible with the fewest strings attached. She may also try to influence the employer to cooperate in structuring the payment in the most tax-effective way — so much for legal expenses, so much for outplacement, so much to be carried over into the next calendar year. That is what the process is all about.

Equal but opposing attempts at influence go on across the table. The employer is trying to influence the employee to reduce the number of months' notice she is claiming or to exclude from her calculation home office expenses that bear no relation to company business after dismissal. The employer may also want to influence the employee to accept that the dismissal "wasn't personal, or anything", while the employee still feels resentful and bitter.

Mutual influence is the stuff of which mediation is made. Mediators try to influence parties; parties try to influence each other, and parties try to influence the mediator whom they hope will in turn influence the other side. In mediation, influence occurs constantly with varying intensity on diverse issues and with variable success. The strength of any participant's influence can change from moment to moment. The mobile swings and bobs this way and that as the participants act and react.

Thus, it can be seen that a mediator is not merely a wooden spoon that stirs the pot and then rests passively on the spoon holder. A mediator is a full participant in the mediation system and, as such, both affects and is affected. Whether the mediator is conscious of it or not, whether the mediator admits it or not, he or she has an impact on the parties' negotiation, and, fairly frequently, this influence relates to the content of the dispute.

Here are some additional mediator tactics, ways in which a mediator can influence the mediation system:

1. A mediator tries to destabilize people's perceptions and narratives, particularly their interpretations and attributions concerning the other

side. "He served that notice of dissolution last month to deliberately destroy my son's inheritance", says the company founder of his former partner. "You resent the fact that he took the initiative", says the mediator. "However, he tells me that the two of you had not been getting along for two years and that you returned his letters unopened and refused to attend meetings."

2.   A mediator tries to influence people's predictions of success if they take their dispute to arbitration or court. The mediator does this by standing in as a proxy for an arbitrator or judge. "I know that you think this clause in the tender documentation is clear so that you had no duty to enquire, but when I read this the first time, I saw it differently. Would you be interested in hearing how I interpreted it?"

3.   A mediator insists upon or encourages certain standards of behaviour to ensure that parties control their emotions in order to foster logical problem-solving. "Listen, counsel", says the mediator, "It might not be a good idea to use the word 'extortion' again. Come to think of it, I don't recommend the phrase 'shaking the tree' either."

4.   A mediator tells people what they can and cannot talk about or the way in which they can talk about subjects. "You can unwind the cobwebs one strand at a time", she says to the long-time business associates. "Or, you can blast them off all at once with 200 lbs per square inch of pressure. That's me — 200 lbs per square inch."[9]

5.   A mediator provides or provokes new information, sometimes tentatively, sometimes boldly. "Have you talked to your lawyer about the costs of taking this thing through to trial?" or "Sir, I know you want your job back, but if you were successful at this tribunal, you'd be sent back to grievance arbitration, not put directly back to work."

6.   A mediator helps people frame offers and proposals to make them attractive or palatable to the other side. "You don't need to say you screwed up", the mediator advises. "I don't think she's looking for an admission. I think it's more important for her to hear you say that you see the consequences of what you did and how it affected her life. Let's just play with some words here."

7.   A mediator transmits or reformulates information in more diplomatic terms. A mediator does not run off and repeat words like "malingerer", "welfare bum" or "crook" because the mediator can see with greater clarity that the other side will not accept or like them.

8.   A mediator excavates interests and picks up on topics that get lost or overlooked in the heat of the moment. "Wait a minute", says the mediator, "He just said that he won't stand in the way of selling this in-

---

[9]   Paraphrased from an entertaining and educational address to the ADR Section of the Ontario Bar Association by Justice Warren Winkler of the Ontario Superior Court at the Annual ADR Award of Excellence Luncheon (June 2003).

vention. He just wants to make sure everyone knows that he's the inventor. You've said that your primary goal is to generate income. If the licence goes ahead as planned, will you have any difficulty identifying Mr. Sylvester as the inventor?"

As the above list demonstrates, there are all kinds of ways in which mediators can influence what goes on. This is tied to their philosophy, self-confidence, levels of tolerance for ambiguity as well as conflict and training.

WHO MAY CALL THEMSELVES A MEDIATOR?

The answer to this question is the same today as it was for the first edition of this book. Anyone may call himself or herself a mediator: there are no barriers to entry in this field, no standard process of approval and no single set of criteria to be met, educational or otherwise. Unlike dentistry or law, mediation has no licensure — meaning no governmental grant of permission to practise based on prescribed levels of education, training, experience or performance. It would be familiar territory for Descartes: "I think I am a mediator, therefore I am one." Anyone can start a mediation business and hold himself or herself out to the public as a mediator.

However, things have changed when it comes to particular applications for mediation. Many informal and formal forms of certification exist by which mediators are admitted to rosters, named in standing offers for government services, made members of mediation groups or granted designations by private mediation organizations like Family Mediation Canada or ADR Canada Inc.

Context-specific criteria have been developed for these many and varied initiatives. There are specific things that mediators must show in order to qualify. These range from minimal educational or training criteria, demonstration of skills through role playing, videos, peer review or a practicum, examinations, detailed descriptions of work done and specific, detailed reference letters. In addition to the proliferation of context-specific requirements, what has changed the most in the last 10 years is that mediators are now required to prove that they can actually do what they claim to do. Their word is no longer enough because programs need to be accountable to the people who use a mediator's services.

By way of example, to be added to the Toronto roster of mediators for the Ontario Mandatory Mediation Program,[10] which mediates civil and estate cases, a candidate must satisfy the program (through written application and discretionary interview) that he or she has completed a minimum of 40 hours of mediation training and has conducted a minimum of five mediations as a

---

[10]   See online: Ontario Ministry of the Attorney General <http://www.attorneygeneral.jus.gov.on.ca/english/courts/manmed/guidelines.asp>.

sole or co-mediator. Mock mediations in training courses do not count, nor does mere observation or bag-carrying for an established mediator. The candidate must also provide three reference letters, and two of those must specifically state that the referee (in the capacity of mediation participant, participant's lawyer or co-mediator) has actually seen the candidate perform work as a neutral mediator (not arbitration or some other ADR service). A candidate must also satisfy the program that he or she is familiar with the civil justice system, where the mediations originate.

The criteria are similar but more demanding for ADR Canada's Chartered Mediator[11] designation which signifies a generalist mediator competence not specific to any field. Those criteria include at least 80 hours of mediation training, the conducting of 10 mediations (five of which are fee-paying), with the applicant having been the sole mediator or the mediation chairperson at least five times, plus a skills assessment, which is usually a combination of direct peer observation/assessment and interview.

Family Mediation Canada's criteria for the national certification of family mediators[12] seems to be more demanding. They include a minimum of 80 hours of basic mediation training, an additional 100 hours of training related to specific family issues, an approved mediation practicum or two positive peer evaluations, a videotaped role play assessment and a final written examination. Detailed lists of what are considered to be mediation competencies are set out on the website noted below.

These various criteria do not represent a single, unified standard of practice but reflect common ways of establishing who can call themselves a mediator for what purposes. A candidate must establish a certain level of training, skill and experience.

Of course, all of this assumes that mediation is a discrete, identifiable activity carried out only by "mediators". That is not necessarily the case and we caution against becoming too exclusive about what constitutes "legitimate" or "real" mediation for a number of reasons.

First of all, the categories between different ADR processes are indistinct, and the words used are capable of different applications. Take, for instance, the process of facilitation. The word *facilitate* (to make easier) is commonly used to describe the task of managing group discussions. Chairs of meetings are *facilitators* because they keep things moving along. It is also increasingly and confusingly used by mediators and their clients as an alternative way of referring to a mediation, a way that avoids any need to acknowledge that there is a conflict or a dispute among the participants. One example is the process mandated by the Ontario Health Services Restructur-

---

[11]   See online: Arbitration and Mediation Institute of Manitoba <http://www.amim.mb.ca/medcertif.html>.

[12]   See online: Family Mediation Canada <http://www.fmc.ca/index.php?page=18>.

ing Commission. Hospitals ordered to close, merge or restructure were afforded a *facilitator* to assist them in reconfiguring the puzzle of programs, staff, facilities and funding. It was a situation rife with conflict and it required specific resolution in order for the hospitals and the communities to move on.

There are a number of differences between mediation and facilitation, but the most significant is probably the goal of the intervention: settlement versus working together. The parties to a mediation have been unable to settle their differences on their own and are seeking assistance to help them resolve the dispute. The parties to a facilitation want to improve their ability to work together effectively.

Some other processes called mediation oblige the mediator to be more evaluative in his or her approach to the dispute. In the Alberta Court of Queen's Bench, the DR process offered by the judges is sometimes referred to as *judicial mediation*, for example. We categorize such processes as forms of neutral evaluation, but mention the mediation label to underscore the blurring of the edges between the various forms of dispute resolution. While the emphasis in this book is on interest-based mediation, all of the foregoing variations are legitimate DR processes. We think it is important that people be aware of other possibilities and adapt the relevant process to their needs.

A second reason to avoid an exclusive attitude about mediation is that there are other professions and practices that involve substantially the same work without using the same label. One area that comes to mind is the area of organization development ("OD").

Consider the following situation. An OD practitioner completed a mandate in a large national organization where two co-workers in a particular department had a conflict. The mandate was to see whether and how the employees could come to their own amicable resolution, which they eventually did. In bringing the parties to resolution, the OD practitioner:

1.   clarified her mandate and the respective roles of those involved;

2.   met individually with the two co-workers first;

3.   got some sense of what the parties were looking for and assessed their levels of flexibility and willingness to compromise;

4.   convened and led a plenary session with both co-workers;

5.   facilitated communication at the plenary session and promoted mutual understanding;

6.   brokered the delivery and acceptance of an apology from one co-worker to another; and

7.   helped the parties frame a practical agreement for how they would interact and work together in the future.

This mandate is remarkably similar to the mediation used to illustrate exceptions to the three-stage mediation model. It also resembles many workplace mandates that we ourselves have performed as mediators. The difference is that as far as the other practitioner was concerned, this was an OD intervention and not a mediation. It has most of the hallmarks of a mediation, but the OD practitioner:

1.   would never be labelled a mediator; she calls herself an organizational development consultant and always has;

2.   does not offer mediation as one of her services and has no intention of doing so;

3.   has never taken a mediation course, learned a mediation model or been taught any "mediation skills" by anybody;

4.   has no familiarity with the term "interests" or any of the associated vocabulary and no working knowledge of this concept;

5.   has no experience of mediation, has never seen or participated in one in her life and likely never will; and

6.   knows something about psychology, consulting, counselling, change management, organization development, human resources and adult education from her own education, background and experiences.

The OD consultant's mandate is a reminder that mediation is actually an amalgam of skills, models and theories imported from many other fields, such as psychology, counselling, law, change management, organizational development, industrial relations and so forth, with a level of folk wisdom thrown in. In the last two decades, this combination has been packaged with a label marked "mediation" but the packaging remains permeable. Perhaps mediators need to be careful about their claims of exclusivity and their zeal to exclude others who do not meet criteria or operate under their limited or particular frame of reference. After all, what's in a name?

AUTHORITY ISSUES AND SPECIALIZED KNOWLEDGE IN MEDIATION

Despite the fact that mediation has matured considerably in Canada in the last decade, tension persists around the definition of "real" mediation. One prong of the debate concerns employed mediators like human resources advisors, dispute resolution officers or staff mediators who work at public or private organizations. Can a manager ever be a mediator with respect to staffing disputes? Do members of administrative tribunals have any business mediating? When regulatory staff broker a settlement, can that be called mediation?

In each of these examples, the mediator brings a mandate or agenda that directly relates to the dispute and this frequently involves some kind of authority over individual disputants. The manager, for example, may be able to dictate the outcome of the dispute if individual staff cannot agree. The tribunal has a statutory mandate to decide disputes within its jurisdiction. And regulatory staff may have obligations pertaining to the regulatory body.

It is obvious that in these cases the mediator has an interest of some kind in the dispute. One might even say that the mediator is simultaneously a facilitator and a party or a mediator and a negotiator. This may sound like a contradiction in terms, but it need not be. The mediator is playing a hybrid role.

When a mediator has authority by virtue of position or law, "real" mediation can still be taking place. But the mediator is not what the literature calls an "independent mediator", in that the mediator has a direct connection to the parties (maybe even an agency relationship) and is not indifferent as to specific outcomes.

There is no practical use in debating whether these mediations can accurately be called "real mediations". That is just energy wasted over labels. In his formative text, *The Mediation Process*, Christopher W. Moore[13] helpfully reframes the debate. He identifies different types of mediators based on the type of relationship that they have with the involved parties. For example, the manager with a staffing dispute may be classified as an "Administrative/Managerial Mediator". Such a mediator has an ongoing authoritative relationship with the parties before and after the dispute. That mediator seeks a solution jointly developed with the parties but within mandated parameters, and may have the authority to advise, suggest or decide, and even the authority to enforce an agreement.

As another example, the staff at a regulatory body may be classified as a blend of "Administrative/Managerial Mediator" and "Vested Interest Mediator". This mediator also seeks a solution within mandated parameters (the governing statute) and works for a body with the ultimate authority to enforce the agreement. He or she also has a strong interest in the outcome of the dispute in accordance with the mandate of the regulatory body and may have resources to help in monitoring and implementing the agreement.

In either case it is still possible for the mediator to work with the parties to develop a solution that meets needs, including those of the mediator or the mediator's institution. The expectations of the parties need to be consistent with the configuration of this kind of mediation.

Another persistent (and related) area of debate concerns mediators with specialized or substantive knowledge. Are they supposed to actively use it or resist using it?

---

[13]   C.W. Moore, *The Mediation Process: Practical Strategies for Resolving Conflict*, 2d ed. (San Francisco: Jossey-Bass Publishers, 1996).

Some people argue that in order to be credible the mediator must know about the subject matter of the dispute, *e.g.*, a labour mediator must know about labour relations; a mediator in a construction dispute must be an engineer or design professional; an intellectual property dispute calls for an intellectual property lawyer. Mediators with substantive knowledge can more quickly understand terminology used by the participants. They can also more readily determine when one party or the other is taking a position, advancing an argument or proposing a solution that is not realistic. This permits them to "challenge" unrealistic expectations or behaviours, and to be an "agent of reality" who helps keep the discussion on a practical, achievable level. Mediators with substantive knowledge are also better equipped to suggest solutions.

In contrast to the foregoing approach, others argue that a mediator with substantive knowledge is a dangerous thing. As one person put it, "A little knowledge is a dangerous thing, but a lot of knowledge is profoundly dangerous!" While knowledgeable mediators may indeed understand the language and the issues, they run the risk of imposing their notions and their solutions on the parties, and of inhibiting creativity with their urge to maintain a practical, achievable reality. Thus they function more as evaluators or arbitrators. The objection is twofold. First, such mediators preclude full participation of the actual disputants by virtue of the authority implied in their substantive expertise, and, second, they put a damper on creativity and option creation. To some, this is inconsistent with a party-driven process like mediation.

Once again, we question this "either/or" framing. Many mediators bring substantive knowledge to the table and yet are able to facilitate interest-based outcomes. Other mediators lack substantive knowledge, yet credibly and effectively assist negotiations. The only generalization we concede is that many buyers of mediation services identify subject-matter expertise as their criteria for selecting a mediator. However, this preference is not unanimously endorsed by sellers of mediation services; during one panel discussion on marketing, several mediators acknowledged that they were selected for their subject-matter expertise but stated that the expertise was irrelevant to them in their function as mediator.

Admittedly, there are issues surrounding the mediator's use of authority regardless of whether that authority comes from a managerial position, a statutory base or substantive expertise. Accordingly, it is more helpful to address the issues than to argue about definitions. The real question with respect to mediator authority concerns *how* the mediator makes use of it and what expectations the parties can *reasonably* have of the mediator. There are ways to integrate authority into interest-based mediation.

- *Terminology and understanding.* Obviously, it is helpful for the mediator to understand what the dispute is about, but that kind of understanding should not be confused with an appreciation of the parties' interests. If one side alleges patent infringement and the other denies it, an intellectual property lawyer may know what that litigation entails, but may not know what motivates the two sides. What if one side had a need to be recognized as an inventor but the other cared only about market expansion? Knowing patent law alone will not reveal that difference. Knowing how to elicit interests will.

- *Evaluating the parties' cases.* As discussed at length in this chapter, some mediators express opinions about the merits of a party's case or create doubt about the prospects of success. Sometimes the parties specifically ask that this be done. Other times, as in court-connected civil mediations, the expectation is implied. When a mediator evaluates, substantive knowledge helps. A mediator who does not know the range of notice for the dismissal of a two-year employee might have difficulty commenting on a request for seven years' notice. Seven years might seem perfectly logical within the plaintiff's subjective frame of reference. It might just not be realistic in court. It all depends on how the mediator uses knowledge to check the realism of the plaintiff's expectations. Immediately labelling the demand as unreasonable may not be as helpful as inviting the plaintiff to justify the request for seven years' notice in light of recent court decisions.

- *Offering solutions.* Some interest-based mediators never put options (solutions) on the table for the parties. Others do, saying that if a solution was obvious to the parties, a mediator would not be needed. Mediators with substantive expertise are well positioned to help the parties develop solutions. Mediators who are staff at agencies, boards or commissions are particularly well-suited to assist with this task. They are able to tell the parties what other kinds of solutions they have seen, what kind of solutions the tribunal has contemplated or what usually happens. The staff mediator at the National Energy Board, for example, can tell the parties how landowner objections to pipeline locations have been resolved in other cases. Interest-based mediators can offer solutions as one of a number of options for the parties to consider. Offering a suggestion is not the same thing as imposing a solution.

- *Institutional mandate.* Many institutions, including government agencies and administrative tribunals, use mediators who are their employees. They do not contract with "independent" mediators who are nominated by all concerned. Essentially, these institutions use "internal mediators", who typically bring the institution's mandate and interests to the table such that the mediator is simultaneously the facilitator and negotiator, or facilitator and agent for the institution. In practical terms, this means that settlements generally take place within mandated parameters and that the needs of the institution are to be met in any settlement agreement. For example, suppose a patient made a complaint against a regulated health professional such as a doctor or a nurse. The complaint is made to the regulatory body whose job it is to be concerned about professional competence and public safety. If the regulatory body assigned a staff person to work out a settlement of the issues in the complaint, an interest-based settlement would need to meet the interests of the patient, the health professional and the regulatory body. If the complaint suggested that the health professional could put other members of the public in danger, then a settlement which simply treated the complaint as a "personality dispute" or a "communications issue" between the patient and the doctor would not address the regulatory body's need to ensure public safety.

THE MEDIATION AGREEMENT

Private, voluntary mediations are generally conducted pursuant to written mediation agreements, examples of which are found at the end of this chapter. These agreements essentially set out the parameters and rules of mediation, such as the date, time and place; the issues to be mediated; the amount and allocation of mediation costs; and the conditions of confidentiality that are to prevail. Agreements to mediate need not be complex, but can be very helpful because they clarify what the parties and the mediator can expect of one another.

Court-connected mediations or mediations associated with administrative tribunals are usually governed by public documents like legislation, regulations, court rules, public notices or practice directions. Written mediation agreements may also be used. The wide variety of supporting documents requires a specific enquiry in every case.

By way of example, the Canadian Human Rights Tribunal posts on its website a 14-page document in PDF format called "Mediation Procedures".[14] This document comprehensively sets out the Tribunal's mediation options in question-and-answer format, and it is relatively easy to find on the Tribunal's home page.

However, other tribunals have less obvious or accessible ADR protocols. The Canadian Radio-television and Telecommunications Commission[15] published "Practices and procedures for resolving competitive and access disputes" in May of 2000 and "Expedited procedures for resolving competitive disputes" in February 2004, but these can be accessed on the website

---

[14] Canadian Human Rights Tribunal, *Mediation Procedures* (13 May 2004), online: <http://www.chrt-tcdp.gc.ca/pdf/mediation-may13-ef.pdf>.

[15] See online: <http://www.crtc.gc.ca>.

most easily by knowing of and searching for a specific CRTC Public Notice or Telecom Circular.[16]

In Ontario, estate mediations are governed by Rules 75.1 and 24.1 of the Rules of Civil Procedure,[17] under the *Courts of Justice Act*.[18] However, a court referral to mediation also results in a court order specific to the mediation that may set out the issues to be mediated, the parties required to attend and other relevant issues desirable to facilitate the mediation.

THE COST OF MEDIATION

The cost to the parties of engaging in a mediation has the same three components as the other DR processes discussed in this book:

1.   the cost of the mediator to prepare for and conduct the mediation plus associated disbursements;
2.   the internal business cost of preparation and attendance; and
3.   the cost of the lawyer and/or other professional advisor's preparation and attendance.

In court-connected or government-sponsored programs, the fees are fixed or capped. For example, in the Ontario Mandatory Mediation Program, the cost of the mediator for the three-hour mediation session and an hour of preparation is fixed at the rate of $600 for one hour of preparation and up to three hours of mediation in a two-party lawsuit. The cost is divided equally among the parties.

In private mediations, the mediator is paid either at an hourly, a half-daily or a daily rate, and some mediators are beginning to publicly disclose their fees on their websites. We would estimate the range to be from $750 to $5,000 per day. The total estimated fees are typically set out in the mediation agreement and split equally among the parties regardless of the outcome of the mediation. Mediators charge for preparation as well as for leading the mediation session(s), and disbursements such as room charges or travel expenses are in addition to the fees. The elements of cost to be considered can be seen in the sample mediation agreements at the end of this chapter.

---

[16]   See C.R.T.C., Telecom Circular 2004-2, "Expedited procedure for resolving competitive issues" (10 February 2004); C.R.T.C., Telecom Circular 2007-16, "A guide to the CRTC processes for telecommunications applications" (11 June 2007); C.R.T.C., Broadcasting Circular 2005-463, "Expedited procedure for resolving issues arising under the *Broadcasting Act*" (18 April 2005); C.R.T.C., Public Notice 2000-65, "Practices and procedures for resolving competitive and access disputes" (12 May 2000); C.R.T.C., Broadcasting and Telecom Information Bulletin 2009-38, "Practices and procedures for staff-assisted mediation, final offer arbitration, and expedited hearings" (29 January 2009). These are available online: Canadian Radio-television and Telecommunications Commission <http://www.crtc.gc.ca/>.

[17]   R.R.O. 1990, Reg. 194.

[18]   R.S.O. 1990, c. C.43.

The typical court-based mediation in the commercial context lasts from two to three hours, while the average private mediation is usually booked for a day. Telephone mediations usually take less time, and complex issue or multi-party cases generally take more.

Another factor to be considered is the cost of resolving the dispute if it is not taken to mediation or other appropriate DR process — not just legal and court costs, but also the internal and personal costs associated with discovery and preparation and attendance throughout an adversarial process. In most cases, these costs include anxiety about testifying and having colleagues and customers testify, and also anxiety about having an uncertain outcome at an unpredictable time in the future. Sometimes this anxiety is the most significant factor and will materially affect the outcome of negotiations. This can be ameliorated to some degree by informing the party of exactly what to expect in the course of the lawsuit.

Experience has shown that parties rarely have a true picture of the full financial costs they are facing in litigation, or an understanding that there will always be significant non-recoverable costs even if they are completely successful at trial. Because solicitor and client costs[19] are frequently claimed, and lawyers fail to explain how infrequently costs are awarded on that scale, parties too often enter settlement negotiations with unrealistic expectations of what can be achieved. Wise and durable settlements will not be concluded unless the parties are fully advised of the risks as well as of their rights. Only then can they make informed decisions and instruct counsel appropriately.

WHAT KIND OF DISPUTES CAN BE MEDIATED?

In the late 1980s and early 1990s, it took significant energy to bring people together for mediations. The value of mediation was far from self-evident, and the process was unfamiliar. People needed to be convinced of its benefits and assured that they would not be harmed if it did not result in a settlement. They were openly afraid that it was a sign of weakness even to suggest mediation to the other side of a dispute.

In the early days, some mediators were given mandates to bring people to the table. They were paid a flat fee or an hourly rate by insurance companies, for example, to telephone and write the lawyers involved in the case in order to get them to agree to give mediation a try. Sometimes, mediators played a dual role — introducing and explaining the process of mediation and offering themselves as mediators if the parties agreed. As mentioned in the first and second editions of this book, these mediator-convenors would generally:

1.   explain how mediation works;

---

[19]   A request for almost complete reimbursement by an opposite party of litigation costs.

2.   emphasize confidentiality in group and caucus sessions;

3.   stress the low-risk nature of the process in that nothing is binding unless agreement is reached by all the parties;

4.   reiterate that participation has no effect on legal rights if settlement is not achieved;

5.   talk about creative solutions tailor-made for the parties;

6.   mention that compared to any other process in litigation it is efficient (often takes only a half-day) and cost-effective (costs often split among parties); and

7.   discuss success rate of mediations.

Although the mediators tried to approach convening with openness and honesty, they frequently met with resistance. Not surprisingly, people found the approach self-serving. We still have a copy of an angry letter that one lawyer wrote to a mediator with engineering qualifications who had been asked to convene a mediation and act as co-mediator for an insurer in a construction file. The letter told the engineer to stop interfering in a perfectly good lawsuit because all this talk about mediation was impertinent and unnecessarily wasted lawyer time and client money.

Fortunately for all concerned, those days of convening are gone. Full-time commercial mediation administrators seem to have disappeared and mediators no longer need to market their services in this way.

The environment for mediation has changed in a number of ways. First, lawyers (and to a lesser extent clients) are proactively seeking out mediation to help settle disputes. Second, the courts themselves are actively encouraging or requiring people to take part in mediation as a standard part of a lawsuit. And third, mediation has been integrated into administrative tribunals and workplaces in formal and informal ways.

People are generally more comfortable and familiar with mediation. Mandatory mediation programs and the proliferation of negotiation and mediation courses throughout the country have enhanced the level of public awareness about mediation. Furthermore, many more people have had the actual experience of mediation, instead of just a theoretical introduction.

In our experience, almost any kind of case can be mediated. It is not really the type of case that determines suitability. It is the attitude of the players and whether or not their unilateral self-help remedies are any good.

Certain cases seem to be naturals for mediation, such as conflicts be-tween family members or co-workers, grievance disputes involving union and management, disputes between franchisor and franchisee, shareholder disputes, and the contestation of estates by beneficiaries. These can all be described as relational disputes, where the people involved have an ongoing relationship at the present and likely off into the future. However, mediation can be equally useful in one-time disputes, where the parties have no desire or inclination to interact again and earnestly wish to end their current interaction. An example would be a personal injury claim arising out of a motor vehicle accident. In fact, the British Columbia Notice to Mediate process was first introduced in motor vehicle accident cases, where the parties are unlikely ever to interact again. The resolution rate of 71 per cent is a strong indicator of the effectiveness of mediation in these circumstances.

As early as 1995 and based on the Ontario Superior Court ADR pilot project's outcome data, its external evaluators[20] recommended that there be "presumptive" mediation in all civil, non-family cases (*i.e.*, that it is generally a suitable process unless it is rejected for an expressly understood reason). This recommendation was acted upon in the design of the project's successor, the Ontario Mandatory Mediation Program, where every kind of civil case has been successfully mediated at a very early stage, subject only to special concerns around personal injury and medical malpractice cases, which need time for a proper prognosis of a plaintiff's medical condition.

Still, there remain some common objections to the use of mediation. Let us examine some of them:

1. when fraud is alleged;
2. when a precedent is required;
3. where domestic violence is involved or alleged;
4. when a declaratory judgment is required;
5. when the parties are not willing to settle; and
6. when the damages are not yet quantifiable.[21]

Mediation should not automatically be rejected for cases falling within these categories. That should happen only if one or more parties hold expectations or needs inconsistent with mediation. For example, if bank fraud is alleged and is substantially backed up by evidence, and the bank's insurance policy requires a judgment, a settlement in mediation is unlikely. However, if fraud is alleged by a father against his son with whom he has been in business for 30 years, the fraud involves moving funds around the family companies in ways that have been countenanced for a decade and the allegation is made just after the father and son had a falling out on other issues, that case may well settle with the help of a skilled mediator.

With regard to a precedent, this is a decision of a state-sanctioned body used to govern the conduct of future cases. The need for a court judgment to

---

[20] J. Macfarlane, *Court-Based Mediation for Civil Cases: An Evaluation of the Ontario Court (General Division) ADR Centre* (Toronto: Queen's Printer for Ontario, November 1995) at 15.

[21] This is a fairly typical list put forward in T. Sourdin, M. Scott & J. David, *Court-connected Mediation: National Best Practice Guidelines* (Sydney: Centre for Dispute Resolution, University of Technology Sydney, 1994) and the Centre for Court Policy and Administration, University of Wollongong, in association with the Law Council of Australia.

be used as a precedent is often the reason given for diverting constitutional and products liability cases from mediation. You should avoid automatically rejecting either precedent or mediation without a careful examination to assure yourself that your case is the right case with the right evidence to enable you to establish your point before the Supreme Court of Canada. Mediation is often used as a low-risk way to test a case's potential precedential value. Also, sometimes two concepts are confused. Taking a case to court to establish a precedent is very different from taking a case to court on a matter of principle. To understand the difference, ask yourself whether you would accept a settlement offer that is double your claim. If the answer is yes, then it is clear that you do not need a decision to govern the conduct of future cases, and mediation may be a good option for you.

Where there is a genuine, *bona fide* need for a decision, and the choice is an informed, thoughtful one, that choice should be respected. Factors which may indicate an adjudicative process include:

1. genuinely frivolous or opportunistic claims that should be tested for *bona fides*;

2. legal precedents that are unavailable and genuinely needed to guide future similar cases; and

3. the need for coercion to ensure participation in the process or adherence to outcome.

All *necessary* information must be known about the dispute in order for it to be successfully mediated. This is quite different from requiring all possible information to be known, as it would be after discoveries had been conducted in a lawsuit. If the amount of damages is not yet known, mediation is probably premature. A typical example is a medical negligence case where the patient is making progress, but has not yet recovered the use of her right thumb at the time mediation is being considered. The decision might well be made at that point to postpone going to mediation until the patient's condition has reached a plateau, and medical reports containing a long-term prognosis are available. Until that occurs, the reasonable range of damages for the injury cannot be ascertained. Contrast that with a case where the 2010 value of a building is in issue. The amount of damages is not known because the parties have not yet had the 2010 value of the building assessed by an expert. That case can be readily mediated, with the issue of how and from whom to obtain the expert valuation forming part of the solution.

If we were to identify one factor which does contra-indicate mediation, however, we would have to identify attitude or frame of mind. A stubborn, self-centred and withholding person (even if stubborn, self-centred and withholding for good reason) is not a very good prospect for mediation. Mediation involves a level of flexibility and openness to new information and to change. It requires that a person not only be able to articulate, prioritize and seek to actualize his or her own needs, but also be able to perform the difficult balancing act of considering and acknowledging those of the other parties at the same time. It is a multi-dimensional exercise and it means that the other side has to be taken into account, too. If a person is unable or unwilling to take into account what is going on across the table, it will be difficult to get anywhere; as we have stressed, mediation involves cooperative problem-solving, not unilateral actions or demands.

An analysis of "successful" and "unsuccessful" mediations has been reduced to chart form and can be found as Table 6 at the end of this chapter. It shows that unless a party is, on some level, able to recognize aspects of the controversy *beyond itself*, then the chances of a successful mediation are significantly reduced. This includes an ability and willingness to consider, entertain, examine and listen to other points of view — whether of the facts, the law, the inferences to be drawn from the facts, the motivations of another party, the meaning that can or might be attached to words used, the technical explanations for the problem and so on. The party that is unable to acknowledge these possibilities beforehand or with the assistance of the mediator is a difficult mediation candidate. That party is unlikely to be able to perform a related task which involves an ability and willingness to consider possible ways to resolve the controversy that take into account the multiple aspects of the problem, including needs, wants or concerns of another party.

This analysis does not identify as suitable the party that is so anxious for a deal or to preserve a relationship that it capitulates entirely to the other side without taking stock of its own needs. Rather, it identifies the party which, while appreciating its own needs, can extend itself to give *recognition* to another party. In our experience, it does not matter whether this recognition is given out of enlightened self-interest or whether it is a genuine extension of the self, based on strength or compassion. The presence of some form of recognition, even if it is weak, seems to predict success. Without recognition, the success of a mediation (in the sense of achieving a voluntary agreement) is in peril.

The term "recognition" has its origins in the book *The Promise of Mediation*.[22] The authors argue that fostering recognition is a moral imperative for mediators, but that doing so is incompatible with a mediation model that aspires to bring about settlement. Leaving aside the moral issue for the moment, our view is that recognition and settlement are *not* mutually exclusive but that recognition is a necessary condition for settlement.

Consequently, to assess whether a particular controversy is suitable for mediation, some preliminary and continuing sense of a party's attitude and flexibility, of its ability to give recognition to the other side, is critical. The

---

[22]   R.A. Baruch Bush & J.R. Folger, *The Promise of Mediation: Responding to Conflict Through Empowerment and Recognition* (San Francisco: Jossey-Bass Publishers, 1994).

table at the end of this chapter is compiled from a random sampling of mediations. The analysis showed a correlation between settlement and recognition. Wherever there was a failure to achieve settlement through mediation, there was also an absence of recognition by at least one party at the table. While this is not the result of a scientific study, it certainly accords with our experience in mediation.

There are no litmus tests to tell you when a case is going to be resolved through mediation. What can be said, though, is that for most kinds of cases, mediation gives you a better than even chance of settlement in a process that does not involve high cost, delay or high risk if settlement is not achieved. With those odds, and the business need to get conflicts resolved and move on, it should not be surprising that more and more Canadians are choosing mediation as their dispute resolution option.

THE PARTIES' DIRECT ROLE IN MEDIATION

From time to time, we come across mediations where an argument is made for conducting a mediation where the ultimate decision-maker will not be present. It is proposed to exclude the one who actually "owns" the dispute. Someone will suggest that a proxy, such as a lawyer who stands in for a client, a son who represents his parents or the attorney for property who takes part for the principal, is adequate. While we have mediated cases to resolution without having the real parties there, this generally does not work. At the very least, it makes such mediations more difficult. The substituted person can only approximate the thoughts and feelings of the missing participant and often confuses his or her own risk tolerances and priorities for those of the principal.

The best situation at mediation is for the actual parties to participate directly. Each party to the dispute has a significant level of involvement in a mediation — much greater than in the litigation and trial process generally. In some mediations, the parties are the only participants apart from the mediator. If they work with professional advisors, they work in partnership, each playing different but necessary roles.

The party's involvement begins with the decision to mediate. Is this the right case? Whose presence would be the most constructive, *i.e.*, who would be able to make a helpful, positive contribution to moving things along instead of obstructing, deflecting or deferring necessary talk? Who would be a negative influence? Whose approval is needed before a settlement can go through? Who can veto a deal? The party has the answers to all of these questions, which are critical to the success of the mediation.

Whether to negotiate at all is a party's decision. In court-connected programs where referral is mandatory, the parties must attend the mediation session, but once there, any party can decide not to negotiate and walk away.

This does not happen often. For perhaps the only time in the lawsuit, all of the principals are around the table, and it makes sense to use the opportunity to try to settle. There is little to lose, since it is all "off the record", and a lot to gain in terms of time, money and finality if an acceptable resolution can be achieved. Most people who find themselves enmeshed in a dispute are looking for a reasonable solution to the problem, not a Supreme Court of Canada precedent, and mediation is a process which affords them the most say in arriving at that solution.

Parties know the details of their case and will be able to answer the mediator's questions as to the facts. Also, having read Chapter 2 and understanding that their interests are the motivations, needs or concerns that lie behind their positions (the why behind the what), parties will be able to identify their underlying interests. Examples might be an interest in continuing a business relationship within a small industry, or an interest in a quick resolution before a potential sale is completed. Parties will also know what barriers stand in the way of a resolution, such as a financial squeeze that precludes a substantial payment in the next 60 days, or feelings that are so hurt by an allegation of bad faith that without an apology, the other substantive issues cannot be addressed.

Parties have the information that enables them to be very active in generating creative options for settlement of the dispute. Their knowledge of the business or situation obviously extends beyond the confines of the conflict. They know what is possible and what might create value in the settlement for another party. Add to that mix an understanding of both the party's own and the other side's interests and barriers in the negotiation, and it is easy to see that the parties are an essential ingredient in a successful mediation.

Parties will also be asked difficult questions by the mediator. Along with their more significant role in the process comes more responsibility for the outcome. Parties will be asked to consider options that do not just satisfy them, but which potentially meet the other side's needs as well. The mediator may ask a party to stop repetitive behaviour that is interfering with the productivity of the mediation. The mediator may ask all parties to stop spending so much time convincing one another that they are right and to move on to what needs must be met before the dispute can be resolved. The mediator is skilled in facilitating communications between the parties, and his or her job requires that parties be appropriately informed of behaviour that threatens to derail the process. It should not be taken as a personal affront.

Throughout the mediation, parties and their professional advisors are continually reassessing their alternatives to a negotiated solution. This happens every time new information is shared, every time another party's situation is understood in a different light, and every time the mediator plants a seed of doubt as to the relative strength of the party's case. It is an active process that will feel like work for all participants. No more sitting back while counsel does all the talking.

Finally, only the parties can make the decision to enter into a settlement agreement. It is the job of the mediator and the lawyers to make sure that the decision is an informed one, but only the principals can ensure that the outcome is one they can live with, and that it is binding — by signing on the dotted line and making the necessary moral, financial or other practical commitment. With this increased role and responsibility for outcomes, are parties shying away from mediations? On the contrary, they seem to like having more say. Perhaps that is one of the reasons that mediation is a growth area in the DR spectrum, both in the public and in the private sectors, as is more fully covered in Chapter 10.

After each mediation in the Ontario Superior Court ADR pilot project, parties were asked to rate the experience in confidential questionnaires. In the first six months of operation, with an exceptional survey return rate, 84 per cent of the participants polled reported that they were satisfied or very satisfied with the mediation process, and 98 per cent reported that they perceived the process to be fair.[23] These results closely match those of Washington's Superior Court Settlement Week,[24] in which more than 700 civil cases were mediated. Eighty-four per cent of the parties were satisfied with the experience; 95 per cent thought it was fair; and more than 90 per cent would recommend the experience to others.[25]

Mediation clearly appeals to people as a way of resolving disputes. Its discussion format and its emphasis on constructive problem-solving are more familiar than the litigation preoccupation with assigning blame. It gives the parties a real measure of control over their own disputes, throughout the process. Once that is experienced, the difficulties in persuading people to try mediation melt away.

THE LAWYER'S ROLE

It would be a mistake to think that a more substantial role for the parties in mediation leaves lawyers on the sidelines. In fact, where lawyers do take part, they play such an important role that they can make or break a mediation. Their participation can significantly increase the chances of success.

---

[23] Alternative Dispute Resolution Centre Release, Vol. 1, No. 2 (Winter 1995).

[24] This was an early ADR initiative, when large numbers of civil cases were sent to mediation; sort of a "mass-mediation" event.

[25] L.R. Singer, *Settling Disputes: Conflict Resolution in Business, Families and the Legal System* (Boulder: Westview Press, 1990) at 79.

Good lawyers are a delight to work with at mediation. They serve their clients well and make the mediation process palatable for everyone, no matter how far apart the parties seem to be. Even when the mediation does not result in a settlement, they can make the process a pleasant experience.

It is impressive to watch such lawyers during mediation. They are unfailingly courteous and poised. They show respect for everyone in the room, even in the face of rude, obnoxious or infantile behaviour from the other side. They model for their clients how to disagree without being disagreeable and how to have a constructive discussion on a difficult topic.

Such lawyers have discernible boundaries between themselves and their clients. They readily separate their own interests from those of the client and do not lose perspective by getting caught up in the client's cause, reactions or moods. At the same time, they are sensitive to the client's situation. They respect their clients' unique characteristics and do not confuse or impose their own attitudes and risk tolerances.

Good lawyers are scrupulously honest with their clients. They deliver good news and bad; they do not withhold unpleasant advice or distort it because the client will find it unpalatable. They recognize their natural self-interest on the matter of fees, particularly in contingency cases, and deal with the matter as clearly and comprehensively as they can.

Lawyers who get the most out of mediation learn to work in partnership with the mediator and to find mediators that they trust. They understand and respect the mediator's role and relay useful and reliable information to help the mediator do the job, such as what they think of the case, what they need to get a deal or what is standing in the way. They appreciate that the mediator has a different vantage point and welcome the mediator's feedback and observations even if these differ from their own.

They do not waste time arguing and trying to prove a point. They concede what should be conceded, even their errors and oversights, and hold firm when they should hold firm. Above all, they come with open minds and are prepared to be influenced by what they hear.

Unfortunately, it is easy to draw a caricature of a bad lawyer in mediation. Though rare, the bad lawyer's impact on the process and the outcome is so profound that they stand out. Bad lawyers make mediation an unpleasant experience for some or all of the people involved.

However, there are some lawyers who are rude or obnoxious. They are snide, sarcastic and dismissive to everyone, including the mediator. They talk about someone present in the third person, oblivious to the person's feelings, and may snort or roll their eyes to emphasize their disdain. They hit below the belt by disparaging the experience level or competence of the other lawyer — frequently in front of the clients. These lawyers have ego issues and create unnecessary bad feelings that seriously inhibit settlement.

Others identify completely with their clients or the cause. They are champions to the exclusion of everything else. They treat the opposing client and lawyer like their personal enemies and interpret their words and actions one way only — the worst way. They exaggerate the state of the law and resist suggestions that other interpretations or other outcomes are possible in their case. These lawyers lack perspective and deprive their clients of objective or realistic advice. Everyone has to work against their negative energy and often this is a futile task.

Others lack spine. They give the clients the answers they want to hear and deliberately or carelessly overestimate their chances of success. They withhold negative information, like the non-recoverable costs of taking something through to trial, or give incomplete or careless calculations. Unfortunately, they sometimes also let their own financial interests take precedence over the interests of the clients.

And some are woefully unprepared. They have not checked out the necessary facts, assembled the necessary paperwork, or considered the prospect of evidence. Their lawyering is a succession of spontaneous responses to the unanticipated demands of the moment.

Fortunately, bad lawyers are few and far between. The majority of lawyers make a positive contribution to settlement. Their energy and intelligence help create the momentum for everyone to move to resolution.

Lawyers have always been employed in resolving the 95 per cent or more of lawsuits that settle before trial across Canada. The growth of DR processes and their institutionalization as part of the civil justice system is a recognition of that fact. What is new is that the lawyering skills most likely to assist a party in mediation are being analyzed and taught. As part of a team where these skills are brought to bear in preparing for the mediation as well as in the session itself, the client will be afforded the very best opportunity of resolving the dispute at an early stage.

In preparation for mediation, the lawyer's most important function is to help focus the client on the goal of the session. That goal is not the litigation ideal of achieving the best possible result at trial. The aim is to resolve the case in a way that is acceptable to an informed party and to the other side. Once the lawyer and party agree on what they hope to achieve through the mediation, its preparation falls into the realm of common sense, dealt with in more detail in the next section.

The skills and abilities which a lawyer brings to a mediation include:

1.   gathering all the facts relevant to the dispute and probing for holes and inconsistencies;

2.   analyzing the problem within the framework of the law, evaluating the facts and predicting what a court is likely to do and giving accurate in-

formation about how the court system works and what its various stages cost;

3. knowing and realistically exploring with the client the best and worst alternatives to settlement, including an assessment of the non-recoverable business, personal and legal costs of litigation through appeal;

4. unearthing his or her client's barriers to settlement, which might include a limitation on authority to settle, a need for a judgment before settlement funds can come out of the right pot, or an inability because of a written policy to make any form of apology or expression of regret;

5. assessing who is the right party representative to participate in the mediation, given the goal of the session and the need for appropriate authority to settle;

6. advising how and with what aids the client's presentation can have the most impact on the other party;

7. developing with the party a flexible negotiation strategy that takes into account that new information will be learned, and previously known information will come to be viewed in a different light;

8. identifying with the party the realistic boundaries of the negotiation field;

9. communicating to the party the power of apology and acknowledgment;

10. setting a courteous, conciliatory tone in the mediation to help foster the goodwill necessary for the parties to settle their differences;

11. listening carefully and observing body language during the mediation to be able to really understand all that is being communicated by the other party;

12. appreciating the far greater impact when the story is told directly and specifically by the party rather than the lawyer, and knowing when not to talk or argue;

13. continually re-evaluating offers and responses with the party — testing the mediation goal against the party's interests and options; and

14. if a settlement is achieved, ensuring that the memorandum of settlement includes all of the terms essential for durable resolution between the parties.

Mediation lives up to its optimum potential when parties and their professional advisors function as partners, each bringing different strengths to the table. What will guarantee its failure is the gladiator mode of felling all comers. Treating all participants with courtesy and respect is a more effective strategy when the goal is resolution. The next section contains a sample problem to illustrate the partnership approach to preparing and conducting the mediation in the way most likely to achieve successful results.

STRATEGIC PREPARATION

Preparation for the mediation is a key ingredient in its success. However, because the idea of the process is to get people to talk to one another directly or through the mediator, the preparation is not just about paper or assembling legal research. Conventional mediation is principally an oral process, akin to storytelling, so a different approach is called for — one that involves more listening than reading or summarizing.

Because there is such a significant component of party involvement, there is no substitute for "talking it through" in advance. The aim is a tailor-made solution for the party's circumstances, and no tailor worth his or her reputation would deliver a custom suit without one or two try-ons. With a better than even chance that you can settle your case in mediation, why not give it your best effort?

If counsel are involved, the lawyer attending the mediation should be the one doing the preparation with the party. It does not involve mounds of paper, but it does mean more than a cursory meeting. In the nature of the mediation process, lack of preparation will be immediately apparent to everyone in the room. In an estate dispute, for example, the estate trustee will be expected to know the nature, value and location of the assets. It slows everyone down and leads to negative inferences to hear, "I didn't bring that with me today" or "Gee, I'm not sure".

Ideally, preparation includes an uninterrupted discussion at the party's office or home. That helps everyone focus on the business or personal issues involved in the dispute, and it is probably much more comfortable for the client. That is important because the most effective preparation requires the party to talk freely.

The focus of the meeting is not the conflict that gave rise to the dispute, but how to resolve it in a way acceptable to all parties. Write that down and keep coming back to it. It too easily eludes the grasp.

Now, follow the preparation of a hypothetical dispute using the interest-based approach more fully discussed in Chapter 2, and the mediation worksheet that follows the case study discussion below.

Case Study Three

In this two-party employment dispute, Anita Patel, aged 63, is suing her employer of 24 years, XCO, for wrongful dismissal. XCO says Anita Patel was dismissed for cause because she failed to show up at a weekend management meeting as required. Anita Patel's employment file has nothing in it except notices of change under the benefit plan.

XCO has recently been experiencing financial difficulties. Anita Patel's counsel, Christina Macleod, elicits these facts and the circumstances of the weekend meeting. Ms. Macleod advises Anita Patel based on the most recent law as to the range of possible outcomes after a trial, including the effect on damages of finding a job and collecting employment insurance. They discuss the witnesses needed to prove Anita Patel's case at trial, and project the number of trial days it will take for both Anita Patel's and XCO's evidence, as well as the number of days of discovery and possible motions.

A realistic estimate of Anita Patel's time needed for preparation, discovery and trial is given. Christina Macleod gives her estimate of the budget needed through to the end of the trial, and the time it takes to get to trial and for the decision to be handed down in this jurisdiction.

Christina Macleod discovers that Anita Patel's greatest need is for her pension to begin immediately, and reviews her pension documents for potential early retirement provisions. Anita Patel is very upset at the manner in which she was unexpectedly fired after so many years of loyal service, and with no chance to tell her side of the story or to say goodbye to her friends. She felt insulted by being publicly escorted from her office when she left. That makes her see red and she cannot get the idea of punitive damages out of her mind. Anita Patel is very worried about a trial being so many years away, since she has a chance to move in with her sister in Florida, but not until the case is resolved. She is also worried that XCO might not survive that long.

On the following page is an example of how Christina Macleod and Anita Patel can use the worksheet in preparing for the mediation which is scheduled to take place shortly. See Appendix 3 for the blank template of this worksheet.

MEDIATION WORKSHEET

PARTY'S NAME: **Anita Patel**
COUNSEL: **Christina Macleod**

CONCERNING: **Wrongful Dismissal**

I. PARTIES		
WHO ARE THE PARTIES AND WHO SHOULD BE PRESENT AT THE MEDIATION?		
YOUR SIDE		
(a) Anita Patel	individual	full authority
(b) name	position/status	authority
(c) name	position/status	authority
OTHER SIDE		
(a) Mr. Dupont	VP Operations	authority
(b) Ms. Topping	HR Manager	authority
(c) Mr. Shaw	President	full authority, on advice from Operations and HR
OTHER PARTIES		
(a) name	position/status	authority
(b) name	position/status	authority
(c) name	position/status	authority
WILL ALL NECESSARY PARTIES BE PRESENT? CAN THEY BE INDUCED/PERSUADED TO ATTEND? HOW? IF NOT, CAN THE MEDIATION PROCEED?		
Anita Patel's attendance is obvious, but there may be someone else without whose advice she will not settle. It may be her sister or her accountant, but the question should be asked and that person should attend, or, at the very least, be readily accessible by phone. If pension or tax planning advice may be necessary, that should be sought in advance or lined up and available by phone during the mediation.		

Mr. Dupont fired Anita Patel. Ms. Topping generally looks after these matters for XCO but it is Mr. Shaw whom Anita Patel worked with for 24 years and reported to for the last five years as Manager, Special Projects. She really wants to tell him her side of the story. What would induce him to come?

II. SUITABILITY & COMMITMENT

WHAT IS THE LEVEL OF COMMITMENT TO SETTLEMENT?

YOUR SIDE: It is high. Anita Patel can't find a job and needs money to live. Cheaper living in Florida is not available until case over.

OTHER SIDE: It is probably low because of its financial difficulties.

IS THIS CASE SUITABLE FOR MEDIATION?

✓ yes because:

Establishing cause will be problematic for XCO, it will incur legal fees to defend the case, Anita Patel was well-liked by the staff and her firing has caused a big morale problem at a difficult time, and XCO is likely to be courting new investment and doesn't need the distraction or the publicity of a lawsuit.

__ no because: [*provide explanation*]

__ don't know because: [*provide explanation*]

III. PURPOSE

PURPOSE OF THE MEDIATION SESSION AND EXPECTED WORK PRODUCT

__ signed settlement agreement

__ signed agreement in principle

✓ resolution of some issues and target dates for next steps

Anita Patel wants this over and done with but doesn't think the company can commit to a settlement on the spot. See note below.

___ other

WORK PRODUCT NEEDS FINAL APPROVAL OR RATIFICATION?

✓ yes

Because of its financial difficulties XCO may need ratification of any settlement agreement by its board of directors and/or its investor. Anita Patel as a principal will not.

___ no

IV. MEDIATOR & TERMS OF MEDIATION

ISSUES

1.   WHO IS THE MEDIATOR AND HOW SELECTED?

Possibly from panel of experienced mediators who do employment work or (only if we cannot agree) randomly assigned by a court-connected program.

2.   IS THERE ANYTHING YOU WOULD LIKE TO KNOW ABOUT THE MEDIATOR:

✓ background?   Substantive knowledge of employment field

✓ qualifications? Training & experience in mediation

✓ style/mediation model? *e.g.*, evaluative or not

___ other?

3. WHAT ARE THE COSTS ASSOCIATED WITH THE MEDIATION?

✓ administration fee or court filing fee $250

✓ mediator preparation fees $350 × hours

✓ mediator mediation fees $3,000/day

__ mediator expenses
   (mileage, flights, hotel, *etc.*)   N/A in this case

✓ room rental $400

✓ refreshments $150

✓ counsel fees $400 × hours

__ expert fees   N/A in this case

__ other expenses   N/A in this case

4. IS THERE A WRITTEN MEDIATION AGREEMENT FOR TERMS OF REFERENCE?

__ yes

If yes, is it adequate?

__ no

If no, who will draft?

[*See Mediation Agreement, pp. 132-136.*]

5. WHERE WILL THE MEDIATION TAKE PLACE?
   Office of Mediation Inc.

6. WHO IS RESPONSIBLE FOR ARRANGEMENTS?
   The mediator

V. MEDIATION SUMMARY/PRE-MEDIATION INFORMATION
WHAT INFORMATION IS BEING EXCHANGED IN ADVANCE?
ARE WRITTEN SUMMARIES BEING PREPARED FOR THE MEDIATOR?
BY WHOM AND WHEN?
The employment file and pension information will be exchanged for Anita Patel's job search record. Each party will prepare a short summary of the essential facts and the issues in dispute to be in the mediator's hands a week before the session.

VI. OUTSTANDING ISSUES
1. WHAT ISSUES ARE OUTSTANDING BETWEEN YOU AND THE OTHER PARTY?
• Did Anita Patel's conduct amount to cause for termination?
• If not, what amounts to reasonable notice of termination?
2. WILL THESE ISSUES HAVE ANY RELEVANCE/IMPACT ON THE MEDIATION?
They provide the positional starting point for the negotiation.
3. HOW CAN YOU MOVE FORWARD TO SETTLEMENT WITHOUT CONCLUSIVELY RESOLVING THESE ISSUES?
By finding a solution that satisfies enough of the underlying motivations or needs ("interests") to be acceptable to both parties.

VII. INTERESTS *Identify and Prioritize*			
YOU		**THEM**	
Money to live on	Priority # 1	Low cost solution	Priority # 1
Speedy resolution	# 2	Speedy resolution	# 2
Ameliorate the insult	# 3	Stop plunge in morale	# 3

[See Chapter 2 for a full discussion of interests and how they may be identified.]

VIII. OPTIONS

ISSUES

1. WHAT MIGHT SATISFY SOME OF THE IDENTIFIED INTERESTS?

    Income might be provided by an early retirement with pension, possibly with a top-up amount. The feeling of insult might be addressed by some form of recognition of long service.

2. HOW DO THESE OPTIONS SATISFY YOUR INTERESTS AND THEIRS?

    Early retirement could be a low cost alternative for XCO if it can be brought within the current pension plan. A form of recognition could satisfy the morale problem and the insult. Both want speedy resolution.

IX. ALTERNATIVES

EXPECTATIONS

1. IF SETTLEMENT IS NOT ACHIEVED IN THE MEDIATION, WHAT ARE YOUR ALTERNATIVES? HOW PALATABLE ARE THESE?

✓ BEST ALTERNATIVE:

    Payment for the maximum notice of termination period under the law minus any unemployment benefits received in the time waiting for trial, minus anything earned by Ms. Patel in the period, minus the amount of legal fees and disbursements not payable by the losing party.

✓ WORST ALTERNATIVE:

    XCO declares bankruptcy before trial and Anita Patel collects nothing, while still being responsible for legal fees and disbursements.

2. WHAT ARE THE COSTS OF THE ALTERNATIVES?

✓ Legal fees and disbursements to end of trial:

Portion that is non-recoverable, even if successful:

✓ TIME:

Trial may be more than two years away.

✓ RELATIONSHIP:

Internal:

Failure to move to Florida right away may harm relationship with her sister.

External:

Friendships at XCO affected.

✓ Opportunity cost:

Delays plans for a new business.

✓ Party's time and resources:

Depletes both.

✓ Emotional costs:

Anita Patel is dreading a trial.

✓ Publicity:

Idea is upsetting to Anita Patel.

___ Other:

X. THE MEDIATION PROCESS

ISSUES

1. CAN YOU SUMMARIZE YOUR VIEW OF THIS CONTROVERSY SUCCINCTLY?

   Constructively, without using emotional red flag words, and signaling cooperation in finding a solution that works for all the parties.

2. WHAT TOPICS DO YOU THINK NEED TO BE DISCUSSED IN MORE DETAIL?

   Possibly cause, pension entitlements.

3. **WHO WILL DO THE TALKING FOR YOUR SIDE?**

Both counsel and parties generally participate. Christina Macleod will probably open with a summary of the issues, and Anita Patel might talk about how the summary dismissal made her feel after so many years of her life were devoted to XCO. She will likely answer many of the mediator's questions. Both will work with the mediator in the caucus to generate settlement options.

4. **WHAT ROLE WILL THE PARTY PLAY?**

(In mediation, parties act as partners with their professional advisors, employing the strengths of each. A very effective opening can be made by an articulate party. More often the lawyers start off, but parties will quickly jump in when asked questions or when they have something to add.)

5. (a) **WHAT CAN THE MEDIATOR/OTHER PARTY EXPECT OF YOU?**

(That you will be prepared, behave with courtesy and will allow everyone to have a say without interruption.)

(b) **WHAT ARE YOUR EXPECTATIONS OF THE MEDIATOR?**

(The mediator will be impartial, will not tell any party how the case should be settled, will listen to and understand each party's perspective, and will work diligently with the parties to help them analyze their risks and options for potential resolution.)

(c) **WHAT ARE YOUR EXPECTATIONS OF THE OTHER SIDE?** *AS IN 5(a).*

6. **WHAT USE DO YOU PLAN TO MAKE OF THE MEDIATOR?**

(The mediator can be most helpful by taking a fresh look at the problem and finding "openings" previously overlooked or ignored, and by testing complainant's view on punitive damages.)

7. **IS THERE ANYTHING YOU ARE CONCERNED ABOUT DISCLOSING IN THE MEDIATION? IF SO, WHAT ARE THE RISKS AND REWARDS OF DISCLOSURE?**

MEDIATION AGREEMENT

- SAMPLE 1 -

NAMES OF PARTIES AND COUNSEL:

AGREED MEDIATOR: Christine Hart

Accord/hart & associates inc.

TIME AND PLACE OF MEDIATION:

PRE-SESSION CONFERENCE CALL: [to discuss who will attend, dates for disclosure and summaries, and other procedural matters]

PRE-MEDIATION SUMMARIES: Short statements of fact and issues in contention to be exchanged and sent to mediator by _____.

PARTICIPATION/AUTHORITY TO SETTLE: Appropriate representatives of each party will attend with authority to settle the dispute in the mediation session.

CONFIDENTIALITY: All aspects of the mediation including prior disclosure shall be treated as confidential settlement discussions, and the mediator shall not, in any event, be asked to testify in court. He or she will retain no record of the mediation.

DISCLOSURE: Key documents to be exchanged prior to the session.

ROLE OF MEDIATOR: The mediator will at all times act impartially toward all participants and will maintain confidentiality with respect to the dispute. The mediator will not provide legal advice or therapy, will not coerce a settlement and will not impose his or her judgment on any party.

TERMINATION: Any party may withdraw from the mediation at any time and for any reason. The parties may agree to terminate the session, either because a settlement has been reached, or otherwise. The mediator may terminate the mediation if he or she believes that the process has become unproductive or that settlement is unlikely.

COSTS AND FEES: [mediator and room costs, whom to pay and when]

We agree to the above terms and indicate our intention to make a serious attempt in the mediation to resolve this dispute:

DATE: _____

MEDIATOR: _____

MEDIATION AGREEMENT

- SAMPLE 2 -

GENEVIEVE A. CHORNENKI

LL.B., LL.M. (ADR), C.Med., F.C.I.Arb.

Conflict Management Services since 1989

55 St. Clair Avenue West, Suite 255
Toronto, Canada, M4V 2Y7
Telephone: 416-975-9898
Facsimile: 416-975-9352
E-mail: gac@chornenki.com

AGREEMENT TO MEDIATE

1. PARTIES:

agree to mediate certain differences with Genevieve A. Chornenki as mediator.

2. DATE:

3. TIME:

4. PLACE:

5. TERMS OF MEDIATION:

The parties agree to abide by the Terms of Mediation, attached.

6. ISSUES:

The issues to be mediated as understood at this time are summarized as follows:

7. COSTS OF THE MEDIATION:

The costs are as set out in Schedule "A". Unless there is an exception set out below, the parties agree to share the fees and expenses related to the mediation equally, but shall be jointly and severally responsible to Genevieve A. Chornenki for any unpaid or outstanding fees and expenses. The parties shall each bear their own legal expenses, if any.

Exceptions:

8. SIGNING INDIVIDUALLY:

Each party may sign a separate copy of this agreement, which, when so signed and delivered to the mediator, shall be an original copy even though not signed by the other parties. All such separately signed copies shall together constitute evidence of all parties' consent to be bound by this agreement.

9. CONSENT TO THIS AGREEMENT:

Each of us has read this agreement and willingly agree to proceed with the mediation on the terms contained in it.

DATE:

per:

_____

per:

_____

_____

_____
Genevieve A. Chornenki, Mediator

Schedule "A"

COST SCHEDULE

Mediator Fee:	$ [rate] per 7 ½ day or part thereof, plus GST	
Estimated Fees:	0 days @ $ [rate] for mediation	$ 000.00
	Plus GST	00.00
	0 days @ $ [rate] for preparation	000 00
	Plus GST	00.00
	TOTAL ESTIMATED FEES:	$0,000.00

not to be exceeded without the
prior consent of the parties.

Expenses:	Boardroom & Breakout Room	00.00
	Meals (lunch)	00.00
	Photocopies - $0.25 per page	
	Facsimiles - $0.25 per page	
	Other - at cost	
	Mileage - $0.30 km.	
	Plus GST	00.00
	ESTIMATED EXPENSES:	$ 000.00

TOTAL ESTIMATED FEES & EXPENSES: $0,000.00

Cancellations bear the following charges:

- ✓ One (1) business day before scheduled date — *Full estimated fee and any out-of pocket expenses incurred by the mediator, plus GST*

- ✓ Two (2) to five (5) business days before scheduled date — *One-half of the estimated fee and any out-of pocket expenses incurred by the mediator, plus GST*

- ✓ Over five (5) business days before scheduled date — *$500.00 and any out-of pocket expenses incurred by the mediator, plus GST.*

TERMS OF MEDIATION

1. Mediation is a voluntary and informal settlement process by which the parties try to reach a solution that is responsive to their joint needs. Their participation in the process is not intended to alter their existing rights and responsibilities unless they expressly agree to do so.

2. The mediator is a facilitator only, is not providing legal advice, legal representation or any other form of professional advice or representation, and is not representing any party. The mediator's role is to assist the parties to negotiate a voluntary settlement of the issues if this is possible.

3. The parties will send to the mediation representatives with full, unqualified authority to settle and understand that the mediation may result in a settlement agreement that contains binding legal obligations enforceable in a court of law.

4. The parties will discuss the matter with the mediator individually or together, in person or by telephone, with a view to achieving settlement.

5. Throughout the mediation the parties agree to disclose material facts, information and documents to each other and to the mediator, and will conduct themselves in good faith.

6. Statements made by any person, documents produced and any other forms of communication in the mediation are off-the-record and shall not be subject to disclosure through discovery or any other process or admissible into evidence in any context for any purpose, including impeaching credibility.

7. The parties will deliver to the mediator and exchange with each other a concise statement of the issues and the problem as they see it in a reasonable period of time prior to the first mediation session, which in this case is on or before [*insert date*].

8. No party will initiate or take any fresh steps in any legal, administrative, or arbitration proceedings related to the issues while the mediation is in progress.

9. Either during or after the mediation, no party will call the mediator as a witness for any purpose whatsoever. No party will seek access to any documents prepared for or delivered to the mediator in connection with the mediation, including any records or notes of the mediator.

10. Other than what is stated above, the mediation is a confidential process and the parties agree to keep all communications and information forming part of this mediation in confidence. The only exception to this is disclosure for the purposes of enforcing

any settlement agreement reached. The mediator will not voluntarily disclose to anyone who is not a party to the mediation anything said or done or any materials submitted to the mediator, except:

a.   to any person designated or retained by any party as a professional advisor or agent;

b.   for research or educational purposes, on an anonymous basis;

c.   where ordered to do so by a judicial authority or where required to do so by law;

d.   where the information suggests an actual or potential threat to human life or safety.

11.   The parties are responsible for obtaining their own independent professional advice, including legal advice or representation, if desired; the mediator is not providing same. The mediator has no duty to assert or protect the rights of any party, to raise any issue not raised by the parties themselves or to determine who should participate in the mediation. The mediator has no duty to ensure the enforceability or validity of any agreement reached. The mediator will not be liable in any way, save for his/her wilful default.

Table 6: Criteria for Successful Mediation Checklist*

Type	No. of Parties	Deal	No Deal	Reason (Contributing Factors)	How Mediator Helped	Recognition	Empowerment	Individuals	Institution(s)
Shareholder Dispute	4	X		• Parties genuinely wanted to disassociate • Good faith on all sides • Alternative (litigation) too costly with too limiting an outcome	• Depersonalized dispute • Expanded/crystallized outcome	X	X	X	
Professional Relationship	3	X		• Parties wanted closure • Participation and outcome for alternative (adjudication) too limiting	• Surfaced parties' needs, wants, concerns • Worked with parties to meet them • Facilitated understanding	X	X	X	X
Contract Dispute	3	X		• Amount in dispute too small relative to cost of alternative (litigation)	• Provided a focus for problem solving	X	X	X	X
Contract/Tort/Relationship	5	X		• Parties flexible • Important relational concerns satisfied • Parties wanted closure • Alternative (litigation) too costly	• Convened parties; provided event/focus • Surfaced parties' needs, wants, concerns; worked with parties to meet them • Divided complex problem into manageable parts • Modelled/encouraged stamina	X	X	X	X

* In the preceding table, "recognition" and "empowerment" have the meanings ascribed to them by Robert A. Baruch Bush & Joseph P. Folger, *The Promise of Mediation* (San Francisco: Jossey-Bass Inc. 1994). Briefly, "recognition" is the ability of one party to be open and responsible to the situation and needs of the *other* party, whereas, "empowerment" relates to a party's own capacity to participate in mediation, namely the clarity, confidence, organization and decisiveness that a party achieves about its *own* situation and needs.

Table 6: Criteria for Successful Mediation Checklist — cont'd

Type	No. of Parties	Deal	No Deal	Reason (Contributing Factors)	How Mediator Helped	Recognition	Empowerment	Individuals	Institution(s)
Construction	10	X		• Alternative (litigation) too costly and time consuming	• Convened parties; provided event/focus • Identified impasse and devised solution • Explored alternatives	X	X	X	X
Tort	2		X	• Unrealistic expectations or misunderstanding of mediation process • Inflexible • Preference for alternative (litigation) despite cost	• Surfaced needs, wants, concerns of parties • Explored alternatives and parties' preferences for them		X	X	X
Personal	3		X	• Ultimate decision maker not present • Party unable/unwilling to see other aspects of problem	• Surfaced needs, wants, concerns of parties • Explored alternatives and parties' preferences for them		X	X	X
Contract/Tort/ Relationship	5		X	• Party unable/unwilling to see other aspect of problem — using prior mediation as standard or precedent	• Surfaced needs, wants, concerns of parties • Explored alternatives and parties' preferences for them		X	X	X
Professional Relationship	3		X	• Party preferred alternative (adjudication) despite risks	• Surfaced needs, wants, concerns of parties • Explored alternatives and parties' preferences for them • Ensured adequate information flow	X	X	X	X

Table 6: Criteria for Successful Mediation Checklist — cont'd

Type	No. of Parties	Deal	No Deal	Reason (Contributing Factors)	How Mediator Helped	Recognition	Empowerment	Individuals	Institution(s)
Professional Relationship	4		X	• Party unable/unwilling to see other aspects of problem (other party's needs) • Vindication (through alternative process) preferred	• Surfaced needs, wants, concerns of parties • Explored alternatives and parties' preferences for them	X	X	X	X
Contract/Tort/ Relationship	4	X		• Alternative (litigation) too costly and uncertain • Parties want closure	• Depersonalized dispute; absorbed tension • Modelled/encouraged stamina • Clarified available deal and its advantage over alternative	X		X	X
Contract/ Construction	2	X		• Parties wanted closure • Alternative (litigation) too costly and uncertain	• Depersonalized dispute • Surfaced needs, wants, concerns of parties • Explored alternatives and parties' preferences for them • Modelled/encouraged stamina • Identified major impasse and devised solution	X	X	X	

4

NEUTRAL EVALUATION

INTRODUCTION

Neutral evaluation is a DR technique that can stand on its own or be integrated with other dispute resolution processes, such as mediation, as an aid to achieving settlement. *Early neutral evaluation, expert evaluation, quick ruling, pre-trial, settlement conference* and *rent-a-judge* are some of the names given to processes involving neutral evaluation. They may be court-connected or privately available, and the timing of their use in the life of a dispute may differ, but they share several key characteristics.

As the name suggests, a neutral evaluation is undertaken by an impartial person who is either an expert in a field relevant to the dispute or an expert in the law. Judges are considered to be general experts in the law, but some disputes may require specific legal expertise (*e.g.*, intellectual property or admiralty law). An issue or an entire case is put to the evaluator by the parties on a confidential basis. The evaluator typically explores with the parties the relative strengths and weaknesses of their positions, and then offers a reasoned, often written, opinion of each party's likelihood of success on the merits. It may also include an assessment of the probable range of damages. The opinion is confidential and non-binding unless the parties agree otherwise.[1]

Neutral evaluation is used in many different contexts where parties need some expert advice to help them resolve an issue or a dispute. It is a process that is incorporated in contractual relationships. Architectural evaluation and approval is a routine provision required to be implemented in construction contracts before the project is considered complete and funds are released. More recently, parties in relationships that extend over a period of time, such as major building projects, franchises or dealerships, include neutral evaluation in the dispute resolution systems that they agree to be bound by over the course of their contract. Other examples of the range of issues and evaluators making private neutral evaluations are:

- a medical ethics expert giving an opinion whether a nurse acted ethically in providing a patient's family with certain information;

---

[1] For a useful summary, see Department of Justice Canada, *Dispute Resolution Reference Guide: Neutral Evaluation,* online: <http://www.justice.gc.ca/eng/pi/dprs-sprd/ref/res/drrg-mrrc/eval.html>.

- an engineer giving an opinion whether the roof of a condominium's parking garage was leaking because of faulty workmanship or design;

- a retired judge giving an opinion as to a limitation period and whether it stands in the way of bringing an action to court;

- an accountant giving an opinion whether a cost allowance treatment is consistent with generally accepted accounting principles;

- a trademark lawyer giving an opinion whether a corporate logo is so similar to another as to create an infringement; and

- an independent claims consultant giving an opinion on the extent and validity of a construction claim by a trade contractor.

CONFLICTING AIMS IN COURT-CONNECTED NEUTRAL EVALUATION

The courts have introduced neutral evaluation into the litigation cycle for various, sometimes conflicting, reasons. It is helpful to understand those goals in considering whether it would be a useful technique in any particular case.

One of the first early neutral evaluation ("ENE") pilot projects, in the United States District Court for the Northern District of California, did not have immediate settlement as its principal objective. The primary purposes of this program were to promote early, efficient and meaningful communication about disputes, and to move parties and counsel to confront early, and to realistically assess, their situations.[2]

Only as that pilot progressed were the goals expanded to include the fostering of early settlements. A study of the project found that ENE did not live up to expectations that it would streamline the litigation by producing agreed statements of fact and discovery plans, and identifying key motions for early resolution. The participants believed overwhelmingly, however, that the process significantly increased their understanding of and ability to assess their own and their opponent's case and to identify key issues actually in dispute.[3]

Expectations for the pilot were exceeded in terms of case dispositions. The Levine study[4] found that the ENE sessions led to settlement in

---

[2]   W. Brazil, M. Kahn, J. Newman & J. Gold, "Early Neutral Evaluation: An Experimental Effort to Expedite Dispute Resolution" (1987) 69 Judicature 279 at 284.

[3]   J. Rosenberg & J. Folberg, "Alternative Dispute Resolution: An Empirical Analysis" (1994) 46 Stan. L. Rev. 1487 at 1489.

[4]   D. Levine, "Northern District of California Adopts Early Neutral Evaluation to Expedite Dispute Resolution" (1987) 72 Judicature 235.

over one-third of the cases. Levine has pointed out that this statistic is itself an important reason that the process was not more productive of tangible outcomes such as agreed statements of fact and discovery plans. Such litigation product is useful only if the litigation is continuing. A settled case is a closed case.

Levine postulates from the results of the project that there are two different kinds of ENE sessions — one focusing on settlement, and the other on case management.[5] Because this could just as aptly apply to other applications of the neutral evaluation process, it is critical for the participants to know beforehand the focus of the session they are engaging in. The preparation and outcomes are very different. When either focus is possible, as it was in the California project, then it is up to the parties to decide which addresses their needs, and to communicate that to the evaluator and to each other before the session.

The tension between the goal of streamlining the case going forward and the goal of settling the case can be seen in a number of court-connected processes in Canada. In Ontario, the pre-trial was introduced in the mid-1970s as a way of achieving both goals. A judge gave what amounted to a neutral evaluation of the most likely outcome at trial of each case, as the last step before sending it on to trial. It was designed to give the parties a frank and objective assessment of their case and to encourage them to resolve it. In the early days, the parties were present, and the pre-trial very often resulted in a settlement. In recent years, however, counsel usually attend without the parties, and, more often than not, it is a session to facilitate the trial by scheduling the exchange of appropriate notices and documentation. Consequently, people treat pre-trials in a perfunctory way, recognizing that they are not very effective as a settlement process.

The settlement and case management goals for a pre-trial are incompatible, one being about problem-solving and the other about running an adversarial process. That both need to be addressed was explicitly recognized by the Ontario Civil Justice Review Task Force in recommending that there be two separate processes — a trial management conference and a settlement conference, which takes the form of a neutral evaluation by a judge.[6] This recommendation was adopted by the Ontario

---

5   D. Levine, "Early Neutral Evaluation: The Second Phase" (1989) 1 J. Disp. Resol. 1 at 15, 41.
6   R.A. Blair & S. Lang, *Civil Justice Review: First Report* (Toronto: Publications Ontario, 1995) at 230. Confirmed in Ontario, *Civil Justice Review: Supplemental and Final Report* (Toronto: Publications Ontario, 1996) at 42. Please see online: Ontario Ministry of the Attorney General <http://www.attorneygeneral.jus.gov.on.ca/english/about/pubs/cjr/>.

Superior Court of Justice and is now enshrined in the Rules of Practice,[7] although that division is less clear with the recent amendments to the Rule.

The Ontario Court's ADR pilot project had already separated the case management function from its early neutral evaluation process. The ENE followed a mediation, and was convened only if the participants and the mediator agreed that an evaluation by a judge of one or two specific issues would very likely lead to settlement of the case.[8] Since the Ontario Mandatory Mediation Program was implemented, ENE has not been available to cases in the early stages.

WHEN TO USE NEUTRAL EVALUATION EFFECTIVELY

A neutral evaluation is primarily used as an aid in settling a dispute. It is an *informative* technique as more fully described in Chapter 1, which may or may not influence the outcome of the negotiations between the parties. Depending on the evaluator's opinion, one or other of the parties may alter the position that they first brought to the table. Standing alone, however, neutral evaluation does not resolve the issue or dispute in question. It merely informs the parties' efforts to find resolution.

A neutral evaluation may take place early (Prince Edward Island, Saskatchewan) or late in a court process (pre-trials/settlement conferences in most provinces), or it may be convened completely outside the court system (rent-a-judge, expert evaluation). In some instances, such as court-sponsored settlement conferences, participation is mandatory. Private neutral evaluations are voluntary or contractual. When there is a choice of DR processes, the question to be answered is: In what circumstances is neutral evaluation the right one?

Little has been written on choosing cases for neutral evaluation. The Northern California District Court project on early neutral evaluation found that the participants were positive about the benefits of ENE regardless of the category of the case. The Ontario Court's ADR pilot project included ENE as one of its dispute resolution techniques, but its results were not evaluated. Indications from the judges who acted as

---

7   See Rule 50 of the Rules of Civil Procedure, R.R.O. 1990, Reg. 194, as am. by O. Reg. 438/08, in force January 1, 2010. See online: ServiceOntario e-laws <http://www.e-laws.gov.on.ca/html/statutes/english/elaws_statutes_90c43_e.htm>.

8   See *Practice Direction Concerning the Alternative Dispute Resolution Project in the Ontario Court (General Division)* [now the Superior Court of Justice] (1995), 24 O.R. (3d) 161 at 168-69, paras. 4.9, 4.10 (Ont. Gen. Div.).

neutral evaluators were that case type did not help in predicting whether neutral evaluation would aid in generating a settlement.

Some of the important questions to ask in making the choice are as follows:

- Are there really only one or two issues in dispute?
- Can the disputed factual or legal issues be clearly and concisely presented?
- Are the disputed factual issues dependent on the credibility of witnesses or on differing opinions based on the same facts?
- Do any of the parties have a very unrealistic view of their best possible outcome of the litigation?
- Can the issues in dispute be separated from the people?
- Will any of the parties be so surprised/wounded by the evaluation that it is as likely to lead to a greater polarization as to a settlement?
- Is the issue of law relatively settled or in flux?
- Are there only a few parties?
- Will the opinion of the evaluator help you to formulate an offer after the session that, if not bettered after a trial, will yield a higher level of costs for your case?

Experience has shown that in cases with one or two clearly stated issues, neutral evaluation can be a valuable aid to settlement. Legal issues where the law is not in great flux, and factual issues not dependent on findings of credibility, are suitable candidates. More parties present more difficulties, though this is not determinative. Greatly differing expectations of the outcome of the litigation may be either resolved or reinforced by neutral evaluation. These difficulties will be magnified if the people involved in the dispute have an emotional investment in the outcome. On the other hand, neutral evaluation can assist in depersonalizing an issue. Its characteristic reliance on presentation by lawyers and through documents is useful in creating distance between the parties. Neutral evaluation can also help in tempering one or more parties' expectations of the outcome at trial, if they are persistently unrealistic.

Some examples where neutral evaluation has been an effective aid to settlement are:

- a neutral expert evaluates who pays for storm damage to telephone poles after hearing differing opinions from engineers as to the appropriate type of pole support;
- a senior employment lawyer evaluates whether an employer had sufficient cause to terminate an employee's job without notice;

- a judge evaluates whether a cause of action exists against a municipality for failing to include a contractor in a call for tenders under a by-law;

- a retired judge (rent-a-judge) evaluates the appropriate range of damages in a personal injury case after reviewing the full medical reports; and

- a judge gives a quick ruling after reviewing a franchise agreement as to who pays accounting fees arising from a joint project of franchisor and franchisee.

Keep in mind that such an evaluation will not end the dispute unless the impasse between the parties truly relates to an absence of *information*. Few impasses are quite that simple. The overriding consideration in choosing a neutral evaluation is whether the opinion of the evaluator will significantly help you in achieving your goal of bringing resolution to all or part of the case. However, the evaluation may be only one piece of your DR strategy. If you believe that the information received from the evaluator will come as a surprise to at least one of the parties, you may decide to follow up the evaluation with a mediation. The mediator, who may or may not be the evaluator, will assist the parties to get past the polarization that is the characteristic response when an evaluation is not in line with expectations, and to refocus them on the goal of resolution. The experience of the Ontario Court's ADR pilot project was that the combination of the two DR processes is effective in those circumstances.

THE COST

The cost to the parties of engaging in a neutral evaluation has three components: the internal business cost of preparation and attendance; the cost of lawyer preparation and attendance; and the cost of the evaluator. All of these costs are based on time and will vary by the amount of time required, as well as by region. They would be roughly analogous to the costs of an interlocutory motion in the courts.

The time and cost of the neutral evaluation session itself will generally be known at the time of booking. Court-connected processes of neutral evaluation, pre-trial and settlement conferences seldom take more than an hour. In Canada, the cost of the judge or evaluator is covered by the filing fees paid by both parties. In the U.S., where several of the court-connected evaluations take two hours or more, and are provided by private attorneys, the costs are divided among the parties, regardless of outcome. Private processes are generally booked in half-day increments, and even the most complex of neutral evaluations are completed in less than two days. The cost is split equally by the parties, regardless of outcome.

TIMING CONSIDERATIONS

Neutral evaluations can be initiated at any time in the life of a dispute. Those built into a contract will be governed by the provisions of the agreement between the parties. In litigation, they are generally convened before the institution of the action, as soon as the lawsuit is defended, immediately after discoveries or just before trial.

In the mandatory court-connected evaluations, there is no choice as to timing, but the courts have chosen the intervention to coincide with points in a lawsuit where settlement is usually discussed — when the action is defended (Ontario Superior Court of Justice in Toronto and Ottawa), and just before trial (pre-trial/settlement conferences in Nova Scotia, New Brunswick, Ontario, Manitoba, Saskatchewan, Alberta and British Columbia).

If your goal for the evaluation is to settle the case, you should first consider whether the parties are ready to settle. Do they have enough information about the issues to feel confident about negotiating towards a resolution? Can an informal exchange of documents be agreed upon, and is that enough to create the necessary confidence? If that comfort level is not achieved, the evaluation will be a wasted effort.

The experience in the Ontario Court ADR pilot project, which offered a range of ADR processes, including neutral evaluation, was that parties were often ready to settle sooner than their counsel. They are perhaps more accustomed to negotiations where all the facts are not fully known. Lawyers may prefer to negotiate after discoveries have given them the opportunity to exhaustively explore the facts. These differing interests and preferences should be considered in determining the optimum timing for the evaluation.

The other factor that often precipitates a neutral evaluation is where settlement negotiations have been proceeding but the parties have reached an impasse. In that circumstance, the evaluation can be creatively used to overcome the barrier to settlement. It is a short process. It can be convened very quickly, and the parties can choose an evaluator who is an expert in the very subject that has caused the difficulty.

PARTY INVOLVEMENT

The parties to a dispute have a very low level of involvement in neutral evaluation sessions that occur as part of the court process. They are generally present and listen to their counsel's presentation of the issue and to the evaluator's opinion. If the evaluation is in writing, the parties will get a copy. It is only after the session that their participation becomes more active — in the ensuing settlement negotiations.

Neutral evaluations which take place in a private or contractual context may be quite a different story. In construction, or many other kinds of technical disputes, the parties are the ones with the expertise to be best able to put the issues to the evaluator. The format can be informal, and the process may indeed take place in the office trailer on the site. Since the parties have designed the process, they can also decide what their role in it will be. In those circumstances, the parties are more likely to be the major participants, and often the only participants along with the evaluator, in the neutral evaluation process.

LAWYERS' ROLES

Counsel play the leading roles in neutral evaluations that take place in the context of litigation. Except in a mandatory process, counsel advise their clients if, when and before whom to engage in an evaluation. They carefully craft the issue(s) to be submitted to the evaluator. They prepare their clients and have instructions for various negotiation strategies, depending on the opinion of the evaluator. They prepare and present oral and written submissions to the evaluator that are models of brevity and clarity. They are nimble and creative enough to be able to capitalize on whatever opinion the evaluator gives and to work with it to move the parties towards settlement.

Each court process has its own approach to setting out the issues for the evaluator. A sample submission that includes the information usually sought by the evaluator can be found below. Ontario's Superior Court of Justice no longer offers early neutral evaluation, so the form under the former ADR Pilot Project Practice Direction is no longer used. In the Alberta Court of Queen's Bench in Calgary and Edmonton, a form of neutral evaluation is offered, but under the name of Judicial Dispute Resolution or Judicial Mediation. No form is prescribed there. Instead, each judge presiding over the process sets the requirements for materials to be filed in advance. In a private process the parties can agree on the documentation to be submitted, but the underlying reasons for the written submission in both public and private processes are the same.

The evaluator needs a succinct statement of the issues on which an opinion is sought. If the issue is legal, the argument is required in summary form, with copies of the relevant excerpts of the leading cases. If the issue is to choose between competing expert opinions, the full opinions and their rationale are needed. The emphasis should be on brevity. If you feel it necessary to submit more than one document book or legal brief, your case may not be the best candidate for this process.

[General Heading]

ISSUES FOR NEUTRAL EVALUATOR

[To be filed with the evaluator at the time he or she specifies]

The parties and counsel acting on their behalf have participated in negotiations and believe that a neutral evaluation by a judge [*or state expert's name*] on the one or two outstanding issues will assist them in concluding a settlement of the dispute. The parties state that the following issues are to be submitted to the neutral evaluator for an opinion. [*Please be brief*]

1.   Can Tenant sue Subtenant for unpaid rent under the 2009 agreement, which was an oral agreement respecting land and may be contrary to the Statute of Frauds?

2.   Since the 2001 letter agreement is not under seal, does the six-year limitation for actions founded on contract apply as between Tenant and Subtenant?

A brief summary of the agreed-upon facts follows:

Landlord and Tenant entered a written lease in 1990 for a 20-year term. In 1995, Tenant, in a written document, subleased part of the leased premises to Subtenant for a term of 10 years. In 2005, by a letter agreement, Tenant extended the term of the Sublease for a further 3 years, all other terms of the Lease to apply. In 1998, Tenant and Subtenant orally agreed to add another 1,000 square feet to the subleased premises at the same rent per square foot. No rent was paid for the additional space. In 2000, Tenant demanded payment on that space and settled with the Subtenant on the amount owed, which amount was paid. In 2010, when the lease expired, Landlord claimed that Tenant had underpaid its Additional Rent (proportionate share of utilities, *etc.*) and brought an action for payment. In 2010, Tenant also brought action against Subtenant for underpayment of its Additional Rent for the expanded premises that it occupied from 1998 to 2010. The parties have agreed on the amount of Additional Rent outstanding if the action is maintainable.

Submissions as to what the contentious evidence will be if the matter proceeds to trial, including "will-say" statements, expert reports, and corporate and/or medical records relating to the issues to be determined, will be exchanged and filed by the parties with the evaluator at least 7 days before the scheduled date [*or by the date set by the evaluator or judge*].

Supporting argument and authorities relating to the issues to be determined will be exchanged and filed by the parties with the evaluator at least 7 days before the scheduled date [*or by the date set by the evaluator or judge*].

Dated: June 1, 2010

_____   _____

Counsel for the Plaintiff   Counsel for the Defendant

DESIGN OPTIONS

Many of the available design options for a neutral evaluation process have already been described. It may be court-connected or privately offered. It may take place early or late in the life of a dispute, or any time in between. The evaluator may be a judge or an expert in the subject matter of the dispute, or anyone else in whom the parties repose confidence to give a reasoned, impartial opinion. The documentation submitted to the evaluator may be more or less voluminous. An expert for each party may or may not participate at the session. The opinion of the evaluator may be written or oral.

One option which is available but which tends to change the character of the neutral evaluation process, bringing it much closer to arbitration, is to make the evaluation binding on the parties. This can be done in a private neutral evaluation by their prior written agreement. The only Canadian court that offered a binding neutral evaluation process, now referred to as a *binding JDR*,[9] is the Alberta Court of Queen's Bench. Binding expert evaluation is quite commonly used in England as a private process.

The Alberta *binding JDR*, is not resorted to very often. Since the *L.N. v. S.M.* case,[10] a *binding JDR decision* is no longer available. A *binding JDR opinion* is available as a matter of contract between the parties. Any party wishing to challenge the opinion, however, must sue on the contract. The appeal process of the court is not available to them.

_____

[9]   For a discussion of whether the court has the jurisdiction to enable a "binding JDR decision", as opposed to a "binding JDR opinion" following the decision in *L.N. v. S.M.*, [2007] A.J. No. 888, 284 D.L.R. (4th) 1 (Alta. C.A.), see Justice J.D. Rooke, "Improving Excellence: Evaluation of the Judicial Dispute Resolution Program in the Court of Queen's Bench of Alberta" (1 June 2009) at xxii, 120-124, online: Canadian Forum on Civil Justice <http://cfcj-fcjc.org/clearinghouse/hosted/22338-improving_excellence.pdf>.

[10]   *Ibid.*

Before a *binding JDR opinion* is undertaken, there is a signed agreement by all parties and counsel, and a full vetting of the ramifications of having a binding opinion made by the same person who has heard the parties' settlement positions as well as other information that could not otherwise come out at a trial.

When the evaluator essentially decides the outcome of the dispute, the question arises as to whether the rules of natural justice apply. Is the evaluation session a "hearing"? Is the evaluator conducting an "investigation"? Must the parties be given a right to cross-examine? Does the duty of fairness apply? These issues are beyond the scope of this discussion, as binding evaluation is not used in Canada as part of a public process, but their ramifications should be considered before choosing neutral evaluation as a design option. You will find some assistance in Chapter 7 of this book, which deals with the legal issues raised by different DR processes.

One hybrid neutral evaluation option was tested at the Ontario Court ADR pilot project, but has since been discontinued as being impractical under the private-sector managed Mandatory Mediation Program. Mediation was the primary dispute resolution technique offered at the project; neutral evaluation by a judge was available if the parties and the mediator agreed that it would be helpful in bringing about settlement. Because there were judges hearing commercial list motions on the same floor as the ADR Centre, a practice arose in which the judges' expertise as evaluators on a more informal basis was used. In mediations where an impasse had been reached in the negotiation and the barrier to settlement was a legal issue, the mediator would ask a judge to assist in the breaks between motions. The judge heard briefly from each party its position on the issue, then gave a "read" on how the issue might be decided at trial. It was not a full-fledged opinion, as it was offered before discoveries and before counsel had a full opportunity to work up the law, and it was obviously not binding on the parties. The judge then left the session, and the mediation continued.

Some work was required by the mediator to help the parties in overcoming any polarization and in moving them beyond any loss of face caused by the judge's "read" on the issues. The parties may have had unrealistic expectations of the potential outcome of the litigation, causing the judge's relative risk analysis to come as a shock to them. The project's experience was that these issues did not long stand in the way of the settlement of the case. This quick evaluation, provided early in the process as an adjunct to the mediation, proved to be a very successful aid to the parties in achieving settlement. Although no longer available in the same informal way, the experience is a useful one to draw on in making the choice of whether to convene your own neutral evaluation privately.

OUTCOMES AND ENFORCEMENT

There is very little data on the effectiveness of neutral evaluation as an aid to settlement of disputes. The Northern District of California pilot project in early neutral evaluation reported a settlement rate of one-third of the cases evaluated. Even in the cases that did not settle, nearly 60 per cent of the attorneys agreed that participation in ENE contributed to the settlement negotiations, and that those settlement discussions took place earlier because of the ENE.[11] There is as yet no comparable Canadian data.

The Canadian courts have few statistics showing the settlement rates for cases that have engaged in a pre-trial/settlement conference. It is generally reported that between 95 and 97 per cent of all civil actions filed settle before trial. However, there is little information as to when in the litigation cycle those settlements occur.

The Ontario Court, in designing its ADR pilot project to intervene early in the process, acted on the assumption that many more cases than necessary settle just before trial, and too often for the wrong reasons. Justice George Adams, one of the designers of the project, described the problem as follows:

> Thus, where an action settles on the eve of trial, although the costs of the actual trial are saved, large amounts of time, money and effort have already been expended, leaving the parties exhausted, embittered and often impoverished.[12]

The ADR pilot project's settlement experience with early neutral evaluation was, unfortunately, not part of its formal evaluation. Anecdotally, it was generally thought to be most useful when followed up with a continuation of the mediation to help parties and counsel get through any polarization, which is inevitable when an evaluator's opinion is more favourable to one party than another.

Enforcement is a consideration in neutral evaluation only when a settlement is concluded. The evaluation given does not decide the issue for the parties. Since it is confidential and non-binding, the parties can accept or reject it as they choose. If, however, they use it as the basis for concluding a settlement agreement, it can be enforced in the courts in the same manner as any other binding contract. Where the settlement agreement is in writing, the province's summary judgment rules may be invoked to secure relief.

---

[11]   D. Levine, "Early Neutral Evaluation: The Second Phase" (1989) 1 J. Disp. Resol. 1 at 41.

[12]   G. Adams & N. Bussin, "Alternative Dispute Resolution and the Canadian Courts: A Time for Change" (1995) 17 Advocates' Q. 133 at 144.

PREPARATION

As with all dispute resolution processes, preparation for a neutral evaluation session is the key to a favourable outcome. It generally has at least four discrete phases: choice of evaluator; work up of evaluation statement; preparation of client; and negotiation strategy.

CHOICE OF EVALUATOR

At present in Canada, the choice of evaluator is mostly available in private evaluations, although in Alberta you have some capacity to choose your judge for a JDR. When a choice is available, though, you should choose carefully by keeping in mind your goal of facilitating settlement of the case.

Is the real issue in dispute in the case a technical one? For example, if it is a question of whether a marine navigation system was appropriately designed for the use to which it was put, it might make some sense to have an evaluator who is impartial and without conflicts with an expertise in the design and/or use of marine navigation systems. If the main issue is one of law, you will want to consider a retired judge or a senior lawyer with expertise in the relevant area of law. If the issue is a medical/legal one, you may choose a lawyer who is also a physician. The overriding consideration is always whether the parties will give credence to an opinion rendered by the potential evaluator.

The choice should not be made on the basis of subject expertise alone. The individual's experience in doing neutral evaluations is important, and his or her reputation for being able to make reasoned decisions and render written opinions on a timely basis should be considered. Whether the potential evaluator requires an evaluation statement of issues is indicative of how seriously the task is taken. Also, he or she must be prepared to spend the time before the evaluation to consider the written submissions. None of these factors comes with a guarantee of satisfaction, but they will give you some idea of the questions to ask when you are choosing a private neutral evaluator.

WORK UP OF EVALUATION STATEMENT

Each court has its own requirements for its pre-trial/settlement conference, although the content is very similar throughout the country. It includes a concise statement of the issue to be evaluated, a brief outline of the facts, expert reports, if any, the law and argument upon which each party relies together with extracts of the leading cases, and anything else that may assist the judge.[13]

Written evaluation statements required by private evaluators generally follow the same format as that of the courts, although the participants may change the content of the agreement. One essential addition is a confidentiality agreement because private evaluations are not covered by court rules. Such an agreement will ensure that the session is "off the record" and that the evaluation cannot be used at trial or for any collateral purpose, should settlement negotiations fail. An example of a precedent confidentiality agreement is included below.

[General Heading]

CONFIDENTIALITY AGREEMENT

The parties will participate in a Dispute Resolution session in the nature of a Neutral Evaluation. Through their counsel or individually, the parties agree that:

(a) statements made and documents produced in the session or in the pre-session conference and not otherwise discoverable are not subject to disclosure through discovery or any other process and are not admissible into evidence for any purpose, including impeaching credibility,

(b) the notes, records and recollections of the judge or neutral evaluator conducting the session are confidential and protected from disclosure for all purposes, and

(c) the judge or neutral evaluator presiding over the session has the immunity described in s. 82 of the Ontario *Courts of Justice Act*, R.S.O. 1990, c. C43, with necessary changes to points of detail.

Dated: June 1, 2010

_____   _____
Counsel for the Plaintiff   Counsel for the Defendant

---

[13] For example, see Nova Scotia, Civil Procedure Rules and Related Rules, Alternate Dispute Resolution Procedures, online: Courts of Nova Scotia <http://www.courts.ns.ca/practice_memoranda/memo_5.pdf>, Release No. 1, Practice Memorandum No. 5.

Other steps in your strategic preparation that can be usefully included in the evaluation statement are as follows:[14]

1. identify the party representative who will attend the session and assert his or her decision-making authority;

2. identify the legal or factual issues whose early resolution would significantly narrow or settle the dispute;

3. prepare a chronology of significant events;

4. specify information needed from another party that is necessary for meaningful settlement negotiations;

5. identify any person from another party whose presence at the session would greatly improve or greatly diminish the prospects for a productive session; and

6. identify documents whose availability would materially advance the purposes of the evaluation session (*e.g.*, contract out of which the suit arose, or expert reports).

Whether it be a private or a court evaluation, the consideration of what to include or exclude should always be measured against your goal of settling the case.

PARTY PREPARATION

Depending on whether professional advisors are involved in the particular neutral evaluation process, the responsibility for preparation may fall to the party itself or be shared with the party's professional advisors. The party should come to an understanding of the neutral evaluation process and the need for the party's presence at the session with authority to settle. The party should consider whether the presence of others, such as financial advisors, would be useful. If legal arguments will be made, the party should be briefed on them along with their strengths and weaknesses. The role of the evaluator and of the lawyers in the process, if any, should be clarified. There should be a clear understanding of the party's role at the session and in the negotiations which follow. A realistic estimate should be made of the time the session and the negotiation will take. The object is to eliminate as many surprises as possible from what may be a first-time experience.

---

[14]   This list is largely taken from U.S., District Court for the Northern District of California, *Early Neutral Evaluation* (General Order No. 26) (1989) at 4.

NEGOTIATION STRATEGY

A very important aspect of party preparation is the formulation of a negotiating strategy. This can be developed by examining several possible outcomes of the neutral evaluation: the one most favourable to each party, the least favourable outcome and something in between. The worst alternative should not be glossed over as being unlikely. Putting a case to a decision-maker is always fraught with risk, and that risk should be confronted realistically before the evaluation begins.

Time is another issue that the professional advisor should consider in his or her strategy. In litigation, the advisor should factor in the time it takes to get to trial, the length of the trial, the time it takes for a decision to be rendered and the potential for and the time it takes to have an appeal heard and decided. Outside the litigation context, the advisor should consider what impact delay will have on the construction project, the financing or perhaps the continuing relationship of the parties involved in the dispute. Time can work against the advisor and his or her client for many reasons (*e.g.*, financial difficulties, the unresolved dispute holding up business progress, key witnesses leaving the company or being fired). These risks should be discussed and quantified.

Another factor to be considered is cost — not just legal and court costs, but also the internal and personal costs associated with discovery, preparation and attendance throughout an adversarial process. In most cases, personal costs include anxiety about testifying and having colleagues and customers testify, and also anxiety about having an uncertain outcome at an unpredictable time in the future. Sometimes this anxiety is the most significant factor and will materially affect the outcome of negotiations. This can be ameliorated to some degree if the advisor informs the party of exactly what to expect in the course of the lawsuit.

Experience at the Ontario Superior Court Mandatory Mediation Program has shown that parties rarely have a true picture of the financial costs they are facing in litigation, or an understanding that there will always be significant non-recoverable costs even if they are completely successful at trial. Because solicitor and client costs are frequently claimed, and lawyers fail to explain how infrequently costs are awarded on that scale, parties too often enter settlement negotiations with unrealistic expectations of what can be achieved. Wise and durable settlements will not be concluded unless the parties are fully advised of the risks as well as of their rights. Only then can they make informed decisions and instruct counsel appropriately.

Once the party fully appreciates the potential risks and rewards of the case, the formulation of a negotiating strategy will be easier. It will also minimize the possibility that the party will be so surprised by the outcome of the neutral evaluation that negotiations are brought to a halt. The aim for the strategy is to keep moving towards a settlement, regardless of outcome.

While the advisor cannot minimize the risk that the opposite party is unprepared and shocked by the opinion of the neutral evaluator, the advisor can consider ways to help that party save face and to get on with the negotiation. One tactic is to immediately focus on whatever was said by the evaluator that was positive about the other party's case. Another is to set aside the evaluator's opinion as being an interesting exercise, but now it is time for the parties to roll up their sleeves and craft a settlement package that is a positive one for everyone. It will be of great assistance if the advisor has already identified some elements of a potential settlement that create value for the other party at little cost to the advisor's client.

The negotiating strategy will be tied to the needs and interests of the parties in each case. No two are ever the same. What the advisor is striving for is to find some common ground on which to found a settlement. Although the advisor will formulate some parameters before the neutral evaluation session, they will not remain fixed throughout the negotiation. The assumptions on which they are based will change constantly, and the advisor will be compelled to continually reassess his or her client's positions in light of new information. The parties are a valuable resource in this endeavour because of their knowledge of the business. Careful consideration by the parties of their best and worst possible outcomes in the negotiation will optimize their chances of achieving their settlement goals.

NOTES

NOTES

5

PARTNERING

WHAT IS PARTNERING?

Partnering is a tool in the dispute resolution workbox that is most often used in conjunction with complex or long-term contracts that involve two or more organizations working together to achieve a common goal. Partnering has been variously referred to by commentators as an *attitude*, a *strategy*, an *approach*, a *relationship*, a *commitment* and a *process*. It can be all of these things.

Partnering is a strategy for dispute prevention, a team attitude, a "win-win" or mutual gains approach to working together, a working relationship among multiple organizations in an enterprise, a long-term commitment to mutually agreed-upon objectives and a collaborative process for resolving issues.

There are two aspects to every contract: the written contractual agreement (the "what") and the unwritten working relations of the parties that enable the contract to be carried out (the "how"). Typically, much more negotiation time is spent by the parties on the "what" of the contract than on the "how". Large multi-party, multi-year enterprises are no exception. Partnering focuses on those working relationships that usually comprise the "how", and seeks to enhance them. This is done in a collaborative way by creating a range of activities and informal agreements that encompass the legal and contractual documents, but have no legal force and effect. They are based primarily on trust.

In the late 1980s, it became apparent to many in the construction industry that the spectre of litigation, in an arena where unforeseen problems are all but inevitable, was better at creating defensive, positional behaviour than it was at solving the problems and keeping projects on time and on budget. Partnering required a different attitude, and emphasized cooperation when addressing problems. To assess its risks and potential benefits, the construction industry convened a Task Force. The Report of the Task Force was instrumental in bringing partnering before a much broader audience, and further legitimizing its use.

The Construction Industry Institute Task Force defined partnering as:

> ... a long term commitment between two or more organizations for the purpose of achieving specific business objectives by maximizing the effectiveness of each participant's resources. The relationship is based upon

trust, dedication to common goals and understanding each other's individual expectations and values. Expected benefits include improved efficiencies and cost effectiveness, increased opportunity for innovation and continuous improvement of quality products and services.[1]

As partnering is also employed beyond the construction context, a broader definition may be useful: *partnering* refers to the intentional, designed process of establishing working relationships among different organizations or teams engaged in a joint enterprise, through a mutually developed formal strategy of commitment, communication and issue resolution, to help them achieve separate but mutually complementary goals. The objective of partnering is to forge a stronger bond among the teams working together, in order to prevent most disputes before they surface, and to quickly resolve the few that do. The foundational premise on which partnering depends is that the trust the participants build with one another in the process, encourages the early and continued disclosure of needs and interests. This enables parties to more easily negotiate interest-based solutions when problems arise, and to recognize that those solutions must be fair for all participants for the undertaking to survive and prosper. The trust fosters a cooperative working environment, and facilitates the achievement of the objectives of the joint enterprise.

THE CHOICE TO PARTNER

Partnering should be considered in any enterprise where the risks/stakes are high, when there are many unknowns about the relationship and when there are many stakeholders. Examples would be ventures developing new processes or technologies, or public/private ventures that involve stakeholders with a range of interests.

Partnering is commonly used in large construction projects, as they involve many different organizations and levels of authority within those organizations, all working to achieve the mutual objective of completing the project on time and within budget. Examples of successfully partnered construction projects include: the Greater Toronto Airport Authority's new Terminal One at Pearson Airport; the fixed link between Prince Edward Island and New Brunswick; the Clearnet/Motorola/Morrison Hershfeld project constructing a wireless telecommunications corridor from Windsor, Ontario to Quebec City, Quebec; the decommissioning and rehabilitation of the DEW Line site on Cape Hooper in Baffin Island; and the Metro Toronto Trade Centre. Some regular participants in construction projects have been so satisfied with the partnering process that they partner all of their large

---

[1]   Construction Industry Institute, *In Search of Partnering Excellence*, Partnering Task Force Report (Austin, TX: Construction Industry Institute, 1991). The Task Force was established for the purpose of determining the risks and potential benefits of partnering and to provide guidelines for American engineering and construction firms.

projects. The U.S. Army Corps of Engineers mandates partnering in all of its projects with budgets over $1 million. B.C. Hydro has been committed to partnering for many years, as has Defence Construction Canada. On its website, Defence Construction Canada trumpets that they were "pioneers in partnering" and that "alternative dispute resolution has become part of our culture".[2]

The partnering concept started in the retail/manufacturing sector, not in the construction industry. The best-known example was the strategic partnering that began in the mid-1980s between Proctor & Gamble ("P & G") and Wal-Mart. It was the partnering process that led to a dramatic change in the working relationship between these two powerful giants, who had been merciless adversaries. Each was accustomed to dictating the terms of its relationships. Wal-Mart *required* customized electronic data exchange technology from all of its suppliers. P & G *informed* its retailers how much product it would supply and at what prices. There was no sharing of information, no joint planning and no systems coordination. As Sam Walton put it, "We just let our buyers slug it out with their salesmen."[3]

A mutual friend organized a canoe trip that included Walton and the Vice-President of Sales at P & G. Discussions led to a partnering process, and a new, enduring relationship was created. It is a relationship based on mutual trust and respect, which has led to greater profitability for both. Now the two companies share information, plan jointly, and their systems are coordinated to the extent of an orderless ordering system, which means that P & G manufactures to demand rather than to inventory. This has greatly increased the speed of the order-to-delivery cycle.[4]

As the foregoing illustrates, the joint undertaking may take a variety of forms. It may be a long-term arrangement involving a number of projects or contracts, such as strategic alliances between organizations important to one another: retailer/suppliers/distributors, manufacturer/dealers and franchisor/ franchisees, to name a few. The joint undertaking may also arise under a single contract or project with a multi-year duration. Examples include a complex technology development contract or a large-scale construction project. Partnering is especially suited to technology and multinational projects, because the rapid rate of technological change and an international scope render dispute resolution by a court or arbitration procedure an impractically slow option.

Another impetus for working together may come from within organizations. Partnering is effective in organizations experiencing a pervasive

---

[2] See online: Defence Construction Canada <http://www.dcc-cdc.gc.ca/english/ci_industry.html>.
[3] S. Walton & J. Huey, *Sam Walton, Made in America: My Story* (New York: Doubleday & Co., 1992) at 186.
[4] See N. Kumar, "The Power of Trust in Manufacturer-Retailer Relationships: Two Tough Companies Learn to Dance Together" (1996) 74:6 Harvard Business Review 92 at 102.

change, such as a merger of entities with different corporate cultures, or bringing on a new chief executive officer from outside the organization. Partnering has also been used successfully in organizations under stress, that are reeling from conditions such as low morale, bad publicity, long-festering unresolved conflict or the loss of too many productive employees at once. In short, partnering can be considered a viable option in any organization or venture that requires the establishment or the re-establishment of an ongoing cooperative effort by multiple teams throughout the life of a venture.

ESSENTIAL ELEMENTS

Although partnering is a flexible concept which can be designed to meet very different needs, a typical partnering arrangement contains certain key elements.[5] They are as follows:

- commitment
- equity
- communication
- conflict resolution

Commitment

Commitment to the collaborative partnering attitude and issue resolution process must exist and be actively demonstrated by the most senior executives of each participant or team constituting the joint endeavour. Also, that commitment must endure for the life of the working relationships between the parties. In our society, adversarial attitudes and positional negotiations are much more familiar and comfortable than cooperative approaches based on needs and interests. Changing the paradigm to one focusing on mutual interests takes leadership at all stages of the relationship. Leaders can go beyond endorsing the process and empowering their representatives. They can instill enthusiasm for the success of the joint undertaking throughout their organizations. They can and should commit the human and financial resources necessary to permit the partnering relationship to work. Without that leadership, early optimism dissipates as soon as inevitable problems are encountered. Old, defensive attitudes re-emerge. Lukewarm commitment is probably the most significant reason why a partnering effort does not achieve its objectives.

The other kind of commitment that is essential is *individual* commitment. How the individual participants in the partnered venture act and

---

[5]   This list is an elaboration of one found in Associated General Contractors of America, *Partnering: A Concept for Success* (Arlington, VA: ASC of America, 1991) at 2, and abbreviated in its video of the same name (1994).

treat each other is key. Their personal commitment to the process and to a shared vision of the outcome cannot be understated.

Equitable Collaboration

Partnering effectively acknowledges that in long-term relationships, the traditional arm's-length model of dealing must give way to a mutual commitment to shared (or complementary) goals, in an atmosphere of mutual trust and cooperation.[6] All of the participants' interests must be considered in creating those mutual goals. Organizations that rely on their power to subject others to punishing terms do so at their own peril.[7] "Weaker" parties often develop into "stronger" parties, and memories of unfair treatment never fade. They also provide a powerful incentive to be the winner "next time". In the partnering context, that would present a major challenge.

Communication

Better communication is the first step toward preventing disputes. The partnering process seeks to establish improved communication by bringing the participants together to collectively create a statement of the values and objectives that will govern the project (partnering charter). They also clarify one another's expectations and work to more fully understand the concerns, interests and expertise of each participant. An early outcome of the partnering process is to create a practical communications tool or protocol that clearly identifies whom to call, at what numbers and when. It reinforces the typical partnering value of encouraging decision-making and problem-solving at the lowest practical levels of authority.

Building improved communications among the participants usually starts in the partnering workshop, but it is an ongoing effort throughout the life of the enterprise. It takes a conscious effort by each individual participant to pick up the telephone and call his or her corresponding participant when problems arise, rather than resorting to the old-style flurry of defensive emails or faxes. Experience shows, however, that it is only through this type of effective communication that potential conflicts are identified early, and that the creativity and expertise of the right people are used to solve them.

---

[6]   L. Cook & D. Hancher, "Partnering: Contracting for the Future" (1990) 6 J. of Management in Engineering 431 at 433.

[7]   For a general discussion of the most likely outcomes of exploiting power, see N. Kumar, "The Power of Trust in Manufacturer-Retailer Relationships: Two Tough Companies Learn to Dance Together" (1996) 74:6 Harvard Business Review 92 at 92-97.

Conflict Resolution

Partnering plans for conflict by establishing a foundation for conflict resolution that includes an acceptable procedure for discussing and resolving disputes at the lowest possible levels of decision-making authority. The procedure is typically an array of dispute resolution options in which the participants are encouraged to seek the expeditious and inexpensive resolution of disputes in an informal setting through negotiation. This may require assisted negotiation, which may take several forms. If no resolution is achieved, the final step in the process is adjudication, usually a type of arbitration. These options are all alternatives to litigation.

There is no "cookie-cutter" approach to the conflict resolution processes employed in partnering. The best ones recognize conflict resolution as a *process* rather than a *discrete event*. For example, the St. Mary's Hospital experience in Hong Kong in 1991 changed the very nature of construction conflict processes when it demonstrated the effectiveness of an early, disciplined conflict system design that involved the project participants.[8] The successful system featured the parties' joint appointment of a specific neutral construction expert with conflict management skills, called a dispute resolution advisor ("DRA"). The DRA helped the parties build support for cooperative problem-solving, made monthly site visits throughout the project to facilitate discussions of tough issues and had the authority to employ third party assisted processes with site representatives, *e.g.*, mediation, mini-trials and expert fact-finding. If these efforts failed, the DRA could prepare a report identifying the key issues in the dispute, the positions of the parties and the barriers to settlement, and could provide either a recommendation for settlement or a non-binding evaluation of the dispute. The DRA's report would be used by senior off-site representatives in further negotiations. If those failed, the parties resorted to a sculpted arbitration procedure or other mutually acceptable means recommended by the DRA.[9] The effectiveness of the process was demonstrated in the litigation-free outcome. Despite hundreds of owner-ordered changes and the usual problems of building on an old site while the hospital continued to operate, no disputes reached the level of non-binding evaluation.[10]

Another example of a successful conflict resolution process came out of the partnering for the construction of the Greater Toronto Airport Authority's ("GTAA") Airport Development Program ("ADP"), which began in

---

[8]   T.J. Stipanowich, "The Multi-Door Contract and Other Possibilities" (1998) 13 Ohio St. J. Disp. Resol. 303 at 387, quoting at 328, note 65, C.J. Wall, "The Dispute Resolution Advisor in the Construction Industry" in P. Fenn & R. Gameson, eds., *Construction Conflict Management and Resolution* (London: E & FN Spon, 1992).

[9]   T.J. Stipanowich, "The Multi-Door Contract and Other Possibilities" (1998) 13 Ohio St. J. Disp. Resol. 303 at 335-38.

[10]   C.J. Wall, "The Dispute Resolution Advisor: A New Approach to Preventing and Resolving Construction Disputes" *DART News* (August 1993) 1.

1998. The first phase of the design-build project was carried out while Toronto Pearson International Airport (the busiest airport in Canada and one of the busiest in North America)[11] continued to operate and to process almost 30 million passengers per year. The ADP included a virtually complete redevelopment of all of Toronto Pearson Airport's infrastructure, including all access roads, bridges, a central utilities plant, a parking garage, aprons, airport services and the new Terminal One, at a budgeted cost of $4.4 billion — one of the largest building projects in North America at the time.

Some of the unusual issues encountered during the construction period, that had a major effect on either or both of passenger/freight traffic volumes and airport design were: a fast-track design and construction schedule; the terrorist attacks on September 11, 2001 and heightened security regulations; SARS and infectious disease awareness; the demise of both Canadian Airlines and Canada 3000; and the insolvency of Air Canada, the airport's largest tenant. Under the circumstances, there was a high potential risk of expensive and protracted construction claims. Despite the challenges, the new Terminal One opened in 2004 as planned. It was completed within budget, under extremely difficult circumstances.

One of the critical factors that senior managers at the GTAA credit with having a significant impact on the successful completion of the project is the partnering it employed under the leadership of David Aitken,[12] the partnering facilitator. Despite hundreds of changes mandated either by the GTAA or by various governments, only a very small number of claims made it even as far as the formal mediation stage of the dispute resolution procedure formulated by the participants in the partnering.[13]

Many partnered projects employ an *issue resolution* process. The process is given concrete shape by means of a living document often called a dispute or issue resolution matrix or chart. It involves designating project participants by name from each organizational participant, with a commitment for involvement in the conflict resolution process. Another key element is the commitment to a maximum length of time for an issue to be considered before it is escalated to the next level of decision-making. Complex projects typically have a separate *issue resolution chart* for each major contract. Sometimes there are five or more per contract, depending on the number of categories of issues identified as likely to arise. For example, requests for information,

---

[11] Greater Toronto Airports Authority, *Airport Development Briefing Paper #4* (2002) at 1.
[12] David Aitken, David Aitken Associates Inc., Vancouver, British Columbia.
[13] The key conflict management options available under the GTAA's *Airport Development Program Charter 2000* were partnering, the issue resolution process, risk analysis by trade package (identification of major risks, and negotiations to mitigate those risks before contracts are awarded), involvement of an independent claims consultant, and negotiation, mediation and arbitration. The actual DR process was prepared by a stakeholder taskforce post-charter to enable parties to adopt the dispute settlement method(s) best suited to the ADP and its implementation team. We were given access to the charter and process with the kind permission of the GTAA.

quality and contemplated change orders might have charts developed for issues/disputes falling under each of those three categories. A simple example of such a matrix from the construction industry is set out below.[14]

				DISPUTE RESOLUTION MATRIX	
Level	Time	Owner	Contractor	Construction Manager	Architect/Engineer
1	2 hr.	-----------	General Foreman	Field Inspector	Architect/Engineer
2	2 hr.	Oversight A/E	Superintendent	Field Engineer	Project Engineer
3	2 days	Project Manager	Project Manager	Resident Engineer	Department Head
4	2 days	Construction Director	Project Officer	Division Manager	Manager of Projects
5	2 days	Program Director	Executive Officer	Project Director	A/E Principal

Rules of Engagement

   1.   Attempt resolution at the lowest level.

   2.   Do not by-pass levels.

   3.   Do not ignore the issue. Abandon self-interest and review the issue fairly.

   4.   Escalate unresolved issues to the next higher level of authority in the time specified.

Project Management Institute, *PM Network*, Project Management Institute, Inc., 1999. Copyright and all rights reserved. Material from this publication has been reproduced with the permission of PMI.

Conflict is inevitable in any relationship, and the partnering relationship is no exception. It is how that conflict is handled that is the measure of success of the partnering venture. That is where the opportunity for significant savings of cost and time lies. Rick Russell, a well-known facilitator, aptly summed up the conflict resolution potential of partnering when he wrote:

> When people know each other and have an opportunity to relate as people, they find it easier to trust each other and work things out when problems arise.

> When expectations are made clear and objectives are discussed in detail, there are fewer surprises and those that come up are dealt with more proactively.

> When people agree beforehand about what they will do when problems present themselves, they respond more thoughtfully to situations and act rather than react.[15]

---

[14]   This is an elaboration of a matrix found in C.R. Rohan, "Partnering: For Better and Worse" *PM Network Magazine* (February 1999) 55 at 56.

[15]   Reproduced with permission of R. Russell, "Key Elements of Partnering" *The Undergrounder* (Summer 1997), a seasonal newsletter of the Ontario Sewer and Watermain Construction

Timing

Successful partnering most often begins at the very beginning of the joint endeavour, before negative attitudes and destructive patterns of behaviour have a chance to become established, or, in the case of internal partnering, before they become any worse. The notion that partnering principles will be used in a project is signalled even before any contracts are awarded — at the request for proposals stage.[16] Participants committed to partnering now include this request in the contractual documents as well,[17] so there can be no lack of clarity as to the cooperative environment they are working to establish on that project.

Bonita Thompson, Q.C., a pioneering partnering facilitator in Canada, has persuasively written,[18] however, that partnering can be an effective tool even when a construction project is well under way or relationships are already in trouble. She calls this *therapeutic partnering* and outlines a more intensive preparation before bringing the participants together. She has experienced positive outcomes for the partnering

---

Association (OSWCA). This article is also available online: Agree Dispute Resolution <http://agreeinc.com> under "Publications".

[16] The U.S. Army Corps of Engineers introduces partnering in its bid solicitations with language as follows:

> In order to complete this contract most beneficially for both parties, the Government proposes to form a Partnering relationship with the Contractor. The Partnering relationship will draw on the strengths of each party in an effort to achieve a quality project done right the first time, within budget and on schedule. The Partnering relationship will be bilateral and participation will be totally voluntary. Any costs associated with Partnering will be shared equally with no change in contract price.

(R. Steen, "The Construction Industry Experience" (Corporate ADR and the Promise of Partnering, ABA Conference, 16 April 1999) at 61.)

[17] The partnering clause incorporated by the GTAA in the contractual documents for Phase II of its Airport Development Program, used with permission of the GTAA, is:

> 65.1 The Trade Contractor understands and acknowledges that the *Owner* is committed to using the process commonly known in the industry as "partnering" as a tool for fostering (among other things) co-operation, teamwork and avoidance of conflict and dispute among its various contractors working on the *Project*. As such, the *Trade Contractor* acknowledges and agrees that it shall fully participate in and comply with all partnering training, processes, meetings, programs and procedures as may be required of them from time to time by the *Owner* and will implement all partnering procedures or principles as directed by the *Owner* in the execution of the *Work*. The *Trade Contractor* further acknowledges and agrees that it has taken such requirements into account fully in determining its *Contract Price* and any unit prices for the *Work* as set forth in the *Contract Documents* and in determining the *Contract Time*, and accordingly agrees that the *Trade Contractor* shall not be entitled to a *Change Order* for any costs incurred, time spent or delays experienced in respect of the *Work* arising in any way from its compliance with or participation in such partnering training, processes, meetings, programs and procedures, and the *Trade Contractor* shall not be entitled to any extensions in the *Contract Time* or additional compensation in respect thereof.

[18] B.J. Thompson, *Therapeutic Partnering* (Vancouver: Singleton, Urquhart, Scott, October 1995) at 2.

process in giving the participants enough confidence to resolve their outstanding issues and to complete the projects.

THE PARTNERING PROCESS

When the participants contemplate partnering at the contracting stage, the mechanics of partnering begin with building the partnering team for the project. If the participants in an enterprise have not yet all contemplated partnering, the first step is to assess the participants and their organizational culture for receptivity to partnering. Both activities generally involve the assistance of a skilled facilitator.

Another consideration in partnering is the *stakeholder*, who is a person or organization with an interest or concern in the undertaking. It is critical that *all* of the stakeholders of the enterprise are represented on the team. In a construction project, the team would likely include the owner, contractor, major subcontractors, architects and other design professionals. It would also include significant third party interests, such as insurance underwriters and lenders. In a partnering within an organization, the team would include named individuals or department/unit heads, depending on the objective of the undertaking.

Once the facilitator is satisfied that the stakeholders have been identified and that there is commitment to the partnering at the highest levels of the participants, the partnering workshop is convened. The workshop includes the team as well as representation from the most senior decision-making levels of each participant. The facilitator leads the workshop and takes responsibility for ensuring that everyone is heard and that the objectives are accomplished. Depending on the nature and size of the enterprise, there may be a number of partnering workshops for the various levels of the organizations, or as a new phase of the enterprise brings new participants into the mix. The workshops are held away from any participant's place of business, often for a day or two.

The objectives of a partnering workshop are:

* to establish new/stronger working relationships;
* to create a charter for the enterprise; and
* to begin the process of establishing dispute prevention and resolution procedures.

The partnering workshop educates team members about each other's business practices and expectations. It educates them on interpersonal communication, disputing styles and the management of conflict. It clarifies lines of communication, anticipates problems and seeks their commitment to common goals and collaborative problem-solving. The workshop often concludes with the project mission statement or charter. Each participant is asked to join with the others and commit to a relationship of trust and shared goals in approaching the project as an enterprise in which all are stakeholders.[19]

The partnering charter may be a simple statement, developed and agreed to by all participants, about communication, cooperation and conflict resolution at the lowest level of decision-making authority. More commonly, the charter includes a fuller statement of the participants' shared values and objectives for the project in the three key areas of communication, conflict management and performance objectives.

The signing of the partnering charter symbolizes the shared commitment to a new kind of working relationship, but the partnering workshop should not end without concrete plans for follow-up, to reinforce the relationships and mechanisms for reporting and measuring performance in maintaining the charter objectives. The workshop and charter launch the partnering venture. Sustaining the shared commitment over the long term takes work by all of the participants.

THE FACILITATOR'S ROLE

The partnering facilitator is generally considered to be a key ingredient in the successful launch of a partnering initiative. In larger projects, the facilitator is used throughout to ensure that enthusiasm for collaborative working relationships is maintained, and that the issue resolution process is optimized. Ideally, the facilitator should have no vested interest in the decisions made by the participants. Knowledge of the industry involved in the partnering is useful, but not critical. The facilitator's primary role is to manage the partnering process. Consequently, experience in group dynamics, team building and conflict management is essential to guiding participants throughout that process.

ROLE OF LAWYERS/PARTICIPANTS

Partnering is one of the dispute resolution processes where lawyers for the participants are involved to only a minor degree. Indeed, partnering has been described as "an attempt to restore principal parties to centre stage in approaches to conflict, and to limit the role of legal professionals …".[20] A few American commentators have argued for the inclusion of lawyers in the partnering workshop, as they can add to an in-depth discussion of project conflict management and performance goals, and can benefit from a better

---

[19]   T.J. Stipanowich, "The Multi-Door Contract and Other Possibilities" (1998) 13 Ohio St. J. Disp. Resol. 303 at 381-82.
[20]   *Ibid.*, at 384.

acquaintance with the personalities involved.[21] Generally, however, the participants are the players in the partnering process, and lawyers are not involved.

THE ROLE OF INDEPENDENT THIRD PARTIES IN THE CONFLICT RESOLUTION PROCESS

Partnering employs a number of types of independent third parties in its conflict resolution processes — mediators and arbitrators to name two. As seen above, in the discussion of the St. Mary's Hospital dispute resolution advisor, there are more non-traditional independent third party roles being devised. These are to assist participants with the change to a cooperative culture, as well as to reinforce the value of prompt identification and resolution of issues through direct negotiation, at the level at which the dispute originated. Thomas Stipanowich makes the case for a project neutral, which he calls a *conflict manager*:

> The backbone of a relational conflict management system is a neutral who performs a variety of facilitative roles during the course of a relationship ... including educating participants regarding conflict styles, modeling integrative bargaining, ... assist in the conflict diagnosis and advise groups of their dispute processing alternatives ... would continue during the performance of the contract ... as a mediator ... may activate the next stage of the management program, such as submission to early neutral evaluation, or a dispute review board ... important role to play in paving the way for further process.[22]

Although the term *conflict manager* was not used in the ADP, many of these essentially facilitative roles were played by the GTAA partnering facilitator, at least during the early years of the project. The senior manager of the GTAA responsible for the ADP[23] credits those skills and flexibility with keeping the partnering attitude alive in some very difficult and constantly changing circumstances, and for the project's ultimate success.

The same project also employed a more rights-based independent third party to play quite a different role. The GTAA Airport Development Program called this party the *independent claims consultant*. In circumstances where an issue was not resolved directly between the construction manager and the trade contractor, or if the issue was particularly complex or required specialized analytical techniques, the construction manager was empowered to request the involvement of the

[21] K.A. Kunz, "Counsel's Role in Negotiating a Successful Construction Partnering Agreement" (1995) 15 Construction Law 19 at 19.

[22] T.J. Stipanowich, "The Multi-Door Contract and Other Possibilities" (1998) 13 Ohio St. J. Disp. Resol. 303 at 392.

[23] Lloyd McCoomb, then Executive Vice-President, Airport Development, Greater Toronto Airports Authority, now President and CEO.

independent claims consultant ("ICC"). In the GTAA project, that task was undertaken by Revay and Associates Limited.

The role of the ICC is to provide a measure of "objectivity, clarity and understanding", and to assist in achieving a fair but speedy resolution of issues. The ICC evaluates the issues under discussion, establishes the facts, reviews entitlement considerations and analyzes cost, schedule and productivity data. The role often expands to include direct participation in negotiations between the construction manager and the trade contractor.

> It is of major significance in the success of this process that, although these services have been retained directly by the owner, in all cases where it has been required, trade contractors have provided full and open access to their project records in order to facilitate the review. This is a significant departure from the normal adversarial attitudes encountered in construction claim situations, and coupled with the high degree of co-operation from all project participants working towards a common objective of an equitable settlement, has made a significant contribution to the successful track record.[24]

The successful record referred to is that in Phase I of the GTAA's Airport Development Program (seven years, $4.4 billion). No construction claims needed to go as far as the formal mediation and arbitration stages in the project dispute resolution process before they were resolved.

BENEFITS AND DRAWBACKS OF PARTNERING

Research on the partnering process, conducted within the construction industry, identifies these benefits:[25]

1. better coordination among key players resulting in projects that come in on time and at or below cost;

2. improved constructability for better quality projects;

3. more effective communication; and

4. improved working relationships.

In 2006, *An Empirical Study on Incentives of Strategic Partnering in China: Views from Construction Companies* found that through strategic partnering, companies are more likely to access technology, share risks, and improve project-based performance and competitive position.[26]

---

[24]   W.R. Gillan, "Facilitating the Construction Dispute Resolution Process" (March 2004) 23:1 The Revay Report at 4. See online: Revay <http://www.revay.com/eng/publications>.

[25]   Report of the Dispute Avoidance and Resolution Task Force of the American Arbitration Association, "Building Success for the 21st Century" (1996) at 4, online: AAA <http://www.adr.org/sp.asp?id=29169>.

[26]   S. Lu & H. Yan, "An empirical study on incentives of strategic partnering in China: Views from construction companies" (April 2007) 25:3 International Journal of Project Management at 241-249, abstracted online: <http://www.sciencedirect.com>.

Regular adherents of partnering, such as the U.S. Army Corps of Engineers, give it very good reviews:

> Partnering is a strategy for success. In over three years experience we have (1) virtually eliminated time growth, (2) substantially reduced cost growth, (3) experienced no new litigation, (4) reduced paperwork by 2/3, (5) gained new respect for our industry partners, and (6) are HAVING FUN![27]

Partnering, however, is neither a panacea nor a substitute for hard work. It has several vulnerabilities. For example, it is vulnerable to resistance to change — both by participants and by levels within participants. It can also suffer from staff changes within participants, unless the partnering plans for this type of evolution. Partnering represents a cost, and the participants may lose their appetite for that cost if there is a downward shift in business conditions.

Some of the potential challenges arise out of the original design of the partnering. There may have been a failure at the outset to include all of the necessary stakeholders as participants. Just as significantly, there may have been unrealistic expectations stemming from a misunderstanding of the process that were not addressed in the initial partnering workshop. But the most common failure of partnering is the lack of continuous commitment of senior management of all participants. That commitment must be obtained and nurtured over the life of the project, and it does not happen without appropriate planning and adequate resources to follow through.

THE FUTURE

Much of the foregoing discussion of partnering focuses on the process as it is employed in the construction industry. That is certainly where partnering is most usually encountered in Canada. However, as was noted above, partnering did not begin there. It was first used in the manufacturing-retail sector, where there is still enormous potential for partnering to add value to a relationship. Partnering is also especially suited to technology and multinational projects, because the rapid rate of technological change and an international scope render dispute resolution by a court or arbitration procedure impractical.

One of the new ways partnering is being used is to evaluate potential long-term partnership relationships. The partnering model has been applied in a supply chain context, as a way of targeting potentially effective relationships and matching the parties' expectations as closely as possible.[28]

---

[27]   Colonel Charles E. Cowan, U.S. Army Corps of Engineers, Portland District. See the Associated General Contractors of America, *Partnering: A Concept for Success* (Arlington, VA: AGC of America, 1991) at 18.

[28]   D.A. Lambert & A.M. Knemeyer, "We're in this Together" (December 2004) 82:12 Harvard Business Review 114.

The aim was to structure the relationship so that both parties realized the maximum benefit from it.

As we have seen, the future of partnering is very promising. It can be applied and adapted to enhance any venture[29] requiring the establishment of trust by groups of people over the life of the undertaking.

---

[29]   For example, see efforts by the Corporate Partnering Institute, a U.S. think-tank "dedicated to the use of partnering to generate growth and competitive advantage", online: <http://corporate partnering.com>.

6

MINI-TRIALS AND JDR

As was set out in the definitions of the various DR processes in
Chapter 1, the mini-trial takes two very distinct forms, depending on
whether it is convened as a private process or in connection with a court.
With the maturation of the Judicial Dispute Resolution (JDR) Program of
Alberta's Court of Queen's Bench, there is now a third form, which, in some
ways, is a hybrid of the first two.

PRIVATE MINI-TRIAL

The private mini-trial in Canada, sometimes called an executive
settlement conference, is a development of a settlement technique used for
more than 30 years in the United States. The name is confusing because
private mini-trials do not involve a judge or a court. They are conducted
under the authority of a mini-trial agreement negotiated by the parties, and,
consequently, can take many different forms. What they have in common is
abridged presentations about the dispute, and the goal of resolving it on a
more informal basis than a trial.

The evidence and argument are typically heard in brief by a panel of
senior executives from each party and an impartial third party called the
neutral advisor. The neutral advisor acts as a moderator of the proceedings,
taking on whatever role is useful to the parties in their efforts to settle their
own case. At various stages in the mini-trial process, the parties may invite
the neutral advisor to act as a mediator, to ask or answer questions, or to give
an assessment of the strengths or weaknesses of each party's case.
Alternatively, the neutral advisor may only be asked to chair the mini-trial to
keep the parties to their agreed schedule, but not to limit their presentations
in any other way. No two cases are alike.[1]

Some attributes shared with the court model mini-trial are
confidentiality and brevity. What is different in private mini-trials is that
evidence is most often presented in person by key witnesses and experts.
The parties and the neutral advisor also play quite different roles.

In the private mini-trial, the parties are the most significant participants,
not their counsel or the neutral advisor. The senior executive's opportunity to

---

[1] For a good discussion of what the parties may ask the neutral advisor to do for them, see
Alberta Law Reform Institute, *Civil Litigation: The Judicial Mini-trial*, Dispute Resolution –
Special Series, Discussion Paper No. 1 (August 1993) at 2, online: <http://www.law.
ualberta.ca/alri/docs/dp001.pdf>.

assess the impact of his or her own witnesses and the witnesses for the other side, from the judge's front-of-the-room perspective, can be very instructive. It is usually the first time that information about the relative strength of witnesses is not filtered through managers involved in the facts of the dispute. Direct observation of how the key witnesses acquit themselves "on the stand" often leads to settlement discussions. In a very real sense, "the Mini-trial returns the dispute to the businessmen, educates them, and then allows them to use their developed skills — assessing risk and negotiating — to resolve the dispute".[2]

In private mini-trials, the authority of the neutral advisor is conferred by the parties in the mini-trial agreement. That agreement could confine the neutral advisor to a similar evaluative role. In Ontario, where former judges conduct private mini-trials, that does happen. Far more frequently, the neutral advisor is given many roles, each to be carried out when the parties request it. In its more usual form, this is a process which puts the parties in the driver's seat.

MINI-TRIAL IN THE COURTS

As the name suggests, the mini-trial has some of the characteristics of an abbreviated trial, although usually without witnesses being heard. Counsel for the parties put their best case to the judge, with summaries of what witnesses and experts will say, copies of the most relevant documents and records and copies of pertinent authorities supporting their legal arguments. A court-connected mini-trial is actually more similar to a neutral evaluation than a trial. Its purpose is for the judge to evaluate the information provided to him or her in the mini-trial format, and to give the parties an opinion as to how the case would be decided if it went to trial. That opinion is not determinative, because that judge will not be the trial judge. It is informational — to be used by the parties in their ensuing negotiations to resolve the dispute. The very limited exception is the Alberta Queen's Bench "binding mediation" described in Chapter 4.

A typical mini-trial is convened before a judge at the mutual request of the parties, which is made after discovery has been completed. It is an "off the record" session which results in a non-binding opinion as to the probable outcome at trial, rendered for settlement purposes only. The judge's authority to make such an evaluation stems from the office he or she holds. That authority is merely loaned to the parties in a structured way to assist them in their settlement efforts. The mini-trial judge is precluded from hearing the trial, and no record of the opinion may be communicated to the trial judge. No witnesses are called. Evidence is submitted in written form, as is legal argument. Submissions are heard from counsel. The parties are

---

[2]   R. Olson, "An Alternative for Large Case Dispute Resolution" (1980) 6 Litigation 22.

present but have little involvement other than to hear the opinion. That is the end of it as far as the judge is concerned. It is then up to the parties and their professional advisors to engage in settlement negotiations. Costs are usually not assessed.

In British Columbia, the mini-trial may flow directly into a settlement conference.[3] In that case, the judge's role changes from evaluator to mediator. That has proven to be the direction taken in Alberta as well, which has led to the integration of JDR into the court process. This is discussed in more detail later in this chapter.

Because there are no formal mini-trial rules, there are case-by-case variations in the process.[4] In the early days of mini-trials in Alberta, former Chief Justice Moore described[5] the practice of convening pre-mini-trial conferences. Counsel and the mini-trial judge would meet in advance of the session to settle such timing and process issues as the agreed statement of facts, the legal argument brief based on facts expected to be introduced at trial, the exhibits and experts' reports that would be referred to and which summaries of discovery transcripts would be necessary. The recent evaluation of the Alberta JDR processes[6] demonstrated that the practice varied, depending on the "culture of the local bench and bar" where the JDR took place. In Edmonton, for example, most cases in the survey sample (93 per cent), had pre-JDR sessions before a judge. The evaluation study noted as well that evaluative processes such as mini-trial were by far the most predominant forms of JDR held in Edmonton. In Calgary, by contrast, pre-JDR sessions occurred in far fewer cases (32 per cent). There were mixed views in both judicial centres as to the utility of the pre-JDRs in promoting settlement. The parties are able to decide for themselves if the additional expense makes sense for their individual case.

The mini-trial is not currently being used by the Ontario Superior Court of Justice. One variation that was available in Ontario mini-trials a

---

[3]   K.M. Lysyk, *ADR Processes in the B.C. Courts* (Otawa: Canadian Bar Association, March 1994).

[4]   See Rooke, *infra*, footnote 6, who directs us to an overview of how JDRs are conducted in Alberta as set out in several cases: *J.W. Abernethy Management & Consulting Ltd. v. 705589 Alberta Ltd.*, [2004] A.J. No. 483, 25 Alta. L.R. (4th) 326 at paras. 3 and 11 (Alta. Q.B.) (Agrios J.), affd [2005] A.J. No. 370, 253 D.L.R. (4th) 472 (Alta. C.A.); and *Varga v. Sihvon*, [2001] A.J. No. 435, 288 A.R. 1 at paras. 42-49 (Alta. Q.B.) (Burrows J.).

[5]   In Alberta, the former Chief Justice, W.K. Moore, published guidelines which can be found in the appendices of an electronic book — Justice J.A. Agrios, *A Handbook on Judicial Dispute Resolution for Canadian Judges*, version 3.1 (October 2007) (Edmonton, AB: s.n., 2007) [unpublished] at Appendices 2117, 3119 and 4121, online: National Judicial Institute, Judicial Library <http://www.nji.ca/> at 3.

   See former Chief Justice W.K. Moore, Address to the Arbitration Group (6 February 1995) at 8, 14.

[6]   Justice J.D. Rooke, "Improving Excellence: Evaluation of the Judicial Dispute Resolution Program in the Court of Queen's Bench of Alberta" (1 June 2009) at xxii, 120-124, online: Canadian Forum on Civil Justice <http://cfcj-fcjc.org/clearinghouse/hosted/22338-improving_excellence.pdf>.

few years ago was the hearing of testimony. Several of the Ontario Superior Court of Justice judges who conducted mini-trials heard both expert witnesses and a key witness per party. The evidence was not sworn, although that could easily be provided for. There was very limited or no cross-examination of the witnesses. Testimony was heard in instances where discovery transcripts or full experts' reports were not available, or at the request of the parties.

Currently, mini-trials are enabled and being used to some extent in Alberta, the Northwest Territories, Nunavut, Newfoundland and Labrador, and British Columbia.[7] Ontario experimented with court-connected mini-trials several years ago, but it is now committed to mandatory mediation as its primary settlement process. Expanded pre-trial settlement procedures that could encompass mini-trials, even if they are not specifically mentioned, are being implemented in other provinces.[8] As a consensual process, it may well be possible to convene a mini-trial in any province if a willing judge can be found.

A variation on the mini-trial in Prince Edward Island is called a "quick ruling". It has some of the characteristics of a mini-trial, but is available even before an action has been launched, and up to the point that pleadings have closed. If the parties agree to engage in the process, a judge will be assigned and a hearing convened to determine the facts and issues in contention. At the hearing, which is transcribed, the judge may receive evidence in any form. Within 30 days the judge is to give a decision on all or any part of the dispute, including costs.

If it is decided that a "quick ruling" is inappropriate in the case, the hearing may be treated as a conference, and directions may be issued that the judge considers "necessary or advisable with respect to resolving the dispute".[9] The judge's ruling may be accepted or rejected by the parties. If it is rejected and the result at trial is no better, the costs a rejecting party is

---

[7]   Alberta, British Columbia and Ontario courts use or have used the mini-trial. As there is no specific enabling authority under the Ontario Rules of Court, the consent of the parties is a prerequisite. Alberta Rules of Court, Alta. Reg. 124/2010, R. 4.16, effective 1 November 2010, requires a dispute resolution process, which, because of its broad definition, includes mini-trial as one of the potential processes. Newfoundland and Labrador's Rules of the Supreme Court, 1986, S.N. 1986, c. 42, Sch. D, s. 39.05, as am. by Nfld. Reg. 165/94, s. 3, and Nfld. Reg. 9/00, s. 3 enables the ordering of a mini-trial and governs its process. A mini-trial may also be ordered under R. 284(1)(c) of the Rules of the Supreme Court of the Northwest Territories, N.W.T. Reg. 010-96, as am. The same Rule has been adopted by the Nunavut Court of Justice.

[8]   Manitoba Court of Queen's Bench Rules, Man. Reg. 553/88, Rr. 48.01(3), 50.01, as am.; Ontario Rules of Civil Procedure, R.R.O. 1990, Reg. 194, R. 50; Newfoundland and Labrador's Rules of the Supreme Court, 1986, S.N. 1986, c. 42, Sch. D (a regulation under the *Judicature Act*), R. 39, as am. by Nfld. Reg. 165/94, s. 3, and Nfld. Reg. 9/00, s. 3, and Rules of the Supreme Court of the Northwest Territories, N.W.T. Reg. 010-96, R. 284(1)(e). (Note that Nunavut uses the Rules of the Supreme Court of the Northwest Territories.)

[9]   Rules of Civil Procedure (Supreme Court of Prince Edward Island), R. 75, online: Prince Edward Island <http://www.gov.pe.ca/courts/supreme/rules>.

ordered to pay are increased by 50 per cent, and any costs awarded to that party are decreased by 50 per cent. A ruling that is accepted may be enforced as a judgment of the court.

ALBERTA'S JDR

In the early 1990s, the Alberta Court of Queen's Bench began making judicial mini-trials available to litigants in the large centres of Calgary and Edmonton to help them settle cases that were likely to need lengthy trials. At the time, what became known as JDRs took the form of judicial mini-trials, with the judge acting as an impartial evaluator of the case. They evolved as participating judges became more familiar with facilitative and mediative techniques. Today, JDR can encompass a pre-JDR focusing of the issues, a neutral evaluation or risk assessment by a judge of the law and principal facts in the case, a facilitative negotiation assisted by the judge, and, if that fails to produce agreement, with the consent of the parties, a binding opinion or decision on the merits by the judge. It is a consensual, party-initiated process that can be tailored to the needs of the particular litigants.[10]

JDR is available only in the major judicial centres, and the techniques used by the justices depend on the legal culture of the local bench and bar. However, JDR was enshrined in Alberta's New Rules of Court as of November 1, 2010.[11] Unless waived by court order, every case must participate in a dispute resolution process, the goal of which is to settle the claim by agreement. JDR is one of the dispute resolution processes specifically sanctioned by New Rule 4.16(1). As effectively argued by Associate Chief Justice John D. Rooke in his thesis, "JDR has now become an equal partner with adjudication in the Court's dispute resolution process."[12] It was not very many years ago that that statement would have been considered revolutionary.

CONSIDERATIONS IN CHOOSING A MINI-TRIAL

As a settlement technique, a mini-trial can be very effective in cases where a lengthy trial is anticipated,[13] the issues are complex, and there is not much factual dispute. It can reduce trial time to as little as a day, if

---

[10]   J.D. Rooke, "Improving Excellence: Evaluation of the Judicial Dispute Resolution Program in the Court of Queen's Bench of Alberta" (1 June 2009) at xxxiv, 5, 15, 113 and 221, online: Canadian Forum on Civil Justice <http://cfcj-fcjc.org/clearinghouse/hosted/22338-improving_ excellence.pdf>.

[11]   Alberta Courts <http://www.albertacourts.ab.ca>.

[12]   J.D. Rooke, "The Multi-Door Courthouse Is Open in Alberta: Judicial Dispute Resolution Is Institutionalized in the Court of Queen's Bench" (thesis for LL.M. in Dispute Resolution, University of Alberta School of Law, 2010) at 9-10, online: <http://cfcj-fcjc.org/clearinghouse/ hosted/22471-multidoor_courthouse.pdf>.

[13]   Ontario's informal guideline for consideration of mini-trials was that the trial was anticipated to last longer than a month.

successful. It is "off the record". Tailoring the process to the individual case by means of the pre-mini-trial conference is also a significant benefit to the parties. There are some critical differences between private and court mini-trials, which are highlighted in the following discussion. Where no differentiation is made, as in the preparation section, it is because none exists.

An example of a good candidate for a mini-trial is the dispute between a power generator and distributor, Hydro, and its customer, MCO, with whom it has a 50-year guaranteed power supply contract, the price to be renegotiated every five years. There are no timelines in the contract for the negotiations and no clear provision for retroactivity of the price level once it has been agreed to. Nor is there any process specified if negotiations break down. In years six to ten of the contract, there have been several power interruptions to MCO for unusual reasons apart from the weather, and, as well, MCO has been doing some re-engineering of its processes, which now require less power than previously. Because of the political and economic climate, both Hydro and MCO are under pressure. Hydro is dragging its feet in the negotiations because it likes the old pricing, and its negotiator, who is close to retirement, has been given very little authority to effect a resolution. MCO is extremely frustrated with the negotiator and with Hydro because it is losing money every day in very tight money times. As a pressure tactic, MCO brings a lawsuit against Hydro.

Both Hydro and MCO have legal departments, which become involved once the litigation is instituted. It quickly becomes apparent that both parties potentially have a great deal to lose, depending on how the court views the contract. Whatever the result, they would have to live with it for many years. Time is a problem because it would take two years to complete discoveries and two more to get to trial. An appeal would take a further two years. Also, the people involved in negotiating the original contract are at retirement age, and would not necessarily be available to testify when the time comes for trial. Even more troubling, the court's ultimate decision might not solve the parties' problem — how to arrive at a new price every five years.

After some discussion between their counsel, it is decided to immediately submit the dispute to a private mini-trial process. A very senior executive from each company would spend a day sitting on a panel with a respected mediator. They would hear from two witnesses, and one power costing expert from each side. The same executives would participate in the negotiations scheduled for the second day, and they would come with enough authority to agree to a resolution of the pricing issue, and a new process for determining the pricing for the remainder of the 50-year contract term. These provisions, along with a requirement for disclosure of key documents, and for confidentiality throughout, are set out in a mini-trial agreement. The mini-trial takes place within six weeks. With the assistance of the mediator, the negotiations conclude after two days with a settlement agreement. A month later, the parties have signed a contract revision governing price negotiations in the future. Not surprisingly, the contract contains a DR provision, to apply in the event that the future negotiations reach an impasse.

On the other side of the ledger is the expense of the mini-trial. There is significant preparation cost for the parties and their counsel. In court-connected mini-trials, the judge may call for agreed statements of fact, issues in dispute, witness summaries, legal briefs and argument. These add time and cost to the case if the resulting settlement discussions are unsuccessful. In the private mini-trial, there is the additional and significant cost of the time required for the senior executives to sit on the panel and to conduct the settlement negotiations. Balanced against that is the inherent flexibility of a private mini-trial, which can be scheduled at any stage of the dispute, and can involve as little or as much preparation or documentation as the parties choose, and specified in the mini-trial agreement. That flexibility to have an early-stage mini-trial, with a less formal process, can mean significantly less expense for the parties. On the other hand, even if a settlement is achieved after a court-connected mini-trial, because it comes late in the litigation process, the parties have incurred most of the cost of a trial, except the expense of the full number of trial days. For this reason, it is not generally used where small amounts are at issue.

Another consideration to be weighed in choosing a court-connected mini-trial is whether there are serious issues of credibility. Because the judge usually hears the mini-trial based on written summaries of the evidence, without seeing the witnesses, and without benefit of cross-examination, factual disputes cannot be resolved. The judge is asked to evaluate the case and to give an opinion as to how the case would likely be decided if it went to trial. Testing the credibility of witnesses is a very important function of the trial process, because, at the end of it, the judge imposes a decision on the parties that is determinative of their rights. If an assessment as to which witness is to be believed is critical to the resolution of a dispute, then a court-connected mini-trial is not the appropriate DR process.

Credibility as an issue is less of a concern in a private mini-trial, since the function of the executives who "hear" the case is not to decide who is right and who is wrong. Rather, the "evidence" stage of the mini-trial is to immediately *inform* the executives of the issues and positions, and to give them a first-hand look at the key witnesses for both sides *in preparation for* the negotiations which follow. Their first impressions of how the case might play out if it actually went to trial, will probably cause them to modify their approach to the negotiation in a variety of ways. However, since their goal is a resolution that is acceptable to all parties, and not an imposed decision as to who is "right", the credibility of one or more witnesses is only a background consideration.

Another factor to consider when contemplating a mini-trial is the nature of the case or dispute. For example, mini-trials can work very well in highly technical cases with fairly clear legal issues between parties who wish to preserve their business relationship. The process can also be effective where the technical nature of the factual disputes will require a battery of experts at trial. In Alberta, for example, the Court of Queen's Bench has found that mini-trials work exceedingly well in complex personal injury cases involving medical experts.[14] A private mini-trial should be considered when it is important, either for the business or for the case, for a very senior executive to focus on the issues raised by the dispute.

MINI-TRIAL PREPARATION

Marshalling the case for a mini-trial is virtually the same as preparing for trial. It will vary depending on the judge or private panel conducting the mini-trial, and on what is required by the mini-trial agreement, but will typically include the following:

- interviewing all major witnesses and preparing witness summaries;
- reviewing discovery transcripts and preparing index of references to be read to the judge/panel (where discoveries have been held);
- preparing key witnesses and/or experts to testify (where witnesses are to be heard);
- drafting a chronology of events for the judge/panel;
- compiling agreed exhibit books and demonstrative evidence;
- an agreed statement of facts and issues not in contention;
- finalizing expert report(s) and perfecting the understanding of the opinion(s) given;
- reviewing the opposing expert report(s) with experts, to understand the differences of opinion, and the possible reasons for those differences;
- researching and writing legal arguments with a supporting case brief for the judge/panel;
- outlining examinations of witnesses;
- preparing oral arguments; and
- developing a settlement strategy considering various outcomes of the mini-trial.

The aim of a mini-trial is to put forward a mass of material in a condensed form. The case must be boiled down to its essence, and that inevitably takes far more preparation time than the "throw every vegetable in

---

[14]   J.D. Rooke, "Improving Excellence: Evaluation of the Judicial Dispute Resolution Program in the Court of Queen's Bench of Alberta" (1 June 2009), Appendix 6 at 776, online: Canadian Forum on Civil Justice <http://cfcj-fcjc.org/clearinghouse/hosted/22338-improving_excellence.pdf>.

the pot" approach. To take a positive view, even if the mini-trial is unsuccessful at achieving a resolution, parties are fully prepared for trial, and all parties and their witnesses have had the advantage of a "dry run".

COSTS

None of the provinces using the mini-trial assess costs based on any measurement of success. The costs are treated as settlement assistance offered by the court without penalty or reward for outcome.

The question of whether the eventually successful litigant can recover costs for an unsuccessful mini-trial remains unanswered. Some or all of those costs may be recoverable as preparation for trial. In provinces with cost consequences for settlement offers that are similar to or better than the result at trial,[15] making an offer should be carefully considered at the conclusion of an unsuccessful mini-trial.

In private mini-trials, the issue of costs can be addressed in the mini-trial agreement. On the table for discussion should be the cost of the neutral advisor and the cost recovery attendant on success. If the mini-trial process results in a settlement, the parties may wish to bear their own costs. However, the parties could agree that if the mini-trial did not result in settlement, the successful party at trial would be entitled to the usual costs recovery, only if the result was better than the final offer following the mini-trial.

OUTCOMES

There is a dearth of hard data on the success rates of mini-trials in Canada. Very few have been held in British Columbia[16] or in Ontario, although anecdotal reports by counsel are positive. In Alberta, where the greatest number have taken place, as early as 1994, former Chief Justice Moore reported a high degree of success in complex cases.[17] Associate Chief Justice Rooke's evaluation of JDR in 2009[18] confirms success rates of 78 per cent in what are predominantly injury cases. He also notes that as a result of the settlements, "the trial time saved was the equivalent of a whole year of the Court's civil trial capacity, accomplished in ¼ of that time at JDR's".[19]

---

[15]   Rules of Civil Procedure, R.R.O. 1990, Reg. 194, R. 49.

[16]   K.M. Lysyk, *ADR Processes in the B.C. Courts* (Ottawa: Canadian Bar Association, March 1994).

[17]   R. Olson, "An Alternative for Large Case Dispute Resolution" (1980) 6 Litigation 22.

[18]   J.D. Rooke, "Improving Excellence: Evaluation of the Judicial Dispute Resolution Program in the Court of Queen's Bench of Alberta" (1 June 2009), Appendix 6 at 776, online: Canadian Forum on Civil Justice <http://cfcj-fcjc.org/clearinghouse/hosted/22338-improving_excellence. pdf>.

[19]   *Ibid.*, at vi.

The mini-trial as a dispute resolution process is still uncommon in the eastern provinces of this country, but in the West it is thriving. The court-connected model has its drawbacks in terms of cost and timing in the litigation cycle. Also, its focus on presenting to the judge diverts attention away from the goal, which is settling the case. However, the evolution of the Alberta court-connected mini-trial into the more flexible JDR, in many ways, overcomes those drawbacks. For the right case and the right parties, the mini-trial, whether it be private, court-connected or JDR, with its flexibility, confidentiality and relative informality, can provide an appropriate route towards settlement.

FUTURE DEVELOPMENT

We have noted above the evolution of traditional court-connected mini-trials in Alberta and British Columbia, in which the judge renders an opinion after the hearing, to affording the option of a judge-assisted negotiation following the opinion, to provide the parties with an expanded opportunity to settle their cases. Private or executive mini-trials do not end when an opinion is delivered. In fact, they may not involve an opinion as to the probable outcome of the case at all. The panel's task in the hearing phase is information-gathering. Once the facts are in hand, the parties' senior executives on the hearing panel shift immediately into negotiation mode, an accustomed role for them. There is no loss of focus on the settlement goal.

It is this private process that will likely increase in use as we become more familiar with the available dispute resolution choices. It is based on a mini-trial agreement, which can be tailored to meet the needs of the case. The best aspects can be borrowed from the court-connected model and may be combined with the best aspects of mediation. The neutral advisor may be used as a mediator. The mini-trial can be held early in the life of the dispute, before positions harden and relationships deteriorate beyond repair. The points in issue may be narrowed to the one or two needed to settle the case. Paper presentations may be limited or eliminated. This process has enormous potential.

What is appealing to parties in the private mini-trial is the redistribution of the power over the resolution of their dispute. It is not merely a forum for lawyers and judges to perform their usual roles. It is for the parties themselves to hear and form impressions of the evidence, and then to negotiate an informed solution. They will have assistance from counsel and the neutral advisor, but only if it is needed, and only on their terms. In the "Internet Age", in which people are more informed and demand more control over their own destinies, this will be a very viable dispute resolution option.

7

LEGAL CONCEPTS*

INTRODUCTION

As we write this chapter, there is no body of law in Canada pertaining specifically to consensual methods of dispute resolution. Instead, there are time-honoured legal concepts that the courts are adapting and applying on a case-by-case basis. This chapter will present some of these concepts in an elementary form and discuss how the law is emerging, especially as it applies to mediation.

This text is a practical handbook of a general nature as opposed to a legal textbook, so we do not pretend to be exhaustive or authoritative. As we mention in other chapters, it is wise to seek up-to-date professional advice should a specific matter or area of concern have legal implications.

PRIVILEGE

Background

The most salient legal topic is that of privilege, an evidentiary notion that identifies what can and what cannot be used as evidence in court. At first glance, privilege may not seem relevant to negotiation and mediation, because what a court will accept as evidence is not a paramount concern when litigation is not the first priority. However, the concept is important because it provides a protective envelope for settlement discussions to take place during these processes.

To understand privilege, one has to first appreciate that the courts generally receive all relevant evidence in order to have the broadest base of information from which to find facts. Privilege is an exception to this broad-based approach, and is therefore thoughtfully and cautiously carved out.

There are two kinds of privilege, class privilege and case-by-case privilege.[1]

---

* The authors acknowledge and thank Sam Posner of Posner Legal, Toronto for his legal research and contributions to this chapter.
[1] See *R. v. Gruenke*, [1991] S.C.J. No. 80, [1991] 3 S.C.R. 263 (S.C.C.).

Class Privilege

Class privilege concerns communications that occur in a very limited set of relationships, for example, between a lawyer and client or between spouses. If the relationship falls within an acceptable class (of which there are very few), communications within the class are assumed to be inadmissible, and cannot be disclosed or used in legal proceedings. Another term for class privilege is "absolute privilege".

Class privilege does not apply to consensual dispute resolution because the relationships between an individual and a mediator or between one negotiator and another do not fall within a traditionally recognized class. As a result, communications that take place during mediation or negotiation cannot be assumed to be inadmissible. They are only inadmissible if they fall within the second kind of privilege, case-by-case privilege.

Case-by-Case Privilege

As the name suggests, this kind of privilege depends on the facts and circumstances of any particular situation and it evolves one case at a time. The courts determine whether case-by-case privilege exists by applying a general framework called the "Wigmore test", which consists of four criteria. If the court concludes that all four criteria are satisfied, the communication in question is classified as privileged and therefore cannot be compelled, disclosed or used in evidence.

The four criteria in the Wigmore test can be colloquially stated as follows:

1. The communications must have been made in the belief that they would not be disclosed.

2. Confidentiality must be an essential ingredient of the relationship in question.

3. The relationship must be one that society is prepared to consciously and deliberately support.

4. Disclosing the communication would result in more harm to the relationship than benefit to the litigation.

By applying the Wigmore test, Canadian courts have extended case-by-case privilege to a variety of communications such as *bona fide* settlement negotiations in civil disputes or plea-bargaining in the criminal context.[2] The term "without prejudice settlement privilege" or simply "settlement privilege" has evolved from such cases.

---

[2]   For instance, see *R. v. Griffin*, [2009] A.J. No. 1445, 2009 ABQB 696 (Alta. Q.B.).

When people type the words "without prejudice" on their letters or announce that conversations are "without prejudice", they are invoking this type of case-by-case privilege. But the words alone do not have magical effect. Everything depends on the substance of the communication in question.

Settlement privilege, one subset of case-by-case privilege, protects oral and written settlement communication from disclosure or use in court (whether or not "without prejudice" is used) when the following conditions are met:[3]

- Litigation is in existence or within contemplation at the time the communication is made.
- The communication is made with the express or implied intention that it would not be disclosed to the court in the event negotiations fail.
- The purpose of the communication is to attempt to effect a settlement.

Applications for Settlement Privilege

Once the above conditions are satisfied, a person who wants to use privileged settlement material as evidence must show that it is relevant and that the disclosure is necessary.

Settlement privilege allows people to suspend the positional requirements of the adversarial system and openly discuss their concerns without fear that admissions and concessions made during those discussions will be used against them in litigation if they do not resolve their differences. It also lets them resume adversarial positions at a later date should litigation become necessary.

Settlement privilege provides a protective envelope within which settlement can be explored. Canadian courts respect this envelope because they recognize an overriding public interest in favour of settlement. Settlements achieved through direct negotiation or mediation spare litigants the aggravation and expense of trial and reduce the strain on the court system, thus conserving public resources.[4]

Mediation Privilege

As to the mediation process itself, Canadian courts have begun to recognize a "mediation privilege" using the Wigmore test and have classified communications during mediation as privileged whether the mediation is

---

[3]   See *Costello v. Calgary (City)*, [1997] A.J. No. 888, 209 A.R. 1 (Alta. C.A.) or *Inter-Leasing Inc. v. Ontario (Minister of Finance)*, [2009] O.J. No. 4714, [2010] 1 C.T.C. 177 (Ont. Div. Ct.).

[4]   *Kelvin Energy Ltd. v. Lee*, [1992] S.C.J. No. 88, [1992] 3 S.C.R. 235 (S.C.C.).

voluntary or mandatory. In October 2010, Ontario's Court of Appeal affirmed mediation as "an integral part of the civil litigation process in Ontario" and exempted from disclosure mediation materials prepared for a single mediation involving several civil actions, some of which were subject to mandatory mediation, some of which were not. The court stated, "There is no principled reason to treat mandatory and consensual mediations differently, when considering whether they are part of the litigation process."[5]

When deciding whether to protect a communication as privileged, courts have looked at the wording of the relevant agreement to mediate or, in the case of a mandatory mediation process, at the procedural rules of the court or tribunal.[6]

Courts have refused to compel the testimony of mediators[7] or to accept evidence from a mediator as to what occurred at a mediation session.[8] The mediator's evidence can, however, be admitted on the basis of Wigmore's fourth criteria, if there is a compelling social need for disclosure, for example, to protect children at risk from criminal activity.[9]

Questions of mediation privilege do not just concern the courts. They also concern arbitrators, agencies, boards and commissions. For instance, in 2009, Prince Edward Island's Information and Privacy Commissioner used mediation privilege to decide that a school district did not have to disclose records of a mandatory mediation concerning a dispute between a parent of a school advisory body and a principal.[10] In 2010, Ontario's Liquor Control Board was vindicated in its refusal to disclose the complete record of a mediated settlement relating to a mediation between the board and a private company.[11]

Continued Evolution

Settlement privilege and mediation privilege will continue to evolve as decisions emerge on a case-by-case basis. We did not find any Canadian cases that applied or adapted privilege to communications between an ombudsman and an individual, but this may simply be a matter of time.

---

[5]   *Ontario (Liquor Control Board) v. Magnotta Winery Corp.*, [2010] O.J. No. 4453, 102 O.R. (3d) 545 at para. 36 (Ont. C.A.).

[6]   *Delisser v. State Farm Mutual Automobile Insurance Co.*, [2004] O.J. No. 1399, 70 O.R. (3d) 774 (Ont. S.C.J.).

[7]   See *Rudd v. Trossacs Investments Inc.*, [2006] O.J. No. 922, 79 O.R. (3d) 687 (Ont. Div. Ct.) and *Sinclair v. Roy*, [1985] B.C.J. No. 3085, 20 D.L.R. (4th) 748 (B.C.S.C.).

[8]   *Porter v. Porter*, [1983] O.J. No. 2926, 40 O.R. (2d) 417 (Ont. Unif. Fam. Ct.).

[9]   *Pearson v. Pearson*, [1992] Y.J. No. 106 (Y.T.S.C.).

[10] *Eastern School District v. Prince Edward Island (Information and Privacy Commissioner)*, [2009] P.E.I.J. No. 45, 290 Nfld. & P.E.I.R. 282 (P.E.I.S.C.).

[11] *Ontario (Liquor Control Board) v. Magnotta Winery Corp.*, [2010] O.J. No. 4453, 102 O.R. (3d) 545 (Ont. C.A.).

CONFIDENTIALITY

Background

Confidentiality is another legal concept that contributes to the effectiveness of mediation. The law recognizes various kinds of oral and written communications as confidential and protects them from disclosure or imposes sanctions when disclosure is made without authorization.

A duty to keep communications confidential can arise when people consciously consider the issue and agree that their communications are private and off-the-record. This mutual understanding would be the case in mediation when, for example, participants sign an agreement to mediate that contains a confidentiality provision, or when they sign a memorandum of settlement that prevents disclosure of the settlement details.

Duties of Confidence

A written commitment or acknowledgment is not necessary. An obligation to respect confidentiality can be implied or deduced from the circumstances, such as when management invites employees to send commentary in an envelope marked "confidential"[12] or when commercial parties exchange sensitive industrial information in the course of negotiations.[13]

When there is a reasonable expectation of confidentiality, the recipient of restricted information has a duty not to use it for any purpose other than the one for which it was conveyed. A breach of confidence occurs if the information is misused, making the recipient liable to the one who conveyed the information. Canadian courts have imposed damages, resulting trusts and injunctions for breaches of confidence.

Application to Mediation Participants

Mediation participants can breach confidentiality by publishing, posting or otherwise using what was said or agreed to at mediation outside of the mediation process. Canadian courts are evolving various responses when such breaches of confidence occur, such as striking out parts of court documents, refusing to accept mediation communications in evidence and ordering removal of mediation details from a website.[14] To date, contempt of court has

---

[12] *Slavutych v. Baker*, [1975] S.C.J. No. 29, [1976] 1 S.C.R. 254 (S.C.C.).
[13] *LAC Minerals Ltd. v. International Corona Resources Ltd.*, [1989] S.C.J. No. 83, [1989] 2 S.C.R. 574 (S.C.C.).
[14] *Galileo Canada Distribution Systems Inc. v. Asian Travel Alliance Inc.*, [2005] O.J. No. 2127 (Ont. S.C.J.).

not been available as a sanction for compromising the confidentiality of mediation but the deliberate breach of a confidentiality agreement can be conduct relevant to a party's entitlement to costs.[15]

The law of confidentiality serves the same purpose in mediation as does the law of privilege in that it creates a safe container for settlement discussions to occur.

> Effective mediation requires freedom to freely and frankly discuss resolution including a variety of outcomes that may or may not mirror the outcome at trial. It is important that parties have the freedom to discuss strengths and weaknesses of their positions with the mediator and it is critical in order to foster such discussion that the information disclosed in mediation may not be misused.[16]

Canadian courts seem keen to promote the integrity of the mediation process. One decision notes that if mediation discussions are not protected from disclosure or if mediators are required to testify about the mediation communications, then those who have a choice will avoid mediation and those who must take part in mandatory mediation will simply treat it as a formality. In the court's view, this outcome would impede a laudable goal and the resolution of disputes effectively and fairly without the expense of trial.[17]

Application to Mediators

The above discussion focuses on mediation participants, but mediators themselves have a duty of confidentiality. This duty is based on expectations of confidentiality reflected in case-by-case decisions as well as on the promises made by mediators in written agreements to mediate.

It is not wise to assume that a mediator's duty of confidentiality is absolute. Mediators may be required to reveal otherwise confidential information if the mediator is subpoenaed or required to disclose by virtue of applicable legislation.[18] Although there have been no court decisions directly on point, it also seems likely that mediators would be obliged (legally and ethically) to disclose information to appropriate authorities when there is an imminent threat to human life and safety.[19]

---

[15]   *Rogacki v. Belz*, [2003] O.J. No. 3809, 67 O.R. (3d) 330 (Ont. C.A.), supp. reasons [2004] O.J. No. 719, 236 D.L.R. (4th) 87 (Ont. C.A.).
[16]   *Marshall v. Ensil Canada Ltd.*, [2005] O.J. No. 789, 10 C.P.C. (6th) 67 at para. 12 (Ont. S.C.J.).
[17]   *Rogacki v. Belz*, [2003] O.J. No. 3809, 67 O.R. (3d) 330 (Ont. C.A.), supp. reasons [2004] O.J. No. 719, 236 D.L.R. (4th) 87 (Ont. C.A.).
[18]   Such as child protection legislation.
[19]   *Smith v. Jones*, [1999] S.C.J. No. 15, [1999] 1 S.C.R. 455 (S.C.C.).

FAIR PROCESS

Background

Fair process is an evolving concept of administrative law. This body of law concerns how processes like arbitration and fact-finding should be governed.[20] It also concerns the procedural rules for agencies, boards or commissions created by legislation, as well as disciplinary bodies, churches and private clubs.

Existing Applications

Typically, fair process applies to individuals or bodies that carry out judge-like functions and decide people's rights, interests or privileges. It is based on the notion that those impacted by decisions should have the opportunity for input and a chance to influence the decision-making process. That process should be fair, impartial and open, and the individual or body making the decision should be non-partisan, open-minded, disinterested and independent. So important is fair process that when it is missing, a decision has no legal validity.[21]

In Chapter 8, "Arbitration", we outline the elements of fair process,[22] but it is worth repeating them here. The three basic aspects of fair process that pertain to a judge-like function are as follows:

1. The individual assuming the judge-like mandate must bring certain characteristics to the position. He or she must be:

    •   honest;

    •   even-handed as between the parties;

    •   detached and open-minded, willing to listen and be influenced by what the parties have to say without preconception or partisan motives;

    •   independent of the people and the issues; and

    •   free of personal interests that would interfere or conflict with the relevant mandate in any way.

2. In carrying out the judge-like mandate and serving the parties, the individual must:

    •   respect the boundaries of the assigned mandate by not investigating or deciding outside issues;

---

[20]   See also Chapter 8.
[21]   *Cardinal v. Kent Institution*, [1985] S.C.J. No. 78, [1985] 2 S.C.R. 643 (S.C.C.).
[22]   Other labels are procedural fairness and natural justice.

- refrain from delegating the work to someone else (such as an expert witness) or back to the parties themselves (such as by letting one of them evaluate or decide liability or remedy); and

- provide clear and cogent reasons for his or her decisions.

3.   The process in question should be organized and carried out in a way that gives no party an advantage or disadvantage. Specifically, it should ensure that:

- each side receives sufficient notice of any hearings;

- each side receives sufficient, timely and relevant information so that it is prepared to respond to the other side's case (or any issues raised by the individual performing the judge-like function);

- each side has an equal opportunity to present its case; and

- each side has an equal opportunity to rebut and/or challenge the other party's case.

Fair process is a flexible concept, however, and it changes its appearance according to the function and activities spelled out in the decision-maker's mandate,[23] which can originate in a statute, regulation, written agreement or position of authority. In her 2004-2005 report, the ombuds for Ryerson University illustrated this flexibility by means of a checklist for decision-makers who do not decide legal rights but who nevertheless exercise power or authority over others.[24]

The farther the decision-maker's mandate moves away from a judge-like function, the more relaxed the requirements of fair process will be. At the far end of the range, the duty will be minimal for a person who issues a report for use as evidence in an adversarial process. In such a situation, the report has implications for the rights of the parties but does not represent a final outcome. Furthermore, the parties still have a chance to challenge or rebut the report before it is used to reach a decision. To give fair process, the report writer may simply have to ensure that interviewees know the nature and purpose of meetings and are not misled in any way.

Different factors can influence what is required to discharge a duty of fairness including the importance of the decision to the person affected, the nature of the decision, how prejudicial the decision is, and any legitimate process expectations that participants had.[25]

---

[23]   *Imperial Oil Ltd. v. Québec (Minister of the Environment)*, [2003] S.C.J. No. 59, [2003] 2 S.C.R. 624 (S.C.C.).

[24]   See online: Ryerson University <http://www.ryerson.ca/ombuds/> and search for "Administrative Fairness Checklist for Decision-Makers".

[25]   See *Baker v. Canada (Minister of Citizenship and Immigration)*, [1999] S.C.J. No. 39, [1999] 2 S.C.R. 817 (S.C.C.).

Mediation Adaptations

Many aspects of fair process have been imported into consensual dispute resolution processes like mediation. For instance, a mediator is considered to occupy a neutral and impartial role and is expected to run an even-handed process. These expectations are nourished by the general discourse of mediation, by standards of practice developed by mediation associations and by the contractual obligations that mediators voluntarily assume. However, they do not amount to a common law duty of fairness because a judge-like function is missing from mediation. Mediators have neither public nor private authority to decide legal rights, and, accordingly, the rationale for a common law duty is absent.

Aspects of fair process are incorporated into mediation as a matter of philosophy and effectiveness, rather than law. Like confidentiality, these aspects are considered necessary ingredients of a credible, effectual process. Simply put, people need to place trust and confidence in a mediator and will not do so if the mediator gives preferential treatment to one party or if the mediator's words and actions convey self-interest, partisanship or closed-mindedness.

Continued Evolution

How the law of fair process will evolve is anyone's guess. Perhaps a different rationale will emerge and give rise to a refinement or unanticipated application. At the time of writing, however, we found no Canadian case that imposed a duty of fairness on a person or body carrying out the role of mediator or other similar mandate. A 1999 trial decision applied a duty of fairness to a public consultation process, but that decision was overturned on appeal because a judge-like function was not involved.[26]

MEDIATOR LIABILITY

Background

One would expect that like most service providers, mediators could be subject to lawsuits for negligence or breach of contract in respect of the performance of their mandates, but we were unable to find any reported cases dealing with mediator liability or immunity on any basis at the time of writing. Whether this is because of the absence of claims or the absence of trials, we cannot say.

---

[26] *Carpenter Fishing Corp. v. Canada*, [1997] F.C.J. No. 1811, 155 D.L.R. (4th) 572 (F.C.A.), leave to appeal refused [1998] 2 S.C.R. vi (S.C.C.).

Immunity of Experts and Arbitrators

Expert witnesses in civil, tribunal and arbitral proceedings are immune from suit by people whose only relationship with the expert comes from the judicial proceeding. This immunity exists to protect the integrity of the judicial process, not to benefit the witness, so that experts are not intimidated from testifying for fear of litigation. The protection extends to the expert's actions in collecting and considering material upon which the expert may later be called to give evidence. Arbitrators enjoy civil immunity too and for similar reasons. They cannot be sued for want of skill or negligence in making an arbitration award.[27]

No Mediator Immunity

It does not seem reasonable to expect that these kinds of immunity will be extended to mediators because they neither give expert testimony nor make legally binding decisions about people's rights. Mediation may have become a standard feature of the civil justice or tribunal procedures in some jurisdictions by virtue of mandatory mediation programs, but it is still materially different from the adversarial process. A mediator listens to what people have to say but does not decide the substance of the dispute or the outcome for them.

Mixed Mandates

Dispute resolution practitioners sometimes assume mixed mandates such as med-arb (where the same person sequentially mediates and arbitrates a dispute),[28] or pre-hearing mediation where an expert tries to bring the parties together before issuing an expert report, or even a combination of mediation, assessment and counselling. In such situations, matters of liability will be more complicated, and much will depend on how the mandate is characterized.[29]

Mixed mandates are a potential minefield of liability and should be undertaken with caution and clarity, because different dispute resolution processes create different expectations and have different practical or legal consequences for participants. If the dispute resolution practitioner is ignorant or confused about these differences, the participants are poorly served. For example, if the process blends mediation and investigation participants may let down their guard and be frank, only to find that the practitioner does not treat their concessions as privileged communications.

---

[27] *Sport Maska Inc. v. Zittrer*, [1988] S.C.J. No. 19, [1988] 1 S.C.R. 564 (S.C.C.).
[28] Med-arb is dealt with in more detail in Chapter 8.
[29] *Varghese v. Landau*, [2004] O.J. No. 370, 3 R.F.L. (6th) 204 (Ont. S.C.J.).

One of our colleagues shared an example directly on point. He was working with a complaint system where the people handling complaints carried out mixed mandates. They acted as investigators, mediators and informal facilitators of settlement discussions, and moved freely between these mandates without clarifying their role sufficiently with participants. In this ambiguous environment, those complaining and those complained about would share information candidly only to find that their remarks were later used for or against them when the complaint handlers changed roles. The resulting feelings of betrayal gave rise to many objections to the complaint handling system and could also result in legal liability. The law of fair process may well apply because in transitioning from mediators to investigators without warning or consent, the people handling complaints exposed the unwitting participants to prejudice.

CONCLUSION

Mediators sometimes have an uneasy relationship with the civil justice system. Although it is a source of paid work from those who want or need to settle, it arouses disapproval because it endorses an adversarial model, makes differences overt and tends to escalate disputes. And, to be fair, litigation can exact high monetary, emotional and opportunity costs.

Nevertheless, there are positive aspects to an open, publicly funded civil justice system and these can easily be overlooked or taken for granted.

The civil justice system articulates and evolves precedent. It articulates ideas and guidelines that are available to all citizens and can be used by everyone to govern their affairs. This has social significance and, as this chapter illustrates, helps consensual dispute resolution to develop in a thoughtful and principled way.

8

ARBITRATION

ARBITRATION — A COMPLEMENT TO MEDIATION

In 1996, when we wrote the first edition of *Bypass Court*, we confined ourselves to consensual methods of dispute resolution like interest-based negotiation and mediation which were in their infancy. We excluded arbitration because it was fairly well documented and understood. We were not motivated by a sense of disapproval of the arbitration process.

Fifteen years later, the time has come to make this a more complete handbook by integrating arbitration as another valid way for people to "bypass court". In the right hands, arbitration takes people to a final solution more directly and more assuredly than any other method, including everybody's favourite, mediation. Arbitration has momentum and moves towards a legally enforceable outcome with a minimum of outside interference. We tend to think of it as an impasse-breaking mechanism when consensual methods fail or are unsuitable.

In this chapter, our intention is to provide an overview of the arbitration process as it applies to Canadian civil disputes. This is not a legal text on the law of arbitration, nor is it a marketing piece that advocates for arbitration as a preferred dispute resolution process. We aim to be descriptive so that readers can see what arbitration involves and how it applies when consensual methods do not work. We will take a focused approach and give practical insights about the process based on our experience. However, we will not — indeed cannot — be exhaustive on the topic because arbitration has applications as disparate as spousal support, copyright contracts and malfunctioning farm machinery, and because Canadian courts continue to evolve the relevant law.[1]

ARBITRATION DEFINED

Arbitration is similar to civil litigation. It replicates the decision-making function of our public court system in a setting that is not open to the public. It is a private dispute resolution process where a person chosen by or for the parties (the "arbitrator") performs a judicial function. The arbitrator's mandate is to listen to and review presentations from the parties and to issue

---

[1] For this reason, always seek up-to-date professional advice should your topic or area of concern have legal implications.

a legally binding decision in favour of one or the other based on those presentations.

The mandate to serve as an arbitrator can be given to a single individual or to a group of individuals who work as a team, in which case they are called an arbitration panel. The arbitrator may or may not have subject matter expertise, and need not be a lawyer.

The parties' presentations to the arbitrator can take various forms, as will be discussed, but basically consist of facts and logical argumentation put forward in an effort to convince the arbitrator to rule in their favour. Before the presentations occur, the two sides prepare and exchange information about the issues to be decided, the positions they will take and what kind of decision they want the arbitrator to make.

The arbitrator leads everyone through the process in a fair and even-handed way and decides all issues of fact, law, process and evidence that emerge as the arbitration proceeds. At the end of the process, the arbitrator delivers a reasoned written decision that finally resolves the stated issue between the parties by imposing an outcome on them. This final decision on the merits is called an "award". Decisions on matters relating to the conduct of the arbitration are not awards but, rather, are called procedural orders or directions.

All of the arbitrator's decisions (final awards and procedural orders or directions) can be enforced through the court system, but procedural orders and directions cannot be appealed or otherwise challenged in court. In practical terms this means that once the arbitration train starts moving, it does not stop for bystanders or supervisors until it reaches its destination.

Because it replicates many features of civil litigation, arbitration is often a comfortable forum for lawyers trained and experienced in court work. Their backgrounds can be an advantage, because knowing how to organize and present a compelling case to an arbitrator is necessary for effective participation in the process.

From a participant's point of view, the purpose of arbitration is not to compromise or negotiate a settlement agreement but to win a favourable ruling from the arbitrator. Thus, arbitration is a contest and can quite properly be characterized as an adversarial process (not to be confused with an antagonistic one). In an adversarial process, each side advances its own position to the best of its abilities and tries to undermine or weaken the other side's position, all with a view to convincing the arbitrator to find in its favour.

There are many kinds of adjudication (before tribunals, for instance) but to be classified as arbitration, the process should concern a dispute of a civil nature. It cannot be a form of discipline or way to enforce organizational standards. A hearing that imposes a fine or sanction on someone for failing to meet a standard or live up to a constitutional requirement may not be arbitration, even though it employs the same hearing procedures as arbitration.[2] Unless a dispute resolution process is properly characterized as arbitration, the summary enforcement procedures in provincial or territorial arbitration legislation are not available to enforce the outcome.[3]

UNLIKE CIVIL LITIGATION

Although they are close cousins, arbitration must be distinguished from civil litigation in a number of important ways.

Arbitration is voluntary for the participants. Unlike the civil litigation process, one side to a dispute cannot unilaterally compel the other to engage in arbitration; both sides must agree to use the process. Their agreement may occur before a dispute has arisen (in which case it is a future dispute resolution clause) or once the dispute has actually come into being. The parties can even agree that they will not commence a lawsuit unless and until they have been through the arbitration process. The arbitration clause in Figure 8-1 does this.

The arbitration process is fluid and adaptable and the parties tend to have a higher level of participation in shaping the process than they would in a standard court proceeding. As discussed below, if they agree the parties can set mutually convenient timelines and vary the hearing modality to suit personal preference and case demands.

Once the parties have consented to the arbitration process and given the arbitrator a mandate, the arbitrator can impose the process as well as the outcome because the arbitrator is now the captain of the ship. For instance, the arbitrator can direct when and how an oral hearing will occur or if, indeed, an oral hearing is necessary. The parties have the right to input along the way but they do not enjoy the final say, and it is this feature that makes arbitration so appropriate to resolve intractable disputes. No party has a veto or unilateral control, and the momentum of the process carries them inevitably towards a final resolution. Once the vessel leaves port, it continues to its destination under the arbitrator's direction, whether the passengers are homesick, lovesick or seasick. The only way to stop the journey is for the claimant or plaintiff to withdraw its claim or the parties to jointly agree to bring the trip to an end.

---

[2]   See *Universal Workers Union (Labourer's International Union of North America, Local 183) v. Ferreira*, [2009] O.J. No. 639, 95 O.R. (3d) 118 (Ont. C.A.), leave to appeal refused [2009] S.C.C.A. No. 163 (S.C.C.).

[3]   For the necessary components of arbitration, see also *Sport Maska v. Zittrer*, [1988] S.C.J. No. 19, [1988] 1 S.C.R. 564 (S.C.C.).

Arbitration involves out-of-pocket costs not required in a publicly funded court system. In arbitration, the parties are paying the professional fees of the arbitral tribunal plus related expenses like room rental charges and court reporting fees. These expenses are all in addition to the one-sided costs that parties normally bear in litigation such as the fees and expenses of their lawyers or expert witnesses.

As a general rule, arbitration is confidential, meaning that the public does not observe, participate in or even have the means to know that it is taking place. Arbitration occurs behind closed doors and this troubles some people for at least two reasons. First, it means that a system of justice exists that is excluded from public discourse and scrutiny (arbitration awards do not tend to be the subject of editorials or media reports). Second, it can mean that large and powerful institutions avoid public accountability by treating claims (such as product liability cases) as one-off occurrences that are resolved privately, in isolation from other similar claims.

Confidentiality prevents the outcome of the arbitration process from being shared beyond the parties unless they expressly dispense with this level of privacy or accede to an industry practice or convention where awards are routinely published. For instance, the Sport Dispute Resolution Centre of Canada[4] routinely publishes awards rendered by its arbitrators in amateur sport cases.

And finally, in contrast to civil litigation, private arbitration can apply principles and standards other than legal ones depending on the issue, the industry and or the parties' inclinations. The law is the standard that the arbitrator applies by default but the parties can change this by explicit or implicit agreement.

Arbitration may but need not apply the law or involve findings of fact that are based in evidence. For instance, final-offer arbitrations to set the price of agricultural commodities can involve unsworn, competing economic arguments from producers and processors. The arbitrator sets the price that will apply to all transactions of purchase and sale in a given time period by selecting the unit price proposed by one party over the unit price proposed by the other party. This selection is based on the logic of the parties' presentations, not on the law.

CONTEXT COUNTS

Arbitration is used in different contexts and has many permutations and combinations, so the above generalizations may not apply. Always check for special laws, rules, protocols or practices that govern any particular arbitration process because there may be important features or even prohibitions. In

---

[4]   See online: <http://www.crdsc-sdrcc.ca>.

Quebec, for instance, arbitration is not permitted for family disputes,[5] whereas in Ontario family disputes can be arbitrated but special rules must be followed if the award is to be enforceable. Ontario's rules impose a front-end screening process on the participants, prohibit the waiver of appeals on questions of law, and require the substantive law to be applied.[6]

Many other contextual differences exist. Labour arbitration awards are published, followed and cited from one case to another whereas the standard commercial arbitration award has no precedential value or public distribution. The Canadian Motor Vehicle Arbitration Plan specifically states, "The arbitrator is not bound by any similar decision set out in any other award made by an arbitrator under this program."[7]

The point is simple but significant — context counts.

GOOD CANDIDATES FOR ARBITRATION

People who participate in arbitration must accept it as an adversarial process (not unlike a formalized debate) that results in a final, legally binding and enforceable award. They must also be prepared to surrender control of the process and the outcome to the arbitrator.

Arbitration requires a form of commitment not present in consensual dispute resolution processes. In mediation, one can toy with ideas and test out potential solutions. One can entertain contradictory positions, explore hypotheses and change one's mind as the process unfolds. Not so with arbitration. Arbitration involves a presentation with a purpose — convincing the arbitrator. It is not a process where ideas and arguments can be put forward without consequences because everything submitted to the arbitrator counts. This aspect of the process suits some people and some disputes very well.

Since arbitration comes with costs and consequences, it ought to be approached intelligently and with good faith. It is not a vehicle to spin out a dispute or to create delay or obfuscation. To be sure, an arbitrator can correct or control these tendencies if they exist in one or both parties, but every intervention by an arbitrator imposes direct out-of-pocket costs on the parties. The more cooperative the parties are able to be, the more economical the arbitration will be.

In our view, good candidates for arbitration will have the following five general characteristics:

---

[5]   See the *Civil Code of Québec*, S.Q. 1991, c. 64, s. 2639.
[6]   See various provisions in the *Arbitration Act, 1991*, S.O. 1991, c. 17 and the *Family Law Act*, R.S.O. 1990, c. F.3.
[7]   See online: <http://www.camvap.ca>.

1.   Good candidates wish the dispute to come to an end as soon as is reasonably possible. They want or need to minimize the negative costs and consequences of the dispute, such as out-of-pocket expenses, opportunity costs and wasted emotional energy. Good candidates for arbitration are not motivated by the desire to delay or thwart resolution. Nor do they need to prolong a negative connection with the other side. If they have such motives, they can control or suppress them.

2.   Once the arbitrator is selected, good candidates are willing to respect the arbitrator's authority and to abide by the arbitrator's rulings and judgments. In other words, they do not have serious control issues and are not over-invested in the dispute.

3.   Good candidates can cooperate with each other to move the process forward even though there is a serious issue outstanding between them. They are willing and able to voluntarily exchange relevant documents, set and adhere to appropriate timetables and meet their process obligations in a timely fashion. They readily grant reasonable adjournments and extensions to each other when the circumstances support them. Good candidates stand up for their positions but do not unnecessarily antagonize the other side.

4.   Good candidates for arbitration value economy and efficiency and are open to doing things differently if it will move the dispute towards resolution and reduce the resources required. They do not simply default to an oral hearing on the merits because that is most familiar mechanism for them. They will, for example, use affidavits and will-say statements to shorten the time for oral testimony.

5.   And finally, good candidates are prepared to take the time necessary to analyze the dispute and identify just what the arbitrator should be deciding. Such candidates can frame a meaningful and useful question for the arbitrator to decide from issue to issue and stage to stage. They are willing and able to put together an organized and compelling presentation to help the arbitrator decide each issue as efficiently as possible. They use the arbitrator intelligently. They do not simply delegate a mass of disorganized information to the arbitrator in the expectation that the arbitrator will figure it all out.

GETTING ARBITRATION STARTED

There are three basic pathways to arbitration. This dispute resolution process can be reached by means of: 1) a future dispute resolution clause; 2) an *ad hoc* agreement; or 3) a statute.

1.   Future Dispute Resolution Clauses

Businesses and individuals can prospectively agree to use arbitration if a dispute arises between them at a later date and these agreements are known as future dispute resolution clauses. The word "future" is used because at the time the agreement is made, no dispute is in existence. Such clauses can stand on their own, but usually they are part of a bigger agreement that governs the relations or undertaking between the parties such as a licence, distribution agreement, contract for services, or partnership agreement.

Future dispute resolution clauses do not represent an *option* to use arbitration; they embody an *obligation* to do so once a dispute arises because access to the civil courts will be denied if such a clause has been signed. What happens is that if one of the signatories starts a lawsuit for something that is supposed to go to arbitration, the other signatory can go to court and obtain an order "staying" or stopping the lawsuit.[8] As one Canadian court recently noted, the "modern approach" is to require the parties to adhere to their choice and to view arbitration as an autonomous, self-contained and self-sufficient process, presumptively immune from judicial intervention.[9] This judicial attitude is based on some standard assumptions about the autonomy and freedom of contract that the parties enjoy, assumptions that may not apply to consumer contracts, as discussed below under the heading "Mandatory Consumer Arbitration".

Future dispute resolution clauses can be used in almost any context. Figure 8-1, below, is an adaptation of a clause setting out the arbitration mandate given to one of the authors in a shareholders' dispute. Figure 8-2 is an adaptation of a mandatory clause in a Request for Proposals for international mediation training. That clause refers to rules for international arbitration which are outside the scope of this chapter, but it nevertheless shows the use of a future arbitration clause to achieve a final resolution of a dispute that cannot be settled by agreement.

We offer these clauses as illustrations from the real world of arbitration, but we do not endorse or promote them as model clauses.

Figure 8-1: Shareholders' Agreement Arbitration Clause

If any dispute or controversy shall occur between the parties hereto relating to the interpretation or implementation of any of the provisions of this Agreement, such dispute shall be resolved by arbitration. A single arbitrator shall conduct such arbitration. The

---

[8]   Virtually all provincial arbitration Acts contain a provision that gives the court discretion to stay a lawsuit in the face of an agreement to arbitrate, and the courts do not hesitate to exercise this discretion.

[9]   See *Griffin v. Dell Canada Inc.*, [2010] O.J. No. 177, 2010 ONCA 29 at para. 28 (Ont. C.A.), leave to appeal refused [2010] S.C.C.A. No. 75 (S.C.C.).

arbitrator shall be appointed by agreement between the parties or, in default of agreement, such arbitrator shall be appointed by a Judge of the Ontario Superior Court of Justice sitting in the City of Toronto upon the application of any of the said parties, and a Judge of the Ontario Superior Court of Justice sitting in the City of Toronto shall be entitled to act as arbitrator, if he or she so desires. The arbitration shall be held in the City of Toronto. The procedure to be followed shall be agreed to by the parties or, in default of agreement, determined by the arbitrator. The arbitration shall proceed in accordance with the provisions of the *Arbitrations Act* (Ontario). The arbitrator shall have the power to proceed with the arbitration and to deliver his or her award notwithstanding the default by any party in respect of any procedural order made by the arbitrator. It is further agreed that such arbitration shall be a condition precedent to the commencement of any action at law. The decision arrived at by the board of arbitration, howsoever constituted, shall be final and binding, and no appeal shall lie therefore. Judgment upon the award rendered by the arbitrator may be entered in any court having jurisdiction. The arbitrator shall determine who is responsible for paying the costs of the arbitration.

Figure 8-2: Request for Proposals Arbitration Clause

Any dispute or difference arising out of, or in connection with this contract or the breach thereof which cannot be amicably settled between the parties through Alternative Dispute Resolution (ADR) procedures, if any, as may be agreed to by the parties, shall be arbitrated in accordance with the UNCITRAL Arbitration Rules[10] as at present in force. The arbitration shall take place in Vancouver, Canada. Any resulting arbitral decision shall be final and binding on both parties. Judgment upon any arbitration award may be entered in any court having jurisdiction thereof. Such judgment shall be in lieu of any other remedy. In resolving a dispute hereunder, the parties agree that the contract will be interpreted in accordance with the substantive laws of the province of British Columbia, Canada.

2.   Ad Hoc Dispute Resolution Agreements

The parties can commit to using the arbitration process once a dispute has arisen. They can do this for a one-off civil dispute such as an action for wrongful dismissal or they can sign on to an industry-specific program designed for particular disputes. Examples would be the Sport Dispute Resolution Program of Canada, which was developed to resolve disputes in

---

[10]   See online: United Nations Commission on International Law <http://www.uncitral.org>.

amateur sports, or the Canadian Motor Vehicle Arbitration Plan,[11] which was developed to resolve warranty and defect allegations for automobiles and light trucks.

3.   Miscellaneous Statutes

The parties may have either an option or an obligation to use arbitration to resolve disputes within the purview of certain legislation. One example can be found in Part 10 of the *Strata Property Act*[12] of British Columbia, which permits the arbitration of disputes between strata corporations and owners or tenants, including disputes concerning the common property or common assets. Another example can be found in a regulation made under the *Farm Products Marketing Act*[13] of Ontario that enables the Ontario Farm Products Marketing Commission to appoint an arbitrator to resolve negotiating impasses between the producers and the processors of agricultural products.

There are various ways to get an arbitration process started. Most provincial or territorial arbitration legislation provides for the commencement of arbitration by delivery of a written notice that identifies the dispute and demands arbitration or requests the appointment of an arbitrator. There is no prescribed form of notice. This means that to commence arbitration under the clause in Figure 8-1, one of the shareholders would have to invent and deliver a written commencement notice.

Strata corporation arbitrations are also commenced by written notice, but one that has a legally prescribed form called "Notice Beginning Arbitration". The standard notice is supposed to describe the dispute and propose either an arbitrator, a choice of arbitrators or a method for appointing an arbitrator. A party receiving a strata corporation form must respond within two weeks with a Notice of Reply.

In contrast to the previous two examples, arbitration under the Canadian Motor Vehicle Arbitration Plan is commenced when a consumer completes and delivers a standardized claim form to the plan's administrator. The automobile manufacturers and importers who subscribe to the plan have all signed an omnibus agreement to participate in arbitration once a completed claim form is received. The completed claim form triggers the appointment of an arbitrator by the plan's administrator and starts the time running for the manufacturer's response to the claim.

These few examples reinforce the caveat that context counts. Always check for specifics that govern or guide any particular arbitration process.

---

[11]   See online: Canadian Motor Vehicle Arbitration Plan <http://www.camvap.ca>.
[12]   S.B.C. 1998, c. 43.
[13]   R.S.O. 1990, c. F.9.

MANDATORY CONSUMER ARBITRATION

Mandatory arbitration clauses often appear in consumer contracts such as for the sale of electronics, telecommunications services or credit cards. These clauses are relatively easy to find if you have a magnifying glass or strong pair of reading glasses; simply check the fine print in a purchase contract or read the online terms of sale when buying goods and services over the internet. They tend to appear in situations where vendors are in a position to unilaterally impose the terms of doing business with them.

Mandatory consumer arbitration clauses oblige consumers to take individual claims (pre-existing, present or future) against vendors to binding arbitration, and prohibit them from using the civil courts for individual law suits or class actions. This is contrary to the notion of voluntariness which is one of guiding principles of the International Organization for Standardization in ISO 10003:2007, a standard for dispute resolution external to organizations.[14] According to this standard, consent to participate in a dispute resolution process should not be required when individuals purchase or use goods, property or services for personal or household purposes.

Mandatory consumer arbitration can confer a benefit on vendors because it may inhibit consumer claims. Such claims often have a monetary value that is much lower than the time, money and aggravation required to pursue them against an entity with superior economic resources. Low value claims are likely to make sense only if they are aggregated in the form of a class action where claimants can pool resources and benefit from economies of scale. But mandatory consumer arbitration clauses prohibit class actions, and there have been several court decisions upholding that result. When low value claims must be arbitrated, similar claims against the same company are resolved in a legally binding way, privately and in isolation from one another.

This whole topic is in flux however, and no blanket statements can be made about the state of consumer arbitration clauses at this time. At least two Canadian provinces have used consumer protection legislation to prohibit mandatory consumer arbitration clauses and maintain consumers' access to the civil courts, so up-to-date legal information is once again important. Interested individuals should learn how to search e-laws for current legislation and bills, or consult someone who knows how to do so.

---

[14]   For more on ISO 10003:2007, see "International Complaint-Handling Standards" in Chapter 9, "Complaint-Handling and Ombuds".

DOCUMENTING THE ARBITRATOR'S MANDATE

An arbitrator's jurisdiction is unlikely to be found in a single, exhaustive document. More often than not, it comes from a combination of documents plus the applicable arbitration legislation. In many disputes, it is customary for the parties to expand the document that initiates the process and create more detailed terms of reference that add to or limit the arbitrator's authority. These documents take different forms and bear different names including agreements to arbitrate, rules of arbitration, rules of procedure and specialized rules for a specialized programs. Their purpose is to clarify the nature and scope of the arbitrator's powers as they pertain to the parties and the particular issue in dispute.

While some people like to have the arbitrator's mandate contained in a single, tidy document, this is not always practical or advisable. One of the authors handled a civil arbitration that occurred in stages. At the end of the day, her mandate derived from the cumulative effect of the following: 1) a future dispute resolution clause; 2) a written agreement to arbitrate; 3) a supplementary agreement found in correspondence between counsel; 4) a scattering of email exchanges; and 5) the relevant provincial arbitration statute.

1.   Agreements to Arbitrate

As private arbitrators, we tend to use customized but fairly simple agreements to arbitrate that identify the specific issue or issues we are mandated to decide, and add provisions of significance to the parties such as the authority to award or apportion the costs of the arbitration. Of course, participants, counsel and arbitrators differ as to the amount of detail they prefer in an agreement to arbitrate, and you will find many different precedents if you research the matter further. Figure 8-3 below lists potential topics to include in such an agreement.

2.   Arbitration Rules of Procedure

Another approach is for the parties to adopt a set of pre-existing rules such as the National Arbitration Rules of the ADR Institute of Canada[15] or the Maritime Arbitration Rules of Procedure of the Association of Maritime Arbitrators of Canada.[16] These rules are likely to be detailed and address all manner of issues that might arise during the course of arbitration regardless of the likelihood of their occurrence. The advantage of using a set of rules is

---

[15]   See online: ADR Institute of Canada <http://www.adrcanada.ca/rules/arbitration.cfm>.
[16]   See online: Association of Maritime Arbitrators of Canada <http://www.amac.ca/rules.htm>.

that it promotes a comprehensive and consistent approach to the arbitration process.

3.   Specialized Terms of Reference

There are many specialized arbitration programs developed for particular businesses, industries or callings. These are apt to have standardized documentation, including rules of practice, that govern all program arbitrations in a consistent way. A number of these programs are intended to handle customer complaints against providers of goods and services such as the arbitration program of the Investment Industry Regulatory Organization of Canada, which is a national self-regulatory organization that oversees investment dealers and trading activity on debt and equity marketplaces in Canada. That program uses specialized procedural rules for arbitrations that deal with claims of up to $100,000.00.[17]

Many topics can be covered in the detailed terms of reference for arbitration, and the suggestions in Figure 8-3 are by no means exhaustive. In addition, there is no standard way to deal with any topic. Take, for example, No. 5: Confidentiality. The arbitration process may be completely closed to non-parties and decisions may be kept private. Alternatively, the process may be open to observers and decisions can be published electronically or in print.

For No. 7: Costs, one option is for the parties to bear their own costs with a flat division of the costs of the arbitral tribunal. Another option is for them to give the arbitrator the discretion to allocate costs according to the results in the case. A third option (in the case of a specialized program) is for costs to be underwritten by the industry or group setting up the program so that users bear minimal or no costs.

We are not advocating that any particular topic or treatment apply to all arbitrations because of our conviction that "context counts". The terms of reference should meet the needs of the people and the problem involved, and one size does not fit all.

Figure 8-3: Potential Topics for Terms of Reference

1.   Identity of plaintiff (claimant) and defendant (respondent) and order of presentation.

2.   Identity of arbitrator(s) and method of appointment.

3.   Issues or questions to be put to arbitrator.

---

[17]   The rules vary with the program administrator. See online: Canadian Commercial Arbitration Centre <http://www.cacniq.org/en/arbitrage-specialise-consommateurs.php> and ADR Chambers <http://adrchambers.com/ca/arbitration/specialized-services/IIROC/>.

4. Arbitrator's jurisdiction (general and specific) and any limitations such as ceilings on monetary award or restricted remedies.

5. Confidentiality of proceedings and outcome.

6. Time limits and scheduling.

7. Costs — components (arbitrator's fees and expenses, other costs associated with process) and allocation; whether the arbitrator has the power to award or reapportion costs.

8. Nature and forms of evidence (sworn or unsworn), including affidavits, admissions, agreed statements of fact, expert reports and taking a view.

9. Finality of process; whether rights of appeal.

10. Pre-hearing disclosure/discovery and documentary exchanges including identity of witnesses and proposed testimony.

11. Hearing modalities (oral, electronic, other) and specifics, including need for court reporter or translators.

12. Hearing logistics — date, place, time, duration.

13. Interim and final awards, including due date, format, content and reasons.

14. Pre-judgment interest.

15. Settlement, offers to settle and how offers are to be used in assessing any costs.

PROVINCIAL OR TERRITORIAL ARBITRATION LEGISLATION

Every Canadian province or territory has legislation that governs the arbitration process for Canadian arbitrations and that serves as an additional source of an arbitrator's authority. A competent advocate or participant in an arbitration process will have a passing familiarity with, if not a working knowledge of, the relevant legislation. This is advantageous because the legislation:

• provides a general code for the conduct of the arbitration process as it pertains to both the parties and the arbitrator, including practical things like how to get the process started or what to do if the parties do not agree on the arbitrator. To the extent that the legislative code is not modified by agreement, it applies to the arbitration and will often provide an answer to procedural issues arising during the arbitration such as what happens if the parties settle their dispute or if the claimant withdraws the claim mid-process;

• generally codifies the practical and ethical obligations of the arbitrator who is obliged to treat the parties equally and fairly and who can be challenged for bias. The legislation often indicates whether an arbitrator can assume the role of a mediator during the arbitration process;

- sets out the level of supervision (judicial review) to be undertaken by the courts with respect to the arbitration process, and identifies which level of court is responsible for that supervision;

- provides for appeals from arbitration awards where the court concerns itself with the merits of the case as opposed to the arbitration process. The legislation indicates whether appeals are optional or mandatory and, if optional, tells how to ensure that appeals are included or excluded;

- contains provisions for how to enforce an arbitrator's orders and awards if these are not obeyed; and

- incorporates reference to other pieces of legislation that apply to the arbitration process.

The up-to-date text of the various arbitration statutes can easily be located online so there is no barrier to consulting the appropriate arbitration Act.[18]

FAIR PROCESS

In order for the private process of arbitration to have credibility, it has to be fair in appearance and fact. This is generally accomplished by applying the elements of procedural fairness derived from administrative law. What follows are three basic aspects of procedural fairness that apply to arbitration.

1. The individual assuming the mandate must bring certain characteristics to the office of arbitrator. He or she must be:
    - honest;
    - even-handed as between the parties;
    - detached and open-minded; willing to listen and be influenced by what the parties have to say without preconception or partisan motives;
    - independent of the people and the issues; and
    - free of personal interests that would interfere or conflict with the arbitrator's mandate in any way.

2. In carrying out the mandate and serving the parties, the arbitrator must:
    - respect the boundaries of the mandate set by the parties (decide all matters within the mandate and no matter outside the mandate);

---

[18]   See online: Canadian Legal Information Institute <http://www.canlii.org>.

- refrain from delegating the work to someone else (such as an expert witness) or back to the parties themselves (such as by letting one of them evaluate or decide liability or remedy); and
- provide clear and cogent reasons for his or her decisions.

3. The arbitration process itself should be organized and carried out in a way that gives no party an advantage or disadvantage. Specifically, it should ensure that:

- each side receives sufficient notice of any hearings;
- each side receives sufficient, timely and relevant information so that it is prepared to respond to the other side's case (or any issues raised by the arbitrator);
- each side has an equal opportunity to present its case; and
- each side has an equal opportunity to rebut and/or challenge the other party's case.

The purpose of these elements is to create and sustain a process in which both sides can have confidence regardless of the outcome on the merits. An arbitrator is responsible to ensure that the arbitration process is characterized by fairness whether or not the arbitrator has legal training.[19] One Ontario judge captured this obligation succinctly, as follows:

> It is settled law that the right to a fair hearing is an independent and unqualified right. Arbitrators must listen fairly to both sides, give parties a fair opportunity to contradict or correct prejudicial statements, not receive evidence from one party behind the back of the other and ensure that the parties know the case they have to meet. An unbiased appearance is, in itself, an essential component of procedural fairness.[20]

THE STANDARD ADVERSARIAL PATTERN

Arbitration is an "adversarial" process that proceeds like an orderly debate with people taking turns to make presentations. Arbitration hearings often replicate courtroom procedures that are used by opposing lawyers who present contested facts and arguments to a judge. This sounds more formal and intimidating than it needs to be, so we will devote a few paragraphs to simplifying the format.

Adversarial process is like a three-step dance where the steps are *point*, *counter-point* and *reply*. This simple pattern repeats itself over and over in a standard arbitration, and is very easy to follow once it is recognized.

---

[19]   See *Kainz v. Potter*, [2006] O.J. No. 2441, 33 R.F.L. (6th) 62 (Ont. S.C.J.), where the process was conducted by a psychologist.

[20]   *Hercus v. Hercus*, [2001] O.J. No. 534, [2001] O.T.C. 108 at para. 75 (Ont. S.C.J.).

Typically, the initiator of a step (the claimant, moving party or objector) gets to go first and explain to the arbitrator why its position should prevail. This is "Point". Then the opposite party (respondent, defendant, responding party) goes next and has a chance to explain why its position should prevail instead. This is "Counter-point". After that, the initiator gets another chance, not to repeat or embellish its first presentation but to respond to anything raised by the opposite party in its presentation. This is "Reply".

It is worthwhile knowing this pattern because it applies when the parties make oral or written presentations to the arbitrator. It can reliably be used any time a contested issue or point of difference is under consideration, for it is a tried and true way to ensure that the process is fair. So, the parties can follow a three-step pattern to (i) make submissions about the format of the hearing; (ii) manage the exchanged expert reports; (iii) present evidence; or (iv) argue over the allocation of costs. Figure 8-4 shows the choreography of an oral hearing based on this three-step format.

Of course, the pattern need not be slavishly followed and we do not wish to be understood as saying that arbitration simply replicates the courtroom behind closed doors. It does not.

We compare learning the basic pattern of arbitration to mastering the fundamentals of drawing the human form; depicting a realistic human face should precede Picasso-like abstractions. Once the basics are mastered, the trick with arbitration is to recognize when the standard pattern serves the parties well and when it can be modified or dispensed with.

Circumstances will prompt modifications in the interests of efficiency and economy. For instance, the parties could deliver expert reports simultaneously instead of doing so sequentially according to the standard pattern. Fairness will still be served by giving each side a right of response and reply — but at the same time and on the same schedule. This kind of modification can reduce the time needed to complete any particular step in the arbitration process.

Figure 8-4: Conventional Oral Hearing

Conventional Arbitration Hearing Oral Evidence			
[Authors' Note: The parties can use this to present all or part of their cases on the merits. See text for alternative modalities.]			
	CLAIMANT	**RESPONDENT**	**CLAIMANT**
OPENING	What I intend to prove. What I intend to convince the arbitrator of.	What I intend to prove. What I intend to convince the arbitrator of.	N/A

		[*This occurs immediately after claimant's opening or just before respondent's case begins.*]	
EVIDENCE	**N.B.:** CLAIMANT'S CASE GOES IN FIRST. Witness #1 • Examination in chief • Cross-examination • Re-examination *[limited to new matters raised in XE]* Witness #2 • Examination in chief • Cross-examination • Re-examination Witness #3 • Examination in chief • Cross-examination • Re-examination END OF CLAIMANT'S EVIDENCE. CLAIMANT CLOSES ITS CASE. RESPONDENT BEGINS CASE.	**N.B.:** RESPONDENT'S CASE GOES IN AFTER CLAIMANT'S CASE. Witness #1 • Examination in chief • Cross-examination • Re-examination *[limited to new matters raised in XE]* Witness #2 • Examination in chief • Cross-examination • Re-examination Witness #3 • Examination in chief • Cross-examination • Re-examination END OF RESPONDENT'S EVIDENCE. RESPONDENT CLOSES ITS CASE.	*[Right of reply limited to calling evidence to meet issues raised by respondent that claimant could not anticipate.]*
ARGUMENT	How the arbitrator can pull all of this together to find in my favour.	How the arbitrator can pull all of this together to find in my favour.	*[Reply limited to argument that could not have been anticipated before respondent's argument was made.]*

STAGES OF THE ARBITRATION PROCESS

Each arbitration looks different because it is shaped by the personalities and preferences of the people involved, by the nature of the issues in dispute and by the available resources. Nevertheless, the process will pass through three stages depicted in Figure 8-5, namely, the Pre-Hearing, Hearing and Post-Hearing stages. These are arranged like a sandwich with the filling being the substantive stage where the main issues are argued and decided. Unlike mediation where the stages are circular or iterative, arbitration tends to be fairly linear with the stages progressing sequentially.

1.   Pre-Hearing Stage

The pre-hearing stage is the initial phase when the parties and arbitrator come together and clarify their respective roles and duties. It is at this stage that a formal agreement to arbitrate will be signed and the format of the arbitration worked out. If the format is not specified in the agreement for arbitration or if there is dispute about it, the parties make submissions to the arbitrator who sets the format by means of an arbitrator's direction.

The pre-hearing stage also includes all of the supporting and preparatory activities that bring about a hearing for the main, substantive issues. It is here that the parties exchange information about their respective positions, proposed evidence, relevant documents and preferred outcomes. The notion is to put everyone in a position to intelligently deal with the main issues in the next stage.

2.   Hearing Stage

The second stage of a typical arbitration is akin to a trial in a civil proceeding using the three-stage format discussed above. This is where the parties present their evidence and arguments to convince the arbitrator to rule in their favour. The central contest or a debate occurs at this stage.

We use the term "hearing" but stress that this need not be an oral hearing like the one depicted in Figure 8-4. The format will depend on the specifics of the case and should produce the most efficient and economical way to put the necessary facts and arguments before the arbitrator. In some cases, the arbitrator may never convene the parties in a face-to-face meeting because all information is exchanged electronically or in hard-copy written form. It is neither possible nor advisable to be prescriptive as to the format of a hearing because many options are possible based on the circumstances of each case.

If the main issue in the case simply involves competing interpretations of a clause in a contract or the application of a definition to an uncontested set of facts, this is an entirely appropriate case to be done in writing. A documentary hearing makes sense. The parties can make written submissions as to their varying interpretations and applications, and the arbitrator can have the option of convening the parties in person, by telephone or email if further questions arise.

But suppose the issue in the case is, "Did she resign or was she fired?" in circumstances where that question can only be answered by parsing contested recollections of who said what to whom at a series of meetings. Here, a documents-only hearing would be pure fantasy. To determine the issue, the arbitrator has to be able to assess the competing evidence of the people who were at the meetings. But here again, there are options. One option is a full-blown oral hearing with live witnesses who walk through examination in chief, cross-examination and re-examination. An alternative option is to substitute sworn affidavits for examination in chief with the witnesses being available in person for cross-examination.

The point is that this second stage of arbitration need not be a standard meat-and-potatoes hearing with live testimony. It can be as creative and flexible as the parties and the arbitrator wish it to be, subject to the constraints of fair process.

One of the authors completed a lengthy arbitration concerning the dissolution of a business relationship, and only a small fraction of the proceedings were in person. The arbitration took place in phases and much of it was accomplished means of written submissions and rulings. An oral hearing was only needed to resolve factual issues around disputed conversations. In order for the arbitrator to determine the facts, the evidence went in through books of documents and affidavits. Any witness who swore an affidavit was made available for live cross-examination, but only if opposing counsel requested it.

3.   Post-Hearing Stage

The third stage of an arbitration may be minimal or non-existent, but we include it here because it represents duties and responsibilities that survive the release of a final award. Most provincial and territorial arbitration statutes let the parties ask the arbitrator for an explanation at this stage even though the arbitrator would otherwise have exhausted the arbitration mandate. The statutes also give the arbitrator the power to correct errors and injustices caused by an oversight on the arbitrator's part, and this can be triggered by a request from one of the parties or on the arbitrator's own initiative.

Figure 8-5: Stages of Typical Civil Arbitration

1. PRE-HEARING STAGE	
CONTRACTING	• Initial contact with arbitrator
	• Preliminary Meeting (in person or conference call)
	• Agreement to Arbitrate
	• Arbitrator's Procedural Directions

PREPARATION	• Pre-hearing production, disclosure, cooperation • Pre-hearing Motions • Arbitrator and party preparation for hearing stage
2. "HEARING" STAGE	

PRESENTATIONS ON MERITS	• Arbitrator's opening (if oral hearing)
	• Preliminary Issues (if any)
	• Parties' Presentations — varies according nature of case and issues in dispute. Can include:
	   – Oral testimony (sworn or unsworn)
	   – Live cross-examination
	   – Written interrogatories or discovery transcripts
	   – Requests to admit
	   – Affidavits
	   – Videoconferencing
	   – Agreed statements of fact
	   – Agreed books of documents
	   – Oral submissions
	   – Written submissions

DECISION ON MERITS	• Arbitrator's Award with reasons
PRESENTATION ON COSTS	• Parties' Presentations — varies according to case. See above.
DECISION ON COSTS	• Arbitrator's ruling with reasons
3. POST-HEARING STAGE	
• Request for explanation • Correction of errors	

THE SELF-REPRESENTED PARTY

There is no requirement that people have to have lawyers to participate in arbitration, just as there is no obligation to hire a lawyer in order to go to court but the self-represented individual brings challenges to the process.

In theory, arbitration participants should not expect special treatment if they choose to represent themselves. In practice, however, they place a burden on the arbitrator who has to be fair and even-handed toward all while at the same time extending an extra level of guidance to the inexperienced participant. This extra guidance can include directing a participant away from irrelevancies, focusing the participant's presentation, instructing the participant on how to question witnesses, or even taking over the questioning.[21] It can also extend to providing an experienced but self-represented participant with an adjournment to subpoena a live witness when the participant thought that a notarized letter would be sufficient evidence.[22]

The problem is that these additional interventions on the part of the arbitrator may conflict (in fact or in appearance) with the general rule that an arbitrator is not an advocate or opponent for any person, cause or outcome. The general rule is easy to state in the abstract, but much more challenging to apply in practice. There is no clear line indicating where reasonable assistance ends and advocacy begins. Moreover, even if the arbitrator's interventions are well-founded and well-motivated, they may not be perceived that way by the person on the opposite side of the case. This can result in allegations of bias and challenges to the outcome of the process.

This can be a no-win situation, so rather than wrestle with ambiguity and take on additional risk or inconvenience, some arbitrators turn down mandates involving self-represented parties. But this looks at arbitration through the eyes of the dispute-resolver. What about the participants' vantage point?

If an arbitration occurs pursuant to an organized program, the program can acknowledge and assist self-represented individuals by means of education and pre-arbitration support. (Private arbitrators can do this too but out of their own resources.) The point is to educate participants before entry into arbitration and then to help them prepare properly in advance of a hearing. Waiting to do this until participants appear before the arbitrator is too late.

The first step is a voluntary and informed consent to arbitration. This would seem to entail a level of knowledge and understanding about the process and its potential outcomes before the process is agreed to. ISO 10003:2007, referred to in the section on Mandatory Consumer Arbitration,[23] suggests that voluntary consent should be predicated on information that covers the arbitration process, the arbitrator's mandate, the criteria used for decision-making, the possible remedies and whether the participant gives up the right to go to court. To our knowledge, no Canadian court or other authority has provided a comprehensive list of factors to be taken into account when evaluating a party's consent to arbitration.

---

[21]   See *Jimenez v. Azizbaigi*, [2008] B.C.J. No. 2067, 2008 BCSC 1465 (B.C.S.C.).

[22]   *Griffin v. O'Brien*, [2006] O.J. No. 88, 263 D.L.R. (4th) 412 (Ont. C.A.).

[23]   See "International Complaint-Handling Standards" in Chapter 9, "Complaint-Handling and Ombuds".

Arbitration programs deal with the possibility of self-represented participants in different ways. The Sport Dispute Resolution of Canada provides participants with contact information for a list of lawyers with experience in amateur sport. It also publishes its arbitration awards so that participants can see the kinds of issues that are raised, the kind of evidence and argument that an arbitrator finds compelling and what kind of outcomes he or she might expect.

The Canadian Motor Vehicle Arbitration Plan does not publish arbitration awards or provide a list of lawyers, but it has educational resources like guidebooks to help people decide if the program is for them and to assist in preparing for a hearing. In addition, program users can access the periodic bulletins issued to arbitrators so that they can educate themselves about practical program issues and best practices. During the process, the arbitrator has the ability to order a technical expert to assist in the resolution of the dispute at no cost to the consumer.

ARBITRATION VARIATIONS AND MED-ARB

Up to this point, we have been discussing binding arbitration, where binding means an adjudicative process with a legally enforceable outcome. But other variations exist such as non-binding arbitration, arbitration-mediation (arb-med), and mediation-arbitration (med-arb).

1.   Non-Binding Arbitration

Non-binding arbitration is a dispute resolution process that produces an advisory outcome, one that the parties carry out on a voluntary basis. They cannot be compelled at law to obey or fulfill the arbitrator's decision, so they still maintain a high degree of control over the dispute. The process leading to the decision can be a formal hearing like the one in Figure 8-4 above, or it can be more akin to a mediation that results in recommendations from the mediator after an interest-based discussion with the parties.

One of the authors chaired a panel in a non-binding arbitration involving a dispute between a chartered bank and one of its business customers. The other panelists were a representative of the bank and a representative of the customer. At the end of the process, the panel made unanimous recommendations for how the dispute could be resolved, taking into account the interests of both parties, but it had no power to impose its recommendation on either side. The recommendation gave the participants a way to save face and break the impasse in their dealings if they really wanted to alter the status quo.

2.   Arb-Med

Arb-med is an interesting but potentially expensive process. In this process, the parties engage the same person to arbitrate their dispute and subsequently to mediate between them. An arbitration hearing takes place first and the arbitrator renders an award in the usual way, but the award is sealed and the parties do not know what it says. Then, the arbitrator changes into a mediator. If settlement is reached at mediation, the arbitration award is destroyed without being disclosed. If settlement is not reached, the arbitration award is published and the parties are legally bound by the arbitrator's decision.

At this time, the authors do not have any personal experience conducting arb-med, but one of our colleagues advises that he has successfully completed such a mandate and that in his view, apart from the up-front costs, it is preferable to med-arb, below, because it eliminates concerns that the arbitrator was unwittingly or improperly influenced by compromises and admissions made during settlement discussions.

3.   Med-Arb

No chapter on arbitration would be complete at this time without a reference to med-arb. As the hyphenated name suggests, this is a hybrid of mediation and arbitration. It is a process that gives a single person a sequential mandate of mediation followed by arbitration. The parties initially try to resolve their dispute through mediation conducted by one individual. If they do not succeed, they transition to arbitration and the same individual leads the arbitration process and decides how the dispute must be resolved.

Parties can always decide to arbitrate their dispute if mediation does not bring about a resolution, but med-arb is different from the voluntary choice of arbitration once mediation is over. Med-arb involves agreeing to one individual to conduct both processes in sequence so arbitration is mandatory, not optional if mediation does not produce a settlement. Med-arb is a process that has been recognized and enforced at law.[24] It should therefore be chosen thoughtfully.

The med-arb defined in this section sounds elegantly simple, but it is a concept that has generated as much emotional reaction as mediation did when it first appeared on the civil scene. Concerns about med-arb include: 1) whether it is humanly possible for a single individual to transition from a free-flowing process like mediation to a focused process like arbitration without becoming partisan; 2) whether private communications between the mediator and one of the parties at mediation will create a perception of bias;

---

[24]   See *Marchese v. Marchese*, [2007] O.J. No. 191, 219 O.A.C. 257 (Ont. C.A.).

and 3) whether it is wise for parties to make concessions and admissions to a mediator who will later be in a position as arbitrator to use those to the disadvantage of the disclosing party.

As with all other dispute resolution processes, we do not advocate for med-arb; we recognize it as an option. In light of the concerns raised about the process, however, we do offer the following suggestions to strengthen the integrity of the process and the individual carrying out the med-arb mandate:

- Make sure that the mediation and arbitration stages are distinct and are sign-posted so everyone is clear at all times which process is being used. Do not allow the mediator (or the parties) to casually move from one process to another and back again, at will. This is because each process requires different competencies, expectations and behaviours. Arbitration requires notice and fair process, for example, to make sure that the competing parties have an even-handed opportunity to put their cases before the arbitrator and to challenge or rebut the positions of the other side. This level of formality is necessary because arbitration (unlike mediation) decides peoples' rights.

- Have specific terms of reference for each stage to reinforce clarity of roles and responsibilities according to process.

- Explicitly announce/confirm each stage of the process and the transition from mediation to arbitration. Indicate when and by what means the mediation stage will end such as by express agreement of the parties, on the expiration of a pre-set time period, or on the pronouncement of the mediator.

- Take time to frame the issues for decision for the arbitration stage. They may not necessarily be the same as the issues at the mediation stage — in fact, it is better if they are not. The issue for decision could be an altogether different one or a subset of the issues discussed at mediation. For instance, at mediation, the parties could discuss, "How will we dissociate and wind down our joint businesses?" But at arbitration, the question might be, "Was the partnership validly dissolved? By what means?", or "How do we value the assets? Who gets what?"

- Consider inserting a formal break (hours, days, weeks) between the mediation stage and the arbitration stage, depending on the time constraints imposed by the issue in dispute. This emphasizes the end of one stage and the beginning of another. It also gives time to properly frame an issue for decision and allows each side time to prepare for the hearing on the merits.

- Use a neutral person with a working knowledge of both mediation and arbitration. This will ensure that the parties are led through an appropriate process at each stage (as opposed to an improvised one). Furthermore:

- The mediator should bring well-established attitudes and habits of mind to listen to people without judgment or partisanship in the mediation stage, and to elicit trust and confidence by conveying this to people.

- The arbitrator should understand how to find facts and write reasoned awards on the basis of proven evidence using objective analysis. Through intellectual rigor, the arbitrator will expose the evidence on which the decision was based and show that partisan tendencies played no part in the arbitration.

- Give this joint mandate to a person known and respected for their personal integrity. The stronger the parties' confidence in the individual, the more smoothly the process will go.

- If practical and feasible, conduct the mediation in plenary (joint) session only in order to eliminate one-on-one communications with the mediator that could later give rise to accusations of bias.

- Consider prohibiting the mediator from giving any opinions or views about the merits of the parties' cases during the mediation stage on the grounds that if the mediator does not express any view, he or she cannot be accused of pre-judging the case as arbitrator.

Med-arb has its proponents and its detractors, and each has its reasons. As this hybrid process gains more acceptance and use, additional wisdom will arise to refine and adapt the thinking and attitudes towards it.

9

COMPLAINT-HANDLING AND OMBUDS

INTRODUCTION

A complaint is an expression of discontent made in anticipation of a response. When a complaint is not resolved to the satisfaction of the person making or receiving it, the complaint becomes a dispute. Complaint-handling therefore represents fertile ground for the application of dispute resolution activities, skills and principles. In this chapter, we will look at these and discuss some specific complaint-handling initiatives.

We will sweep with a rather broad brush and will look at many sorts of complaints including those made by customers, end-users and employees. Where appropriate, we will add observations or examples from our own experience. But please be warned: there are as many ways to handle complaints as there are complaint types, and readers will probably have ideas, opinions and experiences that exceed what this chapter contains. If this encourages respect for complaint-handling and advances the topic, so much the better.

WHAT IS COMPLAINT-HANDLING?

Complaint-handling means having a predictable system to receive, process and respond to complaints made to any provider of goods or services, including a provider of employment. Whether that system is straightforward or elaborate, it will involve four basic stages:

Intake — how complaints enter the system, are assessed for validity or impact, and assigned to an appropriate person, level or process.

Enquiry — how the relevant facts are collected so that there is an objective basis for responding.

Analysis — looking at and determining what the facts mean and what, if anything, should be done about them.

Outcome — taking (or not taking) action on the complaint, together with appropriate communication and file-closing activities.

These sequential stages are (or should be) common to all complaint-handling systems, but each system will be unique because it is influenced by variables such as context, available resources and the philosophical preferences of those who develop or endorse the system.

A complaint-handling system can be internal, external or both. For instance, Canadian automobile manufacturers publish company-specific internal procedures for complaints in vehicle warranty booklets or owner manuals. A dissatisfied purchaser must exhaust these internal procedures before being able to use the external arbitration program sponsored by the industry for consumer defect and warranty claims.[1]

The general principles and commentary in this chapter apply to internal, external and hybrid systems for the handling of complaints.

PEOPLE VERSUS PROBLEMS

A complaint-handling system should be designed and operated to address the fundamental aspects of all complaints, namely the "people" aspects and the "problem" aspects.

The people aspects have to do with how people feel as a result of making a complaint or being the recipient of a complaint, and what measure of humanity is incorporated into the system. Do people feel respected and listened to? Was the process fair? Does the outcome make sense and seem valid on its face? Was the complaint welcomed as a source of information about products and services? Or did the complaint-handling system give the impression that complaints are a nuisance or inconvenience?

The problem aspects of complaint-handling concern the subject matter of the complaint, what it is about and what can or should be done about it. These tangible parts will vary according to the subject matter of the complaint and the parameters of the system. Sometimes a problem cannot be addressed because the complaint does not have merit, or the problem is outside the purview of the complaint system or even outside the purview of the organization.

THE IMPORTANCE OF COMPLAINT-HANDLING

In late 2009 and early 2010, one of Canada's major transit systems experienced growing pains when members of the public refused to recognize its complaint-handling system as credible or responsive. Public concerns about fare increases, service levels and discourtesy reached a tipping point. People with complaints started bypassing existing avenues of input in favour of social networking sites. Relations with the public became further strained when a few individuals photographed transit employees on the job and held them up to ridicule or contempt by posting the images on the internet.

---

[1]   See online: Canadian Motor Vehicle Arbitration Plan <http://www.camvap.ca>, s. 4.3.7 of the program's Agreement for Arbitration.

This escalating situation concerning public transit illustrates the importance of a customer-focused complaint-handling system that is seen as trustworthy. Ours is a culture of entitlement. Individuals expect their concerns to be taken seriously and addressed promptly by those with control, power or authority, no matter what the area of concern: public transportation, consumer goods, food products, religious rites and rituals, policing, medical or dental care, financial disclosure, or the closing of a local swimming pool. Perceived failure to listen and respond can result in swift and wide-spread retribution.

Over and above societal expectations, there is a pragmatic reason to maintain a reliable complaint-handling system. When purchasers or users of goods and services complain, they give the provider information that it does not already have concerning satisfaction levels. When a credible system is not in place to capture and constructively respond to complaints, the organization loses the opportunity to analyze the input and decide what improvements or adjustments to make. Moreover, the organization still has a dissatisfied user or customer with the capacity to magnify dissatisfaction by communicating and associating with like-minded people. A complaint-handling system cannot prevent individuals from using self-help remedies or control the many forms of electronic communication, but it can offer an effective alternative if it is responsive.

In *A Complaint Is a Gift*,[2] authors Barlow and Moller argue that complaint-handling should be a strategic business tool because complaints essentially amount to free market research. They maintain that businesses and organizations should thank complainants for the gift of this information and cultivate constructive attitudes and procedures to respond to complaints.

Fortunately, the transit system referred to above recognized both the dangers and the opportunities inherent in its public relations problem. It began several initiatives to examine the relationship between its riders and workers with a view to improving customer satisfaction. One initiative was the appointment of an independent "Customer Service Advisory Panel" composed of 10 members of the public with diverse business, customer service and social advocacy backgrounds. The panel spent six months collecting feedback from transit riders, employees and members of the general public, and issued a public report. Many of the report's recommendations are being implemented.[3]

---

[2]   J. Barlow & C. Moller, *A Complaint Is a Gift* (San Francisco: Berrett-Koehler, 2008).

[3]   For the report and other information about this scenario, visit <http://ttcpanel.ca>.

COMPONENTS OF A CREDIBLE COMPLAINT-HANDLING SYSTEM

Organizations that invest in genuine complaint-handling systems want them to be seen as trustworthy and reliable by all concerned. The following eight factors will contribute to such positive perceptions. They apply to a wide range of situations and complaint types:

1.   Emotional Intelligence
2.   Ease of Access
3.   Fair, Defined Process
4.   Objectivity
5.   Understandable Outcomes
6.   Reliable Fact-Finding
7.   Appropriate Confidentiality
8.   Organizational Support

1.   Emotional Intelligence

Complaints are essentially human problems. One person is trying to communicate to another that a system or undertaking failed to deliver as promised or imposed some form of harm or inconvenience. Something motivates the complainant to come forward, a desire for redress, a wish to be heard, a hope for acknowledgment, the prospect of compensation, or an attempt to level the playing field, perhaps.

Making a complaint takes effort and energy and, as a general rule, a complaint is not a happy event for complainants or recipients. People may not be "at their best". They can be aggressive, reactive, self-absorbed, defensive, confused, upset, angry and more. Their capacity to listen and use logic may even be impaired. An effective complaint-handling system recognizes this and does not respond in kind. Instead, it projects genuine openness, empathy and concern. By taking people seriously and treating them with courtesy, the system lowers people's emotional arousal instead of increasing it.

There is a relationship between how people are treated and their level of satisfaction with a complaint-handling process.[4] One of the authors waited some months to complain about how a course instructor treated her after a death in the family. The instructor had asked the author to return the course materials and leave the class unless she could stay for the whole five-day course. The author withdrew, as requested, but nursed a persistent grudge

---

[4]   See also the three dimensions of fairness at page 232.

until she was able to arrange a telephone call with the business owner to discuss what happened.

The owner was the person in charge of customer relations but had no advance notice of what the author was going to say. During the initial stages of the call, the owner simply listened. When the author finished describing her experience and its impact, the owner spontaneously said, "Wow! That's sure not how I would want things to be handled in a situation like that." The owner then invited further discussion about what had happened, what redress the author was looking for and how such a situation could be avoided in the future. The owner indicated what could and what could not reasonably be done all these months later. There was no defensiveness.

After a 30-minute conversation, the matter was resolved to the author's satisfaction without any compensation or tangible consideration being provided. The conversation itself and the owner's attitude and approach comprised a sufficient response.

Respectful listening is not the only way for a complaint-handling system to convey responsiveness. Care and concern are also shown when people are provided with adequate and appropriate information in a timely fashion. Personal respect is embedded in this level of accountability.

If a complaint is found to have merit, an appropriate official should initiate corrective action and communicate with the relevant people to let them know what is happening, when and why. If a complaint is found to lack merit or is outside the scope of the complaint-handling system, that too should be communicated together with an adequate explanation.

People tend to draw negative conclusions when they are not given timely and appropriate information. They fill in the blanks themselves to draw an unflattering picture of the other person, group or company. They may become tenacious and escalate their efforts to gain redress. Anecdotally, we have heard about numerous lawsuits being initiated against hospitals and health care providers by family members who were not told what really happened in the medical treatment of a loved one. Often, the family members assumed that there was a cover-up to protect the hospital or doctor, and/or resented the use of power to deny them access to pertinent information.

Health care providers and their insurers are learning the value of voluntary disclosure and are developing protocols to provide timely and forthright information to family members. The practical result of such pre-emptive responsiveness and care is a reduced number of lawsuits.[5]

---

[5]   For an interesting initiative, see online: Sorry Works! <http://www.sorryworks.net/default>.

2.   Ease of Access

Making a complaint should be straightforward. People should easily be able to find out where and what to do when they want to make a complaint. The complaint-handling system does not need to dominate a company's website, intranet or literature, of course, but relevant information in an accessible format should be within reach when individuals want to communicate their concerns.

A few years ago, one of the authors wanted to raise a concern with her telephone service provider, but nothing on its website pointed to a complaint process, and direct telephone contact was impractical due to automated voice messaging and extended wait times. The author was only able to register a complaint by investing time in research. Eventually, she located a list of senior executives on the company's website (with no contact information) and guessed at identifying the appropriate person. Then she composed and mailed a letter to that person using the company's general mailing address, detailing her the problem and its consequences. A less motivated person would have given up, which might have been the company's intent, but the author's persistence resulted in monetary compensation for the inconvenience identified in her letter.

There are multiple ways for people to make complaints — in person, in writing, by email, by telephone — and the system should choose formats and methods that make sense in the circumstances. One would be more likely to make an oral complaint directly to the retailer if a new steam iron was defective, whereas a complaint alleging fraud or professional misconduct would be more appropriately put in writing to the proper regulatory authority. It all depends on resources, needs and intentions. The authors know of one customer complaint-handling system that is inaccessible by telephone so that potential complainants are forced to put their concerns in writing. But other systems invite complaints in any way that people find convenient.

If a special application form is required for the complaint-handling system, it should be easy to get and to understand. The need for back-up information to start the process should be clearly communicated. If someone will be in touch to obtain more information, that should be spelled out too.

Not every complaint is a proper or relevant one, so it is entirely appropriate for the complaint-handling system to include a screening process to exclude complaints that do not meet the system's criteria. However, the screening process should not form an undue barrier to entry. One complaint-handling system within our knowledge prohibits entry to potential complainants until the target of the complaint gives its approval. This is not a program design that we endorse.

A complaint system is not easy to access when the relevant constituency does not know about it. Some measure of publicity and outreach is required. If a complaint-handling system exists but is archived in someone's credenza, it may not even be a genuine complaint system.

Lack of publicity is not uncommon when it comes to complaint-handling systems. In 2009, one Canadian ombuds canvassed various agencies, boards and commissions to learn their complaint procedures in order to be in a position to make appropriate referrals. Some of those canvassed did not respond at all. Others responded to say that they had established systems, but that these were not publicized or updated. The ombuds who initiated the enquiries observed that lack of reliable contact and intake information impeded her ability to make appropriate referrals for potential complainants.

3.   Fair, Defined Process

A complaint-handling systems can be based on a single dispute resolution process such as arbitration or a combination of the different processes covered in this book. Some systems use a "progressive" approach and move a complaint through steps that are increasingly more authoritative and determinative.

At the first stage of a progressive system, people may have to try to resolve the complaint through direct interaction such as discussion between an employee and a direct supervisor or between a customer and a service provider. This would be a negotiation stage.

If negotiation does not succeed, the next step may involve an objective individual who tries to facilitate a voluntary resolution. This would be a mediation or facilitation stage.

After that, the peak of the notional pyramid in a progressive system may consist of an individual or organization with the mandate to impose an outcome or make a written recommendations with a view to finally resolving the complaint. The ultimate decision-maker in the final stage could be a senior manager, an outside arbitrator or an industry ombuds. This final stage would be an adjudicative or decisional stage.

Potential complainants (and those who are impacted by complaints) need to know what process or combination of processes the system uses, and in what order, as well as what each process involves. This allows potential complainants to make informed choices about whether to initiate a complaint and invest the required time and effort. It also promotes fair process in that participants know what their roles and responsibilities are.

There are a number of ways (including websites, intranet, brochures and telephone personnel) for a complaint-handling system to publish or distribute details about its chosen process(es), the roles and responsibilities of the various people involved in each process, the scope and range of authority given to any decision-maker, and the criteria used to reach an outcome (law, policy, standards, *etc.*). A straightforward process can be conveyed through well-formatted hard or soft text. For a more complex process, a flow chart may be advantageous.

In addition to being publicized and understandable, a credible complaint-handling process will be fair in fact and appearance. In this context, fairness has three aspects or dimensions: procedural, substantive and relational.

Procedural fairness has to do with how decisions are made or outcomes reached such as the steps to be followed before, during and after the outcome.[6]

Substantive fairness has to do with the substance of the complaint (what it concerns) and the extent to which the outcome adequately addresses that substance.

Relational fairness reflects the emotional intelligence of the system. It concerns how people are treated during the complaint-handling process and how they feel about both the process and the outcome. Relational fairness includes an individual's sense of being respected and his or her reaction to the information and explanations provided by the system. Many of the examples we give in this chapter illustrate the importance of relational fairness.[7]

The three dimensions of fairness tend to address the people aspects of complaints and are conveyed through a collection of attitudes and activities such as:

- approaching the complaint with an honest intent to resolve it in an interest-based way;[8]

- giving the person making the complaint and the person complained about full, fair and equivalent opportunities to participate;

- conveying respect and attention to the people involved;

- ensuring that complete information is obtained before deciding what to do about the complaint;

- clearly explaining outcomes before the process is undertaken as well as at the end; and

---

[6]   See also "Fair Process" in Chapter 7.

[7]   For more about the three dimensions of fairness, see Manitoba Ombudsman, "Understanding Fairness: A Handbook on Fairness for Manitoba Municipal Leaders" (2009) at 6, online: <http://www.ombudsman.mb.ca/pdf/Understanding%20Fairness%20Web%20Report.pdf> and the course materials from "Dealing with Unreasonable Complainant Behaviour" (October 7, 2010), presented by Chris Wheeler, Deputy Ombudsman, New South Wales, Australia and sponsored by the Forum of Canadian Ombudsman.

[8]   See Chapter 2 for more about interests.

- being timely and keeping people informed of the progress of the complaint.

The process adopted by the complaint-handling system should offer a level of formality that is appropriate to the situation. The higher the stakes, the more formal or legalistic the process may need to be, giving each party notice and a chance to present its version of events.[9] As always, context counts. A complaint about slow service in a restaurant would obviously not bear the same gravity or call for the same level of fair process as a complaint that a hospital administered the wrong blood type to a patient.

If the complaint-handling system uses progressive dispute resolution stages like those described above, participants must know how and when to transition from one phase to another. The transition should not be controlled by one of the participants. This may sound obvious but one of the authors reviewed a system that included a mandatory negotiating stage. It was in the interests of one constituency to move the matter forward but in the interests of the other to hold back because the next stage involved out-of-pocket expenses. Participants routinely disagreed about completion of the negotiation stage and when to move to the next stage, but the system lacked an impartial way to break such impasses. The author provided several options to improve the system such as removing the monetary incentive for delay, automatically moving the matter to the second stage after a specified period of time, or eliminating the mandatory negotiation stage altogether.

It goes without saying that any complaint process should have milestones and timelines so that a complaint is processed as quickly as possible. Unavoidable or unanticipated delays should be explained to the person complaining and, where applicable, the person complained about.

4.   Objectivity

Objectivity is the hallmark of credible complaint-handling and promotes confidence in the system. It includes a constellation of attributes such as impartiality, detachment, even-handedness, openness, and the absence of subjectivity or bias. When a system is objective, complaints are received, handled and addressed on their merits in a non-partisan way.

Personnel who handle complaints will manifest objectivity through their attitudes and non-partisan behaviours. For instance, they will be indiscriminately courteous and helpful to all participants. They will follow the mandate, as established, and not create exceptions to satisfy participants with influence, status or power.

---

[9]   For the elements of fair process, see Chapter 7, "Legal Concepts" and Chapter 8, "Arbitration".

But the personal attributes of complaint-handling personnel are not sufficient to ensure that the system is objective. The design of the system including its governance structure must also support and protect objectivity. For instance, the system should be free of incentives that would cause personnel to favour one constituency over another. And those who fund or sponsor the system should not be able to influence or direct the day-to-day handling of complaints.

Everyone who works or comes in contact with the complaint-handling system should understand the importance of objectivity, and safeguards should be in place to preserve it.

One of the authors reviewed a complaint about the fairness of a staff selection process pursuant to an established complaint-handling protocol in a workplace. The manager who led the impugned selection process had no supervisory role to play in the author's review, but he was anxious to vindicate himself and attempted to elicit progress reports and make off-the-record submissions by means of private telephone calls to the author. The manager was well-intentioned but did not appreciate or understand the independent nature of the author's non-partisan mandate and how that related to the integrity of the process and outcome of the complaint.

In the absence of education and support from upper management, it was the author who had to establish and maintain the boundaries of her review mandate. In other words, she had to rely on personal attributes to implement objectivity, in circumstances where the system should have taken steps to do so.

As with fair process, objectivity results from an assembly of attitudes and activities. These include:

- making sure that the personnel handling the complaint (from administrators through to top decision-makers) have the skills, training and habits of mind that ensure an objective, non-partisan approach;
- establishing, communicating and maintaining an organizational commitment to objectivity;
- structuring the system so that funding sources do not influence the people, processes or outcomes involved in complaint-handling;[10]
- ensuring that the people involved in decision-making are not aligned with any particular constituency or political agenda; and
- making supportable decisions in all complaints through objective analysis applied to established facts and using known criteria.

Ideally, a complaint-handling system should enjoy a measure of independence from the constituency being complained about. This is a key fea-

---

[10]   For a few structural examples, see the section of this chapter dealing with the ombuds office.

ture of the ombuds office, a complaint-handling system that is examined later in this chapter.

There should be no interference or obstruction in the complaint-handling system from sponsors, funders, or any other person or group with authority or status. The objectivity of the system should not be undermined by policies, compensation systems, operational systems or discretionary control of resources. For instance, outside pressures from funding sources should not motivate a supervisor to instruct an employee on how to handle a particular complaint. Nor should the system permit reprisals against a decision-maker by a disgruntled participant. These things should be obvious, but trust us, they are not.

5.   Understandable Outcomes

The outcome of a complaint-handling system is not just the end product. It is something to address before complaints even enter the system.

Potential complainants should be told the range of possible outcomes and the scope of the complaint-handling system so that they can decide whether to invest their time and energy in the process. For example, can the complaint lead to a binding monetary outcome or will it, at most, offer a recommendation for change? Does the complaint process have the capacity to address the harm or inconvenience alleged by the complainant or will it simply makes things better for others in the future?

If the process involves decision-making by an authorized person, the system should indicate what criteria that person will use to make a decision.

Honest information concerning outcomes contributes to informed, voluntary participation on the part of complainants. In one Canadian arbitration program, some dissatisfied users choose not to complain about the arbitrator because the outcome of a complaint will not change the result in the arbitration or get them a new hearing.

Potential outcomes should be suited to the complaint. There are many possibilities. Informal options include voluntary refunds, replacement, compensation, apology or goodwill gestures. Options for determinative outcomes include specific findings of fact (such as that a service provider fell below an established standard), enforcement of policies or protocols, and legally binding orders to pay money or make repairs.

Once the complaint-handling process is complete, the people involved should know what the outcome is and the basis for that outcome even if nothing is going to be done about the complaint because it is outside the scope of the program or lacks merit. The outcome should be based on an objective analysis of the relevant facts and ought to be explained in plain language so that the logic is clear and explicit. If an individual, department or business is expected to do something as a result of the complaint, the required action should be unambiguous and capable of implementation.

One of the authors reviewed how a workplace complaint was handled. The complaint appeared to be stalled from the vantage point of the initiating employee, who was confused about what really happened and why. Unbeknownst to that employee, the relevant manager had concluded that the complaint lacked merit because, "I know that the other person is a good guy with lots of integrity, so he couldn't have done any of the things alleged in the complaint." The manager had offered the employee no process, had made no enquiries or investigation and had simply formed (but not communicated) a conclusion about the merits based on subjective impressions and information from the past. This is not an example of good complaint-handling for a number of obvious reasons, including the fact that the outcome was not communicated or explained in a forthright manner. Perhaps this happened because the manager knew that such a subjective outcome would not be defensible and hoped to avoid embarrassment.

6.   Reliable Fact-Finding

As the previous example illustrates, the response to a complaint can only be as good as the quality of information that goes into it. A complaint-handling system must recognize when the facts are unclear or contested and must have effective and efficient ways to determine relevant facts.

Complaints typically speak to what happened in the past, what impact that had and what the complainant would like to see happen as a result. Complaints can contain many different allegations such as, "The mediator was biased", "My manager is harassing me" or "My neighbour is making too much noise". Allegations tend to be a mixture of fact and inference plus personal opinion about the way things ought to be. Where more than one individual is involved or implicated, there can be multiple versions of reality or, at the very least, a competing version of events.

There are many ways to find relevant facts. These can be as formal or informal as the situation and the gravity of the issues require. As always, the choice should suit the complaint. Possibilities for where and how to elicit facts include written statements (complaint and response), various documents and records, email correspondence, and telephone or personal interviews with relevant people.

When appropriate sources of information have been pursued and assembled, it may be that the essential facts are not contested and the real issue may be what meaning to attach to the facts. In-person interviews or hearings may not be required as part of a complaint-handling process.

The Ombuds for Banking Services and Investments considers it rare to require a face-to-face meeting. When it receives a complaint from a member of the public, it first reviews the material sent by the individual complaining and the firm complained about. Then it calls the individual to discuss the complaint in detail. After that, it speaks with the firm and completes any other appropriate research. Among the documents reviewed are the last letter that the firm sent to the individual concerning the subject of the complaint, account statements, opening agreements or other correspondence.

The banking ombuds' approach differs significantly from that used by the Special Ombudsman Response Team ("SORT") of Ontario's Ombudsman, which is a group of experienced investigators and staff who conduct systemic investigations. SORT investigations are meticulously planned and include recorded, in-person interviews conducted by two investigators who control all aspects of the investigation.[11] There is a much higher level of formality inherent in a SORT investigation than there is in the fact-gathering approach of the banking ombuds.

This is not the place to debate the merits of each approach or to lobby for one over the other but rather to point out the range of possibilities and to emphasize that appropriate fact-finding should precede analysis and decision-making in any complaint-handling system.

7.   Appropriate Confidentiality

Although complaints can have a positive effect on people and organizations, they do have a dark side. Complaints can stigmatize people and permanently alter reputations. They can disrupt workplaces and undermine morale. They can cause anxiety to individuals and organizations.

To contain these negative costs and consequences, appropriate levels of confidentiality need to be maintained in any complaint-handling system. Identifying information and content details may need to be restricted on a need-to-know basis. The authors are familiar with one complaint system that assigns numbers to respondents and redacts identifying information about the person or organization making the complaint. This is done so that those ultimately deciding what to do cannot be influenced by the identity or status of any of the parties involved. Over and above these reasons for confidentiality, there may be legal reasons that are outside the scope of this text.

When information must be withheld, the reason for doing so should be legitimate and the complaint-handling system should provide a credible rationale in order to indicate that the withholding of information is not capri-

---

[11]   For more information about SORT, see G. Jones, *Conducting Administrative, Oversight & Ombuds Investigations* (Toronto: Canada Law Book, 2009) at 84.

cious or arbitrary. If the rationale is sound, the policy should be applied consistently.

An acquaintance of the authors filed a sexual harassment complaint against some members of a volunteer organization to which she belongs. During the complaint-handling process, the complainant was interviewed by an independent investigator. The organization received a fact-finding report from the investigator and decided the merits of the complaint plus remedial action without further input from the complainant.

The complainant was not given copies of the fact-finding report or any other documents generated in connection with her complaint. The organization explained that distribution was not in the best interests of the individuals or the community and could revive personal animosities. However, the organization disclosed the investigator's general findings, the sanctions that had been imposed and the steps that were being taken to prevent a recurrence of events.

While the complainant would have liked to satisfy her personal curiosity with more details, she did not insist on disclosure of the written report for two reasons. First, she understood and accepted the risks associated with disclosure. Second, she did not need to see details to appreciate that her complaint had been taken seriously and that meaningful corrective action was the result. The complainant had been interviewed by a thorough and courteous investigator, had been kept advised during the process and had been given information about how the merits were being addressed.

This anecdote illustrates an effective complaint-handling system in operation. The system applied an appropriate degree of confidentiality in a transparent and principled way. Coincidentally, it also applied procedural, substantive and relational fairness, and these dimensions of fairness supported the application of confidentiality.

8.   Organizational Support

Resource allocation and organizational attitude are vital to a robust complaint-handling system. There is no use designing and initiating a complaint system if the organization does not provide ongoing support in tangible and meaningful ways.

Support includes the allocation of sufficient resources so that the complaint system can address the "problem" aspects of complaints. It involves the political will to ensure that systemic issues are addressed throughout the organization in order to prevent a recurrence of similar problems.

Support also means cultivating a culture that responds to the "people" aspects of the complaint. Ideally, that culture accepts the inevitability of complaints, receives them graciously and processes them efficiently and effectively.

Case handling should be tracked, analyzed and reported to the appropriate level or person who can make a difference. It sounds trite, but someone within the organization needs to care enough to pay attention and to take a big picture view. Data from the system should ultimately filter towards a level or individual with oversight who looks at the cumulative effect of complaints, assesses the effectiveness of the system, and spots trends.

We know of a volunteer organization that delivers an important public service at several locations. Because of its public profile, it is politically and practically essential for this organization to have a complaint-handling system, and it does — only nobody tracks what happens. When we contacted the organization to find out the number of complaints, the issues complained about and the outcome of the complaints, the leaders and the administrative staff could not tell us. There was neither consistency of approach nor consistency of tracking, and virtually no reporting, even to the supervising authority in government. While the world obviously keeps on spinning without this particular complaint-handling information being compiled, analyzed and publicized, there is still a lost educational opportunity. The people in the field who provide the service on a no-cost or low-cost basis want to know how their services are perceived and what areas of concern their users raise. They want to be able to assess the risks and whether they are worth it. They also want affirmation and support. Without the organizational will and resources, their desires remain unfulfilled.

We know of another complaint-handling system for workplace concerns that is staffed by competent, well-intentioned people who lack both the time and permission to do outreach work. The system is poorly publicized and can only be found by the most motivated and persistent employee. It has a minimal budget and lacks written terms of reference that carve out its independence, responsibilities and reach. Miraculously, the system does receive complaints and has performed valuable and important work on a case-by-case basis, for which employees at all levels have been grateful. A complaint system is not properly nourished when the corporate culture makes the complaint-handling staff timid about identifying systemic issues and inhibits them from publishing a report with annual statistics or case studies.

CONTRASTING COMPLAINT-HANDLING EXPERIENCES

One of the authors was motivated to make complaints to two organizations concerning issues of importance to her. What follows is a description and analysis of her complaint experiences. How would you rate the complaint-handling systems involved? How well did they apply the eight factors identified above? Importantly, to what extent did they manifest procedural, substantive and relational fairness?

The author reports that one day her train trip from Ottawa to Toronto was disrupted by a group of young employees of a major Canadian telecommunications company who were travelling together from a corporate event. Many members of the group were intoxicated and as the trip progressed the volume of their carryings on increased. They were singing, swearing, playing music and talking loudly on their cell phones, mostly to co-workers in another car of the train. (That is how the author learned whom they worked for.) The group was oblivious to the impact of its behaviour and treated the train car as its private party room.

Requests of train staff, including one or more supervisors who passed through the car, produced no results. Group members only shrugged when asked to tone things down.

The next day, the author went on the train company's website and easily found a link for complaints. She sent an email detailing her experience and observations. She explained that the disruption posed a problem because she used the train regularly for business purposes and this kind of noise made concentration impossible.

Within 24 hours the author received a response both by email and telephone. The train company representative indicated that they were looking into the matter and had received other complaints from passengers over the situation. He advised that his company was contacting the group's employer to report the problematic behaviour. The representative asked what train staff and supervisor had done, if anything, and the author told what she knew. When the author then tried to find out which corporate office the noisemakers came from (so she too could complain directly to their boss), the representative politely declined and indicated that they were unable to provide personal information about passengers under these circumstances. A few days later, the train company forwarded a discount coupon for another trip together with an apology for the disruptive noise.

Contrast this with the complaint that the same author made about an eye care provider who failed to perform a standard eye examination on her eye and thus missed an urgent, sight-threatening condition. Months passed after the author wrote to the provider's regulatory body with the facts and her concerns. Then one day she received a telephone call from a representative of the regulatory body. The representative explained that the eye care provider was not disputing the facts and complimented the provider's attitude. The representative went on to say that, as a consent outcome, the regulatory body would look through the provider's paper files to see how similar sight-threatening conditions were handled in the past. When the author asked how looking at paper files was going to protect future patients from a risk of blindness at the hands of that particular eye care provider, the representative began to advocate for his stated solution and dismissed the author's concerns. The author then had to retain a lawyer and appear at a tribunal hearing before the proposed outcome was modified to include steps to address the provider's practical competence.

The author also asked for a copy of the expert's report concerning the treatment of her eye. This request was denied at an administrative level so a motion before the tribunal was required. At the hearing of the motion, the regulatory body had two lawyers, its regular counsel and additional counsel to advise the tribunal, plus a court report to transcribe the proceedings. The tribunal refused to release the expert's report. It was not until the author took steps to commence legal proceedings that she received a copy of the expert's report. Phew!

Of course, there is a big difference between a noisy train trip and an eye care provider who almost lets someone go blind and that difference has to be reflected in the process. The eye care provider has a professional reputation to protect, so the process contains more formal aspects than a complaint about a noise disturbance and therefore takes longer. But, as the person who complained, that is not a material difference from the author's point of view. The people aspects are what stand out for her.

In particular:

- The train company's complaint-handling system showed more emotional intelligence. It lowered the author's emotional arousal, treated her with courtesy and seemed to take her concerns seriously. By contrast, the regulatory body's system perpetuated, indeed increased, the author's emotional arousal (as her friends and relatives will attest). The regulator either did not understand the author's concerns or, more likely, dismissed them as unworthy or impertinent. The regulator was respectful up to the point when it thought its authority was being challenged. Thereafter, it was dismissive.

- The train company's outcomes made sense. The resulting action — having words with the noisemakers' employer — corresponded to the problem. And when the company representative declined to give the author their specific address, his reason seemed genuine and made sense. By contrast, the regulatory body's proposed outcome needed explanation because a file review does not seem to be the most direct way to instill the diagnostic skills that the uncontested record showed to be missing. The eye care provider's cooperative attitude is not an obvious or appropriate justification for the regulator's proposed outcome.

- The train company's response was characterized by objectivity. Its representative was not advocating for or against any person or outcome. He gave the impression of wanting to know the facts in order to determine what should be done next. By contrast, the regulatory body's representative was partial to his proposed solution and personally adverse to the author because her questions challenged his competence. As a result, the regulator's process was fuelled by the emotional arousal of an individual who may have been justifiably upset but who was supposed to play an objective role. The regulator therefore spent time and money opposing the author's requests instead of addressing the merits of the complaint.

- The two scenarios expose different attitudes towards complaints. The train company welcomed complaints as a way to improve service and enhance user satisfaction. By what it said and did, the train company supported the author's right to complain. The regulatory body's words and actions conveyed the reverse. It seemed to resent her complaint and it applied its resources in acts of resistance. Although it did not say so, the regulator was operating under the standard assumption that a complainant is merely a witness with no legitimate interest in the proceedings. The train company showed that they cared about the comfort of passengers. The regulator's behaviour suggested that it cared more about eye care providers and its own powers than it did about members of the public.

Does it matter in the end result that the train company gave the author a monetary reward and an apology? You might suppose so, but if you asked, she would tell you that such tangible tokens were beside the point. Relational fairness such as being taken seriously and respected was more important than any material outcome. Moreover, an apology from the eye care provider would not have been responsive to the complaint. The author would rather have had the eye care provider acknowledge the implications of the misdiagnosis and address the clinical situation in order to minimize the risk of blindness to others. Of course, the author did play a role in provoking adversarial relations with the regulator, but the situation is still a shame because both the author and the regulator shared an interest in public protection.

INTERNATIONAL COMPLAINT-HANDLING STANDARDS

Readers seeking more guidance for the design, development and operation of a complaint-handling system may wish to consult one of the standards developed by the International Organization for Standardization, known internationally as the ISO. The ISO is a worldwide federation of national standards bodies that prepares standards by means of technical committees. Draft standards are circulated to the member bodies for voting and publication, as an international standard requires approval by at least 75 per cent of the member bodies casting a vote.

While the ISO is not the only body concerned with dispute resolution standards,[12] it has developed two standards that are directly relevant to complaint-handling (but not employment-related disputes). These are:

- ISO 10002:2004 — **Quality management – Customer satisfaction – Guidelines for complaints handling in organizations** (23 pages).[13] This standard concerns internal complaint-handling for all types of commercial or non-commercial activities.

- ISO 10003:2007 — **Quality management – Customer satisfaction – Guidelines for dispute resolution external to organizations** (34 pages).[14] This standard relates to external dispute resolution for product-related complaints that are not remedied internally, where the term "product" includes services, software, hardware and processed materials.

Neither standard is well known within Canada's dispute resolution community, probably because distribution is strictly controlled, keeping them out of the public domain.[15] At the time of writing, it cost CDN $225 for a set of licences that permit only a single hard copy to be made of each standard.

These comprehensive standards contain more detail than is possible for us to convey in this overview chapter. They resemble do-it-yourself guides for the development of a complaint-handling system but they do not prescribe what the system looks like any more than a knitting reference book dictates the colour, texture or structure of a hand-knit sweater. Particulars are organized within the standards under headings like:

- Terms and Definitions
- Guiding Principles
- Complaint-Handling Framework
- Planning, Design and Development
- Operations
- Maintenance and Improvement

Canada's Commissioner for Complaints for Telecommunications Services ("CCTS") is an example of a complaint-handling system modelled on ISO 10003:2007. For the purpose of illustration (and without endorsing its

---

[12]   An extensive review of the many and varied organizations interested in dispute resolution standards is beyond the scope of this book. For a specific instance of one standard that recognizes the multiplicity of sources, see the Online Dispute Resolution Standards of Practice: <http://www.icann.org/ombudsman/odr-standards-of-practice-en.htm>.

[13]   See online: International Organization for Standardization <http://www.iso.org/>.

[14]   *Ibid.*

[15]   To purchase a copy, see online: International Organization for Standardization <http://www.iso.org/iso/store.htm>.

scope and mandate), we encourage readers to examine the components of that system by visiting its website.[16]

The commissioner's published standards of performance for complaint-handling include accessibility, fairness, timeliness, confidentiality and continual improvement. The complaint-handling system is based on progressive dispute resolution steps. The penultimate step is a recommendation that the parties can voluntarily adopt to resolve the complaint. If either the customer or the service provider rejects the recommendation, the complaint moves to the ultimate stage where the commissioner can issue a decision that is binding on the service provider.

This particular complaint-handling system resulted from a decision of the Canadian Radio-television and Telecommunications Commission ("CRTC") in 2007, following public hearings. The notion was an independent agency with a mandate to resolve complaints from individual and small business retail customers as a component of a deregulated telecommunications market. The agency's governance structure to ensure its independence from the telecommunications industry with design elements such as a governing body composed of a majority of members who were not affiliated with any telecommunications service provider, a non-affiliated chief executive officer and an adequate budget set by the governing body but funded by industry. Initially, membership was mandatory for all service providers with annual Canadian telecommunications service revenues exceeding $10 million.[17]

In December 2010, the CRTC issued an oral decision extending the mandate of the CCTS to investigate consumer telecom complaints for a further five-year period. It also extended the agency's scope to all Canadian telecommunications service providers, regardless of the amount of their annual revenues.

The CCTS is mandated to investigate complaints that relate to billing errors, contract disputes, service delivery and unauthorized transfer of service but not complaints about customer service, misleading advertising, pricing, a service provider's general policies and whether or not it is fair for a provider to be able to draft a contract that favours itself.[18]

---

[16] See online: Commissioner for Complaints for Telecommunications Services <http://www.ccts-cprst.ca/>.

[17] Telecom Notice of Consultation CRTC 2010-247, "Review of the Commissioner for Complaints for Telecommunications Services" (30 April 2010) and Telecom Notice of Consultation CRTC 2010-241-1, "Review of the Commissioner for Complaints for Telecommunications Services" (12 August 2010).

[18] CCTS, *Annual Report 2009–2010: Talking Solutions and Getting Results*, online: <http://www.ccts-cprst.ca/wp-content/uploads/2010/01/CCTS-Annual-Report-2009-2010.pdf>, especially at 5 and 27.

THE OMBUDS OFFICE

Introduction

An ombuds is a specific complaint-handling model and refers to a position or office, as opposed to a particular process, for the resolution of complaints. There are many such offices in Canada in a wide range of contexts, and more are coming into existence each year.

The original English term, ombudsman, originates from a Swedish word "justitieombuds" and loosely translates as "citizen's defender". Ombuds and ombudsperson now seem to be the terms preferred in Canada by most individuals who occupy this role, but other titles such as "commissioner" are also in use.

The ombuds concept has been in existence for over 200 years and has been developed and adapted in Canada for the past four decades. Simon Fraser University in British Columbia established the first Canadian ombuds office in 1965. Two years later, New Brunswick and Alberta were the first provinces to establish such offices.

At the present time in Canada, ombuds serve an assortment of constituencies in a range of contexts including broadcasting, voluntary ski patrols, unionized workplaces, financial services and universities. Regardless of where the office is situated or who it serves, in general terms an ombuds helps individuals obtain redress from public or private institutions or from those who exercise power, authority or control over them. Often they do this by encouraging and overseeing the appropriate use of established channels of redress.

What the office of any particular ombuds looks like in operation will vary from mandate to mandate and from one individual ombuds to another. Two individuals with the same terms of reference can interpret and implement their mandates in distinctly individualistic ways.[19] For these reasons, it is hazardous to generalize too much about ombuds offices and services.

Typically, an ombuds is empowered to investigate complaints from a defined constituency or identified group or industry, and to facilitate the resolution of those complaints on a one-time and/or systemic basis. Some ombuds can look into issues on their own initiative even if a specific complaint has not been made.

If complaints cannot be resolved informally and with voluntary compliance, many ombuds have a mandate to make and publicize non-binding recommendations. Ombuds do not generally have the power to implement or

---

[19]   Contrast, for example, the present ombudsmen for the provinces of Saskatchewan and Ontario.

enforce their recommendations and rely upon moral suasion to get results, which suasion some exert more aggressively than others.

Operating Principles

We have chosen to isolate three key operating principles (or necessary conditions) that characterize the ombuds office.[20] We state these principles at a high level of abstraction, knowing that they will display a different complexion according to the operating environment and individual ombuds.

For present purpose, an ombuds receives, investigates and resolves complaints consistent with these principles:

Independence — An ombuds enjoys a high level of autonomy and does not take direction or orders about how to carry out its function or perform its day-to-day activities, even if the ombuds has a relationship with an industry, organization or constituency.

Impartiality — An ombuds acts in an objective and non-partisan manner and promotes fair process. The office is neither an advocate nor an opponent for any individual, position, organization or constituency.

Confidentiality — An ombuds does not disclose identifying information or other details concerning those who contact the ombuds office, without permission.

We highlight these operating principles but we recognize that they are not exclusive or exhaustive. Many ombuds publicize or subscribe to additional principles such as fairness, equity, efficiency, informality, accessibility and safety.[21] To the extent that additional principles have already been covered in our general discussion of complaint-handling, we consider them to be implied with respect to an ombuds.

Multiple Functions

Ombuds perform many functions. Some functions are highly visible, perhaps even notorious such as publishing reports and organizing press conferences to expose the excesses or failings of public authorities. Other om-

---

[20]   The International Ombuds Association considers these three principles plus a fourth, informality, to be key, and it classifies them as "ethical" principles rather than operating principles. See <http://www.ombudsassociation.org>. Informality is not a necessary feature of the ombuds office, however. For instance, the Ombuds of Ontario has an infrastructure and methodology called SORT (Special Ombuds Response Team) that is dedicated to conducting formalized investigations of systemic issues; see G. Jones, *Conducting Administrative Oversight & Ombuds Investigations* (Toronto: Canada Law Book, 2009) at 83-94.

[21]   For one particular example, see the Value Statement of the ICANN ombuds online: Internet Corporation for Assigned Names and Numbers <http://www.icann.org/ombudsman/articles/value-statement.pdf>.

buds functions are administrative, routine, mundane or somewhat unremarkable. Nevertheless, these more commonplace activities are part of the day-to-day functioning of an ombuds office that routinely receives, processes, looks into and resolves complaints.

One less visible function of an ombuds is responding to requests for information and making referrals to people or programs best suited to help those who bring forward concerns. Private and public institutions can be intimidating places and people are often uncertain as to where to go or who is responsible for what. An ombuds plays a valuable role by simply pointing people in the right direction and helping them navigate the relevant organizational system.

Ombuds also promote communication among appropriate individuals, departments or organizations, and work to resolve issues informally. The extent to which an ombuds intervenes in conflicts and disputes varies from office to office. Some ombuds are comfortable with direct and active engagement and are willing to play the role of mediator or facilitator for disputing parties. Others are more hands-off. They encourage direct dealings between people at the lowest possible level, failing which they suggest the use of established channels of resolution and only get directly involved at a future date if established channels of redress are not respected or carried out fairly.

If these and other functions were gathered together, a composite list of activities would look something like this. In no particular order, an ombuds:

- provides relevant information;
- makes referrals to people, programs or procedures best suited to help;
- requests assistance on behalf of people who contact them;
- educates people about existing avenues of redress;
- reviews how existing avenues of redress were carried out to ensure that they were fair and compliant with their mandates;
- does outreach and raises awareness;
- performs conflict coaching: supports people to take steps on their own behalf;
- teaches people conflict resolution skills;
- makes recommendations to correct one-time problems;
- identifies systematic or emerging issues;
- performs dispute resolution interventions such as mediation or shuttle diplomacy;
- investigates allegations of unfairness, arbitrariness, *etc.*;
- makes and publishes non-binding recommendations;
- classifies, tracks and compiles case management data; and

- prepares and publishes annual reports to relevant constituents.

Varied Complaints

There is no standard complaint type dealt with by ombuds offices due to the variety of contexts and constituencies served by ombuds. To appreciate this variety, consider the following lists. Figure 9-1 shows the kinds of complaints made to an ombuds who serves the municipal level of government. Figure 9-2 shows the kind of complaints made to an ombuds at a university or community college.

Figure 9-1: Municipal Complaints

- Customer service
- Adverse impact or discriminatory consequence of a decision or policy on an individual or group
- Failure to adequately or appropriately communicate with a member of the public
- Unreasonable delay
- Failure to adhere to process, guidelines or policies or to apply them in a consistent manner
- Denial of service
- Wrong or unreasonable interpretation of criteria, standards, guidelines, policies, information or evidence
- Insufficient reasons for a decision or no reason given
- Failure to provide sufficient or proper notice
- Failure to keep a proper record

Figure 9-2: University Complaints

- Academic Advice
- Academic Appeals
- Academic Misconduct
- Accessibility
- Advancement and Development
- Admissions (Undergraduate and Graduate)
- Conduct — Instructor, Staff, Student
- Confidentiality
- Convocation and Awards
- Curriculum Advising

- Enrollment Services
- Fees

Kinds of Ombuds

As if there has not been enough reference to variety, readers also need to understand that there are two fundamentally different kinds of ombuds:[22] 1) legislative ombuds (also known as classical ombuds) who deal with complaints against public authorities; and 2) non-legislative ombuds who deal with internal or external complaints relating to a particular organization, workplace, industry or other non-governmental entity.

Legislative Ombuds

As the name suggests, this kind of ombuds is appointed pursuant to legislation and paid from the public purse. A legislative ombuds handles complaints concerning the actions (or inactions) of members of the public service, and is empowered to investigate allegations of arbitrariness, abuse of authority or other wrongdoing, and to recommend corrective action on a one-time or systemic basis. If the relevant public authority does not implement the recommendations of the ombuds, then public exposure can follow in the form of a report to the legislature or other kinds of publicity and exposure.

The legislative ombuds is intended to provide citizens with redress that is not practical from the courts, the legislature or the executive branch of government, given the size and nature of the modern state. Many people now regard the legislative ombuds as a standard part of accountable government, and the Supreme Court of Canada has explicitly recognized its function and necessity.[23]

There are legislative or classical ombuds with different mandates at all jurisdictional levels in Canada: national, provincial and municipal.

Whether or not a legislative ombuds can properly accept public complaints about agencies, boards, commissions and tribunals, depends on the empowering provisions of the statute creating the ombuds office. The answer differs from one jurisdiction to another. For instance, the mandates for the ombuds of British Columbia and Alberta include child protection ser-

---

[22] There is no consistent classification system because sorting criteria can vary. The Forum of Canadian Ombudsman identifies three types of ombuds: legislative, organizational and hybrid. Its classification mixes the origins of the ombuds' authority with the functions. See online: <http://www.ombudsmanforum.ca>.

[23] *British Columbia Development Corp. v. Friedmann (Ombuds)*, [1984] S.C.J. No. 50, [1984] 2 S.C.R. 447 (S.C.C.).

vices and public hospitals, but at the time of writing this is not the case for Ontario's ombuds.

Canada has 10 legislative ombuds at the provincial and territorial level, established between 1967 and 2001. There is one in each province (except Prince Edward Island) plus Yukon. These ombuds differ widely in terms of their jurisdiction, resources and size. The smallest (Yukon) has a staff of three and a budget just over $500,000. The largest, being the Quebec Ombuds, has a staff of 132, a budget in excess of $11 million, and an extensive and far-reaching mandate.[24]

Federally, there is no comprehensive ombuds empowered to receive complaints concerning all aspects of the federal public service. Instead, there are a number of special purpose ombuds with restricted and focused mandates. The Office of the Taxpayers' Ombuds is one example.

In 2008, Canada's first Taxpayers' Ombuds was appointed by Order in Council pursuant to the *Public Service Employment Act*[25] that allows for the appointment of a special adviser to the Minister of National Revenue.[26]

The mandate of this specialized ombuds is to:

- provide an impartial, independent and efficient system for handling individual complaints from taxpayers about the service or treatment they receive from the Canada Revenue Agency ("CRA");

- identify and investigate emerging and systemic service issues related to CRA programs and processes and make recommendations for improvements or corrective action directly to the Minister of National Revenue;

- facilitate taxpayer access to CRA; and

- develop awareness of something called the *Taxpayer Bill of Rights* and the role of this ombuds' office.

In the first year of operation it was estimated that the Office of the Taxpayers' Ombuds would receive contact from 2,700 taxpayers. This was an underestimate. The office was contacted by almost 4,853 taxpayers in its 2008–2009 year, and completed more than 500 investigations in that time.

By all accounts, the Office of the Taxpayers' Ombuds is satisfying just the kind of role that an ombuds is intended for. One of its early cases concerned a "Notice to Pay an Outstanding Debt" that was sent to a taxpayer on Government of Canada letterhead, indicating that unless the debt was paid,

---

[24] For a snapshot of provincial and territorial ombuds as at the summer of 2008, see S. Hyson, ed., *Provincial & Territorial Ombudsman Offices in Canada* (Toronto: University of Toronto Press, 2009) at 18-19.

[25] S.C. 2003, c. 22, Part 3.

[26] For the complete terms of reference of this ombuds, see Order in Council P.C. 2007-0828, online: Taxpayer's Ombudsman <http://www.taxpayersrights.gc.ca/rdrncncl-eng.html>.

the taxpayer's tax refund would be withheld. The notice listed a toll-free number for the Ontario Ministry of Revenue but no one there — or at any of the other government departments or agencies contacted — could identify the origins of the letter or the basis for the claim. (We are not making this up.) It took intervention on the part of the ombuds to finally learn that the Canada Revenue Agency was collecting on behalf of a provincial program and that the taxpayer should not have been in the collection database to begin with.

Non-Legislative Ombuds

Public and private institutions, including industries and businesses, wield considerable power over the individual and, like modern government, have the potential to act in an arbitrary, high-handed or ill-advised way. To meet these concerns, the second type of ombuds, non-legislative, was developed from the basic attributes of the legislative ombuds.

Non-legislative ombuds tend to serve large workplaces or large organizations and industry groups. They can have an internal organizational focus such as employee complaints, or an external focus such as customer complaints, and they often perform a risk-management function by facilitating dispute resolution so that complainants do not seek determinative outcomes from arbitrators, administrative tribunals or the courts.

As their name suggests, non-legislative ombuds do not derive their authority from statute but from written terms of reference, charters or organizational policies. There are many possible ways to document and design the non-legislative ombuds office. The content of the terms of reference for an ombuds office could form a separate chapter, as there are many legal and practical issues to take into account such as whether notice of an issue that is given to the ombuds office is notice to the organization itself.[27] For present purposes we will simply point out that written terms of reference can cover all aspects of the ombuds office, including:

- the method of appointment of the ombuds;
- the ombuds' remuneration;
- the indicia of independence that attach to the office;
- the nature and structure of the ombuds accountability;
- staffing and resourcing the ombuds office;
- the constituency and scope of the ombuds mandate;
- the ombuds powers including access to information, making recommendations, or undertaking investigations on its own initiative;

---

[27] For sample terms of reference applying to the university and community college context, see online: University of Western Ontario <http://www.uwo.ca/ombuds>.

- operating procedures and principles, including confidentiality and impartiality;
- tracking and reporting obligations; and
- the relationship between the ombuds office and other existing complaint-handling mechanisms such as grievance procedures in unionized workplaces.

As an example, the Office of the Ombudsperson at Dalhousie University in Halifax, Canada finds its mandate in written terms of reference that are six pages long.[28] The terms create a multi-stakeholder advisory committee and specify that the ombuds' appointment is effective when the Dalhousie Student Union, the University Senate and the Board of Governors approve the committee's hiring recommendation. The terms of reference also give this particular ombuds the authority to assess and investigate complaints from a broad constituency consisting of past or present students, faculty members, staff members, administrators and outsiders, provided the complaint relates to the university or its community. Labour relations grievances are outside the ombuds mandate, however, as they are governed by one or more collective agreements.

The Internet Corporation for Assigned Names and Numbers ("ICANN") also has an ombuds. ICANN is a not-for-profit public-benefit corporation with participants from all over the world dedicated to keeping the internet secure, stable and operable. Its ombuds has jurisdiction over complaints concerning decisions, actions or inactions by staff members or by the ICANN board of directors. By accessing its website, interested readers can review the mandate of this ombuds, which is set out in a written framework.[29]

Non-legislative ombuds exist to investigate and redress complaints in an impartial and independent way much like classical ombuds. Investigations may be triggered by specific complaints or on the initiative of the ombuds, depending on the scope of the ombuds mandate.

Typically, a non-legislative ombuds intervenes only after other forms of complaint-handling have been attempted via established forms of redress. For example, if an employee contacts a workplace ombuds with concerns about unfair treatment in the workplace, the ombuds would most likely refer the employee to established workplace procedures such as a human rights and harassment procedure, and put the individual in touch with relevant forms of internal assistance such as union representatives or human resources consultants. A workplace ombuds would not become the employee's advocate and directly investigate the employee's allegations. Only after the

---

[28]   See online: Dalhousie University <http://ombudsperson.dal.ca>.
[29]   See online: Internet Corporation for Assigned Names and Numbers <http://www.icann.org/ombudsman/framework.html>.

employee had used relevant workplace procedures might the ombuds look to see that such procedures were applied fairly and consistently. So, this kind of ombuds is more appropriately viewed as a place of last resort rather than a knight in shining armour.

Non-legislative ombuds perform several important functions on behalf of their organizations or industries. When they intervene effectively on behalf of individuals, they promote good customer or employee relations. When they de-escalate conflict and bring about settlements without lawsuits and grievances, they reduce the monetary and opportunity costs of conflict. When they spot trends and identify systemic issues, they help manage risk. And when they objectively determine that a complaint does not have merit, they support the work and morale of those complained about.

In the financial services industry, there is a cluster of ombuds offices that investigate customer service complaints that cannot be resolved at the local level. The Ombuds for Banking Services and Investments looks at complaints about most banking and investment services and products, such as errors in accounts, poor disclosure and inappropriate advice. The Ombudservice for Life and Health Insurance deals with concerns about life and health insurance, including disability. The General Insurance Ombudservice covers issues of car, property and business insurance. These three are part of the Financial Services OmbudsNetwork, an arrangement of dispute resolution services to address industry-specific customer complaints.

There are also ombuds at Canadian universities and community colleges similar to the one at Dalhousie University.[30] These ombuds handle complaints from students and other members of the educational community that may arise against the institution or anyone at the institution that exercises authority. They are set up to be independent of the administrative structures of their particular educational institution as well as independent of students' associations. At Simon Fraser University, the university and two associations, the Simon Fraser Student Society and the Graduate Students Society, jointly fund the Office of the Ombudsperson.

The ombuds at the Canadian Broadcasting Corporation ("CBC") is an example of an organizational ombuds with an external mandate. It serves as an appeal authority for complainants who are dissatisfied with the responses they received from program staff or management about programming. The office of this ombuds is independent of the program staff and management, and reports directly to the president and through the president to the board of directors.

The CBC ombuds determines whether the journalistic process or broadcast in question violated the corporation's journalistic policies and standards,

---

[30] Most belong to the Association of Canadian College and University Ombudspersons; see online: University of Western Ontario <http://www.uwo.ca/ombuds>.

and makes its findings public.[31] In 2004, the findings of this ombuds were used as evidence to assign civil liability to the corporation in a defamation action.[32] The current terms of reference for the office state, "the ombuds does not examine the civil liability of the Corporation or its journalists".

We have previously mentioned that the ombuds concept can apply in the workplace. The office can serve as a place for employees to raise concerns about staffing, corporate governance, work environment, compensation and benefits, career development, and similar concerns. Employees can also complain that existing corporate mechanisms such as human rights and harassment procedures were not adhered to or administered fairly.

There are probably dozens of workplace ombuds and it would require considerable time and resources to research them fully because they do not do public outreach or publicly distribute their reports. Workplace ombuds tend to be accessible only to employees of the company sponsoring the ombuds office.

An exception to this is the ombuds for Hydro-Québec, whose annual report is readily available online.[33] In the period between 2000–2008, that office handled an average of 168 complaints per year from unionized and non-unionized employees concerning matters such as discrimination, staffing, compensation and benefits and harassment. This ombuds' mandate extends to employment equity and complaints relating to Quebec's *Charter of Human Rights and Freedoms*.[34] It resolves cases in various ways including mediation by the ombuds, referral to other authorities, management intervention, payment of compensation or other forms of redress, and staff changes like transfer, relocation or promotion.

Contentious Classifications

The most important substantive difference between a legislative and a non-legislative ombuds is the degree of autonomy and authority (real and apparent) that each office enjoys.

A legislative ombuds is an independent body whose autonomy is a matter of law. It is funded by all taxpayers and has public, not partisan, accountability. A legislative ombuds is not aligned or funded by any particular industry, organization or interest group.

---

[31]   See online: Canadian Broadcasting Corporation <http://www.cbc.ca/ombudsman>.
[32]   *Gilles E. Néron Communication Marketing Inc. v. Chambre des notaires du Québec*, [2004] S.C.J. No. 50, [2004] 3 S.C.R. 95 (S.C.C.).
[33]   See online: Hydro-Québec <http://www.hydroquebec.com/publications/en/protectrice_personne/index.html>.
[34]   R.S.Q., c. C-12.

By contrast, a non-legislative ombuds is deliberately designed by those who sponsor or fund the office and its mandate is aligned and/or responsive to the needs of one or more identifiable constituencies. Consider, for instance, the Financial Services OmbudsNetwork, the Commissioner for Complaints for Telecommunications Services or the workplace ombuds described above.

The differences between these two types of ombuds give rise to debate in the field about the extent to which non-legislative ombuds are "true" ombuds. Detractors point to the fact that non-legislative ombuds have less autonomy, face more restrictive mandates and are essentially captive creatures. The office of a non-legislative ombuds can be occupied by a past or current executive or employee who may have an allegiance to funders or sponsors, and the office may also play a customer relations role.

We agree that non-legislative ombuds can be subject to corporate or partisan interests. If those interests are not recognized and subordinated to those of the office, they will rob the ombuds of credibility. But this is a matter of design, not definition. As with "true" mediation, we prefer to avoid polarizing labels. We tend to take a broad and inclusive view of what an ombuds is, using our three key operating principles of independence, impartiality and confidentiality.

We suggest that the term "ombuds" can legitimately be used by any position that investigates and resolves internal or external complaints from one or more constituencies in a non-partisan way and maintains the confidentiality of those who seek assistance, provided there is an adequate, not absolute, level of independence. To assess independence, one has to go behind the ombuds label and examine the underlying structures, including how governance and funding are handled.

Several structural ways have been developed to support the independence of non-legislative ombuds offices and some of these have already been alluded to. These include one or some combination of the following:

- obtaining funding from various constituencies served by the ombuds;
- making the ombuds accountable to multiple constituencies;
- providing ombuds services through an arm's-length body with a governance system that is not controlled by corporate or partisan interests;
- ensuring that the ombuds office is adequately funded to support its operations and the implementation of its mandate;
- employing arm's-length contractors who have no allegiance to any particular constituency to provide ombuds services;
- ensuring that the ombuds reports directly to the highest level of authority in the organization; and

•   giving the ombuds a long, fixed-term contract.

This is not an exhaustive list or a how-to prescription, just an indication of some of the options available to address legitimate concerns about the independence of the ombuds office in fact and appearance.

We add that structure and design of the office is one factor to look at when assessing independence. The personal integrity of the individual occupying the office is also important. That individual should bring appropriate personal attributes such as openness and a non-partisan attitude towards complainants. His or her attitudes, words and actions should not betray an allegiance to or preference for funders, sponsors and others who occupy positions of power, authority or control. As with any complaint-handling system, both the structure and the personnel are important to the integrity of the system.

Concerning the public relations aspects of an ombuds office, we doubt that it is fatal to independence or credibility if an ombuds office is available to accept compliments in addition to complaints or if it is mandated to promote goodwill and favourable relations. After all, Canada's highest court has observed that it is legitimate for an ombuds to validate the work of others and thereby increase organizational morale.[35] This suggests that public relations could legitimately be an aspect of an ombuds office provided it is one component of an overall program and that there are appropriate structures and personnel to support independence.

By this point, it should be obvious that use of the term "ombuds" is no assurance of the nature of the office, regardless of the personal attributes of the individual using that title. In one Canadian financial institution, the ombuds' internal function is predominantly as a repository of whistle-blower complaints. The ombuds office is identified as a place for employees to report concerns about suspected fraud, questionable accounting or business practices, internal controls over financial reporting or auditing matters. The ombuds notifies the chair of the audit committee of all concerns relating to accounting or auditing matters and the chair of the audit committee determines any next steps.

The function performed by this "ombuds" is, of course, a valid organizational function but it does not meet our definition of an ombuds. Our inclination would be to classify this particular office as part of a regulatory compliance framework designed to meet the needs of the financial institution. The office is a subordinate position with a mandatory obligation to transmit concerns to the chair of the audit committee. All in all, this particular office does not fulfill the three operating principles of independence, im-

---

[35]   See *British Columbia Development Corp. v. Friedmann (Ombuds)*, [1984] S.C.J. No. 50, [1984] 2 S.C.R. 447 (S.C.C.).

partiality and confidentiality, demonstrating that even the elasticity of our generous definition of an ombuds has its limits.

CONCLUSION

This chapter has outlined the features of a credible complaint-handling system and examined the office of the ombuds as one particular example. In the future, we anticipate that new and different forms of complaint-handling will develop and that existing ones will continue to be refined. We do not expect complaint-handling to become any less relevant than it is today. After all, we live in an individualistic culture of rights and entitlements where people feel at liberty to complain when they perceive that their needs are not met. Whether this is a good or a bad thing does not matter. What matters for present purposes is that this is not likely to change any time soon, thus ensuring the relevance of complaint-handling.

10

CANADIAN INITIATIVES AND ONWARD

An interested dispute resolution practitioner or student could happily disappear into cyberspace for hours at a time while surfing the web for Canadian dispute resolution initiatives. The searching would not be in vain. A basic or advanced search with a popular search engine will quickly produce protocols, policies, frequently asked questions, application forms, guidelines, annual reports and more. These documents are the concrete elements of Canadian DR programs and projects.

Canadian DR initiatives have grown exponentially since the first edition of this book. There are now so many Canadian applications for DR in so many different contexts that only a devoted and independently wealthy researcher would have the time to visit the websites that are publicly accessible on the internet. That still would not cover the universe of Canadian programs because some DR initiatives do not maintain websites or make their DR documents available to the public.

For the most part, websites for Canadian programs and projects are easy to locate. Type in the search term "mandatory mediation" in an advanced search and you will be taken directly to the link for the Ontario Mandatory Mediation Program. Type in "notice to mediate" or the relevant bulletin of British Columbia's Dispute Resolution Office. Type in "insurance complaints Canada" to get the links for the Financial Consumer Agency of Canada and the General Insurance OmbudService.[1]

It helps, of course, to know that a program exists. Sometimes, that knowledge plus persistence and luck are necessary to find a particular program. DR initiatives can be incorporated into some other document with a different focus, like general by-laws, or can appear under non-descriptive labels. The location or indexing of DR tools may not be intuitively obvious, although the ability to search is definitely improving. An important initiative of the Alberta Energy Resources Conservation Board, for instance, used to be hidden behind the words "Public Information". Now all of the Board's "appropriate" dispute resolution initiatives are easily accessed by typing in "ADR".[2] Similarly, a quick

---

[1] See online: Ontario Ministry of the Attorney General <http://www.attorneygeneral.jus.gov.on. ca/english/courts/manmed/>, British Columbia Dispute Resolution Office <http://www.ag.gov.bc. ca/dro/publications/bulletins/general.htm>, Financial Consumer Agency of Canada <http://www. fcac-acfc.gc.ca/eng/consumers/Complaints/default.asp> and General Insurance Ombudservice <http:// www.gio-scad.org>, respectively.

[2] See online: Energy Resources Conservation Board <http://www.ercb.ca>.

search from the home page of the Immigration and Refugee Board easily reveals a detailed, evaluated ADR protocol for sponsorship appeals.[3] In both cases, there is an abundance of clear information to help searchers access and understand the program.

As we explained in the previous editions of this book, there are DR initiatives in industry, government (including agencies, boards and commissions), licensing and disciplinary bodies, communities and schools. There are even DR initiatives for the members of various faith communities, not to mention proliferating programs connected with the civil courts.

Canadian DR initiatives are appearing, disappearing, evolving or mutating all the time.[4] They rest on over two decades of practical experience, monitoring and evaluation.

In 1992, Canada's Department of Justice created the Dispute Resolution Services with the mandate to serve as the "leading centre of DR excellence in Canada". Part of that included a DR Fund established in 1998 as a joint initiative with the Treasury Board. Between 1998 and 2002, a total of $6.9 million was disbursed to federal organizations as seed money to support the design and implementation of DR projects. Many DR initiatives began as a result. Some still exist. Some have been discontinued.

Cost savings were reported as a result of the federal DR Fund. The Canadian Human Rights Tribunal reported a savings of approximately $957,000 in the period 1998–2003 on a grant of $63,990. Fisheries and Oceans reported avoiding costs of $1.7 million in the period 1999–2000 on a grant of $180,929. The Canadian Food Inspection Agency reported a $2.5 million savings in direct litigation costs in the period January 1, 1999 to March 31, 2003, on a grant of $208,500.[5]

The Insurance Corporation of British Columbia ("ICBC") has been involved in mediating cases since 1986, when it jointly sponsored a pilot project with the Canadian Bar Association in mediating personal injury claim files. ICBC reported in its cost/benefit analysis that in 1994 over 1,000 cases were mediated. Of those, 82 per cent were resolved.[6] The study recommended that ICBC endorse and encourage the use of mediation

---

[3]   See online: Immigration and Refugee Board of Canada <http://www.irb-cisr.gc.ca>.

[4]   For a lengthy illustrative list of B.C. regulatory bodies with established dispute resolution procedures, see online: The Trade Investment Mobility Agreement <http://www.tilma.ca/pdf/ListOfRegulatorsWithDisputeMechanisms_BC.pdf>.

[5]   All data taken from Department of Justice, "DR Fund Evaluation: Overview of the Return on Investment from the DR Fund as of March 2004", online: <http://www.justice.gc.ca/eng/pi/dprs-sprd/ref/eval/peval-evalp.html>.

[6]   D. Crosby, *The Use of Mediation in Settling Injury Claims: A Cost/Benefit Analysis* (Vancouver: ICBC, 1995) at 1; see online: Terry Harris <http://www.terryharris.com/Crosby%20ICBC%20Report.htm>.

throughout the corporation, and found that mediation used early in the litigation process was a cost-effective settlement alternative.[7]

More recently, the Court of Queen's Bench of Alberta engaged with Associate Chief Justice John D. Rooke in a formal evaluation of all of the court's Judicial Dispute Resolution (JDR) cases (606) held in Alberta in the year ending June 30, 2008. The JDR process encompasses a variety of DR mechanisms, ranging from facilitative to evaluative, and is defined broadly in the Evaluation Report as being "a voluntary and consensual process whereby parties to a dispute, following the filing of an action in Court (and, most typically, close to trial), seek the assistance of a JDR justice to help, in a facilitative, meditative and/or evaluative way, to settle the dispute before trial".[8]

Depending on the judicial centre involved, the Evaluation Report found success rates of upwards of 80 per cent on all issues. Nor were these rates dependent on case type or the particular JDR process used. It also found that "the trial time saved was the equivalent of a whole year of the Court's civil trial capacity, accomplished in ¼ of that time at JDR's, leaving available judicial time to devote to new cases in the queue and other expanding judicial responsibilities ... [and that] the trial time saved also reduced Alberta clients' estimated legal costs by $10,000,000".[9]

Many Canadian communities have also initiated community justice programs to mediate between victims and offenders in certain property damage cases. One of the oldest of these, Community Justice, begun by the Mennonite community in Kitchener-Waterloo, Ontario,[10] reports a high degree of success in restoring damaged property to good condition, but, even more important, in bringing about reconciliation between the victims and the offenders. Without that there is every chance that the same behaviour will recur. If you search under "community justice in Canada" you will find thousands of community and restorative justice initiatives across the country that build on that important beginning.

To even approach staying current about new or changing Canadian programs and projects, not to mention books, courses and designations, DR practitioners need to belong to ADR organizations, read newsletters in hard copy or electronic format, attend meetings and other get-togethers, take part in online chat groups, volunteer on committees, swap books and generally stay connected to others in the field. Even then, it is an ongoing

---

[7]   *Ibid.*, at 17.
[8]   J.D. Rooke, "Improving Excellence: Evaluation of the Judicial Dispute Resolution Program in the Court of Queen's Bench of Alberta" (1 June 2009) at xxiv, 171-72, online: Canadian Forum on Civil Justice <http://cfcj-fcjc.org/clearinghouse/hosted/22338-improving_excellence.pdf>.
[9]   *Ibid.*, at iii, vi, viii.
[10] See online: Community Justice Initiatives <http://www.cjiwr.com>.

commitment. The DR universe is still expanding in Canada at an accelerating rate.

Links (from one website to another) and databases are other ways to try to stay up-to-date. These provide useful sources of information. For example, in April 2002, the Canadian Forum on Civil Justice[11] launched the Civil Justice Clearinghouse database, which includes thousands of bibliographic records and a growing number of full-text documents. You only need to scan the list of award-winning ADR papers to see the range of ADR applications and to appreciate the futility of trying to track the development of all of them.

It is not that DR skills and knowledge are becoming unrecognizable and outpacing practitioners. It is that new applications come into being and old ones take on new configurations all the time. The issue is the rate and magnitude of program change. The state of DR in Canada is extremely fluid.

The reasons for change can also be complex or obscure, as was the case with Ontario's Mandatory Mediation Program. In the summer of 2004, there were rumours that mandatory mediation would end abruptly in a matter of weeks. This was perplexing, since no consultation had taken place and an arm's-length evaluation of Ontario's mandatory mediation initiative in 2001 found significant cost savings for litigants.[12] As it transpired, there was a proposal for change prompted by the perceptions of the judiciary that urgent action was required to address pressing problems facing civil cases in Toronto. A draft practice direction was eventually circulated to lawyers and mediators in the fall of 2004. The practice direction made several significant changes to mandatory mediation in Toronto for actions started after December 31, 2004, which were incorporated into Rule 24.1 of the Ontario Rules of Civil Procedure.[13] These changes are discussed in the section on court-related initiatives later in this chapter, but the most significant one was that the typical timing of the mediation changed from the beginning to the end of the litigation cycle.

Inevitably, keeping up with ADR in Canada will be limited by each individual's personal interests, location (geographic or jurisdictional) and practical time constraints. There is also the phenomenon of information overload. There is more going on than one person can reasonably process.

For all of these reasons, this chapter will take a selective approach to Canadian initiatives. Rather than sending readers off to the internet to get dizzy and oversaturated with data, we will confine ourselves to a small

---

[11] See online: Canadian Forum on Civil Justice <http://www.cfcj-fcjc.org>.

[12] J. Macfarlane, *Court-Based Mediation for Civil Cases: An Evaluation of the Ontario Court (General Division) ADR Centre* (Toronto: Queen's Printer for Ontario, November 1995), cited in Ontario's *Civil Justice Review's Supplementary Report*, c. 5 (1996); see online: <http://www.attorneygeneral.jus.gov.on.ca/english/about/pubs/cjr/suppreport/ch52a.asp>.

[13] R.R.O. 1990, Reg. 194.

number of programs. We will examine some of the features of these DR initiatives and suggest what might be noteworthy about each one. There is no judgment implicit in our selection. We are not saying that the chosen initiatives are good and that others are not. We are simply showing a little of the range and diversity of DR in Canada.

INITIATIVES OUTSIDE THE CIVIL COURTS

Canadian Motor Vehicle Arbitration Plan: Neutral Expert Opinion plus Arbitration

One of the early Canadian DR initiatives is the Canadian Motor Vehicle Arbitration Plan ("CAMVAP"), a DR program for consumer warranty and defect claims against automobile manufacturers and importers.[14] This program has been written up and reproduced elsewhere, so the intention here is not to replicate those efforts. Instead, after a brief description, we will look at how it uses an informative process as a subroutine in arbitration by providing neutral expert opinions from independent technical inspectors.

CAMVAP came into existence in 1994 as a proactive response to the prospect of "Lemon Law" legislation. By initiating their own dispute resolution program, automobile manufacturers and importers have avoided consumer protection legislation. CAMVAP is designed to be a "fast, fair, friendly and free" alternative to litigation over warranty and defect claims.

As the name suggests, CAMVAP is an arbitration program, not a mediation program. The results of the process legally bind both consumers and manufacturers.

CAMVAP has roster arbitrators across the country. These arbitrators have a defined mandate with limited discretion and a set menu of available remedies[15] for proven warranty and defect claims.

In 2007, CAMVAP handled a total of 267 cases. Monetary awards for that year totalled $2,091,692. Its availability is an important public service, as a vehicle (car, truck or van) represents a significant monetary investment for the average Canadian. The website does note that because vehicles are built better all the time, the number of claims has decreased over the years.

---

[14]   See online: Canadian Motor Vehicle Arbitration Plan <http://www.camvap.ca/eng/consumers_guide.htm>. Reference has already been made to this program's policy for complaints about roster arbitrators, which is informed by the principles of procedural fairness.

[15]   The detailed *Agreement for Arbitration*, which sets out both eligibility criteria and jurisdiction, can be found online: Canadian Motor Vehicle Arbitration Plan <http://www.camvap.ca/downloads/camvap_agreement_arb_eng_2010.pdf>.

CAMVAP operates in both official languages in all Canadian provinces and territories. It is funded by the automobile industry and governed by a multi-stakeholder board with representatives from government, consumer groups and the automobile industry.

In Chapter 1, we mentioned that DR processes can be combined and ordered in different ways. A program does not have to confine itself to a single DR process like mediation. CAMVAP inserts an informative process into an adjudicative one.

A central question in most cases is whether or not there is a defect in vehicle assembly or materials specific to the vehicle as delivered by the manufacturer to an authorized dealer.[16] To decide that, an arbitrator has the option of referring technical automotive questions to an independent technical inspector at any point in the arbitration process. This can be done on the arbitrator's initiative or on the request of either or both parties.

The technical inspection is an informative process that takes the form of a subroutine in the arbitration process. The CAMVAP program contracts with third party experts for this purpose and makes technical inspectors available at no cost to either party.[17]

Relevant program documents for technical inspections are available online.[18] Article 10 of the *Agreement for Arbitration* outlines the arbitrator's discretion to order a technical inspection, and the relevant time frames.[19] Basically, the arbitrator sets out the symptoms to be examined by the independent expert and asks what those symptoms mean and what can be done about them. The expert's response helps the arbitrator interpret the facts of the case and draw appropriate inferences.

A technical inspection is purely informative. The expert's mandate is to be independent and not to act as an advocate for any party. The expert's report does not bind the parties or the arbitrator, but is used as assistance in reaching an appropriate result on the facts of the case. The parties receive a copy of the expert's report before the arbitrator rules, and they have the opportunity to make comments on it. Technical inspectors do not usually participate in hearings, although they are available for clarification and, if need be, for cross-examination.

The employment of experts to examine the vehicle and report back to the arbitrator is helpful in a DR program that uses non-expert arbitrators.

---

[16] See s. 4.2.2 of the *Agreement for Arbitration, ibid.*

[17] Keep in mind, however, that the program is ultimately funded by vehicle manufacturers and importers.

[18] See online: Canadian Motor Vehicle Arbitration Plan <http://www.camvap.ca/eng/camvap_getting_ready.htm#Stage%207%20-%20Inspecting%20the%20Vehicle%20and%20the%20Test%20Drive>.

[19] See online: Canadian Motor Vehicle Arbitration Plan <http://www.camvap.ca/eng/agreement_for_arbitration_2010.htm>.

The technical inspector assists the non-expert decision-maker to interpret and process technical information.

Technical inspections are also of assistance in a consumer-oriented DR program. CAMVAP has many one-time users (consumers) and a few repeat users (manufacturers and importers). Consumers may not have the financial resources or wherewithal to hire their own technical experts. This feature of the program makes independent technical expertise available at no cost to the consumer. It thus goes some distance to balancing power in the arbitration.

General Insurance OmbudService: Non-Binding ADR at Lowest Level

CAMVAP can be compared and contrasted with a DR initiative in the insurance industry, the General Insurance OmbudService ("GIO"). General insurance (property and casualty insurance) refers to all types of insurance other than life and health insurance. It includes automobile insurance, insurance for homeowners and tenants as well as business-oriented insurance, such as business interruption coverage. GIO concerns itself with disputes between customers and general insurance companies.

Unlike CAMVAP, which was a proactive initiative to avoid legislation, GIO is the result of legislation. The federal *Insurance Companies Act*[20] governs all federally incorporated or registered insurance companies. Section 486(1) of that Act requires all insurance companies to put in place a procedure for handling customer complaints about their products or services and to designate someone within the company to implement those procedures. That plan must be filed with a federal agency called the Financial Consumer Agency of Canada.

Section 486.1 of the *Insurance Companies Act* requires that each insurance company also be a member of an organization that is not controlled by it and that deals with those complaints that have not been resolved to the customer's satisfaction at the company level. For the property and casualty insurers, GIO is that independent organization. It was launched on July 1, 2002.

GIO is designed to comply with 10 standards or principles for complaint-handling set by the Centre for Financial Services OmbudsNetwork,[21] namely accessibility, timeliness, courtesy, clarity, accuracy, consistency, knowledge, fairness and impartiality, confidentiality and independence and objectivity.

---

[20]   S.C. 1991, c. 47.
[21]   See online: General Insurance OmbudService <http://www.giocanada.org/whosgio.html>.

GIO members are insurers and reinsurers licensed in Canada to carry on the business of general insurance and that have agreed to abide by the organization's standards. GIO is governed by a seven-person board of directors, five of whom are independent. Like CAMVAP, however, GIO is funded by industry.

Dispute resolution through GIO is of a non-binding nature. It uses direct negotiation followed by independent mediation. The parties are not legally bound by the outcome unless they reach a mutually satisfactory agreement. If the consumer is still dissatisfied after going through GIO's process, he or she has access to legal options.

GIO has a three-step dispute resolution process. It is straightforward with minimal documentation required,[22] unlike CAMVAP, which has an elaborate agreement to arbitrate and a guidebook.[23]

GIO's first step is described as *Consumer Assistance*. Consumers are assigned to a Consumer Service Officer (CSO) who will work with them to determine how the problem might be resolved. Consumers may be invited to first contact their insurance company, a GIO member,[24] to determine if the issue can be resolved with a phone call. If not, the CSO will guide the consumer through the complaint-handling process.

Step two is described as *Informal Conciliation*. The CSO will provide assistance with reducing the complaint to writing and discussing the issues with the company's Complaint Liaison Officer. At the end of this step, the insurance company issues a Final Position Letter stating how it intends to resolve the complaint. The consumer has the option of accepting or rejecting the proposal. Essentially, this is a process of offer and acceptance (or rejection, as the case may be). It is also an attempt at achieving resolution at the lowest possible level, the company level, before escalating the dispute to another form of authority.

Step three is described as *Mediation or Senior Adjudication*. If the consumer is not satisfied with the insurance company's settlement proposal, the matter may proceed either to mediation or to adjudication before GIO's Senior Adjudicative Officer. The CSO will assist the consumer with the choice of process and facilitate its progress.

Mediators are selected from rosters that were established independently of GIO for the purposes of this initiative. For Atlantic

---

[22]   See online: General Insurance OmbudService <http://www.gio-scad.org> and click on "How the Process Works" and on "Getting Started".

[23]   This is a consequence of the legalistic nature of CAMVAP as compared to the informal, non-binding nature of GIO. An adjudicative process that decides rights and entitlements and incorporates natural justice will call for more paperwork.

[24]   This is the national trade association that represents the companies that insure Canadian homes, cars and businesses.

Canada, Ontario, the Prairie provinces and British Columbia, rosters were established by ADR Canada Inc., and for Quebec by le Barreau du Quebec. Neither of those organizations administers the mediations, but the mediators are professionally accountable to them, not to GIO. For instance, complaints about a mediator on a panel established by ADR Canada Inc. would be handled by that organization's discipline procedure.[25] The mediator's external accountability is a feature intended to uphold GIO's independence from the insurance industry.

GIO mediations are two hours long and have an interesting feature: if settlement is not reached, the mediator can issue a non-binding report with recommendations. Here is an example of informative DR integrated into a consensual process, this time at the end of the process and with the same practitioner assuming both mandates. In CAMVAP, the informative process (technical inspection) takes place as a subroutine during the arbitration, and is performed by someone other than the arbitrator.

If the Senior Adjudication route is chosen, both the consumer and the company have the opportunity to submit more documentation, but there is no attendance by the parties before the Senior Adjudication Officer. It is a paper hearing unless the Officer requires clarification on an issue. The Officer reviews the case and delivers a report containing a non-binding recommendation. If the recommendation is not acceptable to either party, the next step is litigation in the courts.

To date, GIO has handled a low volume of cases. Its 2008–2009 Annual Report cited 1,300 consumer calls about claims from across Canada, resulting in 66 cases handled by GIO. Of the 66, 12 were settled at the company level, two went to mediation, one escalated to Senior Adjudicative Officer and two went through both mediation and adjudication.[26]

Immigration Appeal Division: Tribunal-Led ADR

In addition to industry uses, there are significant applications for ADR at Canadian agencies, boards and commissions. One well-developed application exists at the Immigration Appeal Division of the Immigration and Refugee Board ("IRB").

The IRB is made up of three tribunals or "divisions". The Immigration Appeal Division ("IAD") is one of them. It decides appeals of sponsorship applications that have been refused by officials of Citizenship and

---

[25] See ADR Institute of Canada, *Regulation No. 1: Discipline Procedure*, online: ADR Institute of Canada <http://www.adrcanada.ca/rules/complaints.cfm>.

[26] See online: ADR Institute of Canada Inc. <http://www.giocanada.org/pdf/GIOAnnualReport09_EN_WEB.pdf>.

Immigration Canada, and appeals from removal orders.[27] Sponsorship is a way for Canadian citizens or permanent residents to reunite their families in Canada. The original decision refusing the sponsorship request would have been made by a visa officer overseas.

In the ordinary course, a sponsorship appeal is resolved by a tribunal hearing and a decision. However, in July 1998, the IAD began a pilot ADR project for these appeals. This project was subsequently expanded, evaluated and refined. It is now offered across Canada.

To our eyes, the IAD initiative is simply a standard, conservative mediation process appropriately adapted and integrated into the workings of an administrative tribunal. This is clear from a review of its written protocol.[28] The protocol contains extremely detailed basic directions for the conduct of ADR conferences, including how to meet and greet the parties and how to scrupulously allocate equal time to private meetings with the parties. The purpose of the protocol is to ensure consistency of approach from one location to another and from one session to another. Consistency of approach is apparently something the tribunal or its consultants value.

Early on, the IAD got caught up in semantics, with some people arguing that its resolution process was not "really" mediation. The linguistic debate became a focal point for resistance to the program by some users. Accordingly, the IAD decided to sidestep theory in favour of practice by calling their resolution process an "ADR conference" instead of mediation.

An *ADR conference* is an informal, in-person, hour-long meeting. The participants include the appellant (Canadian citizen or resident who applied to sponsor a relative) and his or her lawyer, a lawyer representing the federal Department of Citizenship and Immigration (which denied the sponsorship application) and a tribunal member of the IAD. The IAD tribunal member plays a dual role during the meeting, leading the ADR process and offering an evaluative opinion if and when appropriate. A support person for the appellant may also be present, but in a secondary, not a primary role.

From the IAD's point of view, ADR conferences divert cases. That is to say, they help reduce the number of sponsorship appeal hearings. From the appellant's point of view, an ADR conference provides an opportunity to be listened to, as well as a chance at early resolution, without the costs and risks of a hearing. Resolution will result if the lawyer for Citizenship and Immigration Canada is prepared to recommend that the appeal be allowed. For that to occur, the lawyer must become convinced that the appeal would

---

[27] See online: Immigration and Refugee Board of Canada <http://www.irb-cisr.gc.ca/eng/tribunal/ iadsai/Pages/index.aspx>.
[28] See online: Immigration and Refugee Board of Canada <http://www.irb-cisr.gc.ca/eng/brdcom/ references/legjur/iadsai/adrmarl/Pages/protoc.aspx>.

likely succeed at hearing. Thus, like so many mediations in so many other contexts, ADR conferences are not purely interest-based procedures.

If the IAD's ADR initiative was rated for transparency, we would give it a high grade. There is an abundance of clear and complete information available to users of this program. There is a publicly accessible summary of the ADR initiative, an explanation of the traditional hearing process that applies if settlement is not reached, an appellant's guide to ADR conferences and even the detailed protocol intended for the tribunal members who lead ADR conferences, which is something that would not ordinarily be shared. The public also has access to a summary of the independent consultant's evaluation of the program in 2002.[29]

The IAD's program competently addresses basic concerns about integrating mediation into an administrative tribunal. This alone is a reason to study ADR conferences.

The IAD opted to have tribunal members conduct their mediation sessions. When these members do so, they are called dispute resolution officers, or DROs. This immediately creates the potential for natural justice concerns. How do you ensure fair hearings if tribunal members take part in settlement discussions where admissions and concessions may be made? This problem is addressed in several ways in the IAD's Rules and its ADR Protocol.[30] First of all, members who lead ADR conferences are disqualified from hearing the matter if the mediation fails and it goes on to a hearing. Second, the DRO's notes do not go in the hearings file. Third, DROs do not share information with members who could hear the case if it does not resolve. These aspects of the program serve to protect adjudicators from being challenged for bias, promote fair hearings and encourage the necessary trust and confidence in the ADR process.

The use of tribunal members as mediators is one of the mediation variations that we discussed in Chapter 3, where we pointed out that not every mediator is completely at arm's length. In the IAD program, the DRO is a paid member of the very body that will adjudicate the appeal if it does not settle. That is a close connection. The DRO's position brings with it power and authority. Fair hearings have been preserved by isolating the DRO as described above, but the essential value of a tribunal-mediator has been preserved. That value consists of authority, knowledge and experience.

A DRO has typically adjudicated other sponsorship appeals. He or she knows how these appeals work, what can be compelling, what can be influential in winning a case. He or she can distinguish relevant considerations from irrelevant ones. The DRO's knowledge and experience

---

[29] See online: Immigration and Refugee Board of Canada <http://www.irb-cisr.gc.ca/eng/tribunal/iadsai/adrmar/Pages/sum.aspx>.

[30] Immigration Appeal Division Rules, SOR/2002-230, R. 20.

in the context of sponsorship appeals help the parties when the DRO gives an authoritative opinion about what can happen if the matter proceeds to a hearing. The opinion is binding on no one, that is, on neither the parties nor the IAD, but it can be influential. It can help both sides to the appeal consider their alternatives and determine whether to take the risk of going forward.

To digress for a moment, in the context of administrative tribunals we would argue that this is precisely where tribunal-mediators and staff-mediators can add value. They can inform the mediation with relevant knowledge and experience. They can help the parties form realistic projections instead of idealistic or wishful ones. Opinion-giving may offend some mediators philosophically but we would argue that personally held theories should not deprive ADR participants of practical choice. We are convinced that tribunal users want and need informed opinions from the people who conduct ADR processes.

In 2002, a written survey was conducted to obtain feedback from users of an ADR initiative at another federal tribunal.[31] Cases that went to ADR there had a commercial character. ADR was a staff-led process and consisted of a range of processes from staff mediation through to non-binding written opinion, but parties were supposed to try mediation with outside mediators before accessing tribunal staff. However, 71 per cent of respondents disagreed with the requirement to use outside mediators as a condition of entry into ADR, and 28 per cent strongly disagreed with this prerequisite. By contrast, survey respondents were very favourably disposed to staff-led processes and many wanted staff to play an even stronger role. Ninety-three per cent of respondents said that tribunal staff were helpful throughout the ADR process, and the same percentage said the ADR process was fair. Key phrases used by respondents when describing staff involvement included "forthright", "unbiased opinions", "in-depth understanding" and "authority of tribunal's framework". Eighty per cent of respondents preferred an ADR process over a traditional one. In their sounding-board role during ADR, staff served as a suitable proxy for the tribunal. Respondents would dispense with a traditional hearing if they could get the next best thing — a timely, reliable opinion or view from staff which could inform a compromise outcome.

As will be seen in the discussion of an ADR initiative at the Alberta Energy Resources Conservation Board, participants in that tribunal's ADR processes also favoured the involvement of staff from that tribunal.

The IAD's ADR conferences are also intended to be without prejudice settlement conferences, although the label "confidentiality" is used instead. Participants are assured that the conferences are "confidential" and that

---

[31]   The survey was prepared and administered by Genevieve Chornenki.

nothing said in a conference can be used against them at a later date. The explicit "explanation of confidentiality" used at each ADR conference states, "ADR is a confidential process. If your case does not settle through ADR, what is said during the ADR process cannot be used by either party against the other during the hearing." Consent is, of course, an exception.

This protection is not unconditional, however, and brings us to one other important feature. The IAD's program places explicit limits on the protection given to without prejudice and confidential communications. If the information is independently available, the protection does not apply. Nor will there be protection if the information relates to an offence under Canadian Immigration legislation or a breach of the IAD Rules.

The last two exceptions are common and acceptable exemptions for all statutory bodies. A tribunal like the IAD has public interest obligations and governing legislation. Attending to these is not optional. Condoning illegality is not appropriate.

Along the same lines, another feature of the program is that outcomes from ADR conferences are not final outcomes. They are provisional only. The lawyer for Citizenship and Immigration Canada determines whether to recommend that the appeal be allowed. A tentative agreement is reached allowing the appeal. This is subject to a final order of a member of the tribunal. A settlement form is filled out and this is put before a tribunal member (different from the DRO), who approves it, but without a file review or an investigation into the merits. Through this mechanism, the tribunal has properly (albeit formally) dealt with an issue before it, without illegally delegating its authority.

Alberta Energy Resources Conservation Board: Staff-Led Facilitation

The IAD initiative can be compared and contrasted to the initiative at another administrative tribunal, the Alberta Energy Resources Conservation Board ("ERCB").

The ERCB's dispute resolution initiative began in January 2001, when a three-year pilot project was launched. A multi-stakeholder task force developed and endorsed a framework for introducing ADR concepts and tools into Alberta's energy sector.[32] The pilot project was monitored and evaluated, and now is an ongoing dispute resolution program at the Board.

The ERCB's dispute resolution initiative is extremely well documented, monitored and reported. There is an impressive amount of

---

[32]   See Energy Resources Conservation Board, *Report for Implementation of an Appropriate Dispute Resolution System for Alberta's Upstream Petroleum Applications* (May 2000), available online: ERCB <http://www.ercb.ca/>.

documentation available online — from promotional and informational materials about ADR through to detailed report forms.[33] There are also local, toll-free or email helplines.

Like the IAD, the ERCB uses the term "ADR" for its initiative but for a different reason. At the ERCB, ADR means *appropriate dispute resolution* and reflects a range of process choices available to participants, including processes involving ERCB staff. The notion is to promote the "right process" for the "right situation", not just to graft mediation onto conventional board adjudications.

While the IAD decides sponsorship appeals between a Canadian citizen and the state, the ERCB operates in a totally different context. It is a regulatory body in the energy industry. Issues before the Board concern proposed facilities or modifications to existing facilities in the energy industry, such as wells, pipelines, production facilities, electrical substations or transmission lines. There can also be issues between competing companies.

The ERCB values collaboration, interest-based approaches and participation, and these ideals are consistently reflected in its documentation. In the first instance, companies are expected to inform potentially impacted parties of the nature of their proposal or significant changes in operations, respond to questions and concerns and seek understanding through collaborative efforts. The ERCB maintains that effective early and low-level intervention minimizes subsequent disputes.

ADR is used at the ERCB when consultation or direct negotiation has not resolved concerns and objections. Thus, ADR, which is voluntary, is an extension of the ERCB's expectations for public-to-industry and industry-to-industry contact, consultation and disclosure. Many of the disputes involve multiple parties and technical or scientific information.

There are two types of ADR: *staff-assisted facilitation* and something called a *preliminary ADR meeting*, which is run by a paid, arm's-length ADR practitioner and follows an unsuccessful staff-led process.

The assistance of ERCB staff can be sought at any stage of a dispute, even before a formal application has been made. In addition, an application for a hearing will be processed and moved forward at the same time as ADR proceeds, unless the parties agree otherwise. This is an important feature of ADR at an administrative tribunal. Even where ADR is used to shorten hearings or eliminate them altogether, it must not be, or appear to be, a means of delay, nor can it interfere with a party's right to a fair, timely hearing. When that happens, ADR conflicts with the tribunal's jurisdiction

---

[33]   See online: ERCB <http://www.ercb.ca/portal/server.pt/gateway/PTARGS_0_240_2546932_0_ 0_18/> and ERCB, *Finding Solutions* (2008), online: <http://www.ercb.ca/docs/Documents/ reports/ADRAnnualReport-2008.pdf>.

and natural justice obligations. The ERCB is aware of this. It states that participation in ADR does not preclude access to a hearing or diminish the parties' rights. Its attitude is: "Hearings where necessary but not necessarily hearings."

Staff-assisted facilitation is what we would call staff-led mediation, using our broad and elastic definition of mediation.[34] ERCB staff offer both procedural and substantive leadership in ADR. In ERCB facilitations, staff use mediation techniques to facilitate interest-based outcomes and apply relevant ERCB knowledge and experience. This is similar to the IAD's process, where tribunal members play both a procedural and a substantive role in ADR conferences.

The ERCB's ADR guidelines make it clear that staff can be asked for regulatory and other information. In addition, "Staff can facilitate parties' communications to help clarify issues, identify key concerns and interests, and assist the parties in understanding and accessing appropriate ADR options. They can also evaluate consultation efforts and provide feedback."[35]

High success rates and positive feedback from participants attest to the value of staff-led resolution at the ERCB. In its 2007 Annual Report, the Board reported that of the 156 facilitations and 19 third-party mediations that were completed, 92 per cent were resolved. As we would have predicted, participants also observed that ERCB staff added credibility to ADR, clarified regulatory requirements, and helped ensure that complete and reasonable agreements were reached.[36] It should also be noted that there is no charge for staff-led sessions.

If staff cannot bring about resolution at an early stage, the ERCB encourages participants to use outside ADR service providers. The first stop after a staff-led process is a *preliminary ADR* meeting, or PADR. These are essentially convening sessions[37] with a paid ADR professional. At a PADR, the parties discuss dispute resolution options, plus practicalities like the identity of necessary parties, what information is needed and how to obtain it. They also discuss logistics, costs, cost allocation and timing of the next step. Most, but not all matters proceed from a PADR to an interest-based mediation. Parties may choose from a list of mediators on the ERCB website

---

[34]   By contrast, the ERCB defines a mediator as a person who is at arm's length in every way. With that stricter definition, the ERCB makes it clear that "ERCB will not take on a mediation role" even though ERCB staff may attend meetings with the parties.

[35]   Alberta Energy and Utilities Board, Informational Letter IL 2001-1 (8 January 2001), online: ERCB <http://www.ercb.ca/docs/ils/ils/pdf/il2001-01.pdf> at 7. The Energy and Utilities Board was the predecessor of the Energy Resources Conservation Board.

[36]   See the Alberta Energy Resources Conservation Board, *Appropriate Dispute Resolution Review: Finding Solutions* (2007) at 1, online: ERCB <http://www.ercb.ca/docs/Documents/reports/ADRAnnualReport-2007.pdf>.

[37]   See K.A. Slaikeu & R.H. Hasson, *Controlling the Costs of Conflict: How to Design a System for Your Organization* (San Francisco: Jossey-Bass Publishers, 1998) at 110.

or from any other source. In 2003, the average cost of mediation was $4,900 and the average time was eight hours. More recent information has not been reported.

ADR at the ERCB is intended to be without prejudice and confidential. However, as with the IAD, this does not extend blanket protection. The guidelines make it clear that any agreement must conform to regulatory and statutory requirements. That means that certain technical, scientific or other information or components of an agreement may have to be disclosed to the ERCB or other regulatory authorities.

The guidelines speak generally to ADR outcomes and how they will be enforced. A distinction is drawn between matters that fall within the ERCB's jurisdiction and those that do not. The guideline states that: "The EUB may evaluate and enforce only those components of the agreement within its jurisdiction to ensure that the agreement is in the public interest, does not constitute an environmental or public safety risk, and is compliant with regulatory requirements."[38]

Other Combination Programs

Before moving on to look at ADR initiatives in Canadian courts, we will briefly mention just two other programs from vastly different contexts. Both of these happen to contain consensual and adjudicative DR options and both are well documented. They have many features in common but they show how widely ADR concepts and skills may be applied.

One of these combination programs is that of the Ismaili community,[39] which has developed a dispute resolution mechanism that is available for the voluntary resolution of differences among community members and by community members. In 1987 (the early days for Canadian ADR), Conciliation and Arbitration Boards ("CABs") were established. In Canada, there is a National Board and five Regional Boards.

As the title suggests, this dispute resolution initiative consists of both mediation (conciliation) and arbitration, but to date most cases handled by CABs in Canada have been conciliations. Conciliation is defined as "a process of dispute resolution in which a neutral person assists the parties to a dispute in reaching their own settlement. The neutral person does not have authority to make a binding decision on the parties. As the process is entirely

---

[38]   See Alberta Energy and Utilities Board, Informational Letter IL 2001-01 (8 January 2001), online: ERCB <http://www.ercb.ca/docs/ils/ils/pdf/il2001-01.pdf>.

[39]   The Ismaili Muslims form a sect of the Muslim faith. They are widely dispersed around the globe, with communities in North America, Eastern and Western Europe, Asia and Africa. The Canadian Ismaili community has about 75,000-80,000 members.

voluntary, the parties may withdraw from the process at anytime."[40] Matters coming to conciliation may concern marriage breakdown, wills and estates, commercial issues or other civil disputes.

Appendix 4 contains some of the relevant documentation for CABs in Canada in respect of the conciliation process. Students of mediation will find there many of the features they have come to expect in mediation protocols, including ethical standards for conciliators, confidentiality provisions and process directions.[41]

The second ADR initiative to consider is the Sport Dispute Resolution Centre of Canada (SDRCC).[42] This is an independent resource centre for the prevention and resolution of disputes in amateur sport in Canada, established by federal legislation (the *Physical Activity and Sport Act*[43]) and launched on April 1, 2004.

SDRCC specializes in sports-related conflicts that arise in the Canadian amateur sport community. It offers resolution facilitation, mediation, med-arb and arbitration through its rosters, as well as a resource centre and a disputes secretariat to administer hearings. Apart from a small initiation fee, the costs of these ADR services are paid for by the centre.[44] SDRCC also administers all hearings and appeals flowing from the Canadian Anti-Doping Program.

COURT-RELATED INITIATIVES

All across Canada, at all levels from small claims court to appeal courts, there is a growing recognition that ADR can resolve issues earlier and more efficiently than litigation, saving both litigants and the public system time and money. Although private ADR is always available to willing parties, this section concentrates on initiatives where the court exercises jurisdiction and brings ADR under its wing in one way or another.

Mediation is the process most often linked to the civil courts. There are many ways to provide mediation in this context — by government-employed mediators, to a combination of volunteer mediators and government paid

---

[40] His Highness Prince Aga Khan Shia Imami Ismaili National Conciliation and Arbitration Board for Canada, *Rules for Conciliation Proceedings* at s. 1.1 (see Appendix 4, as there is no online source as of yet).

[41] For an interesting essay containing more detail about this initiative and which compares the Beth Din in Judaism, the Conciliation and Arbitration Boards of the Canadian Ismaili community and the Dispute Resolution Policy of the United Church of Canada, see K. Johnston, G. Camelino & R. Rizzo, "A Return to 'Traditional' Dispute Resolution" (2000), online: Canadian Forum on Civil Justice <http://cfcj-fcjc.org/clearinghouse/drpapers/traditional.htm>.

[42] See online: SDRCC <http://www.crdsc-sdrcc.ca/eng/home.jsp>.

[43] S.C. 2003, c. 2.

[44] For its process, see online: CSDRC <http://www.crdsc-sdrcc.ca/documents/eng/CODE2009 FINALEN.pdf>.

administration, through to free market, user-pay systems, and everything in between. Here, we will look at a number of models used in Canada. Once again, our intention is to be neither exclusive nor exhaustive. There is no judgment implied in our choice. We simply want to show something of the range and diversity of ADR in the civil courts.

Because some court-connected programs are *voluntary* and others are *mandatory*, a short discussion of the difference may be useful. There has been a heated debate in the DR community about the appropriateness of *mandatory mediation*, arguing that voluntariness is an essential component of ADR, and that it is counter-productive to force parties to try to settle a case that they have no interest in settling.[45] That there is a value in bringing the parties to the table at all, is succinctly put in the *Ontario Civil Justice Review Supplementary Report*: "As to the mandatory nature of the referral, the literature on the subject reveals that parties do not opt-in to voluntary systems."[46] In the mandatory court-connected programs under consideration, what is mandatory or required is that the participants come to the table to *try to* resolve their disputes, not that they *must* settle. Independent evaluations of these and other mandatory programs have shown repeatedly that the mandate *to the table* has little or no impact on the success of the programs.[47] Noted writer and thinker in the field of DR, Julie Macfarlane, has gone so far as to say in her recent book that the mandate is a good thing:

> The advent of mandatory mediation programming in the courts has created a growing group of personal clients who are asking questions about the traditional parameters of the lawyer-client relationship. Mandatory mediation means that clients who have no knowledge or experience of mediation are finding themselves attending sessions with the mediator, along with their lawyers ... . Studies have consistently demonstrated that the vast majority of clients welcome the chance for mediation and see it as a valuable opportunity whether or not settlement follows. Further, there is no significant difference in satisfaction levels, which remain consistently high, between clients mandated into mediation and those who chose the process voluntarily.[48]

We agree with Professor Macfarlane, having seen the dynamic at work in the Ontario Mandatory Mediation Program, but whatever your view, as

---

[45]   For a recent example, see C. Menkel-Meadow, "Maintaining ADR Integrity" (January 2009) 27:1 Alternatives to the High Cost of Litigation 1 at 7-9, online: Social Science Research Network <http://papers.ssrn.com/sol3/papers.cfm?abstract_id=1340185##>.

[46]   *Ontario Civil Justice Review: Supplemental and Final Report* (November 1996), c. 5, online: http://www.attorneygeneral.jus.gov.on.ca/english/about/pubs/cjr/suppreport/ch52a.asp>.

[47]   R.L. Wissler, "The Effects of Mandatory Mediation: Empirical Research on the Experience of Small Claims and Common Pleas Courts" (1997) 33 Willamette L. Rev. 565, online <http://papers.ssrn.com/sol3/papers.cfm?abstract_id=1724817>; J. Macfarlane, *Court-Based Mediation for Civil Cases: An Evaluation of the Ontario Court (General Division) ADR Centre* (Toronto: Queen's Printer for Ontario, November 1995).

[48]   J. Macfarlane, *The New Lawyer: How Settlement is Transforming The Practice of Law* (Vancouver: UBC Press, 2008) at 135.

you can see from what follows, mandatory mediation in connection with the courts is here to stay.

Ontario's Mandatory Mediation Program

In 1994, Ontario led the way in court-sponsored mediation, beginning with a pilot project, known as the ADR Centre Project, on a select-case basis (4 in 10 of Toronto actions). The project developed as a response to a growing public perception that litigating civil disputes was too complex, too costly and too time-consuming.

This pilot went through a number of iterations and evaluations, and matured into early mandatory mediation for every case-managed civil action in the major judicial centres in Ontario. The initiative came to be known as the Ontario Mandatory Mediation Program ("OMMP").

Under the earliest version of OMMP, mandatory mediation had to occur within 90 days of the filing of the first defence subject to a 60-day extension on consent or a longer delay on order of the court. There was a presumption in favour of early mediation, as close as possible to the time when an action was initiated, and the court kept up the momentum. The parties had 30 days from the first defence to select their own mediator, failing which the court automatically assigned a mediator from a roster maintained for that purpose. Roster mediators were obliged to charge set fees for the first three hours of mediation plus one hour of preparation.

Mandatory mediation still operates in Ontario, but it has a somewhat more limited application and less stringent timelines. The most recent reforms resulted from the Civil Justice Reform Project that was initiated in June 2006 and culminated in a report on November 20, 2007.[49] The reforms became law in January 2010.

Mandatory mediation continues to be geographically restricted to Toronto, Windsor and Ottawa and applies to some, but not all civil actions as of January 2010. Exemptions from mandatory mediation include Toronto Commercial List actions, bankruptcy and insolvency actions, certified class proceedings and actions relating to estates, trusts and substitute decision.[50]

Under the 2010 revisions to OMMP, mediation must take place within 180 days after the first defence is filed, unless the parties agree or the court orders otherwise. Cooperative parties can therefore delay mediation until well into the litigation process, right up until the action is set down for trial.

---

[49]   See the Honourable C.A. Osborne, Q.C., Ontario Ministry of the Attorney General, *Summary of Findings and Recommendations of the Civil Justice Reform Project* (November 2007), online: <http://www.attorneygeneral.jus.gov.on.ca>.

[50]   For fuller details about mandatory court-connected mediation in Ontario including flow charts, see Ontario, Ministry of the Attorney General, "Fact Sheet Mandatory Mediation Under Rules 24.1 and 75.1", online: <http://www.attorneygeneral.jus.gov.on.ca>.

A roster of approved mediators is still maintained by a Local Mediation Coordinator in each geographic centre. Roster mediators continue to be limited to the court-approved rates.[51] If the parties choose their own mediator on consent, they are not obliged to pick from the roster and may select a private-sector mediator with qualifications and rates acceptable to the parties.

The appointment of mediators is less frequent and less aggressive than it was in the early versions of OMMP. As of January 2010, the Local Mediation Coordinator will only appoint a mediator if within 180 days of the filing of the first defence, the parties have not filed documentation indicating: (i) their consent to postpone the mediation date; (ii) the particulars of an upcoming mediation; (iii) a court order postponing the mediation; or (iv) that the action has been settled.[52] If, despite the parties' consent or a court order, mediation has still not occurred by the time the action is set down for trial, a mediator will then be assigned from the roster.[53]

Ontario Mandatory Mediation in Estates, Trusts and Substitute Decisions

Mandatory mediation still exists in Ontario for litigation relating to estates, trusts and substitute decisions. This includes cases where multiple parties often argue over the appropriate distribution of the assets of the deceased, whether by way of will challenges, monetary claims or dependants' relief applications. These mediations are governed by Rule 75.1 of the Rules of Civil Procedure[54] and as with civil cases, roster mediators are obliged to charge court-approved rates.[55] Initially, Rule 75.1 applied on a pilot project basis, but following a positive evaluation, it was made permanent on July 1, 2004.[56]

A unique feature of mediations under Rule 75.1 is that they take place pursuant to a court order. An applicant must bring a motion for directions regarding the conduct of the mediation within 30 days after the last day for serving a notice of appearance. If the parties do not come to agreement on the identity of the mediator, one will be assigned by the Local Mediation Coordinator, although this rarely happens in practice.

---

[51] O. Reg. 451/98, s. 4(1).
[52] Rules of Civil Procedure, R.R.O. 1990, Reg. 194, R. 24.1.09(6).
[53] Ibid., R. 24.1.09(6.1).
[54] R.R.O. 1990, Reg. 194.
[55] O. Reg 43/05, s. 4(1).
[56] For fuller details about mandatory court-connected mediation in estates matters, see Ontario, Ministry of the Attorney General, "Fact Sheet Mandatory Mediation Under Rules 24.1 and 75.1", online: <http://www.attorneygeneral.jus.gov.on.ca>.

The court issues an order that governs the mediation. This order does not replace the agreement to mediate, but addresses the logistics and scope of the mediation. It can cover the issues to be mediated, the parties required to attend the mediation, the identity of the mediator, the allocation of mediation costs, the timing of the mediation and the production and disclosure required. A sample of an order giving directions is included at Appendix 5.

At first glance, interest-based mediators may find the content to be inappropriate for mediation or to represent a contradiction in terms. The court not only identifies who has "carriage" of the mediation, but also sets out the "issues to be mediated". The issues are framed as legal questions seemingly more appropriate to an arbitration or a trial. For example, the issues in Appendix 5 are as follows:

1. Is Loretta Gilbreth a "dependant" of the deceased, as defined in s. 57 of the *Succession Law Reform Act*, R.S.O. 1990, c. S.26?

2. Did the deceased make adequate provision for Loretta Gilbreth's proper support?

3. What provision is adequate for Loretta Gilbreth's proper support?

The issues are questions of fact and law, legal positions — the very thing that mediation is designed to work around and is ill-equipped to conclusively resolve. One would expect these framings to polarize the parties around their legal positions, but, in fact, they provide a useful focus. The reality is that estate mediations happen in much the same way as other civil mediations. They are a blend of positions and interests, legal and non-legal considerations, monetary and non-monetary concerns along with the usual array of psychological, procedural and substantive concerns. The court order does not materially impact the conduct of the mediation. It facilitates its administration.

Mandatory Mediation in Alberta

Mediation, as one of a list of enabled DR processes, will soon be a required feature of litigation in Alberta.[57] Alberta's New Rule 4.16 states in part:

> **4.16(1)** The responsibility of the parties to manage their dispute includes good faith participation in one or more of the following dispute resolution processes with respect to all or any part of the action:

---

[57] Alberta Rules of Court, Alta. Reg. 124/2010, R. 4.16(1), effective 1 November 2010. See also R. 8.4. New Rules 4.16 and 8.4 can be found in J.D. Rooke, "Improving Excellence: Evaluation of the Judicial Dispute Resolution Program in the Court of Queen's Bench of Alberta" (1 June 2009), Appendix 7, online: Canadian Forum on Civil Justice <http://cfcj-fcjc.org/clearinghouse/hosted/22338-improving_excellence.pdf>.

(a) a dispute resolution process in the private or government sectors involving an impartial third person;

(b) a Court annexed dispute resolution process;

(c) a judicial dispute resolution process described in rules 4.17 to 4.21 [Judicial Dispute Resolution];

(d) any program or process designated by the Court for the purpose of this rule.

Although the requirement may be waived on motion to the court (sub-rule 2), the parties must attend the motion, not just their counsel (sub-Rule 3), and waiver will only be ordered for substantial reasons. Without a waiver order, the companion New Rule 8.4 denies a trial date to any party failing to engage in a dispute resolution process required by New Rule 4.16.

What a long way the field has travelled! Courts are no longer suspicious of the full range of DR options. In fact, some have embraced them as full partners in the quest to find effective, cost-efficient ways of resolving disputes, that recognize and balance participants' rights of self-determination and their enjoyment of the rule of law. Associate Chief Justice John D. Rooke puts it best in his Master of Laws in Dispute Resolution thesis:

> One size does not fit all, and the parties can choose. While adjudication is unilateral at the instigation of one party (the plaintiff), both ADR (privately or court annexed) and JDR (within the Court currently) are based on the consent — indeed, the agreement — of all parties to the dispute. Therefore, I believe that this new institutionalized normative ordering has been established — adjudication and JDR (with its broad range of services) within the Court. Accordingly, as others have done, I declare that the "multi-door courthouse" is open in Alberta.[58]

For a discussion of Alberta JDR or *judicial dispute resolution*, which encompasses a full range of DR processes, not just mediation, see Chapter 6, "Mini-Trials and JDR".

At the time of writing the third edition, Alberta was about to begin a two-year pilot project for court-annexed mediation in its Small Claims Court "to promote private, user pay, interest based mediation in Alberta".[59] (Contrast this with Saskatchewan, where three-hour mediation sessions are free of charge.[60]) The Civil Claims Mediation Program is now offered in Edmonton, Calgary, Lethbridge, Medicine Hat, Red Deer, Grande Prairie

---

[58] J.D. Rooke, "The Multi-Door Courthouse Is Open in Alberta: Judicial Dispute Resolution Is Institutionalized in the Court of Queen's Bench" (thesis for LL.M. in Dispute Resolution, University of Alberta School of Law, 2010) at 77, online: <http://cfcj-fcjc.org/clearinghouse/hosted/22471-multidoor_courthouse.pdf>.

[59] See Court of Queen's Bench of Alberta, Civil Practice Note No. 11, Court Annexed Mediation (effective 1 September 2004), online: <http://www.albertacourts.ab.ca/qb/practicenotes/civil/pn11CourtAnnexedMediation.pdf>.

[60] See online: Saskatchewan Justice and Attorney General <http://www.saskjustice.gov.sk.ca>.

and Wetaskiwin to parties with civil claims ($25,000 or less) in the Provincial Court. Those claims are reviewed, and appropriate cases are referred to the Mediation Program. Any party may initiate mediation by serving a notice, called a *Request to Mediate*, on the other parties. This requires the parties to participate in a three-hour mediation within 120 days of service of the request, unless an objection is filed and an exemption is given. The evaluation of the former pilot project demonstrated that approximately 65 per cent of cases referred were resolved following mediation.[61]

Alberta Justice and the Alberta courts both have user-friendly and informative websites, the former with a good list of links to organizations in the DR field.[62]

Mandatory Mediation in Saskatchewan

Saskatchewan was a pioneer in Canada in the use of mediation to resolve civil disputes. It began as a practical approach to the farm debt crises in the 1930s, when farmers could not pay their loans and there was little point to bankers foreclosing on the properties as there was no one to buy them.

Saskatchewan's experience with the farm debt mediation program (which has reached settlement rates of 70-80 per cent) opened the door to further legislative advancements.[63] In 1994, mandatory mediation was instituted for most civil, non-family cases in the Court of Queen's Bench. It now includes cases in the judicial centres of Regina, Swift Current, Saskatoon and Prince Albert, and applies to 80 per cent of the designated cases in that court.[64] In all cases not exempted, a mediation must be held at the close of pleadings and before any other step can be taken in the action.

The Saskatchewan program differs from other court-connected programs in that the mediation generally takes place earlier in the litigation cycle, and the process is supported by government funding of the Dispute Resolution Office. Mediators from that office perform many of the mediations without charge to the participants.[65]

---

[61] See online: Alberta Justice and Attorney General <http://justice.alberta.ca/programs_services/mediation/Pages/mediation_services.aspx#civil>.

[62] See online: Alberta Justice and Attorney General <http://justice.alberta.ca/programs_services/mediation/Pages/default.aspx#com_questions> and Alberta Courts <http://www.albertacourts.ab.ca>.

[63] For the history, see online: Encyclopedia of Saskatchewan <http://esask.uregina.ca/entry/mandatory_mediation.html>.

[64] *Queen's Bench Act, 1998*, S.S. 1998, c. Q-1.01, s. 42.

[65] See online: Saskatchewan Justice and Attorney General <http://www.justice.gov.sk.ca/mediation>.

Mediation in the Courts of British Columbia

British Columbia has implemented mandatory mediation, but on the initiative of one of the parties, not by default fiat of the court at a certain stage in the action. In civil actions in B.C., mediation is initiated by delivering a Notice to Mediate to every other party in the action and to the Dispute Resolution Office in the Ministry of the Attorney General. This permits any party "to make an informed assessment that mediation would be productive, and then to require the other parties to attend a mediation session".[66]

The application of the Notice to Mediate has been expanded since its introduction in April 1998. It began as a dispute resolution option for motor vehicle actions, one of the earliest and most obvious applications of mediation in Canada. In the first four years, over 6,000 cases were mediated, with a success rate of 74 per cent. An additional 10 per cent of cases settled after delivery of the Notice to Mediate, but before a mediation took place. When the initiative was evaluated, 88 per cent of lawyers serving or receiving notices felt that the process could usefully be expanded to other types of civil cases. This commended the process for other contexts.

In May 1999, the Notice to Mediate was extended to actions concerning residential construction. Section 2 of the Notice to Mediate (Residential Construction) Regulation[67] provides that "any party to a residential construction action may initiate mediation in that action". This gives homeowners the option of early and economical resolution in residential construction cases that could otherwise take years and be very costly.

In 2001, the Notice to Mediate was expanded by the Notice to Mediate (General) Regulation,[68] to include a wide range of civil actions in the Supreme Court of British Columbia. The general regulation, however, does not apply to family law actions, applications for judicial review, monetary claims for physical or sexual abuse or actions to which other Notice to Mediate regulations apply.

A Notice to Mediate can be served at any time between 60 days after filing of the first statement of defence and 120 days before trial, unless the court makes an exception. The mediation must occur within 60 days after the appointment of the mediator but not later than seven days before the date of trial.

---

[66] See British Columbia, Dispute Resolution Office Bulletin (June 2002), online: <http://www.ag.gov.bc.ca/dro/publications/bulletins/general.htm>.

[67] B.C. Reg. 152/99, s. 2(1).

[68] B.C. Reg. 4/2001.

Once the notice is served, the parties have a limited number of days (14 or 21, depending on the number of parties) to agree upon a mediator. Otherwise, any party may apply to the Dispute Resolution Innovation Society (formerly the British Columbia Mediator Roster Society) to appoint a mediator. In appointing the mediator, the Society has a number of criteria to take into account, including the fees, availability and qualifications of the mediators and the parties' preferences.[69] The Society is jointly funded by the provincial government and the British Columbia Law Foundation.

Like the Ontario program, roster mediators may charge market fees. All parties must complete a mediation fee declaration, setting out the identity of the mediator, the costs and their allocation.

Mediators have the option of calling a convening meeting, called a "pre-mediation conference", if in the mediator's opinion the matter is sufficiently complex to warrant it.

The Notice to Mediate requires parties to attend mediation (and pre-mediation conferences), although it does not (and cannot) require a party to settle. It makes mediation mandatory, but only one may be compelled under the Regulation. Once the process is initiated by delivery of a notice, every party must attend. The Notice to Mediate gives parties and their lawyers discretion as to when mediation takes place. Also, if none of the parties serve a Notice to Mediate, then mediation is not required. That element makes it quite different from the other court programs, such as Ontario's, which require attendance even if none of the parties want it.

In November 2004, British Columbia's Court of Appeal began a two-year pilot project similar in nature to that of the Quebec Court of Appeal, described more fully below. The project remains in force and operates under Civil Practice Directive #8, revised February 1, 2005. If the parties make a joint request for a settlement conference, one of the participating justices is assigned to the case and it is taken out of the regular stream of cases. An initial telephone conference is convened to determine the suitability of the case for a settlement conference. If directed to go on, the settlement conference is conducted using an interest-based approach. Of the small number of cases that proceeded to the settlement conference as of September 2007, all were settled, either at the conference or shortly after it.[70]

Before leaving this section it is worth noting that mandatory mediation has been incorporated into the Small Claims Court of British Columbia (jurisdiction up to $25,000), at least in downtown Vancouver.[71] The format is a two-hour mediation session offered at no cost to the parties. The pilot is

---

[69] See online: Mediate BC <http://www.drinnovation.ca/>.

[70] G.S. Pun, "Note on the Court of Appeal Judicial Conference" (June 2008) 20:3 BarTalk, online: Canadian Forum for Civil Justice <http:cfcj-fcjc.org/inventory/reform.php?id=134>.

[71] For details of the pilot project, see online: Small Claims BC <http://www.smallclaimsbc.ca/mediations.php> and Small Claims Rules, B.C. Reg. 261/93, R. 7.4.

administered and the mediators are provided by the Dispute Resolution Innovation Society. If the plaintiff does not attend (and has not applied for and been granted an exemption), then the claim can be dismissed, or judgment can be granted, as the case may be. This initiative has produced excellent and clear literature which can be viewed online.[72]

Voluntary Judicial Mediation in Quebec

There is no mandatory mediation of any kind in Quebec at either the Court of Quebec (monetary limit $70,000) or the Superior Court of Quebec, although there is a cheerful page devoted to mediation in civil and commercial matters at the website for Quebec's Department of Justice.[73] Mediation is purely voluntary at all court levels. It may be initiated with a private mediator by *ad hoc* decision of the parties or by implementing a future dispute resolution clause in a contract that requires mediation. It may also be undertaken "as part of a judicial proceeding, with the agreement of the parties". The last option is known as "voluntary judicial mediation". Judges constitute themselves as civil mediators for willing litigants.

In the Court of Quebec, Small Claims Division (monetary limit $7,000), parties are not generally permitted to be represented by counsel. When a claim is filed, a mediation is offered by the clerk of the court to the initiating party. If that party agrees, the party that is being sued will be informed, and will either accept or reject mediation. The one-hour mediation costs the parties nothing and is provided by a lawyer or notary.[74]

In the Court of Quebec, where disputes under $70,000 are litigated by provincially appointed judges, the mediation initiative is called *amicable dispute resolution conference*. A Quebec civil court judge presides over the private, confidential settlement conference, and the service is free. Although one party can take the initiative and propose mediation, the other party is not obliged to attend. The process must be on consent. The Joint Request for Conciliation form is published online.[75]

The Superior Court deals with cases over $70,000 in value and consists of federally appointed judges. In 1999 and 2000, a pilot mediation project was carried out in the Quebec Superior Court to encourage people in lawsuits to use mediation for civil and commercial disputes. Access to mediation was purely voluntary. When litigation was started, a justice of the Superior Court sent a letter of invitation to the litigants. The letter invited and encouraged them to use mediation to resolve their differences. If the parties

---

[72]   See online: Small Claims BC <http://www.smallclaimsbc.ca/mediations.php>.

[73]   See online: Justice Québec <http://www.justice.gouv.qc.ca>.

[74]   See online: Justice Québec <http://www.justice.gouv.qc.ca/english/publications/generale/creance-a.htm#mediation>.

[75]   See online: Cour Supérieure du Québec <http://www.tribunaux.qc.ca/c-superieure/index-cs.html>.

were willing, it was up to them to take the steps necessary to set it up and carry out the process. The letter enclosed a brochure about mediation and explained its features and advantages. It also provided contact information for a mediation coordinator who could provide more information and gave parties the option of participating in an informational session. If necessary, a follow-up invitation was sent to the lawyers and the parties when the matter was ready for hearing.

In the period from November 1, 1999 to October 31, 1999, invitations to mediate were sent out on 14,109 files, resulting in 2,324 requests for information and six mediation information sessions. A total of 119 mediations were conducted, of which 91 settled.[76] That is a 0.6 per cent take-up rate on the invitation letters and a 76.5 per cent success rate for files that did progress to mediation.

The pilot project was not continued. Instead, the court introduced judicial mediation. On January 1, 2003, Bill 54, *An act to reform the Code of Civil Procedure*, came into force in Quebec.[77] This legislation reformed civil procedure, and at least one commentator thought it would "revolutionize" the handling of civil litigation in order to allow for speedier resolutions. There are no publicly available statistics to confirm the impact of the revision at this time.

The *Code of Civil Procedure* reform covers many more aspects of civil procedure than just settlement procedures. It promotes the notion of voluntary mediation and authorizes judges to do it. Section 4.3 specifically provides, "The courts and judges may attempt to reconcile the parties, if they consent, in any matter except a matter relating to personal status or capacity or involving public policy issues. In family matters or matters involving small claims, it is the judge's duty to attempt to reconcile the parties."[78]

The *Code of Civil Procedure* also provides for *settlement conferences* presided over by a judge, at any stage of the proceedings, but only if all parties consent. There is a comparable provision in the Rules of Practice.

Although the word "mediation" is not used, settlement conferences are clearly judicial mediations. They are confidential and take place in private. The legislation provides that, "The purpose of a settlement conference is to facilitate dialogue between the parties and help them to identify their interests, assess their positions, negotiate and explore mutually satisfactory solutions."[79]

---

[76] See "Cour Supérieure du Québec : Service de référence à la médiation en matière civile et commerciale", Rapport final : Évaluation du programme (1 novembre 1999 au 15 juin 2001).

[77] S.Q. 2002, c. 7.

[78] *Code of Civil Procedure*, R.S.Q., c. C-25, s. 4.3.

[79] *Ibid.*, s. 151.16.

A judge conducting settlement conferences enjoys judicial immunity and, as is only proper, cannot preside at any subsequent hearing if the matter does not settle.

Settlement conferences appear to have three specific advantages: they are free; they enjoy the stature and authority of the court; and they provide an easy enforcement mechanism in that a settlement can be immediately converted into a court order on request.[80]

The Court of Appeal of Quebec also has a judicial mediation initiative referred to as *judicial conciliation*. This has been ongoing since 1998, when it began as a two-year pilot project and, as the court sees it, is a natural evolution for judges. Its website states, "As guardians of public order and democratic values, it is fitting that the judiciary participate with the community in transforming the classical justice system so that it is more reflective of social values. In doing so, the justice system bears witness to a lessening of the distance between the judiciary and the public and to the principle that society is better served when it is better understood."[81]

This mediation program at the appeal level operates under the general supervision of the Chief Justice. Conciliation is available to all parties at any stage of a civil, commercial or family law appeal, but only on consent. The Court of Appeal thought that its own members should conduct these mediations, out of respect for the trial judge and the legal process generally, and in order to preclude private mediators from commenting on lower court decisions.

As with the Court of Quebec's amicable dispute resolution conference, parties to an appeal must sign and file a joint request for conciliation. Then the court will schedule a mediation session within 30 days of receipt of the form. Appeal proceedings are suspended when a request for conciliation is made.

The mediation is conducted by a justice of appeal, who will be excluded from the panel should the matter fail to settle and the appeal goes forward. A mediation file is opened and kept separate and apart from an appeal file.

Like mediation initiatives at the other court levels in Quebec, judicial conciliation is free. There are no additional costs to the parties. The Quebec Court of Appeal funds the program through its regular budget. Any settlement achieved at judicial conciliation has the added advantage of immediate enforceability, because a signed agreement can be homologated by the court without additional formality. The settlement agreement is ratified by an independent panel of three judges of the Court of Appeal at no

---

[80]   *Ibid.*, s. 151.22.

[81]   See online: Court of Appeal of Quebec <http://www.tribunaux.qc.ca/c-appel/English/Altres/mediation/mediation.html> and click on "Alternative Dispute Methods" and then "The Judicial Mediation Service Program".

extra cost, and without the need of a written motion. This results in an immediately enforceable judgment.

Judicial conciliation began in 1998, and by the second year of its existence, it had handled over 200 cases, with settlement rates of over 80 per cent.[82] This is about double the success rate of Ontario's Mandatory Mediation Program at the trial level.

The high rate of success flowing from judicial conciliation should not be surprising for at least three reasons. First, by the time an appeal justice mediates, the parties have had prolonged exposure to the costs and consequences of the litigation system. By this point, either litigation fatigue has set in or the economic, psychological and physical stresses have become intolerable. Second, mediation is conducted by a justice of appeal. This adds a level of prestige, authority and status to the mediator that enhances the parties' respect and responsiveness. Third (and perhaps most importantly), participants have already self-selected for mediation and are further screened for suitability by the program. The program manager and the judge-mediator evaluate the likelihood of success in advance of a mediation, so that only parties with a real interest in reaching settlement are welcomed into the program. This is in contrast to Ontario's initiative, where willing and unwilling parties alike are brought to the mediation table.

CONCLUSION

What you see in this chapter is just a tiny sample of the hundreds of DR initiatives that have been undertaken across Canada. Many more are evolving as we write, such as "collaborative practice",[83] an interest-based approach to dispute resolution for family and estate disputes, and "conflict coaching", a way to prepare and equip individuals to have challenging but constructive conversations.[84]

Canadians certainly did not invent alternative approaches to dispute resolution, and are not about to put the courts out of business with "peacemaking". What is happening, though, is that people in every kind of activity are coming to realize that there is a wide range of possibilities for resolving disputes that can be adapted and combined as their particular circumstances require.

---

[82] See the Honourable L. Otis, J.C.A., "The Conciliation Service Program of the Court of Appeal (*sic*) of Quebec" (March 2000) *World Arbitration and Mediation Report*, online: Court of Appeal of Quebec <http://www.tribunaux.qc.ca>.

[83] See, for instance, online: Divorce in Alberta <http://www.collaborativelaw.ca/>. At the time of writing, one or more initiatives are privately under way to explore the application of the collaborative model to estate disputes.

[84] Conflict coaching is established and integrated into human resources and labour relations applications in federal departments or agencies such as Parks Canada Agency or the Department of Agriculture.

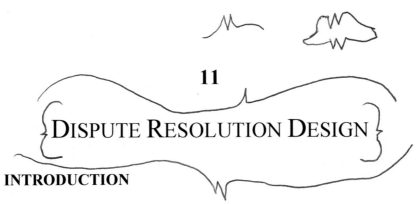

11
DISPUTE RESOLUTION DESIGN

INTRODUCTION

Dispute resolution design or *conflict management systems design* ("DR design") refers to the creation of initiatives which use mediation and other DR mechanisms in an organized way to prevent or resolve disputes. The Canadian initiatives described in Chapter 10 are examples of work products resulting from DR design.

DR design is frequently about institutionalizing dispute resolution modalities in an industry, workplace or organization through the creation of specific programs that are focused towards certain constituents and/or certain types of disputes. A simple example would be a corporate human resources policy that promotes the use of interest-based methods to resolve workplace disputes. Others frequently seen involve a mediation process backstopped by an adjudicative process to resolve customer complaints in a particular industry, trade association or administrative tribunal. DR design can also refer to the creation of a one-time, customized process for a specific dispute. A process to resolve a shareholder controversy, which combines elements of mediation and arbitration, would be such a one-time initiative. Another would be a mediation/trusted umpire combination forming part of a planned process to shut down an office or downsize a business. An arbitration program offered as an alternative process in a class action lawsuit would be another one-time, customized example.

Dispute resolution programs exist in a wide array of Canadian organizations and for many situations. Programs deal with insurance disputes, landowner objections to pipelines, complaints against teachers and interconnect disputes in the telecommunications industry. Just as there is no limit to the subject matter of a program, there is no limit to the parties whom it can serve. Individual workers and managers, personal and class claimants, landlords and tenants, professionals and their clients, victims and offenders can all be the intended participants. The scope of the program and its identified users are specific to every situation.

Typically, DR design is undertaken to address some deficiency in the existing manner of handling disputes. Current processes or procedures, or lack of them, may be seen as too costly, too time-consuming or inappropriate for the people and problem involved. The National Energy Board, for example, decided to offer staff-run mediation to resolve specific complaints by landowners to the location of pipelines because the statutory adversarial hearing was a cumbersome and costly way to address landowner concerns.

Sometimes, DR design is part of a conscious, overall organizational change. Federal agencies created in the late 1990s, such as Parks Canada and the Canada Customs and Revenue Agency, integrated the design of internal dispute resolution programs into the implementation of their agency status. These agencies now have specific mechanisms for workplace controversies.

DR design always involves some measure of organizational or *cultural* change. This is inevitable when an organization seeks to move from a litigation, or authority-based way of resolving complaints, to a more horizontal, interest-based process. One would expect cultural changes in the Department of National Defence or the RCMP, for example, as these military, or quasi-military organizations move forward with interest-based dispute resolution initiatives. Similarly, civil litigation lawyers began to change their approach to handling lawsuits when mediation initiatives were introduced into the civil justice system. Cultural change can also lead to policy change on a broad scale. An example of this is the U.S. Army Corps of Engineers mandating the use of *partnering*, a DR process design, on all of its construction contracts over a million dollars. Because of their size and clout in the market, they have exported their knowledge and potential cultural change to all of their building partners.

THE STAGES OF DISPUTE RESOLUTION DESIGN

The process of DR design can be described in four stages: needs assessment; program design; implementation; and evaluation.[1] Most of the recent Canadian design initiatives resulted from a process that went through these stages in an explicit way. Earlier initiatives sometimes evolved more casually on a case-by-case basis.

• *Needs Assessment.* In this stage, the company, industry or organization considers its "interests" as well as those of its constituents. What are the needs, wants, concerns and fears about current or potential disputes? What are the costs of poorly managed conflict? Typically, some adverse consequences or perception of excessive costs begins the design process. A corporation might have an unacceptably high level of workplace conflict. An industry might be facing troublesome legislation. Or an organization might have received negative feedback about how it has resolved external disputes to

---

[1]   For an alternative way of describing the stages of DR design, see G.A. Chornenki, *The Corporate Counsel Guide to Dispute Resolution* (Aurora, ON: Canada Law Book, 1999) at 220.

date. Whatever the situation, there must be an adequate degree of motivation and support (internal and external) to sustain the design effort. Ideally, energy and commitment for the DR initiative will flow within the organization from top to bottom, from bottom to top and from side to side.

At this stage, statistics about the number and kinds of disputes and how these are currently handled may also be collected or analyzed. Models or precedents from other organizations may be sought by means of a "best practices" review. Consideration will be given as to why new or different dispute resolution procedures should be considered and what benefits are anticipated, as well as to what might be standing in the way of improvements. Legal issues may be considered. The objectives of the program are identified at this stage. These objectives are later tested at the evaluation stage.

- *Program Design.* This stage involves the "nuts and bolts" of design. It begins with decisions about design methodology (how the design comes into being) and who will be involved in the design. Will the design be attempted through a large-group, whole-system intervention, or will there be a select design team comprised of constituent representatives? Will an external consultant be employed or are internal resources sufficient for the purposes of the design? There are many methodologies that seek to elicit the input and participation of relevant parties as part of a design process. No single, recommended methodology exists. Ideally, the methodology adopted should maximize parties' satisfaction with the design process.

   At this stage, discussions and decisions about more tangible aspects of the program occur — "what gets designed" as opposed to "how it gets designed". The program will take on a shape and character as the designers attempt to meet the needs of the constituents within relevant financial, legal or other practical constraints. Issues to be decided at this stage include what DR methods will be used in the program and why; what terms of reference or "rules" will govern; who will perform the DR services; what "gate-keeping" and "record-keeping" will take place; how the program will be funded and administered; how the program will be promoted; how it will be initiated and implemented; what information will be compiled; and what use will be made of it. The list is by no means exhaustive. The decisions on each issue, however, will be reflected in the program documentation that gives the initiative a tangible form.

- *Implementation.* This is the stage that activates the proposed program through a series of implementation steps. These steps might begin with information and education sessions for potential users, and include the appointment or selection of appropriate DR personnel such as roster mediators and arbitrators, administrative staff or institutional DR champions. An implementation plan can identify tasks and timeframes.

Frequently, programs are implemented incrementally, beginning with a pilot project that is restricted to particular kinds of dispute or to a particular locality, but this is not a mandatory prerequisite for implementation. Much depends upon the level of awareness and support for the program, as well as on available resources. Some ultimately successful DR programs were spearheaded by a few persistent individuals who were prepared to make modest efforts on small matters, progressing to more significant controversies with higher stakes as momentum built. Other DR programs represented large corporate initiatives that attempted to engage the whole system all at once. Both can work.

Dispute resolution training is frequently a part of program implementation. Relevant parties are taught dispute resolution theories and skills relevant to the program. For example, a company that wants to deal with human resources issues at the lowest possible level will need to train its employees and managers in the principles of interest-based negotiation. An insurance company that expects its claims analysts to refer files to outside mediators will need to train those analysts in how to appropriately select and prepare cases for mediation and how to participate as advocates in the mediation process.

- *Evaluation.* This stage integrates the program goals that were identified in the beginning stages of the design exercise. Its general purpose is to elicit and synthesize information to help the designers determine whether and to what extent those goals were met. For example, were disputes resolved in a way that users perceived as more satisfactory? Were resolutions less costly or faster? Another purpose of the evaluation stage is to determine whether to continue an existing program, or, if the initiative will be continued, whether and how to modify it.

A sophisticated analysis with respect to mandatory mediation was recently completed in Ontario. It produced data about the early use of mediation in the civil justice system, including the fact that about half of the cases referred were settled at an early stage. While continuation of mandatory mediation is a political decision, this data seems to support the extension of mandatory mediation throughout the province.

Evaluation is not an after-the-fact activity. An evaluation plan is drawn up before a DR program is implemented. The plan articulates the purpose of the evaluation, identifies what is being measured, sets out the proposed source of the data and develops an appropriate evaluation methodology. Data collection takes place throughout the course of implementation, not just when a pilot project is over. In a mediation project, for example, parties and mediators are to be surveyed immediately after a mediation session, not months later when the experience is no longer fresh. Quantitative and/or qualitative data can be collected, and they are compiled, analyzed and interpreted as a source of information for program maintenance or amendment.

There are, of course, as many approaches to evaluation as there are to mediation, and no one approach can be prescribed for all. The complexity and depth of the evaluation stage depends on the needs and the resources of the program and, to some extent, on the philosophical approach of the evaluators. Some established programs are able to pay independent research companies to routinely survey all participants or to conduct detailed statistical analyses. Others can afford only more modest efforts and rely on less formal approaches. Whatever the approach, when an evaluation report is made, the design process continues and the cycle starts anew.

The design process is also an ongoing one. Every program needs and should be open to feedback. As a program is developed or used, new or reconfigured information is generated. This information serves as a basis to amend or enhance the program. In DR design, the designers hope to predict and plan for future issues and uses, but, as both DR designers and DR neutrals, we would observe that this is an elusive goal. For example, even a well-drafted and collaboratively produced "complaints" process will raise questions when it is being implemented. Different people may read or understand the same provision in different ways. Program administrators, program neutrals and program users (who may come in contact with a program well after its design) may interpret its spirit or letter in diametrically opposing ways. Unforeseen circumstances may develop and consideration will have to be given to revisiting the intent of the process or revising the text. Or policy decisions embedded in the design may no longer be appropriate. The fact that a program may be amended from time to time is no indication of design "failure".

THE STRUCTURE OF DISPUTE RESOLUTION INITIATIVES

The structure of any DR initiative charts the path that a dispute follows to resolution.[2] This is a function of the chosen dispute resolution processes and how those processes are ordered. For example, a dispute

---

[2]   For some further sample structures expressed as flow charts, see G.A. Chornenki, *ibid.*, at 216-19.

may go directly to adjudication. Alternatively, it may pass through a series of stages that do not involve decision-making — like direct negotiation or mediation.

There is no single structural template available for all programs. Each program will be structured differently according to the objectives of the program, and the nature of the participants and the disputes. But, however it is structured, the dispute resolution pathway should be clear.

Some dispute resolution programs are single-process programs. For example, the Canadian Motor Vehicle Arbitration Program (CAMVAP) is a long-standing cross-Canada arbitration program for the resolution of consumer vehicle complaints.[3] While that program does produce negotiated outcomes which take the form of consent awards, it is primarily an arbitration program where independent dispute resolution practitioners listen to evidence and argument and make enforceable arbitration awards.

Other programs mix and match dispute resolution processes. The staffing complaint process of the Canadian Food Inspection Agency begins with an opportunity for discussion and negotiation between an employee and the direct manager. It progresses up a chain, ultimately arriving at an independent third party review that decides the complaint, if necessary.[4]

The ombuds programs of Canadian financial institutions provide an internal ombuds for the ultimate appeal to authority, but before the ombuds intervenes, customers and institutional personnel at the branch level are expected to attempt resolution through dialogue and discussion.[5] The ombuds may perform mediation between the customer and the branch, may recommend mediation with an outside mediator or may suggest impasse-breaking procedures such as arbitration.

In contrast to single process or mixed process programs, some dispute resolution programs are not built around any specific DR choice. Instead, they provide a wide-ranging menu of DR mechanisms and these rely on a case-by-case selection according to individual needs. A pilot project like this, conducted by the federal Department of Justice in the mid-1990s, required litigation counsel to identify likely files for mediation, arbitration or other alternative processes from among existing lawsuits.

---

[3]   For the details of the program design, see CAMVAP's Program Guide online: Canadian Motor Vehicle Arbitration Plan <http://www.camvap.ca/eng/consumer_guide/2008_camvap_guide_lo_res_en.pdf>.

[4]   For Canadian Food Inspection Agency program details, see online: <http://www.inspection.gc.ca/english/hrrh/stafdote.shtml>.

[5]   For example, see the details of the TD Bank internal customer dispute resolution process, online: TD Bank Financial Group <http://www.td.com/ombudsman.jsp>.

Some Canadian corporations have adopted similar programs within their legal or claims-handling departments. One major insurer, for instance, expects its claims analysts to be alert to every possible opportunity for early resolution and to actively move claims to negotiation, mediation, arbitration or litigation, depending on the case. These types of "selection" programs require in-house staff to be familiar with a range of dispute resolution choices and to have a working knowledge of selection criteria.

It is important to note that DR design extends beyond the use of mediation. If the objective of any program is to conclusively resolve a dispute, then impasse-breaking mechanisms need to be included, as not every dispute can be resolved through processes of agreement such as negotiation and mediation. Typically, an impasse-breaking mechanism involves some process of decision-making such as arbitration, an internal tribunal, a statutory body of decision or a civil court, but it can also include an appeal to higher authority such as a manager or an organizational ombuds.

Impasse-breaking mechanisms are included in dispute resolution programs as the ultimate resolution mechanism, or the ultimate form of risk. Sometimes the arrangement is described as a "dispute resolution stairway", where the parties progress from trying to resolve the matter themselves through to having the matter decided for them by an outsider. The progress, of course, does not have to be sequential and linear: the parties may skip up and down the stairs and may loop back and forth, as desired. One party might commence arbitration under the provisions of a commercial contract in order to engage the other party in a discussion. Settlement talks may then occur. If those talks fail, the parties may prepare for an arbitration hearing. Alternatively, they may seek an arbitrator's decision on only a pivotal issue and leave the rest for negotiation. The notion is one of flexibility within the available dispute resolution procedures.

Sometimes, procedures like negotiation and mediation are integrated into existing procedures of decision. For example, Ontario's mandatory mediation program provides parties with an opportunity to discuss settlement before the trial stage of a lawsuit, but if settlement is not possible, they can still proceed to have their dispute adjudicated by means of a trial or application in court. Frequently, the presence of an impasse-breaking mechanism provides incentive or pressures sufficient to induce settlement. Rather than face the risk of an adverse decision, the parties reach their own deal.

THE DOCUMENTATION OF DISPUTE RESOLUTION INITIATIVES

It is sometimes said of DR design that "the process *is* the product". This cannot be entirely correct. While a process of collaboration or genuine consultation can begin to make a difference in how people interact and frame their conflicts, something more tangible is usually required. A program needs to be documented if it is to have an actual presence and if the intended participants are to understand their roles and responsibilities.

Thus, DR design usually involves the creation of certain documents. These will vary in content, complexity and length according to the nature of the program and the intended participants. The documentation for Ontario's mandatory mediation initiative in the civil courts is relatively straightforward.[6] Contrast this with the extensive documentation of The Internet Corporation for Assigned Names and Numbers ("ICANN") in its Uniform Domain Name Dispute Resolution Policy.[7]

DR program documentation is not limited to "external" documentation such as mission statements, terms of reference or "rules" which help participants understand the scope and intent of the initiative. There may also be a body of "internal" documentation relating to administration and support. This includes things like selection guidelines, scripts, internal policy manuals and report forms, which are collateral to or support the actual DR processes contained in the program.

To see an example of the range of documentation that any particular initiatives can generate, here (in no particular order) are some of the types that we, as design consultants, have helped to create:

- Information Bulletin
- Confirmation Form
- Mediator's Report
- Attendance Report
- Hearing Order for Directions on Procedure
- Mediation Intake Guide
- Mediation Intake Form
- Participant Survey
- Mediator Opening Script

---

[6]   For the OMMP Forms, see online: Canadian Legal Information Institute <http://www.canlii.org/en/on/laws/regu/rro-1990-reg-194/latest/rro-1990-reg-194.html>.

[7]   See online: Internet Corporation for Assigned Names and Numbers <http://www.icann.org/udrp/udrp.htm>.

- Frequently Asked Questions
- Agreement to Mediate
- Agreement to Arbitrate
- Preparation Guide for Negotiation
- Preparation Guide for Mediation
- Standardized Training Protocol
- User Handbook
- Practice Directions

DESIGNS TO MEET THE PUBLIC INTEREST

The last decade has seen an explosion in the use of mediation by statutory bodies in Canada. Mediation has been applied to address a wide variety of situations — landlord and tenant matters, human rights, labour relations, economic regulation, land-use planning and self-regulating professions.

These statutory bodies differ from private ones in an important way. Unlike private concerns, these have public interest mandates. That means that by law they must protect or apply certain laws or certain societal norms and values. The meaning of public interest varies from one statutory body to another. For example, a human rights tribunal has an obligation to ensure equal access and to prevent discrimination based on identified grounds such as race or religion. An environmental tribunal has obligations to protect the environment for the benefit of all. A tribunal engaged in economic regulation has an obligation to ensure equal access to a particular commodity within a certain price range. Essentially, each body's statutory mandate highlights a different aspect of public interest, but the unifying theme is the protection or the promotion of the common good.

In *Reference re Amendments to the Residential Tenancies Act (N.S.),*[8] the Supreme Court of Canada supported the creation of DR programs by statutory tribunals, even in the absence of explicit statutory authority. Yet, statutory bodies still face a fundamental and vitally important question — how to participate in alternative dispute resolution in such a way as to ensure that the public interest continues to be met. The concerns usually relate to the integration of mediation into a statutory scheme for adjudication. A simple private interest model of mediation where two or more parties meet in confidence and craft a settlement that satisfies their individual needs is an incomplete model for public interest controversies. Modifications need to be made to the model.

---

[8]   [1996] S.C.J. No. 13, [1996] 1 S.C.R. 186 (S.C.C.).

Statutory bodies in Canada have taken on the challenge of DR design, especially mediation, with enthusiasm and creativity. No standard response has developed; thus, interest-based processes are being adapted through different models. These modifications include some combination of the following features:

- *Staff participation as mediator or representative.* An employee of the statutory body either conducts the mediation or takes part as a representative of that body. The employee's mandate includes ensuring that any settlement reflects the statutory mandate and the public interest. The Ontario College of Teachers addresses this issue by having a staff member participate in any mediation session. The staff person's job is to ensure that the public interest mandate in public protection is incorporated into any settlement.

  To this end, the College may request changes to the settlement agreement. If the complainant or the member rejects the proposed changes, the complaint proceeds as if dispute resolution had not taken place.[9]

- *Approval mechanism.* Facilitated settlement discussions are conducted with all relevant parties, *i.e.*, a complainant, a respondent and the statutory body. The facilitator may be an "outside" or an "inside" mediator. Any settlement reached is tentative only and subject to approval by the statutory body. This approval can be of an administrative nature, or it can result from a hearing into the merits of the proposed settlement.[10]

- *Timing of mediation.* The statutory body is mindful of where mediation occurs in its process. If an investigation is mandated by statute, the investigation is completed first so that an informed decision about settlement can be made. In bodies which involve land use planning or the sustainable use of natural resources, studies and public consultations involving the broad implications of any proposal take place first.

- *Protection of decision-makers.* Where the statutory body has decision-making responsibilities, those who will adjudicate on the issues under discussion do not take part in any mediation. Further, the content of mediation discussions is not relayed to the adjudicators in order to avoid allegations of interference or bias.

- *Specific exceptions to confidentiality.* The statutory mandate is paramount. If violations of the statute or regulations come to the

---

[9]   See online: Ontario College of Teachers, "Dispute Resolution Program" <http://www.oct. ca/publications/pdf/dispute_resolution_general_e.pdf>.

[10]   For example, a committee of the College of Teachers must ratify the settlement agreement before its terms become final and binding, *ibid.*

attention of the body during the course of the mediation, this information will enjoy no protection.

- *Use of settlement agreement.* The statutory body keeps records of settlements for future use if appropriate. For instance, a regulatory body is alert for repeat offenders who place the public at risk. A mediation involving one specific incident will not necessarily be treated in an isolated fashion.

PUBLIC INTEREST MEDIATORS

Chapter 3 contains a discussion which recognizes statutory public interest mediators as "real" mediators, albeit mediators with certain challenges. Mediators who come to the table with a public interest mandate on behalf of the statutory body should not be shy about discussing that mandate. Some statutory bodies have conducted educational programs for their staff where model mediator "scripts" are practised and discussed. This helps to ensure consistency in how internal mediators are using their specialized knowledge and statutory authority throughout mediation. Discussion topics to help public interest mediators with their scripts include:

- acknowledgment of employment with the statutory body;
- knowledge about practices, policies and precedents of the statutory body (*i.e.*, whether it has decided a particular point or what its procedure for something is);
- knowledge of what others have done in the situation;
- anticipated use of knowledge in the mediation;
- clarification of their role (*i.e.*, mediator assists in settlement; no decision-making authority; no ability to bind statutory body with respect to this or future matters);
- approval, filing or ratification process, if any;
- consequences if no settlement: use of information from mediation; and
- mediator reports: content and distribution.

CONCLUSION

Dispute Resolution in Canada has come a long way, and many of Canada's statutory bodies have been leaders in the field. Their willingness to supplement and modify a simple private interest model of mediation sets an example for all DR users and practitioners, for here the versatility of DR really shines through.

12

EPILOGUE: WHY DISPUTE RESOLUTION STILL MATTERS TO US

In this, the fourth edition of *Bypass Court*, we decided to end on a personal note and indicate why the subject matter of our book continues to hold our interest and attention. This proved more challenging and provocative than we had imagined, but here is what we have to say:

GENEVIEVE'S VIEW

As I write this on a clear morning in early February, it is hard to grasp that I have been a dispute resolution practitioner for over 20 years. In my filing cabinet I have a copy of the first cheque paid to me in July 1989 for mediating an insurance dispute. In October of the same year, I formally started a dispute resolution business with a two-line answering machine and a second-hand computer from a big Toronto law firm. I still have the burled walnut chairs that surrounded a used table I bought for mediation, but little else remains of those early efforts.

In the late 1980s and early 1990s so much energy went into education and promotion of consensual dispute resolution. It was tough just getting people to understand what mediation was, never mind getting mediation mandates. And a certain amount of effort went into staring down resistance and overt aggression from individuals and groups enamoured with the status quo.

There was lots of help too. Supportive friends and acquaintances generated opportunities for me that I could not have generated for myself. A colleague went out of her way to discuss my ambitions with a fellow commuter in a parking lot and that conversation evolved into an opportunity to perform many sophisticated public interest mediations. Another person invited me to do an unpaid demonstration at a conference. Shortly after that a member of the audience tracked me down and invited me into his organization. That developed into training and consulting engagements worth thousands of dollars. And once I even got a mandate in a multi-party dispute because someone whom I did not know went to high school with my brother and supposed that, like my brother, I could walk and chew gum at the same time.

In the 20 years since I started a dispute resolution practice, opportunities like these have supplied my groceries, paid my mortgage and allowed for some memorable vacations. For a person as risk averse as I am, this is quite an achievement.

The other day someone asked about my plans for retirement. (It was the dental hygienist; she was standing in proximity to my grey roots.) I really had no plans to report. I do not intend to abandon dispute resolution any time soon even though I have never considered it a vocation or life purpose.

What is it about dispute resolution that still makes it matter to me after all these years? What continues to give it relevance and vitality? Many factors come to mind and I gather them together in a basket without arrangement or design, as follows.

The Variety

I cannot imagine thinking about and experiencing the same professional situations day in and day out. How boring would that be?

I thrive on the variety that my dispute resolution practice provides, even though there are sometimes long intervals between paid assignments. I perform a wide range of mandates: mediator, arbitrator, facilitator, trainer, consultant, contract ombuds, complaint handler, coach. These mandates have commonalities, but at the same time they demand different skills and aptitudes. That is challenging.

I also work in a wide range of contexts and am involved with different topics. In one file I might learn about how green beans are cleaned before processing and what happens if the crop has too many weeds. The next file might show me what goes on behind the scenes when a department store sells an insurance policy to its customer and the customer does not pay the premium on time. The file after that might find me reading a human rights and harassment procedure and trying to figure out if there is merit to an employee's complaint that the manager failed to follow the procedure.

It is invigorating to have to be versatile. It also makes bridge, Sudoku and crossword puzzles redundant.

The Stories

Art imitates life. Dispute resolution has convinced me of that. My work in dispute resolution has given me intimate glimpses into the thoughts, actions and motives of fellow human beings. Paying attention to people in meetings or reading their briefs and documents, I have been endlessly fascinated by what they do and don't do, by what they say and don't say, by what they cannot bring themselves to say or do.

A dispute resolution practitioner sits in an advantageous position and from the vantage point of "neutral" watches human dramas play and re-play. She sees people enact stories in real time, hears them tell and reconstruct stories from the past, and learns of their hopes and concerns for future stories. Often the hope for the future is that the story will have a more palatable plot, more likeable characters and a better ending.

Frequently, my work has been like indulging myself in short stories, one after the other. Often I find myself reading the same story, but it is written from different points of view — the deceased father's view of the son, the son's view of the deceased father, the cousin's view of them both. These are poignant stories that remind me how much suffering we impose upon each other and how often we divest ourselves of the power to be happy.

Serving as a dispute resolution practitioner is a privileged position but not an elite one, because it begets humility and compassion. Or ought to.

The Skills

My late mother was not one to give compliments and certainly not to your face, yet she did tell one of my siblings that she liked me to accompany her to medical appointments because she admired the way I dealt with people like lab technicians, doctors, nurses and receptionists. Since then I have heard similar remarks from clients and referral sources.

What way is that? I think my mother was referring to a constellation of skills that come from repeat opportunities to practise and teach dispute resolution. These include maintaining a measure of calmness in the face of stress, asserting what is important to me without artifice or manipulation, asking genuine questions, and taking into account the other person's reality which might be very different from my own. That is classic interest-based stuff, is it not? And these are life skills, not just dispute resolution skills.

But as the fitness poster says, there is no finish line. It is skill not theory that makes a dispute resolution practitioner effective and, like thinness, one can never be too skilful. Dispute resolution still matters because it provides endless opportunities to refine or acquire skill. As I jotted down on my notepad at a recent course, "Skill is where it's at."

The People

Along with exposure to relevant life skills, dispute resolution has acquainted me with terrific people who have my utmost admiration.

A few weeks ago, I attended a lunch with a leader in the collaborative practice field whom I found to be captivating. From the moment she entered the conversation, she was able to elicit from the others what was deeply meaningful to them on any given topic. Her approach was friendly, genuinely curious and utterly non-invasive. "This is someone to emulate," I said to myself. "Whatever she has, I want."

Sure, there has been a significant level of dysfunction in the dispute resolution field from time to time. There are people who make me grit my teeth just as surely as I make them grit theirs. But that simply shows us to be human. It does not cancel out the fact that dispute resolution abounds with role models and colleagues to admire.

I have also enjoyed working with clients and still anticipate that they have much to teach me. Dispute resolution has allowed me to work in some very functional teams that show what is possible when people with diverse skills and perspectives successfully integrate their capabilities. I am not talking the rhetoric of diversity here. I am referring to insights grounded in real life experience.

A regular work group that comes to mind contains very different individuals: one who always cares what others think, one who doesn't; one who comes to decisions quickly, one who likes to process things indefinitely; one who remembers how similar things were handled in the past, one who is inventive and careless of precedent. There is no uniformity of thought or approach. And yet, when the group comes together and its members are open to influence, there is always a much better result. I think that dispute resolution sensitized me to the value of that.

The Principles

Many sound and useful principles are embedded in dispute resolution. Things such as, "People need to be understood before they can understand" or "structure binds anxiety" or "judge the people, not the problem". Like dispute resolution skills, these principles are useful in life generally, not just in fee-paying work. They can provide a framework for approaching problems that the shovel of life throws up.

Last year I was called upon to negotiate rent as property trustee for a small charity. The lease was about to run out for its longstanding tenant and the job of negotiating a new term fell to me. (Believe me, I did not volunteer.)

How much rent to ask for? The principle of "objective criteria" came to mind and I put my trust in it. I delegated the collection of comparable rents to a paid staffer and relied on his data. Then I proceeded to calculate an eye-popping rent increase.

The tenant was gracious when I presented the new rent but wondered, was that square foot per month or square foot per year? They only asked, they said, because my rent was suitable for a downtown office tower over-looking the lake whereas theirs was a below-grade space next to a mildewed storage room. It turns out that I had grossly over-calculated the new rent because I had been given erroneous data and lacked the background to recognize that it was not credible.

So, the principle of objective criteria remains sound. It was my execution that was questionable.

The situation was embarassing. Did I mention that dispute resolution presents limitless opportunities for personal growth?

The Freedom

This factor flows from the imperative of self-employment. When I started out in 1989, there simply were no dispute resolution jobs and no such thing as a guaranteed income stream. I had to make my own way by finding and performing dispute resolution mandates at a time when mediation, meditation and magic were considered to be synonyms. While this was sometimes burdensome and terrifying, it ultimately provided me with unparalleled personal freedom. One year I took a five-week vacation in Crete, spent ten days on the shore of Lake Huron, and passed three further weeks touring India with a Canadian charity. Between jaunts, I billed and collected more than enough money from paid work to meet my family's needs.

Dispute resolution still matters all these years later because it obligingly lets me do what I want to do when I want to do it — at least most of the time. It permits me to indulge my tendencies as a dilettante. I could enroll in a masters of ADR and do course work or research at the office during the day if I chose. I could spend three consecutive days in a CBC production studio producing "The Trouble With Tolerance" without having to get anybody else's approval. I could affiliate with colleagues I like and dissociate with those I do not like from project to project or year to year. I could accept or decline work in accordance with my personal preferences and my obscene vacation schedule.

Apart from competitive bids for work (some of which I won, some of which I lost), I have avoided the constraints of policies and procedures, forms, reports, approval processes or planning. That suits me: as a dispute resolution practitioner, I only ever wrote one business plan. The year was 1989. After that, the universe was in charge.

The Mystery

Dispute resolution is not always fun for the person occupying the neutral's chair. It can be nasty, tedious and hurtful. Nevertheless, it remains compelling, possibly because it has mysterious aspects that continue to elude mastery. Power is an example.

Dispute resolution practitioners like to talk about power, its sources, uses and abuses, and one of their favoured activities is "power balancing", whatever that means. Twenty years into it, however, I am beginning to wonder whether our efforts to understand and regulate power are superficial and beside the point. I am not even sure that we know what we are talking about.

The power that intrigues me — and the one that I suspect is embedded in all aspects of dispute resolution — is way beyond words, concepts and human activity. It animates, intimidates and perplexes, and is as real and operational as electricity. But unlike electricity, it is impervious to our well-intended, puny efforts to manipulate, control or police its use.

Power is instructive that way.

Not long ago I was helping others work towards the resolution of a long-standing dispute. With the best of intentions, I did many of the usual things, applied many of the usual concepts like objectivity and neutrality, used many of the usual skills, and brought to bear whatever relevant insights and experience I could.

Then something happened that exceeded anything I could have anticipated, something that was right near the top of the "ten worst things people do to each other". The details do not matter, nor does the question of why. What matters is the event's effect. It was ferocious, intense, atomic.

When I awoke the next day this event was the first thing that entered my consciousness, and as the day progressed an unsettling insight emerged: "This, this force that you have just felt. The one you cannot name. *This* is what you have been playing with all these years. Where did you ever get such audacity? And do you know how lucky you are not to have blown yourself and everyone else to smithereens?"

It occurred to me that for 20 years I have been standing outside the cage of an unruly beast, clutching a plastic water pistol and calling "Here kitty, kitty." It was a sobering picture.

And this would keep me interested in dispute resolution, why? Because dispute resolution points to something bigger than I am. Whatever that is, it simultaneously seduces me and keeps me in my place. And for some reason, that matters.

The Future

Although I did not intend to rank them, this factor may be the most compelling one for me. In the dispute resolution field there are always emerging vistas, issues, topics, themes. For a person with an enquiring mind, this is endless fun. There is always something new to wonder about and explore. And always, always new theories and models to learn, new skills to acquire.

As I write this, I am currently doing an internship towards a qualification in one coaching model plus working towards a certificate of proficiency in another. My goal is to be more able to work one-on-one with individuals (not systems) who experience conflict, especially individuals who are tied up in disputes over wills and estates. This aspiration evolved from previous work. As a mediator, I have too often seen the toll that estate disputes take on people and how ill prepared they are for the conversations they long to have. I want to work with willing individuals who are open to acquiring new skills and insights about their dispute and themselves, so I am training further and practising and creating a support system for guidance and feedback.

Dispute resolution matters because all these years later there are still so many opportunities to be of service, and it is exhilarating to identify one specific area and work towards addressing those needs.

Will the world change as a result of my efforts? That is not a pretension I need to endorse. I can only say that if the future bears any relation to the past, "There is no life like it!"

Genevieve A. Chornenki

CHRISTINE'S VIEW

I have had the good fortune of reading Genevieve's View before putting my pen to paper. As always, it is comprehensive, thoughtful, at times provocative, but at its root, it is a story — her story. Maybe it comes from being born and raised in Nova Scotia, but I have always loved a story — even better if it is told in a song! And my 20 years in the DR field have brought me many stories. There is the story of the futile search for mediations to cut my teeth on after travelling to Harvard to be trained, and the serendipitous meeting of Owen Shime, then Chair of the Ontario Grievance Settlement Board, who generously brought me in as a trainee mediator to learn how to mediate grievances. There is the story of building the ADR Centre Pilot Project from an empty office to the independently evaluated success in mediation that it became. There are the countless stories that I heard from participants in mediations and other DR processes over the years. There have been anxious, sometimes horrifying moments, but it is never dull! We, along with many other wonderful, talented and driven people, have been instrumental in building and developing the field of DR in Canada, and it has been great fun. What more can you ask from your working life than that it gives you the opportunity to learn something new and to hear great stories every single working day! As for the future of DR, it is expanding in every direction, being institutionalized in every sphere, and it has the capacity to change our culture. I couldn't agree more with Genevieve. I say: "Bring it on!"

Christine E. Hart

Appendix 1

NEGOTIATION WORKSHEET: Part I — Preparation

YOUR NAME:

CONCERNING:

I-1: WHAT GIVES RISE TO THE DISPUTE?

Looking at the dispute from your own perspective, describe it here. Consider its practical impact on you and what causes it to demand your attention at this time.

DESCRIBE THE PROBLEM

WHAT ARE THE CONSEQUENCES OF THIS PROBLEM?

I-2: SHOULD I NEGOTIATE? — A PRELIMINARY ASSESSMENT

What are the reasons that you and the other side would invest the time and effort negotiating? Are the costs and consequences of negotiating better or worse than not doing so at this time? Complete this analysis for both yourself and the other side.

ABOUT YOU	ABOUT THEM
WHAT ARE THE CONSEQUENCES OF NOT REACHING AGREEMENT? HOW LIKELY ARE THESE TO OCCUR?	WHAT ARE THE CONSEQUENCES OF NOT REACHING AGREEMENT? HOW LIKELY ARE THESE TO OCCUR?
PROBABILITY: HIGH/MEDIUM/LOW	PROBABILITY: HIGH/MEDIUM/LOW
ARE THERE OTHER POSSIBILITIES FOR SOLVING THE PROBLEM THAT DO NOT REQUIRE INTERACTING WITH THE OTHER SIDE? IF SO, HOW DESIRABLE ARE THEY?	ARE THERE OTHER POSSIBILITIES FOR SOLVING THE PROBLEM THAT DO NOT REQUIRE INTERACTING WITH THE OTHER SIDE? IF SO, HOW DESIRABLE ARE THEY?

DESIRABILITY: HIGH/MEDIUM/LOW	DESIRABILITY: HIGH/MEDIUM/LOW
BASED ON THE ABOVE, WHAT IS MY LEVEL OF COMMITMENT TO ACHIEVING A RESOLUTION?	BASED ON THE ABOVE, WHAT IS MY LEVEL OF COMMITMENT TO ACHIEVING A RESOLUTION?
HIGH/MEDIUM/LOW	HIGH/MEDIUM/LOW

I-3: WHO IS INVOLVED IN THIS NEGOTIATION?

With whom are you negotiating? What characteristics do the partici-pants bring? Who else is relevant? Again, complete this part for both yourself and the other side.

ABOUT YOU	ABOUT THEM
NEGOTIATOR'S NAME:	NEGOTIATOR'S NAME:
CIRCLE ONE: Individual / Partnership / Corporation / Institution / Board / Agency / Government Department / Other	CIRCLE ONE: Individual / Partnership / Corporation / Institution / Board / Agency / Government Department / Other
REPRESENTING:	REPRESENTING:
PAST DEALINGS:	PAST DEALINGS:
CHARACTERISTICS (KNOWN & SUPPOSED):	CHARACTERISTICS (KNOWN & SUPPOSED):
IS THERE A READINESS AND WILLINGNESS TO BARGAIN?	IS THERE A READINESS AND WILLINGNESS TO BARGAIN?
IS THERE AUTHORITY?	IS THERE AUTHORITY?
IS THERE AN ABILITY TO BARGAIN?	IS THERE AN ABILITY TO BARGAIN?

WHAT ARE OUR RELATIVE RESOURCES?

Who else is likely to influence any decisions taken in the negotiation? To whom must any outcome be justified and on what basis?

YOU	OTHER PARTICIPANT
IDENTITY OF INFLUENTIAL PARTIES: BASIS FOR INFLUENCE: JUSTIFICATIONS NECESSARY:	IDENTITY OF INFLUENTIAL PARTIES: BASIS FOR INFLUENCE: JUSTIFICATIONS NECESSARY:

I-4: WHAT IS THE ENVIRONMENT IN WHICH THE NEGOTIATION TAKES PLACE?

What else is likely to influence any decisions taken in the negotiation? Is there anything about the circumstances, situation or environment in which you are negotiating that is relevant? This could include family, ethnic, political, economic, geographic, timing, organizational or any number of other factors.

YOU

CONTEXT OF NEGOTIATION:

SIGNIFICANCE OR IMPACT:

I-5: PROCEDURE — HOW WILL I NEGOTIATE?

What is the preferred method of approach to meet your needs? How can the negotiation best be carried out?

YOU	OTHER PARTICIPANT

I-6: INTERESTS — A PRELIMINARY VIEW

What is really at stake in this negotiation? Try to go beneath the pet solutions that each party is lobbying for in order to understand the root causes. Expose as many <u>interests</u> as you can.

INTERESTS

WHAT HAVE I DEMANDED OR INSISTED UPON?

WHAT NEEDS OF MINE LIE BENEATH MY DEMAND?

DO ANY OF THESE NEEDS CONFLICT WITH EACH OTHER?

IF I COULD ONLY HAVE ONE OF THE CONFLICTING NEEDS, WHICH ONE WOULD IT BE?

WHAT HAS THE OTHER SIDE DEMANDED OR INSISTED UPON?

WHAT NEEDS MIGHT LIE UNDERNEATH THE OTHER SIDE'S DEMAND?

I-7: THE LAW AND THE LITIGATION SYSTEM

In considering whether to call upon the law and the legal system in the negotiation, the negotiator may need to consult a lawyer for advice. Such advice should enable the negotiator to complete the following questions as part of preparation for the negotiation.

COURT PREPARATION

IF THIS WENT TO COURT, WHAT QUESTION WOULD THE COURT BE ANSWERING?

WOULD THIS RESOLVE THE DISPUTE?

WHAT ARE THE CHANCES THAT THE QUESTION WILL BE ANSWERED IN MY FAVOUR?

WHAT WOULD MY INVOLVEMENT BE?

HOW MUCH WOULD THIS COST?

HOW AND TO WHAT EXTENT WOULD ANY OF THIS MEET MY NEEDS?

1-8: ANTICIPATED WORK PRODUCT

Without regard to the specifics of the situation, what outcome or work product, if any, is anticipated from the negotiation?

YOU	OTHER PARTICIPANT
WORK PRODUCT EXPECTED:	WORK PRODUCT EXPECTED:

I-9: TRUST AND DISCLOSURE

Before embarking on direct discussions with the opposite side, a negotiator should reflect on related issues of trust and disclosure. How important is trust and to what extent should it prevail? What information should be disclosed and to what extent? In either case, are there concerns that can be addressed without taking the negotiator to extremes?

ISSUES

DO YOU TRUST THE OTHER PARTY? WHY OR WHY NOT?

ARE YOU GOING TO BE PERCEIVED AS TRUSTWORTHY?

WHAT IS IMPORTANT ABOUT TRUST?

WHAT ARE THE RISKS IF YOUR TRUST IS UNWARRANTED?

WHAT ARE THE REWARDS IF YOUR TRUST IS WARRANTED?

BALANCING THE RISKS AND REWARDS, IS THERE ANY WAY TO MEET YOUR CONCERNS ABOUT TRUST?

HAVING THOUGHT ABOUT YOUR INTERESTS (NEEDS, WANTS, CONCERNS) AND THE OPPORTUNITIES THAT YOU HAVE AWAY FROM THE TABLE, LIST ANY CONCERNS YOU HAVE ABOUT DISCLOSURE, TOGETHER WITH THE BASIS FOR THE CONCERNS.

WHAT ARE THE RISKS ASSOCIATED WITH DISCLOSURE?

WHAT ARE THE REWARDS OF DISCLOSURE?

BALANCING THE RISKS AND REWARDS, IS THERE ANY WAY TO MEET YOUR CONCERNS ABOUT DISCLOSURE?

Appendix 2

NEGOTIATION WORKSHEET: Part II — Analysis

YOUR NAME:

CONCERNING:

II-1: INTERESTS REVISITED — MUTUAL NEEDS

Revisit the preliminary list of interests and consider how it can be modified in light of what you have heard. Think about the information you have obtained and how it is meaningful and useful to you in the negotiation.

INTERESTS

WHAT IS THE MOST IMPORTANT INFORMATION THAT YOU LEARNED IN YOUR COMMUNICATIONS WITH THE OTHER SIDE?

WHAT ARE THE IMPLICATIONS OF THIS INFORMATION?

GIVEN WHAT I HAVE LEARNED, WHAT ARE MY MOST IMPORTANT NEEDS?

WHAT ARE THE MOST IMPORTANT NEEDS OF THE OTHER PARTY?

DO ANY OF THESE NEEDS DIRECTLY CONFLICT? IF SO, HOW IS THIS SIGNIFICANT?

II-2: STATING THE PROBLEM-SOLVING EXERCISE

Now, restate what the negotiation is about, this time using a "how to" question and incorporating as many of your needs and those of the other participant as you can. Make this a joint question, such as: How can I protect the unique aspects of my invention while at the same time giving you sufficient information to make a buying decision?

JOINT "HOW TO" QUESTION

II-3: PROBLEM SOLVING — POSSIBLE AND PREFERRED SOLUTIONS

Thinking about the joint "how to" question and working alone or together with the other person, list as many possibilities as come to mind for responding to the question. Construct a composite sketch if you can, incorporating as many ideas from both sides of the table as you can. Try to add new or novel ones. Then step back and examine what has been created.

YOU

RESTATE THE "HOW TO" QUESTION:

POSSIBLE WAYS TO SOLVE THE PROBLEM:

DO ANY COMBINATIONS MAKE SENSE? OF THE ABOVE WAYS, WHICH ONES DO THE BEST JOB OF SATISFYING AS MANY OF OUR CONCERNS AS POSSIBLE?

II-4: MAKING A COMMITMENT — OR NOT

In this chapter, we have defined negotiation as an exploratory, problem-solving process; an interaction through which parties determine whether and to what extent they can make a more desirable outcome than one that exists. Thus, before committing to an outcome available through negotiations, the negotiator needs to compare that result to opportunities. By doing this in an informed, careful manner, negotiators exercise choice.

YOU

IS THERE ANY SIGNIFICANT WAY IN WHICH THE PREFERRED SOLUTION DOES NOT MEET YOUR PRIORITIES AND NEEDS?

LIST THE VARIOUS OPPORTUNITIES THAT YOU HAVE "AWAY FROM THE TABLE" (ELSEWHERE) TO MEET YOUR CONCERNS, ALONG WITH THE RESOURCES, DEGREE OF RISK AND THE POSSIBLE REWARDS THAT EACH WILL ENTAIL.

DO YOU PREFER ONE OF THESE OTHER OPPORTUNITIES?

WHY WOULD THE OTHER SIDE BUY INTO THE PREFERRED SOLUTION?

II-5: RECORDING THE COMMITMENT

WRITTEN AGREEMENTS

TO WHAT EXTENT IS WRITING NECESSARY?

HOW CAN THE DEAL BE RECORDED IN A WAY THAT IS ACCEPTABLE TO BOTH SIDES?

Appendix 3

MEDIATION WORKSHEET

YOUR NAME:

CONCERNING:

I. PARTIES
WHO ARE THE PARTIES AND WHO SHOULD BE PRESENT AT THE MEDIATION?
YOUR SIDE

Name	Position/Status	Authority
(a)		
(b)		
(c)		

OTHER SIDE

(a)		
(b)		
(c)		

OTHER PARTIES

(a)		
(b)		
(c)		

WILL ALL NECESSARY PARTIES BE PRESENT? CAN THEY BE INDUCED/PERSUADED TO ATTEND? HOW? IF NOT, CAN THE MEDIATION PROCEED?

II. SUITABILITY & COMMITMENT
WHAT IS THE LEVEL OF COMMITMENT TO SETTLEMENT?
YOUR SIDE: OTHER SIDE:
IS THIS CASE SUITABLE FOR MEDIATION?
___ yes because: ___ no because: [*provide explanation*] ___ don't know because: [*provide explanation*]

III. PURPOSE
PURPOSE OF THE MEDIATION SESSION AND EXPECTED WORK PRODUCT
___ signed settlement agreement ___ signed agreement in principle ___ resolution of some issues and target dates for next steps ___ other
WORK PRODUCT NEEDS FINAL APPROVAL OR RATIFICATION?
___ yes ___ no

IV. MEDIATOR & TERMS OF MEDIATION

ISSUES

1.   WHO IS THE MEDIATOR AND HOW SELECTED?

2.   IS THERE ANYTHING YOU WOULD LIKE TO KNOW ABOUT THE MEDIATOR:

___ background?

___ qualifications?

___ style/mediation model?

___ other?

3.   WHAT ARE THE COSTS ASSOCIATED WITH THE MEDIATION?

___	administration fee or court filing fee	$	
___	mediator preparation fees	$	× hours
___	mediator preparation fees	$	/day
___	mediator expenses (mileage, flights, hotel, *etc.*)	$	
___	room rental	$	
___	refreshments	$	
___	counsel fees	$	× hours
___	expert fees	$	
___	other expenses	$	

4.   IS THERE A WRITTEN MEDIATION AGREEMENT FOR TERMS OR REFERENCE?

___ yes

If yes, is it adequate?

___ no

If no, who will draft?

5.   WHERE WILL THE MEDIATION TAKE PLACE?

6.   WHO IS RESPONSIBLE FOR ARRANGEMENTS?

V. MEDIATION SUMMARY/PRE-MEDIATION INFORMATION

1. WHAT INFORMATION IS BEING EXCHANGED IN ADVANCE?

2. ARE WRITTEN SUMMARIES BEING PREPARED FOR THE MEDIATOR?

3. BY WHOM AND WHEN?

VI. OUTSTANDING ISSUES

1. WHAT ISSUES ARE OUTSTANDING BETWEEN YOU AND THE OTHER PARTY?

2. WILL THESE ISSUES HAVE ANY RELEVANCE/IMPACT ON THE MEDIATION?

3. HOW CAN YOU MOVE FORWARD TO SETTLEMENT WITHOUT CONCLUSIVELY RESOLVING THESE ISSUES?

VII. INTERESTS
Identify and Prioritize

YOU	THEM
Priority #1 #2 #3	Priority #1 #2 #3

VIII. OPTIONS
ISSUES
1. WHAT MIGHT SATISFY SOME OF THE IDENTIFIED INTERESTS?
2. HOW DO THESE OPTIONS SATISFY YOUR INTERESTS *AND* THEIRS?

IX. ALTERNATIVES
EXPECTATIONS

1. IF SETTLEMENT IS NOT ACHIEVED IN THE MEDIATION, WHAT ARE YOUR ALTERNATIVES? HOW PALATABLE ARE THESE?

___ BEST ALTERNATIVE:

___ WORST ALTERNATIVE:

2. WHAT ARE THE COSTS OF THE ALTERNATIVES?

___ Legal fees and disbursements to end of trial:

Portion that is non-recoverable, even if successful:

___ TIME:

___ RELATIONSHIP:

Internal:

External:

___ Opportunity Cost:

___ Party's time and resources:

___ Emotional Costs:

___ Publicity:

___ Other:

X. THE MEDIATION PROCESS

ISSUES

1. CAN YOU SUMMARIZE YOUR VIEW OF THIS CONTROVERSY SUCCINCTLY?

2. WHAT TOPICS DO YOU THINK NEED TO BE DISCUSSED IN MORE DETAIL?

3. WHO WILL DO THE TALKING FOR YOUR SIDE?

4. WHAT ROLE WILL THE PARTY PLAY?

5. (a) WHAT CAN THE MEDIATOR/OTHER PARTY EXPECT OF YOU?

   (b) WHAT ARE YOUR EXPECTATIONS OF THE MEDIATOR?

   (c) WHAT ARE YOUR EXPECTATIONS OF THE OTHER SIDE? *AS IN 5(a)*.

6. WHAT USE DO YOU PLAN TO MAKE OF THE MEDIATOR?

7. IS THERE ANYTHING YOU ARE CONCERNED ABOUT DISCLOSING IN THE MEDIATION? IF SO, WHAT ARE THE RISKS AND REWARDS OF DISCLOSURE?

Appendix 4

HIS HIGHNESS PRINCE AGA KHAN SHIA IMAMI ISMAILI NATIONAL CONCILIATION AND ARBITRATION BOARD FOR CANADA[*]

MEMBERS' CODE OF CONDUCT FOR CONCILIATIONS

I. PREAMBLE

1. His Highness Prince Aga Khan Shia Imami Ismaili National Conciliation and Arbitration Board of Canada (the "National Board") is committed to fostering and maintaining the highest standards of conduct among its members and the members of His Highness Prince Aga Khan Shia Imami Ismaili Conciliation and Arbitration Boards for British Columbia, Prairies, Edmonton, Ontario and Quebec and the Maritime Provinces ("the Regional Boards"). The purpose of this Code of Conduct is to provide guidance to members on matters touching on their conduct to enhance the Jamat's confidence in the integrity and competence of members, in the conduct of conciliations.

II. APPLICATION AND ENFORCEMENT

1. This Code incorporates by reference the *Rules for Conciliation Proceedings*, promulgated under the Rules and Regulations for Canada ordained on 11th July 1987, by which members are governed. In the event of a conflict between this Code and the *Rules for Conciliation Proceedings*, the *Rules for Conciliation Proceedings* will prevail.

2. The Chairperson of the National Board and the Chairperson of each Regional Board shall administer the members' *Code of Conduct* in accordance with his or her duty to supervise and direct the work of the Boards under the *Rules of Conciliation Proceedings*.

---

[*] The documents in this appendix are reproduced with permission of His Highness Prince Aga Khan Shia Imami Ismaili National Conciliation and Arbitration Board for Canada.

III. GOAL OF CONCILIATION AND ROLE OF PARTICIPANTS

1.   The goal of conciliation is to effect an agreement that is fair and equitable, not a settlement at any cost.

2.   The primary responsibility for the resolution of a dispute rests with the parties. At no time shall a member coerce the participants into agreement or make a substantive decision for any participant.

3.   The role of the conciliator is that of a facilitator, i.e., to assist the parties to reach an imformed and voluntary agreement. A conciliator should attempt to be an active resource person, who may provide both procedural and substantive suggestions and alternatives.

IV. INTEGRITY AND IMPARTIALITY

1.   A member shall have no interest in the outcome of a conciliation or be aware of any circumstances which could raise the likelihood of perceived bias or partiality. He or she shall not mediate disputes involving close friends, relatives, colleagues, supervisors or students.

2.   A member shall determine and reveal to the Chairperson of the Board any problems that may cause possible conflict of interest; or affect the perceived or actual neutrality of the member in the performance of duties. A member shall also comply with the provisions of Article 9 of the *Rules for Conciliation Proceedings* relating to the disclosure of conflicts of interest. A member should maintain the appearance of impartiality and neutrality at all times. Impartiality means freedom from favouritism or bias in word or in action.

V.   COMPETENCE

1.   Members shall perform their services in a conscientious, diligent and efficient manner in accordance with this Code of Conduct and the *Rules of Conciliation Proceedings*.

2.   A member should stay within his or her own area of competence and should not attempt to conciliate disputes without proper knowledge.

3.   Members shall engage in continuing education as offered by the Boards to ensure that their conciliation skills are current and effective.

VI. RESERVE, COURTESY, DISCRETION AND SENSITIVITY

1.   A member should perform his or her duties and responsibilities and comport himself or herself generally with reserve, courtesy and

discretion. A member should strive to resolve disputes in conformity with the Islamic concepts of unity, brotherhood, justice, tolerance and goodwill.

VII.   CONFIDENTIALITY

1. A member shall not voluntarily disclose to anyone who is not a member of the Board and not a party to the conciliation any information obtained through the conciliation process except:

    (a)   non-identifying information; or

    (b)   when ordered to do so by a judicial authority with jurisdiction to compel such disclosure or required to do so by legislation or other law; or

    (c)   when the information discloses an actual or potential threat to human life or safety; or

    (d)   in accordance with the *Rules of Conciliation Proceedings*.

2. Any information so divulged shall be limited to what is absolutely necessary to accomplish such purposes.

3. Parties shall be informed, at the outset, of these and other limitations to confidentiality.

4. A member shall maintain confidentiality of parties' files in the retention, storage and disposal of such records.

VIII.   INFORMATION, DISCLOSURE AND ADVICE

1. A member shall actively encourage the participants to make decisions based on sufficient information, knowledge and advice.

2. Where financial or property issues are involved, the member shall obtain an undertaking from each party to the effect that he or she is making frank and full disclosure of his or her financial and other relevant circumstances at the appropriate time in the conciliation process. The conciliator will assist the parties to achieve such disclosure. A member has an ongoing obligation to advise both parties to obtain legal and other professional advice and assistance in this respect.

3. A member has an ongoing obligation to advise participants of the desirability and availability of independent legal advice.

IX. LEGAL OPINIONS

Under no circumstances shall a member provide a legal opinion or advice to the parties in dispute.

X. SUBMISSION AGREEMENT OR AGREEMENT TO CONCILIATE

1.   The member shall explain the conciliation process clearly to the parties before agreeing to mediate their dispute. In particular, the conciliator shall at the outset:

    (a)   define and explain conciliation and distinguish it from reconciliation counselling, therapy, assessment, advocacy, adjudication and arbitration;

    (b)   discuss the appropriateness of conciliation for the parties in light of their particular circumstances, the benefits and risks of conciliation, and the other alternatives open to the parties;

    (c)   advise the parties that either of them or the member has the right to suspend or terminate the process at any time;

    (d)   inform the parties that he or she will be functioning as a conciliator and not as an adviser for either or both the parties. If the member is also a lawyer, he or she shall inform the parties that he or she cannot represent either or both of them in any related legal action;

    (e)   discuss with the parties the member's specific procedures and practices, such as when:

        (i)   separate sessions may be held; and

        (ii)   there may be separate communications with the parties.

    (f)   require the parties to sign a submission form in accordance with Article 4 of the *Rules of Conciliation Proceedings*.

XI. TERMINATION OF CONCILIATION OR MEDIATION

1.   It is the duty of a member to suspend or terminate a conciliation whenever continuation of the process is likely to harm or prejudice one or more of the participants, such as when the conciliation is misused to:

    (a)   develop a status quo with respect to the custody of the children; or

    (b)   to dissipate or conceal assets.

2. A member shall suspend or terminate a mediation when its usefulness is exhausted.

THESE RESPONSIBILITIES ARE IN ADDITION TO THOSE IMPOSED UNDER THE <u>RULES OF CONCILIATION PROCEEDINGS</u>.

EXTRACT FROM MEMBER'S REFERENCE MANUAL

SECTION 3 — CASE MANAGEMENT

A) RESPONSIBILITIES OF THE BOARD MEMBER

The objective of the Boards is to serve the Jamats in the area of dispute resolutions. In accordance with Article 13.1 of the Constitution and the Hidayats of Mawlana Hazar Imam pertaining to the Boards' Mandate, it is expected that the members of the Conciliation & Arbitration Boards ("The Boards") will serve the Jamat in a professional manner as follows:

- **Fairness and Impartiality**
Members must be impartial and fair to all parties to the dispute.

- **Confidentiality**
Members must maintain strict confidentiality during and after completion of the cases on which they have worked. It is each Board's policy that only the Chairman of the Board and the member(s) assigned to a particular case have access to all the particulars of the case. Cases when discussed in the meetings are referred to by file numbers only, not names.

- **Cost Effectiveness**
The dispute resolution processes/options offered by the Conciliation and Arbitration Boards must be less costly to the disputants than litigation, in terms of the financial, emotional and psychological costs.

- **Speedy Disposition**
It is each Board's policy that every request for service made to the Board by an individual must be responded to by a Board member within 24 hours of the request being made. This is based on the premise that the mostly efficient and effective (time and cost) means of resolving a dispute is to mediate the dispute at an early stage.

- **Prompt Referral**
When cases fall outside of a Board's jurisdiction, the Board has developed the practice of making prompt referrals to the appropriate institution. Special effort is made to ensure that the individual will in fact be assisted by the institution to which the referral is made to avoid the "football" syndrome.

- **Creating Awareness in the Jamat of the Board's Services**
The Boards do not solicit cases. However, it is important that members of the Jamat within the jurisdiction of each Board are aware of the services being offered by the Board. Some of the ways in which each

Board has attempted to create awareness is by visiting local/district jamatkhanas on a regular basis so that the members of these Jamats are able to recognize Board members; presentations to the Mukhi/Kamadia Sahebs and Mukhiani/Kamadiani Sahebas and institutional leaders, and distribution of a brochure describing the Board's services.

- **Reporting Status of Case to the Chair**
To facilitate updating the data base and generating reports required by the National Conciliation and Arbitration Board, members must complete Status of Case form on a regular basis (see Section 4 — Forms).

B) CASE MANAGEMENT PROCEDURE

Proper and regular record keeping of cases will provide accurate data for the Board and it will also facilitate reports generation. It is recommended that the following activities be documented. Forms have been developed for these activities — refer to Section 4 in this manual.

- **Case Assignment**
Cases come to the Board throughout the following routes:

    –   directly from the disputant(s) to the Chairman or the Members

    –   from Councils and other Institutions

    –   from Mukhi/Kamadia Sahebs, Mukhiani/Madiani Sahebas

    –   from family members of the disputants

The following steps must be taken in dealing with a case from the time it is referred to the Board to the time a member is assigned.

Step 1 — All new cases are forwarded to the Chairman or the Member assigned to handle intake. He/she will first determine if both parties are agreeable to come to the Board for mediation and then allocate a file number and assign the case to one or two members as appropriate.

Step 2 — The member(s) to whom the case is assigned opens a new file by completing the file opening form.

Step 3 — The member will contact each of the disputants and arrange to meet with them in a neutral setting. The member usually meets with each disputant separately first, to determine the best method to conduct the case. During the first meeting, the "Submission for Conciliation" must be completed and signed by the disputants. The member will then proceed to assist the parties in trying to solve their problems. The member regularly reports to the Chairman on the status of the case.

Step 4 — When parties agree to a settlement, the member should prepare the Minutes of Settlement. The Member should ensure that the parties obtain independent legal advice before executing the Minutes of Settlement.

Step 5 — The Member will complete a file closing report and inform the Chairman of the outcome of the case.

- **File Opening**

Complete file opening form and ensure that the Submission for Conciliation form is properly completed and executed by the disputants and file.

- **Documenting Discussion**

Document all telephone conversations and/or meetings held with either of the disputants or third parties relating to the dispute. The documentation should set out the issues discussed, information provided by the Board member, the positions taken by the disputants and the outcomes.

- **Logging Time Spent**

Log the time spent work performed on a case, including the time spent with the disputants on the telephone, at meetings, drafting settlement options, etc.

- **Preparing Minutes of Settlement**

When the parties agree on a settlement, assist the parties in reducing the agreement to Minutes of Settlement. Request the parties to obtain independent legal advice (ILA) before signing the Minutes. Copies of the Minutes of Settlement, memorandum of understanding, etc. must be kept in the member's case file.

- **File Closing**

Complete the file closing report form; record the total number of hours spent on the case.

- **Report to the National Board**

Each Member must submit to the Chairman, a complete "Status of Case" form for all the cases he/she handled during the reporting period to assist the Chairman in preparing a consolidated report for the National Board.

DATED: FEBRUARY 24, 2010

RULES FOR CONCILIATION PROCEEDINGS

His Highness Prince Aga Khan
Shia Imami Ismaili
National Conciliation and Arbitration Board
for Canada

Rules for Conciliation Proceedings

BISMI-LLAHI-R-RAHMANI-R-RAHIM

WHEREAS

(A)   From the time of the Imamat of Hazrat Mawlana Ali (AS) it has been a tradition of the Ismaili Muslims that when differences of opinion or disputes arise between them, these should be resolved by a process of mediation, conciliation and arbitration within themselves in conformity with the Islamic concepts of unity, brotherhood, justice, tolerance and goodwill.

(B)   Over the past many decades, this process of mediation, conciliation and arbitration has been entrusted to the Councils and Tribunals (as the case may be) established in different parts of the world through rules of conduct and constitutions given by the Imam of the Ismaili Muslims.

(C)   The accumulated experience of the Councils and Tribunals has clearly demonstrated that the settlement of differences and disputes can be achieved with fairness, speed, confidentiality and without excessive cost.

(D)   The presence of the Ismaili Muslims in different fields of endeavour in various countries of the world requires that the dispute settlement procedures be made uniform as far as possible and be given wider application and an international dimension.

(E)   To this end, and in order to strengthen, consolidate and enhance the beneficial effect of the systems and procedures established and evolved over the past many decades, the Constitution of the Shia Imami Ismaili Muslims ordained on 13th December 1986 has constituted the International Conciliation and Arbitration Board and the National Conciliation and Arbitration Boards to assist in the conciliation process and to act as arbitral bodies.

(F)   The Rules and Regulations for Canada ordained on 11th July 1987 provide that the National Conciliation and Arbitration Board shall have such practice directions and rules of procedure as it may from time to time determine.

(G)   Pursuant to the said Rules and Regulations the National Conciliation and Arbitration Board for Canada desires to introduce Rules for Conciliation Proceedings to ensure achievement of the foregoing aims and to build a strong institution providing a just, prompt, efficient, discreet and cost effective dispute resolution machinery.

NOW THEREFORE

By this resolution and in exercise of the authority vested in the National Conciliation and Arbitration Board for Canada, IT BE AND IS HEREBY RESOLVED that:

The Rules for Conciliation Proceedings hereinafter appearing shall constitute a set of guidelines for conciliations conducted by the Conciliation and Arbitration Board for Canada but shall not be regarded as binding in nature the objective being to achieve an amicable and mutually acceptable resolution of any dispute which is the subject of conciliation whether by adherence to these Rules or otherwise.

Passed by the National Conciliation and Arbitration Board for Canada at a duly convened meeting held this 24th day of February, 2010, being the 10 day of Rabi`Al-Awwal 1431 A.H (Hijrah).

Signed _____
                            Chairman
                            Shehni Dossa

1.   **DISTINCTION BETWEEN CONCILIATION AND ARBITRATION**

1.1   "Conciliation" is a process of dispute resolution in which a neutral person assists the parties to a dispute in reaching their own settlement. The neutral person does not have authority to make a binding decision on the parties. As the process is entirely voluntary, the parties may withdraw from the process at any time.

1.2   By contrast, "arbitration" is a process in which each party presents its case at a hearing before a panel of one or more persons who make a final and binding decision which is subject, under certain very limited circumstances, to review by the courts of law.

2.   **MANDATE OF THE BOARD**

2.1   The board's role as conciliator is defined in Article 13.1(a) of the Ismaili Constitution as follows:

> "to assist in the conciliation process between parties in differences or disputes arising from commercial, business and other civil liability matters, domestic and family matters, including those relating to matrimony, children of a marriage, matrimonial property, and testate and intestate succession".

2.2   It is the Board's duty to handle all disputes confidentially, expeditiously and with the minimum of expense.

3.   **PRE-INTERVIEW**

3.1   All cases shall in the first instance, be referred to the National or Regional Board (as the context requires), together with the following basic particulars:

(a)   Names, addresses and telephone numbers of the parties; and

(b)   the general nature of the dispute.

3.2   The Chairman of the National or Regional Board (as the context requires), after being satisfied that the dispute falls within Article 13.1(a) of the Ismaili Constitution and that the case is not one for referral to some other body (see Rules 3.3 and 3.4 below), shall assign a member of the Board to conduct a preliminary interview.

3.3   Where a party is resident outside Canada, the Board shall for the purpose of conciliation co-ordinate with the National Board having responsibility for the country of residence of the other party, whilst keeping the International Board informed at all times and dealing generally with the matter in accordance with any advice which may be received from the International Board.

3.4   In order to reserve to the Board the task of assisting primarily in the resolution of the more serious disputes (so as not to burden the Board's limited resources by relatively minor disputes) and also to prevent the Board from turning into a "counseling clinic" or "crisis centre", cases shall, where they fall appropriately within the responsibility of other Jamati institutions, such as the Council's Social and Welfare or marriage committees, be referred to those institutions.

4.   PRELIMINARY INTERVIEW

4.1   The interviewer shall promptly contact the parties and obtain from them the relevant particulars on a form such as the one described in the Schedule hereto.

4.2   The interviewer shall request each party to sign a submission form containing the following particulars:

(a)   a brief statement of the issues to be resolved, and the acknowledgement that the dispute is submitted to the Board for conciliation;

(b)   where applicable and if possible, an undertaking that any legal proceedings will be stayed while the dispute is under conciliation, but without restricting the right of a party to take such steps as may be necessary to prevent an action being time barred under any law governing limitations;

(c)   an acknowledgement that any statements made by the parties shall be on a "without prejudice" basis and for the purposes of settlement only;

(d)   a waiver by the parties of any possible claim they may have against the conciliator concerning recommendations that may be made or opinions offered in the course of the conciliation; and

(e)   an acknowledgement that the parties have voluntarily submitted to the jurisdiction of the Board.

4.3   Where a dispute is submitted to the jurisdiction of the Board by only one party to the dispute, the interviewer shall contact the other party by letter or in person to invite that other party to use the services offered by the Board; such contact shall not be in a manner likely to be perceived as partisan and shall emphasize only the advantages to both parties of participating in the conciliation process (i.e. an expeditious and inexpensive resolution of the dispute; handled confidentially).

4.4   Upon completion of the interview, the interviewer shall report to the Chairman who shall assign the case for conciliation, after being satisfied:

(a)   that the dispute falls within Article 13.1(a) of the Ismaili Constitution;

(b)   that the case is not appropriate for referral to some other body; and

(c)   that the parties have executed the submission form referred to in Rule 4.2 above.

5.   **CONCILIATION**

5.1   The Chairman shall select conciliators in accordance with the following criteria:

(a)   the conciliator shall enjoy the respect of the parties, be able to exert moral persuasion and, where technical expertise or other special skills are required in a case, should possess such expertise or skills;

(b)   the conciliator should have no interest in the outcome of the case nor be aware of any circumstances which could raise a likelihood of perceived bias;

(c)   laymen should normally be preferred over lawyers (firstly, so as to leave the lawyers available to handle the dispute should it proceed to arbitration and secondly, in order to avoid the potential problem of a recommendation for settlement by a lawyer-conciliator being construed as a legal opinion);

(d)   members of the Board should be preferred over other members of the Jamat;

(e)   in order to ensure the proper accountability of the conciliator to the Board, where a non-Board member is asked to act as conciliator, that individual shall be assigned to the case jointly with a Board member, whose duty it shall be to monitor the case and report on its progress to the Board periodically pursuant to Rule 10 below; and

(f)   in complex disputes a team of two or more conciliators may be preferred so that each can consult with the other on ways in which to resolve the case.

5.2   Notwithstanding the relative informality of the conciliation process (as compared to the formal hearings involved in arbitration), all conciliations shall be conducted in a dignified setting, wherever such are available.

5.3   The conciliator shall conduct the conciliation in a fair, ethical, orderly and dignified manner, and in accordance with the following guidelines:

(a)   the purpose of the conciliation should be to persuade the parties to a meeting of minds, to resolve their differences amicably, and accordingly the role of the conciliator shall be merely to persuade and under no circumstances to coerce;

(b)   the conciliator shall not offer to the parties any legal or technical advice, nor any valuation or opinion, and as far as may be practicable shall invite the parties to rely on their own judgment in considering any offers to settle;

(c)   none of the parties shall be represented by a legal practitioner. However, if the parties wish they may, with the consent of the conciliator, seek the assistance of a close friend or family member at the conciliation;

(d)   the conciliator shall not participate in or encourage any unethical or illegal settlement;

(e)   the conciliator shall reserve the right to withdraw from the case if the parties conduct themselves in a disorderly or improper manner, or if the parties breach any undertaking to the Board;

(f)   essential facts of the case shall be recorded and retained, along with supporting documentation, in the conciliator's files, which shall be submitted to the Board's custody at the conclusion of the conciliation;

(g)   at all times, the conciliator shall respect the confidence of the parties and shall not, without the leave of all concerned parties, discuss or report (save as contemplated in Rule 10 below) any aspect of the dispute in a manner that might prejudice the parties; and

(h)   the conciliation shall be commenced without undue delay and shall be conducted and concluded expeditiously.

5.4   If the parties have not, within such time as is reasonable having regard to the complexities and exigencies of the case, been able to reach a settlement, the conciliator shall report to the Board and recommend either termination of the conciliation or referral of the case pursuant to Rule 7 below.

6.   SETTLEMENT

6.1   Where the parties have agreed to settle their differences, the conciliator shall prepare a settlement agreement recording all the essential terms of the settlement and shall have the parties sign that agreement to signify their acceptance of the settlement.

6.2   The conciliator, where the complexities of the case warrant it, may request the assistance of lawyers to prepare the settlement agreement – but the drafters of such document shall be mindful not to introduce into it materially new terms that might frustrate the discussed agreement.

7.   CONFIDENTIALITY

All cases shall be treated confidentially.

8   **CONFLICTS OF INTEREST**

8.1   Given that all Board members are entrusted to act responsibly, the Board shall not entertain any dispute in which a party insists that the party's submission of its dispute to the Board is conditional on the Board keeping the facts of the dispute confidential from one of its members.

8.2   When a case is referred to the Board, upon learning of the names of the parties and, where necessary, the general nature of the dispute, members of the Board are expected to declare forthwith if they have or may probably have:

(a)   any conflict of interest; or

(b)   any perceptible bias that could compromise the Board in its handling of the case.

8.3   Where a Board member has a conflict of interest or where, in the opinion of the Board as a whole, there is a serious likelihood of perceived bias that could compromise the Board in its handling of the case, the Board member involved will be expected to abstain from any dealings in the case and from accessing the case file.

9.   **REPORTING**

9.1   The Board member assigned to conduct an interview shall, promptly after conducting the interview, report on its outcome to the Board.

9.2   Upon being assigned to resolve a dispute, the conciliator shall promptly make an assessment of the complexities of the case and flexibility of the parties and shall give the Board an estimate of the anticipated time required to mediate the dispute. In addition, the conciliator shall, at least at each meeting, or more frequently as the circumstances may reasonably require, provide the Board with a progress report of the case. The purpose of the progress report to the Board shall be to enable the Board to ensure that the case is being handled expeditiously and to apprise the Board of, and consult with its members on, any complications in the conciliation process.

10.   **DO'S AND DON'TS OF CONCILIATION**

10.1   The conciliator shall not undertake a case with any persons whom he has previously represented or to whom he has given any prior advice relating to the dispute. If there has been any previous contact with either one or both of the parties on an unrelated matter this should be disclosed to both the parties and the conciliator should proceed only on the written consent of both the parties.

10.2   The conciliator should inform the parties before the case commences that he will be functioning as conciliator and not as an advisor for either or both the parties.

10.3   In order to maintain neutrality, the conciliator should avoid giving specific legal advice and should dispense only general legal information in the presence of both the parties during the proceedings.

10.4   The conciliator should stay within his or her own area of competence and should not attempt to resolve highly contentious disputes without proper knowledge.

10.5   The conciliator should terminate the process if at any time he believes that the conditions for conciliation have been breached or if in his opinion any of the participants is being harmed or seriously prejudiced by the process.

10.6   The Settlement Agreement should be executed in the presence of the Chairman of the Board, if possible, to avoid any appearance of coercion on the part of the conciliator.

10.7   The conciliator should decline to advise any party in subsequent legal proceedings related to the dispute.

SCHEDULE

PRELIMINARY INTERVIEW FORM

Name of Parties

Statement of Background
of Grievance

Litigation (if any)

Any conflicts of interest of Board Members

General: (e.g. details of previous attempts at conciliation; the parties own assessment of
prospects for conciliation; any preferred choice of conciliator; availability of
parties for conciliation and choice of venue.)

Appendix 5

SAMPLE SUPERIOR COURT ORDER GIVING DIRECTIONS FOR THE CONDUCT OF AN ESTATE MEDIATION

Court File No. 04-51154-08

ONTARIO SUPERIOR COURT OF JUSTICE

THE HONOURABLE	WEDNESDAY THE 9TH
JUSTICE DEMARAY	DAY OF NOVEMBER 2009

IN THE MATTER OF THE ESTATE OF JOHANNES GILBRETH, deceased

B E T W E E N:

LORETTA GILBRETH, by her Attorney, Constance Bedwell

Applicant

-and-

WILLIAM HENRY GILBRETH, Estate Trustee
with a Will of the Estate of
Johannes Gilbreth, MARGARET FRASER
And PRECIOUS LARBIE

Respondents

ORDER GIVING DIRECTIONS

THIS APPLICATION was heard this day at the Court House in Toronto.

UPON hearing the submissions of counsel for the Applicant and the Respondent William Henry Gilbreth.

1. **THIS COURT ORDERS that the within Application proceed as an Application or as a trial of the issues, as the parties may agree or as this Court may further order, and that the issues to be tried are as follows:**

   i.   The Applicant affirms and the Respondents deny that Loretta Gilbreth was a "dependant" of the deceased, as defined in *s.* 57 of the *Succession Law Reform Act*, R.S.O. 1990, c. S.26;

   ii. The Applicant affirms and the Respondent denies that the deceased failed to make adequate provision for the proper support of Loretta Gilbreth;

   iii. in the event that an order for the support of Loretta Gilbreth is made, a determination of what provision is adequate for the proper support of Loretta Gilbreth.

2. **THIS COURT ORDERS that each party on the written request of any other party shall serve and file an Affidavit of Documents and shall attend and submit to examinations for discovery in accordance with the *Rules of Civil Procedure*.**

3. **THIS COURT ORDERS that the Respondent William Henry Gilbreth, Estate Trustee with a Will of the Estate of Johannes Gilbreth provide the Applicant with a statement, including values, of all assets owned by the deceased at the time of death, including all assets which may be available for charging pursuant to s. 72 of the *Succession Law Reform Act*, within 30 days of the date of this Order.**

4. **THIS COURT ORDERS that within 90 days of the date of this Order the parties shall attend for mediation before a mediator pursuant to Rule 75.1 of the *Rules of Civil Procedure* and makes the following directions:**

   a.   The issues to be mediated are as follows.

        i.   is Loretta Gilbreth a "dependant" of the deceased, as defined in s. 57 of the *Succession Law Reform Act*, R.S.O. 1990, c. S.26?

        ii. Did the deceased make adequate provision for Loretta Gilbreth's proper support?

        iii. What provision is adequate for Loretta Gilbreth's proper support?

   b.   The Applicant and Respondent William Henry Gilbreth are Designated Parties with the Applicant having carriage of the mediation and the Respondent William Henry Gilbreth responding to it.

c.   The Notice of the Mediator giving the date, place and time of the mediation shall be served on the Designated Parties by an alternative to personal service pursuant to Rule 16.03 of the *Rules of Civil Procedure*.

d.   The fees of the mediator shall be paid out of the estate, on a without prejudice basis and subject to any agreement between the parties or a final decision on costs at the hearing of the Application.

e.   Any matters arising out of the mediation requiring the further direction of the court shall be referred to me or to such other judge who is available.

f.   The mediation shall take place prior to Examinations for Discovery.

g.   The Parties shall use their best efforts to provide each other with all relevant information and documentation prior to the mediation.

5.   **THIS COURT ORDERS that the Application shall be heard or the issues shall be tried without a jury at Toronto at a date to be fixed by the Registrar and the Trial Record shall consist of the Application Record, this Order Giving Directions and any other Order for Directions made by this court.**

6.   **THIS COURT ORDERS that the distribution of the Estate of Johannes Gilbreth be and is hereby stayed pending the disposition of the within Application, subject to the consent of the parties or the further Order of this Court.**

7.   **THIS COURT ORDERS that William Henry Gilbreth pay to the Applicant interim support payable directly to Loretta Gilbreth by international money order in the lump sum of $3,600, and in the continuing amount of $400.00 per month commending December 1, 2004, and continuing until the hearing of the within Application, or further Order of this Court.**

8.   **THIS COURT ORDERS that the balance of the Application be adjourned *sine die*.**

9.   **THIS COURT ORDERS that the costs of this motion be reserved to the judge hearing the Application.**

THIS ORDER BEARS INTEREST at the rate of 4% per annum.

INDEX